Official Fundraising Almanac

D0851792

DISCARDED
From Nashville Public Library

Library of Congress Catalog Card Number: 89-61428

International Standard Book Number:
0-944496-07-5

Pluribus Press, Inc.
160 East Illinois Street
Chicago, Illinois 60611

93 92 91 90 89   5 4 3 2 1

Printed in the United States of America

Official Fundraising Almanac

Facts, figures, and anecdotes from and for fundraisers

Jerold Panas

Pluribus Press, Inc., Chicago

A GLORIOUS
BEGINNING. . .

The other day, I heard someone refer to fundraising as "big business." Well, it is. But it's much more than that.

In 1988, Americans gave over $104 billion to a dazzling array of philanthropic endeavors. That represented an unbroken record of increased giving, each year more than the year before. It is philanthropy with the same spirit and heart that Alex de Tocqueville referred to in 1836 as "the great American impulse of compassion, character, and action."

It is a great deal of money, indeed. It reflects $104 billion of love and caring, compassion and action.

A resource such as this Almanac is long overdue. This single source includes most anything and everything that relates to fundraising and giving. Everyone who is involved directly or indirectly in the field should have this book as a handy and immediate resource.

The chances are good that there is an answer in this book to anything you want to know about fundraising. If it isn't here, it's not because we didn't try. My Research Director, Shaundra Bason, and our research staff has worked for months, day in and day out, to assemble the type of material that would be the most helpful, the most interesting, and the most important. The list of people in the field who have assisted, sent material, made suggestions—well, there are simply too many to list.

For the first time, all of the major disciplines and areas are put together. Here, assembled side by side, are the humanities, the arts, health care, education, and social services, all in one valuable source. And there's more. The book is also a reference for firms which specialize in the fields of executive search, planned giving, software, awards, and direct mail.

This is only a start. But what a glorious beginning! The Almanac will be an annual event. And each year, the book will grow in information and reference data because it will respond to your needs and concerns. That is why it will be important that we hear from you—your ideas, suggestions, and additions. And, of course, any corrections.

Here it is: Your Almanac. Keep it nearby, at the corner of your desk or on a handy shelf. I am certain you will find it an indispensable friend and aid. I think you'll find, also, that it's just plain fun for random sampling.

As much as anything, this book celebrates the zealous dedication of those great men and women in the field—those tireless workers—who tell the story, design the folder, write the letter, make the call, and acknowledge the gift. Their work, their commitment, made the $104 billion possible. We are the lucky ones, to be in this joyous adventure of caring and concern, and our rewards are great. As John R. Mott said: "Blessed are the fundraisers for in heaven, they shall stand on the right hand of the martyrs."

Jerold Panas
500 North Michigan Avenue
Chicago, Illinois 60611

September 1989

SERVICE ORGANIZATIONS

This category represents what are considered to be the older and more standard organizations—the old-line community agencies. This includes the United Way, the YMCA and YWCA, Boy Scouts and Girl Scouts, the American Red Cross, the Salvation Army, and other similar groups.

Giving in this classification approached $10 billion in 1988, representing nearly 10 percent of the total philanthropic pie.

Over the years, this designation has shown steady but slow gain—consistently larger than the arts and culture, but ranked fourth in giving behind religion, education, and health.

NORTH AMERICAN YMCA DEVELOPMENT OFFICERS (NAYDO)

The purpose of NAYDO is to strengthen the role of financial development in local YMCAs. The organization helps shape the direction and emphasis of YMCA financial development throughout North America.

The first NAYDO Conference was held in St. Louis in 1981.

The 1989 Conference took place at the Disneyland Hotel in Anaheim, California, April 7, 8, and 9. As usual, the NAYDO Conference was held just prior to the conference of the National Society of Fund Raising Executives.

The original group of men involved in the establishment of NAYDO is comprised of:

Phillip S. Brain
Financial Development
Consultant
Phil Brain Associates Inc.
Minneapolis, MN

George E. Rodger
Vice President of Fin. & Fac.
Dev.
H. J. D. Labatte, Metro YMCA
Toronto, Ontario, Canada

Dick Stoll
Vice President, Development
YMCA of Greater St. Louis
St. Louis, MO

Kenneth C. Isherwood
Senior V.P./Finance & Fin. Dev.
YMCA of Metropolitan Detroit
Detroit, MI

Moss Causey
Retired

Paul Nebsel
Retired

Any further questions regarding NAYDO should be directed to: **Mr. Donald L. Zerwer, V.P./Development, San Diego County YMCA, 7510 Clairemont Mesa Blvd., Suite 204, San Diego, CA 92111 (619) 292-4034.**

CURRENT NAYDO MEMBERSHIP ROSTER

Diane E. Anderson
Executive Director
St. Petersburg Family YMCA
116 Fifth Street South
St. Petersburg, FL 33701
(813) 822-3911

Bruce R. Bethers
Executive Director
Cleveland County YMCA
1801 Halley Ave
Norman, Oklahoma 73069
(405) 364-9200

Malcolm Arnett
Executive Director
Billings YMCA
402 North 32nd
Billings, MT 59101
(406) 248-1685

Jim Bowley
President & CEO
YMCA of Greater Green Bay
235 North Jefferson Street
Green Bay, WI 54301
(414) 435-5361

Phillip R. Baaske
Executive Director
Lake County YMCA
2000 Western Avenue
Waukegan, IL 60087
(312) 623-2350

Bill Botts
Vice President
YMCA of Metro Dallas
601 North Akard
Dallas, TX 75201
(214) 954-0500

Clark D. Baker
Chief Executive Officer
Nashville Metro YMCA
706 Church Street
Nashville, TN 37203
(615) 259-9623

Robert J. Botzum
Associate Executive Director
Akron Area YMCA
80 West Center Street
Akron, OH 44308
(216) 376-1335

Sheryl Barnard
Director of Development
Channel Islands YMCA
591 Santa Rosa Lane
Santa Barbara, CA 93108
(805) 687-7727

Christopher Ray Chase
Executive Director
South Bay Family YMCA
50 Fourth Avenue
Chula Vista, CA 92010
(619) 422-8354

Tim Bergstresser
Executive Director
Effingham Family YMCA
1208 North Wenthe Drive
Effingham, IL 62401
(217) 347-5155

Ben Childers
Executive Director
YMCA of Waycross, GA, Inc.
P.O. Box 1189
Waycross, GA 31502
(912) 285-8660

James R. Cimino
V.P. of Financial Development
YMCA of Pittsburgh
304 Wood Street
Pittsburgh, PA 15222
(412) 227-3823

Thomas M. Colligan
Executive Director
Torrington Area YMCA
259 Prospect Street
Torrington, CT 06790
(203) 489-3133

Harold L. Cook
Metro Executive Director
YMCA of Greater Louisville
501 South Second Street
Louisville, KY 40202
(502) 587-9622

Donald J.L. Coppedge
Executive Director
Phoenixville Area YMCA
400 E. Pothouse Rd.
Phoenixville, PA 19460

Ron Cook
Executive Director
YMCA of the Ozarks
Route 2
Potosi, MO 63664
(314) 438-2154

B. Darrell Corder
General Director
Greater Greenville Metro YMCA
P.O. Box 5697
Greenville, SC 29606
(803) 242-4651

Brian T. Cormier
Chief Executive Officer
Winston-Salem/Forsyth YMCA
775 West End Boulevard
Winston-Salem, NC 27101
(919) 722-1163

Gene Cornwell
National Field Consultant
YMCA of the USA
101 North Wacker Drive
Chicago, IL 60606
(312) 977-0031

John Dabrow
Executive Director
Central YMCA
220 Golden Gate
San Francisco, CA 94102
(415) 885-0460

Don Dalziel
Executive Director
Burlington Family YMCA
2410 Mt. Pleasant Street
Burlington, IA 52601
(319) 753-6734

Leo J. Darwit
Marketing Director
New City YMCA
1515 North Halsted
Chicago, IL 60622
(312) 266-1242

Donald L. Deal
Vice President YMCA of Tucson
516 North Fifth Avenue
Tucson, AZ 85703
(602) 624-7471

Paul Devitt
Senior V.P. of Development
YMCA of Greater New York
422 Ninth Avenue
New York, NY 10001
(212) 564-1300

David R. Donahue
Vice President
Pittsburgh Metro YMCA
330 Blvd. of the Allies
Pittsburgh, PA 15222
(412) 227-3828

Fred Hauser
Executive Director
Appleton Family YMCA
218 East Lawrence Street
Appleton, WI 54911
(414) 739-6135

Bernie Heisner
Director of Development
University of Illinois YMCA
1001 South Wright Street
Champaign, IL 61820
(217) 337-1500

Harold J. Hemberger
Executive Director
Smithfield YMCA
P.O. Box 363
Greenville, RI 02828
(401) 949-2480

Douglas Herron
Director Campaign Associates
YMCA of the USA
661 Moore Road, Suite 120
King of Prussia, PA 19406
(215) 337-3116

Tom Hetrick
General Director
Catawba County YMCA
P.O. Box 280
Conover, NC 28613
(704) 464-6130

Trueman Hirschfeld
Director of Fin. Dev.
YMCA of Greater Vancouver
955 Burrand Street
Vancouver, BC,
Canada V6Z 1Y2
(604) 681-0221

Jimmy Holshouser
Executive Director
Lexington YMCA
119 West Third Avenue
Lexington, NC 27293
(704) 249-2177

Peter P. Hoontis
Executive Director
Rome Family YMCA
301 West Bloomfield Street
Rome, NY 13440
(315) 336-3500

George S. Goyer
Senior Vice President
YMCA of San Francisco
220 Golden Gate Avenue
San Francisco, CA 94102
(415) 775-9622

Gary D. Graham
General Executive
YMCA of Tidewater
312 North Bute Street
Norfolk, VA 23510
(804) 622-6328

Thomas Leon Greenwood
Vice President of Financial Dev.
YMCA of Greater Rochester
444 East Main Street
Rochester, NY 14604-2595
(716) 546-5500

Scott Haldane
Succursale West Island
Executive Director
94 Douglas Shand
Pointe Claire, Quebec,
Canada H9R 2A8
(514) 694-9622

Kathy S. Hamilton
Executive Director
Comm. Services Branch of Metro
Dallas
601 North Akard
Dallas, TX 75201
(214) 954-0655

Jerry Haralson
General Director
Orlando YMCA
433 North Mills Avenue
Orlando, FL 32804
(305) 896-9220

Gail Harmon
Executive Director
Midland Metro YMCA
P.O. Box 1103
Midland, TX 79702
(915) 684-8392

Pat Harris
Executive Director
Anderson YMCA
705 East Greenville Street
Anderson, SC 29621
(803) 224-0263

Dan Logan
Vice President – Financial Dev.
Kansas City Metro YMCA
3100 Broadway, Suite 930
Kansas City, MO 64111
(816) 561-9622

Mark Luchette
Aquatics Director
Madison New Jersey YMCA
1 Ralph Stoddard Drive
Madison, NJ 07940
(201) 377-6200

Harry R. McCarty
President – Transportation
YMCA of the USA
Six Neshaminy Interplex
Trevose, PA 19047
(215) 638-1305

J. V. McKinney
President
Little Rock Metro YMCA
2100 Riverfront Dr., Suite 240
Little Rock, AR 72202
(501) 664-7277

Kenneth McLaughlin
President & CEO
Springfield Metro YMCA
275 Chestnut Street
Springfield, MA 01104
(413) 739-6951

Donald K. Macher
Executive Director
YMCA of Southwestern Indiana
222 N.W. 6th Street
Evansville, IN 47708
(812) 425-6151

Gary Male
Executive Director
MI Youth & Government
719 Lott Road
Coldwater, MI 49036
(616) 544-5915

Floyd G. Mann
General Director
Lansing YMCA
301 West Lenawee Street
Lansing, MI 48933
(517) 484-4000

Dorothy R. Kyle
Executive Director
Somerset Hills YMCA
140 Mount Airy Road
Basking Ridge, NJ 07920
(201) 766-7898

H. J. D. Labatte
President
YMCA of Metro Toronto
15 Breadalbane Street
Toronto, Ontario,
Canada M4Y 2V5
(416) 324-4128

Edward Landes
Vice President – Financial Dev.
YMCA of Metro Minneapolis
30 South Ninth Street
Minneapolis, MN 55402
(612) 371-8705

Mr. Harry L. Lesher, Jr.
Vice President
Greater Rochester YMCA
444 East Main Street
Rochester, New York 14604
(716) 546-5500

Norris D. Lineweaver
V.P. MRC South Texas
YMCA of the Greater Houston Area
P.O. Box 3007
Houston, TX 77253
(713) 659-5566

James Lipscomb
President
Albuquerque Metro YMCA
12500 Comanche N.E.
Albuquerque, NM 87111
(505) 292-0993

Dave Livingston
General Director
San Bernadino YMCA
216 West 6th Street
San Bernadino, CA 92401
(714) 885-3268

Mr. Keith A. Lofties
Vice President Fin. & Dev.
YMCA of Metro Tyler
P.O. Box 514
Tyler, Texas 75710
(214) 593-2433

Thomas J. Patton
Executive Director
Tuscarawas County YMCA
600 Monroe Street
Dover, OH 44622
(216) 364-5511

Ann L. Pearson
Program Executive
Ottawa YMCA/YWCA
180 Argyle Avenue
Ottawa, Ontario,
Canada K2P 1B7
(613) 237-1320

7

John O. Pollock
Director of Field Services
National Council of YMCA's
2160 Yonge Street
Toronto, Ontario,
Canada M4S 2A9
(416) 485-9447

Richard T. Przywara
Director of Fin. Dev.
YMCA of Delaware
11th and Washington Streets
Wilmington, DE 19803
(302) 571-6908

E. Evonne Raglin
President & CEO
Miami Metro YMCA
2400 Biscayne Blvd.
Miami, FL 33137
(305) 576-9622

Jacob Rhodes
Vice President
YMCA of Greater Houston
1600 Louisiana Street
Houston, TX 77002
(713) 659-5566

Karen W. Robinson
Executive Director
Peninsula Family YMCA
240 North El Camino Real
San Mateo, CA 94401
(415) 342-5228

George E. Rodger
Vice President of Fin. & Fac. Dev.
YMCA of Metropolitan Toronto
15 Breadalbane Street
Toronto, Ontario,
Canada M4Y 2V5
(416) 324-4128

Carl F. Muller
General Director
Valley Shore YMCA
Route #166, P.O. Box Y
Westbrook, CT 06498
(203) 399-6296

Robert L. Neal
General Director
YMCA of Metro Hartford
160 Jewell Street
Hartford, CT 06103
(203) 521-2482

Oliver Nelson
Executive Director
Yakima YMCA
P.O. Box 2885
Yakima, WA 98907
(509) 248-1202

Ann M. Nischke
Financial Development Manager
YMCA of Metro Milwaukee
915 West Wisconsin Ave., #100
Milwaukee, WI 53233
(414) 224-9622

Jean-Robert Nolet
Director General
Montreal YMCA Foundation
1441 Drummond Street
Montreal, Quebec,
Canada H3G 1W3
(514) 849-5331

Betty J. Olson
Development Director
YMCA of Metro Sacramento
2210 21st Street
Sacramento, CA 95818
(916) 452-9622

Dale Osterman
Assistant Director
Henderson County Family YMCA
460 Klutey Park Plaza
Henderson, KY 42420
(502) 826-2871

Evan C. Page
Executive Director
Beverly Regional YMCA
245 Cabot Street
Beverly, MA 01915
(617) 922-0990

Bill Taylor
Executive Director
Centre Ville YMCA
1450 Rue Stanley
Montreal, Quebec,
Canada H3A 2W6
(514) 849-8393

Jerry Ten Haken
Director – NMS
YMCA of the USA
101 North Wacker Drive
Chicago, IL 60606
(312) 977-0031

Ried Thebault
President
YMCA of Metropolitan Dayton
117 West Monument Avenue
Dayton, OH 45402
(513) 223-5201

Diane Tetreault
Director of Communications
YMCA of Montreal
1441 Drummond
Montreal, Quebec,
Canada H3G 1W3
(514) 849-5331

Kenneth A. Thiel
General Director
North Suburban YMCA
2705 Techny Road
Northbrook, IL 60062
(312) 272-7250

Joseph M. Thompson, Jr.
YMCA of Metro Washington
1711 Rhode Island Ave., N.W.
Washington, D.C. 20036
(202) 862-9622

Robert Turner
President
Greater Peoria YMCA
714 Havilton Blvd.
Peoria, IL 61603
(309) 671-2714

Bill Van Gorder
YMCA Asst. CEO & Gen. Manager
Box 3024
S. Halifax, Nova Scotia,
Canada B3J 3H1
(902) 422-6437

Darcy Sears Sheehan
Assoc. Director of Fin. Dev.
San Francisco Metro YMCA
220 Golden Gate Ave.
San Francisco, CA 94102
(415) 775-9622

Don Shellenberger
Executive Director
Two State YMCA
Box 975
Framingham, MA 01701
(616) 872-1261

Hwa Stacy
Executive Director
South Oakland YMCA
1016 West Eleven Mile Road
Royal Oak, MI 48067
(313) 547-0030

Dale E. St. George
Senior V.P. – Fin. Admin.
Metro YMCA of Alameda County
2330 Broadway
Oakland, CA 94612
(415) 451-8033

Dick Stoll
Vice President, Development
YMCA of Greater St. Louis
1528 Locust Street
St. Louis, MO 63103
(314) 436-4100

Mae-Ruth Swanson
Assoc. Metro Executive Director
Metro YMCA of Greater Oklahoma
City
125 N.W. 5th Street, Box 1374
Oklahoma City, OK 73101
(405) 235-9622

John Swift
Executive Director
San Pedro Peninsula YMCA
301 South Bandini
San Pedro, CA 90731
(213) 832-4211

Lois Tansey
Executive Director
Culver-Palms Family YMCA
4500 Sepulveda Blvd.
Culver City, CA 90230
(213) 390-3604

Rusty Youmans
Assistant General Director
Downtown Branch YMCA
301 West Sixth
Chattanooga, TN 37402
(615) 266-3766

Marcus T. Young
Vice President – Development
YMCA of Metro Chicago
755 West North Street
Chicago, IL 60610
(312) 280-3407

Mark Young
Vice President of Development
Berkeley Central Branch YMCA
2001 Allston Way
Berkeley, CA 94704
(415) 848-6800

Don Zerwer
Vice President Development
YMCA of San Diego County
7510 Clairemont Mesa Blvd., #204
San Diego, CA 92111
(619) 292-4034

Members Emeritus:

Phil Brain
Moss Causey

YMCA INCREASES REVENUE DURING 1988, BUT DROPS IN CONTRIBUTIONS

During 1988, revenue for YMCAs across the country increased 8.8 percent, but the general contributions decreased 20 percent. The largest gain in total dollars was in sustaining membership. These figures are based on 881 YMCAs that reported last year.

CONTRIBUTIONS BY SOURCE

SOURCE	REVENUE BY GENERAL CONTRIBUTIONS	% CHANGE OVER PRIOR YEAR
General Contributions	$22,246,310	– 20
Special Events	8,680,477	11.9
Legacies & Bequests	12,207,839	– 7.6
Associated Organizations	3,108,440	62.7
United Way	90,866,625	4.4
Other Fundraising Organizations	1,504,750	– 27.8
Sustaining Membership	40,817,897	21.1
Total Contributed Income	179,432,338	3.4

YMCA REVENUE

The total revenue reported nationally for YMCAs was $1,138,853,267. This represents the greatest total revenue reported in the history of the YMCA. Of this, 75 percent comes from earned income—primarily from membership fees and program fees.

The YMCA is the nation's largest voluntary community service organization. Last year, 2,048 YMCAs served 13,413,767 people of all ages, incomes, abilities, races, and religions. Forty-five percent are female and 45 percent are under 18. It is estimated that one out of every six youngsters between the ages of 6 and 11 are members of the YMCA.

The mission of the YMCA is "to put Christian principles into practice through programs that build a healthy body, mind, and spirit for all."

The national headquarters of the YMCA of the USA is located in Chicago. Each local YMCA is autonomous and depends on the national organization solely to provide counsel, training, and resources. There are 361,806 YMCA volunteers and 7,980 full-time staff members in the United States.

Solon B. Cousins, National Executive Director of the YMCA, 101 North Wacker Drive, Chicago, IL 60606 (312) 977-0031

THE FUNDRAISER'S LOT IS A HARD ONE!

It has never been easy!

When America transported its fundraising acumen to Australia, the August 1, 1907, edition of the *Sydney Bulletin* reported that there was a smart Yankee "growing monotonous with his glorious schemes for collecting cash. A report of his recent catchpenny proceedings...disgusted a number of Melbourne capitalists who have given handsome subscriptions...but it isn't good enough to justify the eternal importunities of a begging fundraiser, who presumably draws commission on his 'order' in addition to a fat salary. American methods for raising Australian money for highly moral purposes are no more deserving than...raising a controversy."

In New Zealand, it wasn't any easier. In the *Christ Church Truth:* "A pushful American arrived here on Saturday to shove off a movement which he calculates Americans will extract 15,000 pounds...done in the magic name of 'Christianity'...we hope Christ Church will pause before it allows any bustling stranger to bluff it into subsidizing what is really a very questionable object."

These early campaigns were for YMCA building programs and both were over-subscribed.

30 LARGEST YMCAs REPORT OPERATING REVENUE

The North American Urban Group is comprised of the 30 largest YMCAs in the United States and Canada, based on their annual operations budget. This Table gives the summary of income dollars for 1987.

YMCA NORTH AMERICAN URBAN GROUP
SUMMARY OF INCOME DOLLARS

ASSOCIATION	OPERATING REVENUE YEAR	UNITED WAY INCOME	OTHER CONTRIBUTION	SUSTAINING MEMBERSHIP	GOVERNMENT GRANTS	TOTAL INVESTMENT INCOME	MEMBERSHIP INCOME	OTHER INCOME	PROGRAM REVENUE*	PROGRAM FEES	RESIDENCE REVENUE	RESIDENT CAMP INCOME
TO TEN MILLION												
Santa Clara	7,067,528	403,350	89,676	455,366	461,571	17,995	1,391,151	135,645	4,112,774	3,202,145	0	910,629
Wilmington, Del.	7,115,658	599,438	78,099	184,306	394,594	191,201	2,217,682	178,391	3,271,947	1,951,660	298,725	1,021,562
Denver	7,245,803	483,900	288,041	417,854	18,519	70,614	3,223,891	86,802	2,656,182	2,424,629	231,553	0
Fort Worth	7,258,074	1,154,084	144,540	557,169	340,143	78,506	1,738,637	49,862	3,195,133	2,897,764	0	297,369
Honolulu	7,291,400	366,000	106,100	459,700	274,000	316,000	97,300	696,600	4,975,600	3,450,600	1,119,500	405,500
Atlanta/Metro.	7,299,523	788,178	782,759	226,807	0	215,336	2,697,220	61,669	2,527,554	2,392,611	0	134,943
Saint Paul	7,561,069	545,336	42,774	331,427	0	225,363	3,382,876	303,376	2,729,917	1,047,772	0	1,682,145
Cleveland	7,933,667	1,156,553	899,058	509,976	196,972	295,676	1,634,755	147,773	3,092,904	2,311,074	520,317	261,513
Rochester	8,296,196	800,000	467,496	323,672	6,450	473,426	2,838,805	234,802	3,151,545	2,665,695	0	485,850
Pittsburgh	8,406,346	958,318	45,751	408,289	1,089,631	479,858	1,439,879	980,191	3,004,429	1,443,967	136,146	1,424,316
Hartford	8,791,423	579,597	366,231	320,238	348,959	912,971	1,209,730	75,940	4,977,757	2,833,531	1,069,359	1,074,867
	84,266,687	7,834,754	3,310,525	4,194,804	3,130,839	3,277,046	21,871,926	2,951,051	37,695,742	26,621,448	3,375,600	7,698,694
TEN TO FIFTEEN MILLION												
Detroit	11,093,001	1,617,692	160,100	597,290	0	373,481	3,210,608	279,895	4,853,935	2,945,578	1,241,145	667,212
Boston	11,436,376	938,200	445,417	266,538	1,391,409	206,035	2,801,008	1,442,228	3,945,541	2,733,976	668,634	542,931
Minneapolis	12,007,000	1,148,000	392,000	934,000	259,000	485,000	4,109,000	196,000	4,484,000	2,940,000	509,000	1,035,000
Cincinnati	12,065,292	687,219	173,445	441,912	187,410	201,864	5,221,297	1,917,755	3,234,390	2,947,088	63,585	223,717
Milwaukee	12,336,791	580,000	112,510	605,736	17,672	88,450	5,515,663	749,252	4,667,508	3,294,814	1,037,893	334,801
San Diego	13,513,800	651,800	583,800	963,200	3,189,878	126,000	2,352,735	20,487	5,625,900	5,063,300	0	562,600
Seattle	13,921,773	1,147,703	833,493	462,141	3,643,621	169,837	2,978,902	204,830	4,481,246	2,897,667	663,390	920,189
Dallas	14,018,278	1,148,017	346,224	1,491,561	406,581	329,018	4,744,412	476,176	5,076,289	4,351,616	0	724,673
Saint Louis	14,269,955	1,277,042	475,784	738,246	352,881	395,122	898,780	707,759	9,424,341	7,693,428	0	1,730,913
Philadelphia	14,947,784	1,418,429	1,611,910	364,817	25,750	60,796	3,793,077	48,784	7,624,221	7,624,221	0	0
	129,610,050	10,614,102	5,134,683	6,865,441	9,474,202	2,435,603	35,625,482	6,043,166	53,417,371	42,491,688	4,183,647	6,742,036
OVER FIFTEEN MILLION												
Washington	15,169,761	528,000	58,890	668,967	372,791	34,924	6,679,519	525,593	6,301,077	5,428,329	332,695	540,053
Montreal	15,622,640	798,469	37,529	0	3,102,313	4,916	2,430,653	3,883,937	5,364,823	3,506,829	1,458,346	399,648
San Francisco	15,702,278	447,962	306,228	777,511	590,158	391,838	5,495,390	1,010,322	6,682,869	2,992,225	1,318,237	2,372,407
Houston	18,494,294	1,223,236	752,865	979,343	1,082,250	41,185	6,080,643	1,468,224	6,866,548	5,981,386	425,602	459,560
Toronto	29,972,007	1,185,525	210,809	225,346	9,343,670	202,851	7,696,080	1,368,797	9,138,929	8,563,107	0	575,822
Los Angeles	33,138,000	0	803,600	5,459,400	880,000	1,033,000	8,177,000	1,380,000	15,405,000	14,335,000	454,000	616,000
Chicago	38,451,000	2,903,000	2,627,000	0	7,064,000	2,723,000	9,463,000	1,732,000	11,939,000	4,985,000	5,426,000	1,528,000
New York	48,888,183	883,539	2,885,161	137,284	5,549,169	262,042	8,171,344	1,557,810	29,441,834	7,983,227	19,573,657	1,884,950
	214,838,163	7,969,731	7,682,082	8,247,851	27,984,351	4,693,756	54,193,629	12,926,683	91,140,080	53,775,103	28,988,537	8,376,440
	428,714,900	26,418,587	16,127,290	19,308,096	40,589,392	10,406,405	111,691,037	21,920,900	182,253,193	122,888,239	36,547,784	22,817,170

*TOTAL PROGRAM REVENUE = PROGRAM FEES + RESIDENCE REVENUE + RESIDENT CAMP INCOME

CORPORATE PHILANTHROPY UNDERSTAFFED

Brian O'Connell, President of Independent Sector, reports in a recent position paper that one of the more serious problems in corporate giving is significant understaffing. He made a random sampling of staff sizes of approximately 75 private foundations and 75 corporate grant makers. In these 150 programs of equal grant making size, the private foundations average twice the professional staff of the corporations. A graph illustrating staff sizes of corporations and foundations that give $10–$50 million follows.

CORPORATIONS		PRIVATE FOUNDATIONS	
$ Grants (million)	Prof Staff	$ Grants (million)	Prof Staff
$10–50 million		33	22
36	13	25	17
24	9	27	26
17	6	28	32
15	4	28	9
14	1	18	11
12	3	13	12
12	5	15	7
10	1	14	9
10	4	17	8
		11	6
$150 million	46 staff	10	8
		12	8
		10	4
one staff person for each $3.26 million of grants		$261 million	179 staff

one staff person for each $1.44 million of grants

REVENUE PERCENTAGES FOR 30 LARGEST YMCAs

The third largest YMCA—Los Angeles with revenue of over $33 million—receives no funds from the United Way. The largest, New York, receives only 1.8 percent of its $49 million budget from United Way. The San Francisco YMCA has the largest camp program and derives 15 percent of its revenue from this category. Forty cents out of every dollar of New York's mammoth budget comes from its residence operation. Wilmington and Rochester are the smallest cities to make the list. Chicago has the largest endowment.

YMCA NORTH AMERICAN URBAN GROUP
SUMMARY OF INCOME PERCENTAGES YEAR

ASSOCIATION	OPERATING REVENUE YEAR	UNITED WAY INCOME	OTHER CONTRIBUTION	SUSTAINING MEMBERSHIP	GOVERNMENT GRANTS	TOTAL INVESTMENT INCOME	MEMBERSHIP INCOME	OTHER INCOME	PROGRAM REVENUE*	PROGRAM FEES	RESIDENCE REVENUE	RESIDENT CAMP INCOME
TO TEN MILLION												
Santa Clara	100.00%	5.71%	1.27%	6.44%	6.53%	0.25%	19.68%	1.92%	58.19%	45.31%	0.00%	12.88%
Wilmington, Del.	100.00%	8.42%	1.10%	2.59%	5.55%	2.69%	31.17%	2.51%	45.98%	27.43%	4.20%	14.36%
Denver	100.00%	6.68%	3.98%	5.77%	0.26%	0.97%	44.49%	1.20%	36.66%	33.46%	3.20%	0.00%
Fort Worth	100.00%	15.90%	1.99%	7.68%	4.69%	1.08%	23.95%	0.69%	44.02%	39.92%	0.00%	4.10%
Honolulu	100.00%	5.02%	1.46%	6.30%	3.76%	4.34%	1.33%	9.55%	68.24%	47.32%	15.35%	5.56%
Atlanta Metro.	100.00%	10.80%	10.72%	3.11%	0.00%	2.95%	36.95%	0.84%	34.63%	32.78%	0.00%	1.85%
Saint Paul	100.00%	7.21%	0.57%	4.38%	0.00%	2.98%	44.74%	4.01%	36.10%	13.86%	0.00%	22.25%
Cleveland	100.00%	14.58%	11.33%	6.43%	2.48%	3.73%	20.61%	1.86%	38.98%	29.13%	6.56%	3.30%
Rochester	100.00%	9.64%	5.64%	3.90%	0.08%	5.71%	34.22%	2.83%	37.99%	32.13%	0.00%	5.86%
Pittsburgh	100.00%	11.40%	0.54%	4.86%	12.96%	5.71%	17.13%	11.66%	35.74%	17.18%	1.62%	16.94%
Hartford	100.00%	6.59%	4.17%	3.64%	3.97%	10.38%	13.76%	0.86%	56.62%	32.23%	12.16%	12.23%
	100.00%	9.30%	3.93%	4.98%	3.72%	3.89%	25.96%	3.50%	44.73%	31.59%	4.01%	9.14%
TEN TO FIFTEEN MILLION												
Detroit	100.00%	14.58%	1.44%	5.38%	0.00%	3.37%	28.94%	2.52%	43.76%	26.55%	11.19%	6.01%
Boston	100.00%	8.20%	3.89%	2.33%	12.17%	1.80%	24.49%	12.61%	34.50%	23.91%	5.85%	4.75%
Minneapolis	100.00%	9.56%	3.26%	7.78%	2.16%	4.04%	34.22%	1.63%	37.34%	24.49%	4.24%	8.62%
Cincinnati	100.00%	5.70%	1.44%	3.66%	1.55%	1.67%	43.88%	15.89%	26.81%	24.43%	0.53%	1.85%
Milwaukee	100.00%	4.70%	0.91%	4.91%	0.14%	0.72%	44.71%	6.07%	37.83%	26.71%	8.41%	2.71%
San Diego	100.00%	4.82%	4.32%	7.13%	23.60%	0.93%	17.41%	0.15%	41.63%	37.47%	0.00%	4.16%
Seattle	100.00%	8.24%	5.99%	3.32%	26.17%	1.22%	21.40%	1.47%	32.19%	20.81%	4.77%	6.61%
Dallas	100.00%	8.19%	2.47%	10.64%	2.90%	2.35%	33.84%	3.40%	36.21%	31.04%	0.00%	5.17%
Saint Louis	100.00%	8.95%	3.33%	5.17%	2.47%	2.77%	6.30%	4.96%	66.04%	53.91%	0.00%	12.13%
Philadelphia	100.00%	9.49%	10.78%	2.44%	0.17%	0.41%	25.38%	0.33%	51.01%	51.01%	0.00%	0.00%
	100.00%	8.19%	3.96%	5.30%	7.31%	1.88%	27.49%	4.66%	41.21%	32.78%	3.23%	5.20%
OVER FIFTEEN MILLION												
Washington	100.00%	3.48%	0.39%	4.41%	2.46%	0.23%	44.03%	3.46%	41.54%	35.78%	2.19%	3.56%
Montreal	100.00%	5.11%	0.24%	0.00%	19.86%	0.03%	15.56%	24.86%	34.34%	22.45%	9.33%	2.56%
San Francisco	100.00%	2.85%	1.95%	4.95%	3.76%	2.50%	35.00%	6.43%	42.56%	19.06%	8.40%	15.11%
Houston	100.00%	6.61%	4.07%	5.30%	5.85%	0.22%	32.88%	7.94%	37.13%	32.34%	2.30%	2.48%
Toronto	100.00%	4.04%	0.72%	0.77%	31.81%	0.69%	26.20%	4.66%	31.11%	29.15%	0.00%	1.96%
Los Angeles	100.00%	0.00%	2.43%	16.47%	2.66%	3.12%	24.68%	4.16%	46.49%	43.26%	1.37%	1.86%
Chicago	100.00%	7.55%	6.83%	0.00%	18.37%	7.08%	24.61%	4.50%	31.05%	12.96%	14.11%	3.97%
New York	100.00%	1.81%	5.90%	0.28%	11.35%	0.54%	16.71%	3.19%	60.22%	16.33%	40.04%	3.86%
	100.00%	3.71%	3.58%	3.84%	13.03%	2.18%	25.23%	6.02%	42.42%	25.03%	13.49%	3.90%

*TOTAL PROGRAM REVENUE = PROGRAM FEES + RESIDENCE REVENUE + RESIDENT CAMP INCOME

Source: 1988 Management Information Report, YMCA

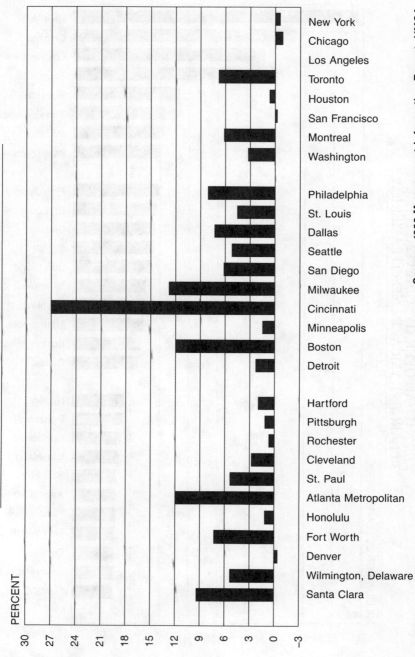

UNITED WAY REVENUE
AVERAGE FOUR YEAR GROWTH
FOR THE 30 LARGEST YMCAs IN NORTH AMERICA

Source: 1988 Management Information Report, YMCA

15

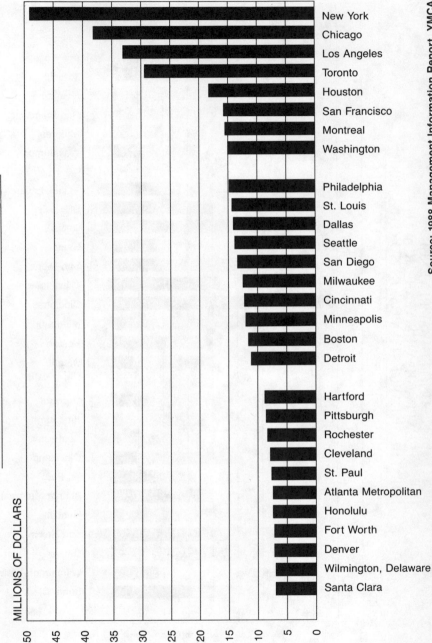

TOTAL OPERATING REVENUE
30 LARGEST YMCAs IN NORTH AMERICA

MILLIONS OF DOLLARS

Source: 1988 Management Information Report, YMCA

New York
Chicago
Los Angeles
Toronto
Houston
San Francisco
Montreal
Washington

Philadelphia
St. Louis
Dallas
Seattle
San Diego
Milwaukee
Cincinnati
Minneapolis
Boston
Detroit

Hartford
Pittsburgh
Rochester
Cleveland
St. Paul
Atlanta Metropolitan
Honolulu
Fort Worth
Denver
Wilmington, Delaware
Santa Clara

50   45   40   35   30   25   20   15   10   5   0

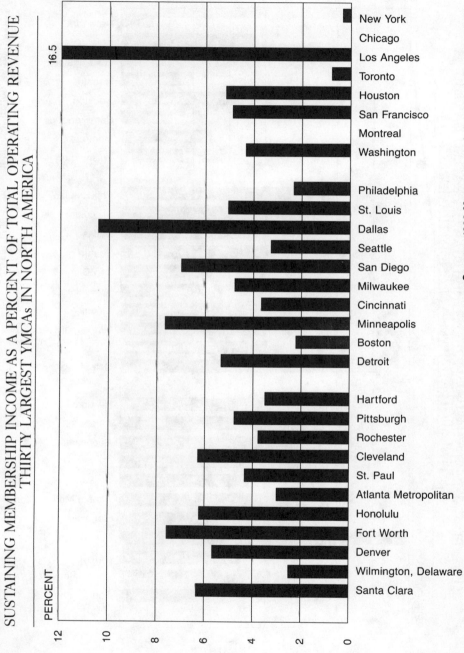

SUSTAINING MEMBERSHIP INCOME AS A PERCENT OF TOTAL OPERATING REVENUE
THIRTY LARGEST YMCAs IN NORTH AMERICA

Source: 1988 Management Information Report, YMCA

PERCENT

New York
Chicago
Los Angeles
Toronto
Houston
San Francisco
Montreal
Washington

Philadelphia
St. Louis
Dallas
Seattle
San Diego
Milwaukee
Cincinnati
Minneapolis
Boston
Detroit

Hartford
Pittsburgh
Rochester
Cleveland
St. Paul
Atlanta Metropolitan
Honolulu
Fort Worth
Denver
Wilmington, Delaware
Santa Clara

16.5

12   10   8   6   4   2   0

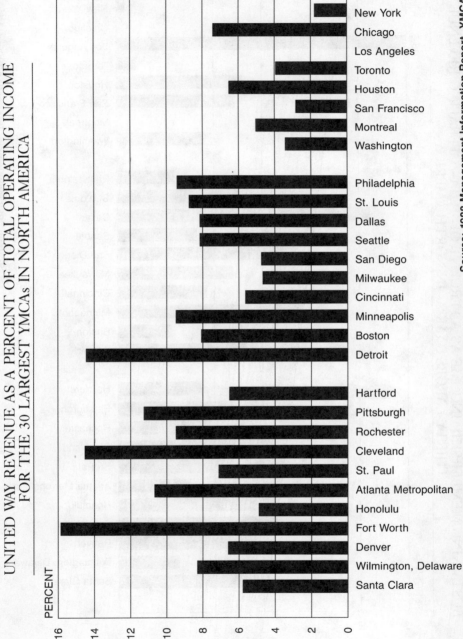

UNITED WAY REVENUE AS A PERCENT OF TOTAL OPERATING INCOME FOR THE 30 LARGEST YMCAs IN NORTH AMERICA

Source: 1988 Management Information Report, YMCA

PERCENT

New York
Chicago
Los Angeles
Toronto
Houston
San Francisco
Montreal
Washington

Philadelphia
St. Louis
Dallas
Seattle
San Diego
Milwaukee
Cincinnati
Minneapolis
Boston
Detroit

Hartford
Pittsburgh
Rochester
Cleveland
St. Paul
Atlanta Metropolitan
Honolulu
Fort Worth
Denver
Wilmington, Delaware
Santa Clara

16 14 12 10 8 6 4 2 0

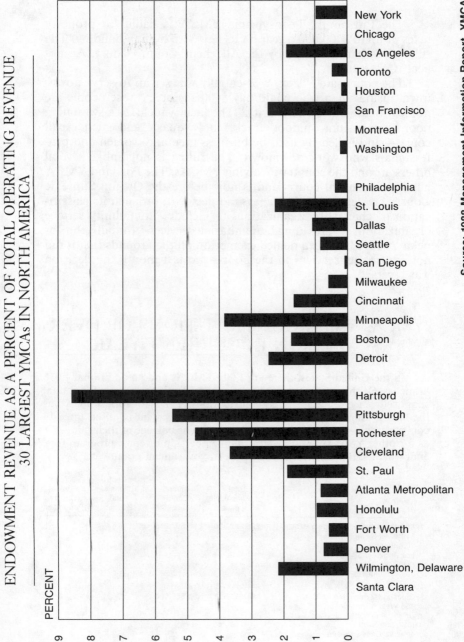

ENDOWMENT REVENUE AS A PERCENT OF TOTAL OPERATING REVENUE
30 LARGEST YMCAs IN NORTH AMERICA

PERCENT

Source: 1988 Management Information Report, YMCA

New York
Chicago
Los Angeles
Toronto
Houston
San Francisco
Montreal
Washington

Philadelphia
St. Louis
Dallas
Seattle
San Diego
Milwaukee
Cincinnati
Minneapolis
Boston
Detroit

Hartford
Pittsburgh
Rochester
Cleveland
St. Paul
Atlanta Metropolitan
Honolulu
Fort Worth
Denver
Wilmington, Delaware
Santa Clara

19

TAX EXEMPT STATUS OF YMCAs CONTINUES TO BE CHALLENGED

The Pittsburgh, Pennsylvania YMCA is liable for property taxes of up to $200,000 a year on its new $7.5 million building. The ruling was handed down by the Allegheny County Court. An appeal is expected.

The court said, "This Y essentially was set up to serve downtown businessmen who could pay $600 a year...those people are not legitimate objects of charity." The facility includes a swimming pool, gymnasium, indoor track, and squash and racquetball courts—and is heavily used by business men and women and professionals who work downtown. The ruling is not unlike several others around the country involving YMCAs. The Portland YMCA has lost in several courts and is now before the Oregon Supreme Court. The legislature in Kansas did decide to broaden its classification of charitable organizations to include "community service organizations...providing humanitarian services." Initially, the Topeka YMCA had been denied exemption on the grounds that it did not confine its services to the poor—and last month the decision was reversed.

YMCAs WITH CONTRIBUTIONS OF OVER $1 MILLION IN CURRENT YEAR

In the United States, there are 1,009 YMCAs and an additional 1,036 branches. Of this group, 26 associations raise $1 million or more for annual support from gifts, grants, and contributions. The New York YMCA has the largest annual operating budget, but only 9 percent is raised through contributions—the lowest among this group. The balance of their budget—as for other YMCAs—is derived from membership revenue, program fees, endowments, residence and food services, government grants, etc.

Association	Total Annual Revenue	Annual Contri- butions	% Contri- butions of Total Budget	Rank of City by Population
1) Los Angeles Metropolitan YMCA 818 West Seventh Street 10th Floor Los Angeles, CA 90017 (213) 489-3200 John G. Ouellet, President/CEO	$28,292,500	$6,507,275	23	2
2) Chicago Metropolitan YMCA 755 West North Avenue Chicago, IL 60610 (312) 280-3400 John W. Casey, President	38,450,615	5,383,086	14	3

3) New York YMCA Metropolitan Board 422 Ninth Avenue New York, NY 10001 (212) 564-1300 William A. Markell, President	47,575,171	4,281,765	9	1
4) Greater Houston Area 1600 Louisiana P.O. Box 3007 Houston, TX 77253 (713) 659-5566 Bev R. Laws, President	18,494,294	2,959,087	16	4
5) Dallas Metropolitan YMCA 601 North Akard Street Dallas, TX 75201 (214) 954-0500 J. Ben Casey, President	14,018,278	2,943,838	21	7
6) Minneapolis Metropolitan YMCA 31 South Ninth Street Minneapolis, MN 55402 (612) 371-8700 James P. Gilbert, President	12,189,085	2,437,817	20	42
7) Greater St. Louis YMCA 1528 Locust Street St. Louis, MO 63103 (314) 436-1177 Larry V. Alvey, President	14,083,202	2,394,144	17	30
8) Detroit Metropolitan YMCA Board 2020 Witherell Street Detroit, MI 48226 (313) 644-9036 Robert W. Davis, President	10,991,571	2,308,229	21	6
9) Philadelphia Metropolitan YMCA 1429 Walnut Street Philadelphia, PA 19102 (215) 963-3700 Richard L. Betts, President	15,150,865	2,272,629	15	5
10) San Diego County YMCA 7510 Clairemont Mesa Blvd. Suite 204 San Diego, CA 92111 (619) 292-4034 Richard A. Collato, President/CEO	13,513,779	2,162,204	16	8
11) Cleveland Metropolitan YMCA 2200 Prospect Ave. Cleveland, OH 44115 (216) 344-0095 Clifford A. Smith, President	7,700,445	2,156,125	28	23
12) Seattle Metropolitan YMCA 909 Fourth Avenue Seattle, WA 90104 (206) 382-5003 William V. Phillips, President	13,985,723	2,097,858	15	25
13) Atlanta Metropolitan YMCA 100 Edgewood Avenue N.E. Suite 902 Atlanta, GA 30303 (404) 588-9622 Fred Hanna, President	7,299,474	1,970,858	27	31

14) Fort Worth YMCA Metropolitan Board 540 Lamar Street Fort Worth, TX 76102 (817) 334-6147 Arthur M. Thompson, President	7,235,724	1,591,859	22	32
15) Greater Boston YMCA 316 Huntington Street Boston, MA 02115 (617) 536-6950 Peter B. Post, President	11,253,087	1,575,432	14	20
16) San Francisco Metropolitan YMCA 220 Golden Gate Avenue San Francisco, CA 94102 (415) 775-9622 David R. Mercer, President	12,969,856	1,556,382	12	13
17) Rochester Metropolitan YMCA Corporate Offices 444 East Main Street Rochester, NY 14604 (716) 546-5500 Marvin E. Reinke, President/CEO	7,461,109	1,417,611	19	*
18) Pittsburgh Metropolitan YMCA 330 Boulevard of the Allies Pittsburgh, PA 15222 (412) 227-6420 Julius Jones, President	8,335,466	1,417,029	17	33
19) Cincinnati Metropolitan YMCA 1105 Elm Street Cincinnati, OH 45210 (513) 651-2100 George H. Edmiston, President	12,065,292	1,327,182	11	38
20) Milwaukee Metropolitan YMCA 915 West Wisconsin Ave. Suite 100 Milwaukee, WI 53233 (414) 224-9622 John H. Turner, President/CEO	12,333,243	1,233,324	10	18
21) Orange County Metropolitan YMCA 13252 Garden Grove Blvd. Suite 120 Garden Grove, CA 92643 (714) 750-2757 Allan D. Shaffer, President	6,351,973	1,206,875	19	*
22) Columbus Metropolitan YMCA 40 West Long Street Columbus, OH 43215 (614) 224-1142 Jerry L. Garver, President	5,189,372	1,193,556	23	21
23) Hartford Metropolitan YMCA 160 Jewell Street Hartford, CT 06103 (203) 522-4183 Robert L. Neal, General Ex. Dir.	8,427,986	1,179,918	14	*
24) Nashville Metropolitan YMCA 706 Church St. Suite 100 Nashville, TN 37203 (615) 259-9622 Clark D. Baker, General Ex. Dir.	5,835,746	1,108,792	19	27

25) Kansas City Metropolitan YMCA   4,605,258   1,105,262   24   29
    3100 Broadway
    Suite 930
    Kansas City, MO 64111
    (816) 561-9622
    Harold E. Dooley, President

*not among top 50 most populous cities

Source: YMCA Year Book

UNITED WAY REVENUE TO TOP 16 YWCAs IN THE COUNTRY

City/State	United Way Revenue	Percentage of United Way Grants to Total Operating Revenue
1) Dallas, TX	$962,738	35.8
2) Chicago, IL	837,762	19.1
3) Minneapolis, MN	814,441	28.1
4) Atlanta, GA	809,668	41.3
5) Los Angeles, CA	702,087	28.3
6) Baltimore, MD	669,871	20.7
7) Cleveland, OH	663,756	28.9
8) Boston, MA	639,333	16.0
9) Pittsburgh, PA	624,064	20.5
10) St. Louis, MO	589,895	38.5
11) Dayton, OH	451,993	32.5
12) Buffalo, NY	433,873	24.0
13) San Francisco, CA	408,723	24.2
14) San Diego, CA	358,122	23.6
15) El Paso, TX	194,174	4.0
16) New York, NY	64,022	1.8

A WONDERFUL TAX

It is not widely known, but Anheuser-Busch imposes a 2.5 cent tax on every case of beer it sells to its distributors. The proceeds go to the Muscular Dystrophy Association. In 1988, the total amount donated through this method amounted to close to $20 million.

In addition, the Anheuser-Busch corporate headquarters also "strongly recommends" that each distributor donate 5 cents to a local charity for every case of beer sold. These accounts are audited by headquarters.

What happens if the local Anheuser-Busch distributor does not allocate the proper amount to charity from beer sales? One local distributor said: "Chances are they would not be a distributor for long."

MEMBERSHIP REVENUE OF TOP 16 YWCAs IN COUNTRY

City/State	Membership Revenue	Percentage of Membership Income to Total Operating Revenue
1) New York, NY	$304,626	8.6
2) Dallas, TX	193,120	6.7
3) El Paso, TX	127,402	2.3
4) Minneapolis, MN	101,093	3.4
5) Cleveland, OH	85,351	4.7
6) Boston, MA	65,714	1.4
7) St. Louis, MO	64,124	4.2
8) Pittsburgh, PA	63,139	2.1
9) Atlanta, GA	50,105	1.2
10) Chicago, IL	41,928	1.0
11) Los Angeles, CA	33,595	1.8
12) San Francisco, CA	31,193	0.0
13) Buffalo, NY	28,328	1.5
14) San Diego, CA	28,061	3.1
15) Baltimore, MD	25,610	0.9
16) Dayton, OH	18,067	1.6

ANNUAL ENDOWMENT INTEREST FOR TOP 16 YWCAs IN THE COUNTRY

City/State	Interest Endowment Revenue	Percentage of Endowment Interest Income to Total Operating Revenue
1) Pittsburgh	$919,783	30.2
2) Chicago, IL	540,316	12.3
3) New York, NY	389,780	10.9
4) Boston, MA	241,000	6.0
5) Dayton, OH	156,877	11.2
6) Minneapolis, MN	131,401	4.5
7) Cleveland, OH	129,242	5.6
8) St. Louis, MO	61,928	4.0
9) San Diego, CA	42,151	2.8
10) El Paso, TX	20,717	0.4
11) Baltimore, MD	17,480	0.5
12) Atlanta, GA	5,676	0.3
13) San Francisco, CA	4,546	0.3
14) Dallas, TX	4,189	0.2
15) Buffalo, NY	382	0.0
16) Los Angeles, CA	175	0.0

NON-UNITED WAY CONTRIBUTED REVENUE TO TOP
16 YWCAs IN THE COUNTRY

City/State	Contributed Revenue	Percentage of Contributed Revenue to Total Operating Revenue
1) Baltimore, MD	$413,098	12.8
2) Cleveland, OH	342,047	14.9
3) New York, NY	328,196	9.2
4) El Paso, TX	326,899	6.7
5) Dallas, TX	259,615	9.7
6) Minneapolis, MN	225,272	7.8
7) Boston, MA	208,978	5.2
8) St. Louis, MO	170,189	11.1
9) Atlanta, GA	155,315	7.9
10) San Diego, CA	149,562	9.9
11) Chicago, IL	126,962	2.9
12) Los Angeles, CA	119,309	4.8
13) Pittsburgh, PA	118,377	3.9
14) Buffalo, NY	117,087	6.5
15) San Francisco, CA	86,206	5.1
16) Dayton, OH	81,523	5.9

GOVERNMENT GRANTS TO TOP 16
YWCAs IN THE COUNTRY

City/State	Government Grants	Percentage of Government Funds to Total Operating Revenue
1) El Paso, TX	$2,666,524	54.8
2) Chicago, IL	1,930,514	44.1
3) Baltimore, MD	1,429,044	44.2
4) Pittsburgh, PA	918,359	30.2
5) Boston, MA	787,060	19.7
6) San Diego, CA	435,849	28.7
7) New York, NY	419,900	11.8
8) Dayton, OH	356,536	25.6
9) Los Angeles, CA	258,300	10.4
10) San Francisco, CA	208,043	12.3
11) Atlanta, GA	188,221	9.6
12) Minneapolis, MN	74,937	2.6
13) St. Louis, MO	55,119	3.5
14) Buffalo, NY	14,285	0.8
15) Cleveland, OH	0	0.0
16) Dallas, TX	0	0.0

AMOUNT OF FOUNDATION FUNDS RECEIVED BY
TOP 16 YWCAs IN THE COUNTRY

City/State	Foundation Grants	Percentage of Foundation Funds to Total Operating Revenue
1) San Francisco, CA	$261,638	15.5
2) New York, NY	219,380	6.1
3) Chicago, IL	214,890	4.9
4) Cleveland, OH	182,023	7.9
5) St. Louis, MO	78,096	5.1
6) El Paso, TX	33,300	0.7
7) Pittsburgh, PA	11,943	0.4
8) Dallas, TX	1,973	0.1
9) Atlanta, GA	0	0.0
10) Baltimore, MD	0	0.0
11) Boston, MA	0	0.0
12) Buffalo, NY	0	0.0
13) Dayton, OH	0	0.0
14) Los Angeles, CA	0	0.0
15) Minneapolis, MN	0	0.0
16) San Diego, CA	0	0.0

THE FIVE SMALLEST UNITED WAYS

The nation's five United Ways reporting the least amount of contributed income.

City & State/Executive	$ Amount Raised
1) Safford, AZ	1,157
2) Crete, NE	1,870
Sarah O'Shea, Secretary, Treasurer	
3) Flomaton, AL	5,000
James R. Jones, Treasurer	
4) Russellville, AL	5,136
Janet F. Blackburn, Treasurer	
5) Pleasant Hill, MO	6,410
Mary Jane Hill, Campaign Chairman	

Source: United Way International *Directory*, 1987-1988

BASIC FACTS ABOUT UNITED WAY

The more than 2,300 United Ways throughout America and abroad are organizations, made up primarily of volunteers, that help meet health and human-care needs through a vast network of local charitable groups and volunteers.

Each United Way is an independent community resource governed by a local board of volunteers.

Through a single community-wide campaign, a United Way raises funds to help meet local health and human-care needs.

But a United Way is much more than a fund-raiser. Volunteers:

Assess current and future community needs;
Bring organizations and people together to address needs;
Distribute resources, through a review process, where they are needed most;
Recruit and train other volunteers;
Put people in touch with the services they need; and
Offer management and technical help to a wide range of community agencies.

Apart from government, United Ways support the greatest variety of human services in the country, reaching people from all walks of life and all income groups.

Voluntary contributions to United Ways support approximately 37,000 programs and services, helping millions of people. United Ways have funded 4,695 new agencies since 1983.

Some of these service providers are nationwide agencies that have local chapters. Some are small one-of-a-kind local agencies. Funding patterns are flexible; they not only serve traditional agencies, but also address new and emerging needs.

United Ways ensure that every group receiving funds is a nonprofit, tax-exempt charity governed by volunteers, submitting to an annual independent financial audit, providing services at a reasonable cost, and maintaining a policy of nondiscrimination.

United Ways are among the most efficient charitable organizations. Because of volunteers and the simplicity of corporate payroll deduction, only 10.5 percent of all funds raised are used for administrative expenses.

United Ways collectively raised $2.6 billion in 1987 through voluntary contributions from individuals, corporations, small businesses and foundations. During the last five years, giving to United Way has steadily increased:

Year	Amount	Percent Increase
1983	$1.95 billion	9.5
1984	2.14 billion	10.0
1985	2.33 billion	9.0
1986	2.44 billion	5.7
1987	2.6 billion	6.4

Source: United Way of America

WILLIAM ARAMONY HEADS UNITED WAY

William Aramony is President of United Way of America, the national association for United Way organizations in 2,300 communities across the nation. He has held the national position since

1970, after 17 years of local service in United Ways in South Bend, Indiana; Columbia, South Carolina; and Dade County (Miami), Florida.

Under his leadership, United Way giving has tripled. The organization has also evolved from primarily fundraising organizations to community problem-solving organizations. In this role, they assume a much larger responsibility in planning for and addressing health and human care needs.

For information call (703) 836-7100.

EVENTS, INSTITUTIONS & EXTERNAL FORCES
AFFECTING UNITED WAY: 1887–1988

1887: In Denver, religious leaders founded the Charity Organizations Society, the first United Way, which planned and coordinated local services and conducted a single fund-raising campaign for 22 agencies.

1888: The first "United Way" campaign in Denver raised $21,700 in November.

1894: Charitable institutions became exempt from the first federal act that imposed a tax on "all corporations organized for profit."

1895: The first independent federation of Jewish agencies was formed in Boston.

1900: Cleveland's Chamber of Commerce formed the Committee on Benevolent Associations to set standards and monitor charities. It was the first effort at charity self-regulation and was established to protect the donor.

1905: Chicago's directory of charities listed 3,000 agencies.

1908: The first community planning program, Associated Charities, was formed in Pittsburgh.

1910: A council was formed in Columbus, Ohio, to prevent overlapping of services and multiplicity of solicitations.

1911: The National Association of Societies for Organizing Charity was formed to help social agencies cooperate and share information.

1913: The nation's first modern Community Chest was born in Cleveland, where a program for allocating campaign funds was developed.

1918: The National Information Bureau, later the National Charities Information Bureau (NCIB) , was established to investigate national charitable organizations.

Executives of 12 fund-raising federations met in Chicago and formed the American Association for Community Organizations (AACO). These men are considered by many to be the founding fathers of what is now United Way of America. The organization's objective was "to encourage and stimulate collective community planning, and the development of better standards in the work of community organizations for social work."

1919: Rochester, New York, used the name "Community Chest," a name widely adopted by United Way organizations and used until the early 1950s. This year began a 10-year growth spurt in the number of Community Chests—39 in 1919; 353 in 1929.

1927: The national AACO adopted a new name, the Association of Community Chests and Councils (ACCC). With the exception of Boston, Chicago, and New York, all larger communities accepted federated financing. Nearly $69 million was raised by 314 communities.

1931: President Hoover permitted the Washington, DC, Community Chest to solicit federal employees. The local Red Cross chapter joined that campaign.

Community Chests mobilized to fight hunger and need created by the Great Depression. The first televised philanthropic appeal to report on campaign progress took place October 10 in the CBS studios. Despite the depression, total funds raised surpassed $100 million.

1933: AACO changed its name to Community Chests and Councils (CCC).

The National Women's Committee, led by Eleanor Roosevelt, joined the mobilization to meet human needs. This was one of the first national responsibilities ever undertaken by a President's wife.

1935: With the support and encouragement of United Ways and their national association, Congress amended income tax laws, allowing corporations to deduct up to 5 percent of taxable income for charitable donations.

1942: AFL and CIO leaders and United Way established labor liaison programs to strengthen the organized labor/United Way partnership in community service. United Way leaders formed the National War Fund to raise and allocate funds for war-related programs. The war sparked fundraising: nearly $167 million was raised, a 53 percent increase over the previous campaign.

1943: The government began withholding social security and federal income taxes from employee pay, paving the way for payroll deduction of charitable contributions.

1944: Almost 800 United Ways raised $222 million during the last full year of the war.

1946: The AFL, and CIO, and the CCC signed an agreement to develop a cooperative relationship between United Way and labor.

1948: The national organization became Community Chest and Councils of America, Inc., though many still called it by its nickname—"Three Cs."

More than 1,000 communities had established United Ways.

1949: Detroit became the first community to adopt the name "United Fund."

1955: The AFL-CIO Community Services Committee was established.

1956: The national organization changed its name to United Community Funds and Councils of America (UCFCA).

1957: President Eisenhower signed the executive order creating the Uniform Federal Fund-Raising Program, which permitted local federated campaigns to ask federal employees for pledges (forerunner of CFC).

The National Council on Community Foundations was incorporated. It became the Council on Foundations in 1964.

1960: The Institute of Community Studies was established (forerunner of the Management and Community Studies Institute, MACSI). The Commerce and Industry Combined Health Appeal (CICHA) was organized in Baltimore.

1961: President Kennedy signed the executive order making health and welfare agencies and "such other national voluntary agencies as may be appropriate" eligible to receive gifts from federal employees.

1963: The National Budget and Consultation Committee, which evolved from the Joint Budget Committee of the Community Chests and Councils and the American War Community Services, published Standards for National Voluntary Health, Welfare and Recreation Agencies.

Los Angeles became the first community to formally adopt the name "United Way." More than 30 Community Chest and United Fund organizations there merged to become United Way, Inc.

1964: The War on Poverty began.

A payroll deduction plan for federal employees started as three fund-raising campaigns were consolidated into one—the beginning of what is known today as the Combined Federal Campaign (CFC).

1966: "Statement of Consensus on Government and the Voluntary Sector in Health and Welfare" developed, urging cooperation among federal government, national agencies, and UCFCA.

Mid-60s: Growth of art and culture concerns; Combined Health Agencies Drives (CHAD) ; International Social Agencies (ISA).

1967: United Way campaigns raised more than $700 million, despite work shortage, civil disturbance, and general unrest. United Ways helped 27.5 million families. 31,300 agencies were affiliated. 8.5 million people were volunteering. 32,800 made donations.

1970: William Aramony became national executive and initiated the Thirteen Point Program for rebirth and renewal of United Way.

The national association reorganized under the name "United Way of America." Volunteer leaders adopted a resolution encouraging members to use the United Way name.

1971: United Way of America relocated from New York City to Alexandria, VA.

1972: The National Academy for Voluntarism (NAV), part of the Thirteen Point Program, was established to provide continuing education to United Way volunteers and professionals, as well as others involved in the management and administration of voluntary agencies.

The Revenue Sharing bill awarded $30.2 billion to state and local governments over a five-year period. United Way's hope that the money would be used for pressing social needs did not materialize (1972-1977).

1974: United Ways raised $1,038,995,000 in America and Canada, marking the first time in history that an annual campaign of a single organization raised more than $1 billion. United Ways undertook the largest public service campaign in the nation's history, as well. A major part of that campaign was "Great Moments," the televised United Way/National Football League public service announcements.

San Diego, California, held the first combined campaign of United Way and CHAD, raising more than $7 million, a more than 10 percent increase over the aggregate amount raised by United Way and CHAD in their 1973 separate campaigns.

Baltimore, Maryland, held the first combined campaign of United Way and CICHA, raising more than $13 million for a 12 percent increase over the total raised by United Way of Central

31

Maryland and CICHA in their separate campaigns the year before.

The National Black United Fund (NBUF) was organized.

1975:   The Filer Commission released its report on Private Philanthropy and Public Needs. It was one of the first and most important studies conducted on nonprofit giving.

1976:   The National Committee for Responsive Philanthropy (NCRP) was created in response to findings of the Filer Commission.

1977:   Annual fund-raising growth, under the Program for the Future, exceeded $100 million for the first time.

1981:   United Ways raised $1.68 billion, a 10.1 percent increase over 1980. Despite high unemployment and economic uncertainty, it was the largest single-year percentage increase in 25 years.

1982:   United Way of America's national service center opened in August, increasing the organization's ability to assist the nation's 2,200 United Ways. It also enabled United Way of America to respond to the needs of new and emerging health and welfare organizations.

1983:   Congress made a first-of-its-kind $50 million emergency food and shelter grant to the voluntary sector. United Way of America was the fiscal agent.

1985:   United Ways raised $2.33 billion, a 9 percent increase over 1984.

1987:   United Way recognized its centennial by saluting the American volunteer through many programs, including the dedication of a United Way postage stamp by the U.S. Postal Service.

In Washington, D.C., more than 3,000 people attended the Centennial Volunteer Leaders Conference, the largest United Way conference ever. At the same time, United Way conducted its first-ever Young Leaders Conference for high-school and college age people from across the country.

United Ways launched the Second Century Initiative (SCI), a collective effort to double funds and volunteers, as well as become a more open and caring organization.

United Ways number more than 2,300 across the country.

President Reagan visited United Way of America in December to receive a report on United Way's progress from the organization's national Board Chairman, James D. Robinson III, chairman and chief executive officer of American Express.

1988:   Supported by United Ways across the country, United Way of

America met with the National Governors' Association to endorse welfare reform legislation that, as of August, was passed by Congress. The reforms would focus on solving the human needs problems that cause welfare dependency.

United Way of America's grant from the W.K. Kellogg Foundation to accelerate minority volunteer involvement and support to minority organizations became even more effective. "Project Blueprint" awarded funds to 18 communities for minority development.

Source: United Way of America

IT HELPS TO HAVE FRIENDS

Henry R. Kravis, the mega-investor, gave $10 million in 1988 to the Metropolitan Museum of Art in New York. It's a pet project of his. And to commemorate the gift, a new wing in the museum will carry his name.

Then others decided to pitch in to demonstrate their friendship for Kravis. Lawrence and Robert Tisch gave $10 million, and they got their name on a gallery in the Kravis Wing. New York City added another $13.5 million. From the estate of Lila Acheson Wallace, co-founder of *Reader's Digest,* came another $1 million. Before it was finished, $51 million had been collected.

To top it off, Henry R. Kravis has been named a Trustee of the museum.

TAKE THEM TO COURT

The Jewish Federation of Southern New Jersey got a lot of attention in 1988. The federation initiated suits against donors who had not completed payments on their pledges. Officials at the federation defended their position, saying that the money pledged was already allocated to many social and welfare programs which provide a wide range of funding to a number of charities serving the Jewish community. It will be interesting to see how well they do this year in their annual campaign!

It is not often that a charity will sue for an unpaid pledge, but it does happen. In 1988 Chapman College (Orange, California) sued the Bentley estate. Mr. Bentley, a board member, had made a sizeable pledge and the family did not wish to acknowledge it. College officials claim that Mr. Bentley was a devoted friend of the college and a board member for a number of years, and his intention was to give the money.

Many organizations are moving toward a "Letter of Intent" instead of a legally binding pledge. Experience indicates that the donor will give more and that there is actually less attrition.

UNITED WAY—WHERE IT ALL BEGAN!

The year was 1887. Denver was experiencing a greater influx of people than ever before. A gold and silver mining boom had swelled the city's population from 5,000 to almost 80,000 in 20 short years! The city was reeling from the rapid change.

Denver was paying a price. Thousands upon thousands of wealth-seekers and soldiers of fortune were streaming in. Beggars filled the streets. Orphans were everywhere—left behind by poor families unable to care for them.

Trainloads of tuberculosis victims flooded in from all over the east—lured by the promise of better health in Denver's dry, thin-air climate. It seemed as if every U.S. city was trying to send its sick elsewhere—and elsewhere was often spelled Denver.

It was an unlikely crib for the birth of the world's largest voluntary human services movement—the United Way, initially known as the Charity Organization Society of Denver.

Denver, to its credit, had developed charities to try to deal with the problems, but local businesses were being overrun by solicitors seeking funds for every cause imaginable: orphans, the elderly, the impoverished, the physically and mentally ill. Not only did everyone have a hand out, but the soliciting was eating up precious work time for both business owners and their employees.

Inefficiency was rife as multiple charities duplicated fundraising efforts. Those early groups spent much of their time soliciting and too little on the human-care problems they were supposed to address.

Like so many important movements before and after, the first United Way was created by men of the cloth—four far-visioned ministers who thought there must be a better way to meet the social needs of the local poor.

The Reverend William J. O'Ryan, a young Catholic priest from England, had recently journeyed to Denver in hopes of curing his tuberculosis problem. While serving in England, O'Ryan had witnessed an interesting new phenomenon in Liverpool—a loosely organized "financial federation" charged with raising money for a variety of different charities.

O'Ryan met three fellow religious leaders in Denver who shared his concerns about the unmet needs of Denver's less fortunate: the Reverend Myron Reed, a Congregational minister; Dean H. Martyn Hart, an Episcopalian minister; and later, the Rabbi William Friedman.

The organizers started what is now the international United Way movement by creating the Charity Organization Society of Denver. They were the first to create an organization that was an effective fundraiser for many charities, and the first to develop a model for organizing teams of workers to solicit employees in a variety of businesses.

Though the founders created their Charity Organization Society in October 1887, the first fundraising campaign was not until 1888, when the society raised $21,700 for 22 charities. Four of the original charities are still Denver United Way agencies 100 years later.

By 1892, eight of the original agencies had dropped out; they were able to raise less money through the federated approach than they could individually. Indecision as to the organization's purpose was demonstrated by four different constitutions within the first five years.

Despite the fundraising society's problems, other cities were catching on to the federated charity idea: by 1895, there were nearly 100 federations nationally.

In 1913, Cleveland took a giant step toward forming the first "modern" United Way organization by creating the Cleveland Federation. The concept was similar to that created by Denver 26 years earlier, but there was no comparing the degree of sophistication.

Workplace employees solicited funds based on intricate strategies. Money collected was allocated to member agencies according to carefully crafted budgeting techniques. A paid public relations officer was highly successful in educating the Cleveland public on the merits of the new organization. And the paid staff was noted for its great efficiency.

Cleveland avoided two mistakes made by Denver: it recognized the need for an able staff and a continuous public education effort. Backers successfully organized a speakers' bureau to educate prospective contributors about the federation's purpose and its agencies' human-care services.

The Cleveland Federation also employed modern research and statistical methods to identify the most urgent service needs of its community.

George Eastman of Eastman-Kodak Company and a group of dedicated Rochester contributors developed the term *community chest* for their city's federated United Way movement, a name that quickly became national.

By the end of World War I, nearly 400 chests dotted the country. The war chest helped establish the present-day model for the combined, community-wide fundraising campaigns that now characterize the United Way movement.

In 1918, federation charity officials from across the country formed the American Association for Community Organizations, the forerunner of today's national United Way trade group, United Way of America.

World War II ushered in changes, as Denver and other U.S. communities resurrected the war chest.

Community Chest agencies were handicapped by the personnel needs of the war effort. Doctors and nurses in particular were in short supply, and even chest recreation agencies and community centers could not meet personnel needs. Health facilities were stretched to the limit. With private hospitals overcrowded and patients discharged earlier than normal, the need for convalescent and Visiting Nurse Association home nursing care skyrocketed.

In the midst of the war, Congress passed far-reaching legislation that would forever change the fact of United Way giving. By mandating compulsory withholding of federal income and social security tax payments from employees' pay in 1943, Congress opened the door for workers to also make voluntary United Way payroll deductions. To this day, employee payroll deductions comprise about 60 percent of funds raised by United Ways.

The 1940s proved a birthing ground for a familiar Community Chest, and later United Fund, symbol: the red feather. The feather, adopted in 1945 as the national Community Chest campaign symbol, was the most familiar United Way identification until the current logo was adopted in the early 1970s.

As the federated charity movement stepped into the 1950s, the modern United Way system was taking shape. In 1950, the phrase "Give the United Way" was coined as the national campaign theme. Over the next 20 years, more than $300 million worth of contributed national media time and space would reinforce the slogan in the national consciousness.

In 1964, the United Fund officially adopted the name United Way, an international movement that boasted more than 2,000 independent chapters worldwide.

The early 1970s ushered in a new United Way identity. In 1972, world-famous designer Saul Bass created the international United Way logo: an outstretched, helping hand, with the rainbow above and a symbol for humanity within.

The hand symbolizes the services and programs supported by United Way that touch so many families and individuals across the world. The mankind image is cradled by the helping hand and shows that many people are supported and uplifted by United Way services. As the rainbow—in a fusion of nature's elements—achieves unity from variety, so does the United Way—in a blending of human diversity—create harmony and unity of purpose.

Source: Condensed from material prepared by Paul Jonas, Associate Director/Communications of the Mile High United Way and *People and Events: A History of the United Way*

United Way

THE OLD FOX CONFESSES!

Someone asked Benjamin Franklin how he managed to be so persuasive and effective in raising funds for the Pennsylvania Hospital—a pet charity of Franklin's and one of the first campaigns recorded in this country.

Franklin said: "I do not remember any of my...proposals or maneuvers...but, after thinking about it, I more easily excuse myself for having made some very wise use of cunning."

UNITED WAY OF AMERICA CHAIRMEN OF THE BOARD OF DIRECTORS 1973-1990

Edward A. Brennan
Sears, Roebuck and Co.
1988–1990

James D. Robinson
American Express Company
1985–1988

Robert A. Beck
Prudential Insurance Company
of America
1983–1985

Donald V. Seibert *(Retired)*
J.C. Penney Company, Inc.
1981–1983

C. C. Garvin, Jr. *(Retired)*
Exxon Corporation
1979–1981

John W. Hanley *(Retired)*
Monsanto Company
1977–1979

C. Peter McColough *(Retired)*
Xerox Corporation
1975–1977

James R. Kerr *(Retired)*
1971–1973

Bayard Ewing *(Retired)*
1973–1975

WHERE THE MONEY COMES FROM

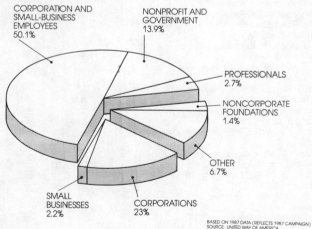

CORPORATION AND SMALL-BUSINESS EMPLOYEES 50.1%

NONPROFIT AND GOVERNMENT 13.9%

PROFESSIONALS 2.7%

NONCORPORATE FOUNDATIONS 1.4%

OTHER 6.7%

SMALL BUSINESSES 2.2%

CORPORATIONS 23%

BASED ON 1987 DATA (REFLECTS 1987 CAMPAIGN)
SOURCE: UNITED WAY OF AMERICA

WHERE THE MONEY GOES

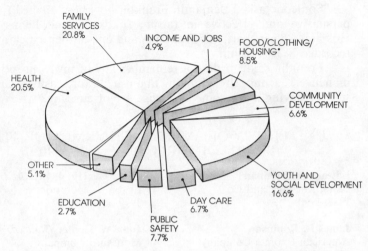

FAMILY SERVICES 20.8%

INCOME AND JOBS 4.9%

FOOD/CLOTHING/ HOUSING* 8.5%

HEALTH 20.5%

COMMUNITY DEVELOPMENT 6.6%

OTHER 5.1%

YOUTH AND SOCIAL DEVELOPMENT 16.6%

EDUCATION 2.7%

DAY CARE 6.7%

PUBLIC SAFETY 7.7%

*INCLUDES HOMELESS ASSISTANCE
BASED ON 1987 DATA
SOURCE: UNITED WAY OF AMERICA

UNITED WAYS RAISING OVER $4 MILLION

City & State/Executive	Population Covered	$ Amount Raised
1) Tri-State*, NY Calvin Green, President (CPO)	11,559,300	92,853,132
2) Chicago, IL Jack Prater, President (CPO)	5,975,149	85,962,065
3) Los Angeles, CA Leo P. Cornelius, President (CPO)	8,811,074	77,750,000
4) New York, NY Calvin E. Green, President (CPO)	7,201,300	64,475,000
5) Detroit, Michigan H. Clay Howell, President (CPO)	3,641,354	58,877,985
6) Washington, DC Oral Suer, Executive Vice President	3,180,500	53,896,158
7) Philadelphia, PA Ted L. Moore, Executive Director	2,644,171	52,005,000
8) Cleveland, OH Jack C. Costello, Executive Vice Pres.	1,590,191	47,154,533
9) Houston, TX Betty Stanley Beene, President (CPO)	3,061,215	42,251,043
10) Boston, MA Robert X. Chandler, President (CPO)	2,371,824	42,216,787
11) San Francisco, CA Joseph W. Valentine, Executive Director	3,459,200	42,071,370
12) Atlanta, GA Donald L. Morgan, President & CPO	2,118,800	39,077,458
13) Saint Louis, MO Martin B. Covitz, President (CPO)	2,032,920	37,265,825
14) Cincinnati, OH Richard N. Aft, Executive Director	1,297,200	35,454,000
15) Dallas, TX J. J. Guise, Jr., President (CPO)	1,764,400	34,718,386

16) Minneapolis, MN	1,240,678	34,301,229
James C. Colville, Executive Director		
17) Seattle, WA	1,341,500	31,475,338
John B. Goessman, President (CPO)		
18) Pittsburgh, PA	1,903,616	30,158,683
Ralph Dickerson, Jr., Executive Vice Pres.		
19) Baltimore, MD	2,262,200	29,789,196
Alan S. Cooper, Executive Director		
20) Rochester, NY	939,260	29,168,058
Joseph Calabrese, President (CPO)		
21) Kansas City, MO	1,306,100	27,006,355
John R. Greenwood, President (CPO)		
22) Columbus, OH	893,100	23,216,823
William H. Schwanekamp, President (CPO)		
23) Denver, CO	1,492,503	22,915,600
Rolland E. Hoffman, President (CPO)		
24) San Diego, CA	2,140,900	22,823,114
W. James Greene, President & CPO		
25) Milwaukee, WI	1,131,238	21,481,680
Henry J. Monaco, Executive Director		
26) Indianapolis, IN	1,084,900	21,220,089
Dan MacDonald, President (CPO)		
27) Hartford, CT	640,871	20,303,105
Dale D. Gray, President (CPO)		
28) Santa Clara, CA	1,393,300	19,259,824
Thomas T. Vais, President (CPO)		
29) Miami, FL	1,771,600	19,007,018
Tanya J. Glazebrook, President (CPO)		
30) Fort Worth, TX	1,045,200	18,422,689
Glenn M. Wilkins, Executive Vice Pres.		
31) Portland, OR	1,290,615	17,709,500
David A. Paradine, President (CPO)		
32) San Antonio, TX	1,106,900	17,406,186
Howard J. Nolan, Executive Vice Pres.		
33) Dayton, OH	730,500	17,257,649
Joel O. Davis, Executive Director		
34) Orange, CA	2,124,000	16,514,227
Merritt L. Johnson, President (CPO)		
35) St. Paul, MN	677,768	15,383,635
Joseph V. Haggerty, Jr., President (CPO)		
36) Memphis, TN	944,840	15,060,000
Harold D. Shaw, Executive Director		
37) Buffalo, NY	963,260	14,224,569
Robert M. Bennett, President (CPO)		
38) Birmingham, AL	835,500	14,175,992
David G. Orrell, Executive Director		
39) Providence, RI	1,031,955	13,962,310
W. Douglas Ashby, President (CPO)		
40) Wilmington, DE	513,100	13,796,986
Thomas L. McFalls, Ed. Dir., Pres. & CEO		
41) New Orleans, LA	1,291,400	13,734,000
G. Gary Ostroske, President (CPO)		
42) Norfolk, VA	587,440	12,221,029
Eugene B. Berres, Executive Vice Pres.		
43) White Plains, NY	954,900	13,501,346
Ralph A. Gregory, President & CPO		
44) Nashville, TN	649,900	13,123,985
Gerald F. Lewis, President (CPO)		
45) Honolulu, HI	828,200	12,934,600
Thomas A. Ruppanner, President (CPO)		
46) Phoenix, AZ	1,356,891	12,841,517
Mark L. O'Connell, President & CEO		
47) Louisville, KY	766,800	12,618,660
Robert C. Reifsnyder, President (CPO)		
48) Richmond, VA	587,440	12,221,029
Larry E. Walton, President (CPO)		

49) Charlotte, NC Donald C. Sanders, President (CPO)	517,000	12,102,130
50) Omaha, NE Dawson Dowty, President (CPO)	566,040	11,501,415
51) Toledo, OH Glenn A. Richter, President (CPO)	622,510	11,409,163
52) Newark, NJ Richard A. Lewin, Executive Vice President	693,631	10,588,671
53) Tulsa, OK Kathleen J. Coan, Executive Director	529,580	10,116,333
54) Sacramento, CA Phillip D. Parsons, Campaign Director	1,214,880	9,600,000
55) Jacksonville, FL Mrs. Virginia L. Burcher, Executive Dir.	707,380	9,436,467
56) Akron, OH Donald J. Frey, Executive Vice President	488,413	9,216,349
57) Flint, MI Randall R. Holcomb, President (CPO)	514,200	8,958,613
58) Long Island, NY Jack J. Sage, President (CPO)	2,701,000	8,867,800
59) Grand Rapids, MI William J. Meyer, Executive Vice Pres.	464,000	8,713,315
60) Chattanooga, TN Paul M. Englemann, Executive Director	311,020	8,249,400
61) Syracuse, NY Harry W. Honan, Executive Director	469,500	7,610,685
62) Winston-Salem, NC Harve A. Mogul, President (CPO)	258,000	7,551,600
63) Des Moines, IA Robert A. Mabie, President (CPO)	281,111	7,511,992
64) Oklahoma City, OK Gregory G. Falk, Executive Director	659,941	7,493,749
65) Wichita, KS Patrick J. Hanrahan, President (CPO)	384,000	7,164,066
66) Tucson, AZ Edmund B. Parker, President (CPO)	399,789	7,115,302
67) Orlando, FL Edward G. Rawa, Executive Director	864,100	5,807,894
68) Columbia, SC John L. Heins, Fr., Executive Director	497,100	6,147,308
69) Raleigh, NC Ronald J. Drago, Executive Director	354,400	6,048,137
70) Morristown, NJ William A. Richards, Executive Vice Pres.	426,000	5,913,536
71) Lansing, MI Robert G. Berning, President (CPO)	361,370	5,912,924
72) Baton Rouge, LA James W. Colvin, Executive Director	476,766	5,852,517
73) Worcester, MA Kevin E. Riordan, President (CPO)	300,957	5,817,897
74) Fort Lauderdale, FL E. Douglas Endsley, Assoc. Exec. Dir.	1,159,100	5,814,657
75) Ann Arbor, MI Vincent S. Buccirosso, President (CPO)	217,360	5,750,830
76) Lawrence, MA Thomas F. O'Leary, President (CPO)	641,980	5,706,585
77) Harrisburg, PA Fritz M. Heinemann, Executive Director	304,220	5,631,878
78) Tampa, FL James E. Rowe, Executive Director	518,070	5,563,157
79) Greensboro, NC Daniel J. Dunne, President (CPO)	246,600	5,552,383
80) Elizabeth, NJ Dell Raudelunas, Executive Director	518,656	5,528,000
81) Albuquerque, NM Michael G. Thompson, President (CPO)	470,200	5,410,000

82) Springfield, MA	304,800	5,394,261
Herbert E. Clauson, President (CPO)		
83) Austin, TX	529,800	5,232,022
Cecil M. Hayes, Executive Director		
84) Rock Island, IL	332,800	5,199,619
Robert J. Garrison, Executive Director		
85) Albany, NY	594,604	5,187,126
John G. Musante, Executive Director		
86) Greenville, SC	308,300	5,107,625
Mack D. Hixon, Executive Director		
87) Fort Wayne, IN	296,200	5,068,713
A. J. Turner, Executive Administrator		
88) Griffith, IN	542,031	5,014,487
John W. Finster, General Manager		
89) Tacoma, WA	521,900	5,007,022
Frank D. Hagel, Executive Director		
90) Hampton, VA	330,200	4,927,860
Erich V. Briggs, Executive Director		
91) Ventura, CA	609,000	4,865,195
Colleen M. Hunter, Executive Director		
92) Camden, NJ	487,300	4,784,733
Arthur D. Diamond, Executive Director		
93) Knoxville, TN	311,400	4,755,196
Wayne Murdock, Executive Director		
94) St. Petersburg, FL	822,400	4,751,000
Richard G. Clawson, Executive Director		
95) Stamford, CT	104,165	4,654,574
Anthony J. Tomanio, Executive Director		
96) Lancaster, PA	368,816	4,627,518
Susan E. Eckert, Executive Director		
97) Mobile, AL	401,600	4,574,281
Darrel L. Miller, Executive Director		
98) Bridgeport, CT	272,306	4,542,846
Richard O. Dietrich, Executive Director		
99) Little Rock, AR	357,000	4,521,809
W. Leon Matthews, President & CPO		
100) Pontiac, MI	226,402	4,517,715
J. Thomas Laing, Executive Director		
101) New Haven, CT	319,456	4,485,642
Douglas L. Higgins, Executive Director		
102) Madison, WI	335,700	4,463,259
John L. Jaco, President (CPO)		
103) El Paso, TX	545,500	4,446,156
Almaron M. Wilder, Executive Director		
104) Binghamton, NY	215,900	4,387,794
John G. Spencer, Executive Director		
105) Portland, ME	201,172	4,378,972
George I. Bahamonde, Executive Director		
106) Milltown, NJ	595,066	4,350,000
Rosalie Burns Davis, Executive Director		
107) Salt Lake City, UT	823,315	4,347,148
Charles L. Johnson, Executive Director		
108) Spokane, WA	357,900	4,339,000
Warren C. Dobbs, Executive Director		
109) Charleston, SC	490,200	4,321,689
John W. Hewell, Executive Director		
110) Lexington, KY	403,000	4,283,180
George W. Hearn, Executive Director		
111) Everett, WA	378,200	4,191,984
Gary L. Smith, Executive Director		
112) Poughkeepsie, NY	258,800	4,129,732
John J. Durkin, President & CPO		
113) Colorado Springs, CO	352,900	4,123,426
Robert A. Parish, Executive Director		
114) Peoria, IL	226,147	4,122,223
David C. Odenback, Executive Director		

115) Erie, PA	267,326	4,106,223
A. Gene Beer, Executive Director		
116) Kalamazoo, MI	215,900	4,100,000
Neil M. Belenky, Executive Vice President		
117) Canton, OH	248,040	4,053,939
Gerard J. Cerny, Executive Director		
118) Savannah, GA	246,900	4,002,541
Brian J. Bowden, President & CPO		

Compiled from: United Way International *Directory*, 1987–1988

*Tri-State, New York United Way is comprised of the following cities: Kingston, Long Island, Middletown, Monticello, New York, Poughkeepsie, West Nyack, and White Plains.

THE UNITED WAYS REPORTING THE HIGHEST PER CAPITA GIVING.

City & State/Executive	Per Capita Giving
1) Stamford, CT	$44.69
Anthony J. Tomanio, Executive Director	
2) Rochester, NY	31.05
Joseph Calabrese, President (CPO)	
3) Cleveland, OH	29.65
Jack C. Costello, Executive Vice President	
4) Winston-Salem, NC	29.27
Harve A. Mogul, President (CPO)	
5) Minneapolis, MN	27.65
James C. Colville, Executive Director	
6) Cincinnati, OH	27.33
Richard N. Aft, Executive Director	
7) Wilmington, DE	26.89
Thomas L. McFalls, Ed. Dir., President & CEO	
8) Des Moines, IA	26.72
Robert A. Mabie, President (CPO)	
9) Chattanooga, TN	26.52
Paul M. Englemann, Executive Director	
10) Ann Arbor, MI	26.46
Vincent S. Buccirosso, President (CPO)	
11) Columbus, OH	26.00
William H. Schwanekamp, President (CPO)	
12) Dayton, OH	23.62
Joel O. Davis, Executive Director	
13) Seattle, WA	23.46
John B. Goessman, President (CPO)	
14) Charlotte, NC	23.41
Donald C. Snaders, President (CPO)	
15) St. Paul, MN	22.70
Joseph V. Haggerty, Jr., President (CPO)	
16) Greensboro, NC	22.52
Daniel J. Dunne, President (CPO)	
17) Portland, ME	21.77
George I. Bahamonde, Executive Director	
18) Richmond, VA	20.80
Larry E. Walton, President (CPO)	
19) Kansas City, MO	20.68
John R. Greenwood, President (CPO)	
20) Omaha, NE	20.32
Dawson Dowty, President (CPO)	
21) Binghamton, NY	20.32
John G. Spencer, Executive Director	
22) Nashville, TN	20.19
Gerald F. Lewis, President (CPO)	
23) Pontiac, MI	19.95
J. Thomas Laing, Executive Director	

24) Dallas, TX   19.68
    J. J. Guise, Jr., President (CPO)
25) Philadelphia, PA   19.67
    Ted L. Moore, Executive Director
26) Indianapolis, IN   19.56
    Dan MacDonald, President (CPO)
27) Worcester, MA   19.33
    Kevin E. Riordan, President (CPO)
28) Tulsa, OK   19.10
    Kathleen J. Coan, Executive Director
29) Milwaukee, WI   18.99
    Henry J. Monaco, Executive Director
30) Kalamazoo, MI   18.90
    Neil M. Belenky, Executive Vice President
31) Akron, OH   18.85
    Donald J. Frey, Executive Vice President
32) Grand Rapids, MI   18.78
    William J. Meyer, Executive Vice President
33) Wichita, KS   18.66
    Patrick J. Hanrahan, President (CPO)
34) Harrisburg, PA   18.45
    Fritz M. Heinemann, Executive Director
35) Atlanta, GA   18.44
    Donald L. Morgan, President & CPO
36) St. Louis, MO   18.33
    Martin B. Covitz, President (CPO)
37) Toledo, OH   18.33
    Glenn A. Richter, President (CPO)
38) Peoria, IL   18.23
    David C. Odenback, Executive Director
39) Boston, MA   17.80
    Robert X. Chandler, President (CPO)
40) Tucson, AZ   17.80
    Edmund B. Parker, President (CPO)
41) Springfield, MA   17.70
    Herbert E. Clauson, President (CPO)
42) Fort Worth, TX   17.63
    Glenn M. Wilkins, Executive Vice President
43) Flint, MI   17.42
    Randall R. Holcomb, President (CPO)
44) Fort Wayne, IN   17.11
    A. J. Turner, Executive Director
45) Raleigh, NC   17.07
    Ronald J. Drago, Executive Director
46) Birmingham, AL   16.97
    David G. Orrell, Executive Director
47) Washington, DC   16.95
    Oral Suer, Executive Vice President
48) Bridgeport, CT   16.68
    Richard O. Dietrich, Executive Director
49) Greenville, SC   16.57
    Mack D. Hixon, Executive Director
50) Lansing, MI   16.36
    Robert G. Berning, President (CPO)
51) Canton, OH   16.34
    Gerard J. Cerny, Executive Director
52) Savannah, GA   16.21
    Brian J. Bowden, President & CPO
53) Syracuse, NY   16.21
    Harry W. Honan, Executive Director
54) Detroit, MI   16.17
    H. Clay Howell, President (CPO)
55) Poughkeepsie, NY   15.96
    John J. Durkin, President & CPO
56) Memphis, TN   15.94
    Harold D. Shaw, Executive Director

57) Pittsburgh, PA   15.84
    Ralph Dickerson, Jr., Executive Vice Pres.
58) San Antonio, TX   15.73
    Howard J. Nolan, Executive Vice President
59) Honolulu, HI   15.62
    Thomas A. Ruppanner, President (CPO)
60) Rock Island, IL   15.62
    Robert J. Garrison, Executive Director
61) Erie, PA   15.36
    A. Gene Beer, Executive Director
62) Denver, CO   15.35
    Rolland E. Hoffman, President (CPO)
63) Newark, NJ   15.27
    Richard A. Lewin, Executive Vice President
64) Knoxville, TN   15.27
    Wayne Murdock, Executive Director
65) Norfolk, VA   15.24
    Eugene B. Berres, Executive Director (CPO)
66) Hampton, VA   14.92
    Erich V. Briggs, Executive Director
67) Buffalo, NY   14.77
    Robert M. Bennett, President (CPO)
68) Chicago, IL   14.39
    Jack Prater, President (CPO)
69) White Plains, NY   14.14
    Ralph A. Gregory, President & CPO
70) New Haven, CT   14.04
    Douglas L. Higgins, Executive Director
71) Morristown, NJ   13.88
    William A. Richards, Executive Vice Pres.
72) Santa Clara, CA   13.82
    Thomas T. Vais, President (CPO)
73) Houston, TX   13.80
    Betty Stanley Beene, President (CPO)
74) Portland, OR   13.72
    David A. Paradine, President (CPO)
75) Providence, RI   13.53
    W. Douglas Ashby, President (CPO)
76) Jacksonville, FL   13.34
    Mrs. Virginia L. Burcher, Executive Dir.
77) Madison, WI   13.26
    John L. Jaco, President (CPO)
78) Baltimore, MD   13.17
    Alan S. Cooper, Executive Director
79) Little Rock, AR   12.67
    W. Leon Matthews, President & CPO
80) Lancaster, PA   12.55
    Susan E. Eckert, Executive Director
81) Reading, PA   12.54
    A. Richard Magliozzi, Executive Director
82) Columbia, SC   12.39
    John L. Heins, Jr., Executive Director
83) Baton Rouge, LA   12.28
    James W. Calvin, Executive Director
84) San Francisco, CA   12.16
    Joseph W. Valentine, Executive Director
85) Spokane, WA   12.12
    Warren C. Dobbs, Executive Director
86) Colorado Springs, CO   11.68
    Robert A. Parish, Executive Director
87) Albuquerque, NM   11.51
    Michael G. Thompson, President (CPO)
88) Mobile, AL   11.39
    Darrel L. Miller, Executive Director
89) Oklahoma City, OK   11.36
    Gregory G. Falk, Executive Director

90) Everett, WA	11.08
Gary L. Smith, Executive Director	
91) Tampa, FL	10.74
Mrs. Virginia L. Burcher, Executive Director	
92) Miami, FL	10.72
Tanya J. Glazebrook, President (CPO)	
93) San Diego, CA	10.66
W. James Greene, President & CPO	
94) Elizabeth, NJ	10.66
Dell Raudelunas, Executive Director	
95) Lexington, KY	10.63
George W. Hearn, Executive Director	
96) New Orleans, LA	10.63
G. Gary Ostroske, President (CPO)	
97) Austin, TX	9.88
Cecil M. Hayes, Executive Director	
98) Camden, NJ	9.82
Arthur D. Diamond, Executive Director	
99) Tacoma, WA	9.59
Frank D. Hagel, Executive Director	
100) Phoenix, AZ	9.46
Mark L. O'Connell, President & CEO	
101) Griffith, IN	9.25
John W. Finster, General Manager	
102) New York, NY	8.95
Calvin E. Green, President (CPO)	
103) Lawrence, MA	8.89
Thomas F. O'Leary, President (CPO)	
104) Los Angeles, CA	8.82
Leo P. Cornelius, President (CPO)	
105) Charleston, SC	8.82
John W. Hewell, Executive Director	
106) Albany, NY	8.72
John G. Musante, Executive Director	
107) El Paso, TX	8.15
Almaron M. Wilder, Executive Director	
108) Tri-State*, NY	8.03
Calvin Green, President & CPO	
109) Ventura, CA	7.99
Colleen M. Hunter, Executive Director	
110) Sacramento, CA	7.90
Phillip D. Parsons, Campaign Director	
111) Orlando, FL	7.87
Edward G. Rawa, Executive Director	
112) Orange, CA	7.78
Merritt L. Johnson, President (CPO)	
113) Milltown, NJ	7.31
Rosalie Burns Davis, Executive Director	
114) St. Petersburg, FL	5.78
Richard G. Clawson, Executive Director	
115) Salt Lake City, UT	5.28
Charles L. Johnson, Executive Director	
116) Fort Lauderdale, FL	5.02
E. Douglas Endsley, Assoc. Executive Dir.	
117) Long Island, NY	3.28
Jack J. Sage, President (CPO)	

Compiled from: United Way International *Directory*, 1987–1988

*Tri-State, NY United Way is comprised of the following cities: Kingston, Long Island, Middletown, Monticello, New York, Poughkeepsie, West Nyack, and White Plains.

Postal officials estimate that one out of every four pieces of mail handled last year by the Postal Service was from a not-for-profit organization or institution.

CAUSE-RELATED FUNDRAISING
BECOMES A MAJOR FACTOR

One of the most significant new dimensions of fundraising was introduced in 1988—cause-related fundraising. Considered a remarkable boon to some, and a curse to others, cause-related marketing is a registered trademark of the American Express Company. It is defined technically as "a mutually beneficial relationship between a corporation and a not-for-profit organization in which the former pursues marketing and promotional objectives and the latter pursues fundraising and public relations objectives."

The major programs thus far have involved the use of credit cards, in which the card is tied to contributions. American Express used their card to tie contributions to the Statue of Liberty program. Proctor & Gamble had a coupon redemption program with Special Olympics.

Most feel that the trend toward cause-related marketing and fundraising will continue and increase. Opponents are not necessarily against the idea, but feel that it no more constitutes true fundraising than does a bingo game.

America's Generosity

Americans are the most caring and generous people in the world. Giving to United Way is proof of that generosity. Since 1981, overall giving to United Way has increased from $1.6 billion to $2.6 billion. That is nearly a 24 percent increase in real- dollar growth.

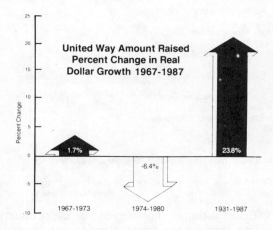

United Way Amount Raised Percent Change in Real Dollar Growth 1967-1987

1.7%   -6.4%   23.8%

1967-1973   1974-1980   1931-1987

TOTAL AMOUNT RAISED BY UNITED WAYS:
1978–1987

Year	Total Dollars	% Increase Over Previous Year
1978	$1,317,745,690	9.4%
1979	1,423,461,336	8.0
1980	1,526,000,000	7.2
1981	1,680,000,000	10.1
1982	1,780,000,000	6.0
1983	1,950,000,000	9.5
1984	2,145,000,000	10.0
1985	2,330,000,000	9.0
1986	2,440,000,000	5.7
1987	2,600,000,000	6.4

TEN LARGEST UNITED WAYS: 1987

City	Rank of City by Population	Dollars Raised
1) Chicago, IL	3	$88,400,000
2) Los Angeles, CA	2	83,509,974
3) New York, NY*	1	66,856,937
4) Detroit, MI	6	59,388,201
5) Washington, DC	17	59,305,763
6) Philadelphia, PA	5	53,253,632
7) Cleveland, OH	23	48,457,102
8) San Francisco, CA	13	47,006,338
9) Houston, TX	4	45,446,338
10) Boston, MA	20	44,352,599

*The United Way of Tri-State, an areawide United Way which includes New York as well as 27 other United Ways, raised $170,000,000 in 1987.

Source: United Way of America Research Services Unit

THE MATCHING GIFT WAS BORN IN 1871

Sophia Smith laid down a condition in her will that she would provide $25,000 to establish a college in the small Massachusetts town of Northampton if the citizens could raise a similar amount in two years. The community responded and over-subscribed, and the college was organized the following year—one of the earliest examples of a matching gift to challenge others. Following that, Smith College launched its first campaign for funds among its alumnae, and between 1888 and 1891, raised $23,500 toward building a $30,000 gymnasium.

RELATIONSHIP OF TOTAL AMOUNT RAISED BY UNITED WAYS OF AMERICA TO THE U.S. ALL-ITEMS CONSUMER PRICE INDEX 1978-1987

In the past ten years, the United Way has consistently increased its giving nationally—each year, more than the year before. But it is only in the last four years that giving has exceeded the consumer price index.

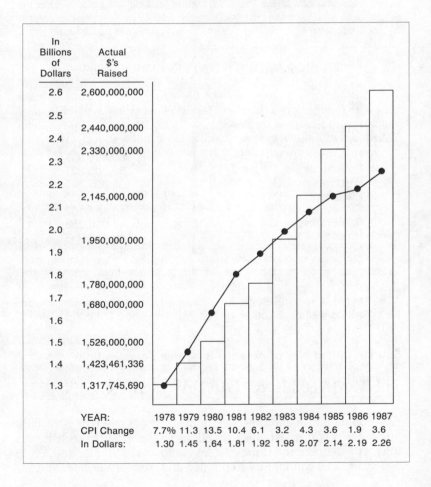

In Billions of Dollars	Actual $'s Raised
2.6	2,600,000,000
2.5	
	2,440,000,000
2.4	2,330,000,000
2.3	
2.2	
	2,145,000,000
2.1	
2.0	
	1,950,000,000
1.9	
1.8	
	1,780,000,000
1.7	1,680,000,000
1.6	
1.5	1,526,000,000
1.4	1,423,461,336
1.3	1,317,745,690

YEAR:	1978	1979	1980	1981	1982	1983	1984	1985	1986	1987
CPI Change	7.7%	11.3	13.5	10.4	6.1	3.2	4.3	3.6	1.9	3.6
In Dollars:	1.30	1.45	1.64	1.81	1.92	1.98	2.07	2.14	2.19	2.26

RECORD OF UNITED WAY CAMPAIGNS IN THE U.S. AND CANADA (IN MILLIONS)

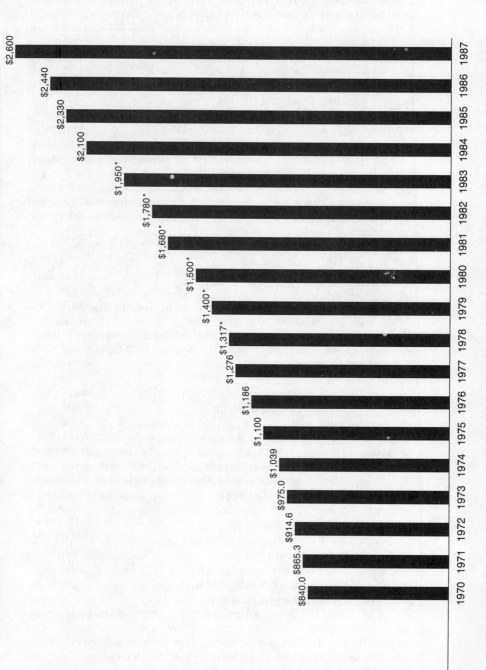

Year	Amount
1970	$840.0
1971	$865.3
1972	$914.6
1973	$975.0
1974	$1,039
1975	$1,100
1976	$1,186
1977	$1,276
1978	$1,317*
1979	$1,400*
1980	$1,500*
1981	$1,680*
1982	$1,780*
1983	$1,950*
1984	$2,100
1985	$2,330
1986	$2,440
1987	$2,600

de TOCQUEVILLE SOCIETY
HONORS $10,000 DONORS

Alexis de Tocqueville was a brilliant young French nobleman and astute political scientist. He came to the United States to study the meaning of democracy in order to understand how it might replace the outworn aristocratic regime in Europe.

De Tocqueville arrived in the United States in May, 1831, and returned to France only nine months later. Yet, for considerably more than a century, de Tocqueville's two volumes entitled *Democracy In America* have provided readers an unparalleled description, analysis, and prophecy concerning almost every aspect of American life.

Democracy In America, in two volumes, analyzes the impact of democracy on the structure and dynamics of American society and culture, while examining the essential nature of our freedoms.

Alexis de Tocqueville's concern was for the development and survival of both freedom and democracy. He interviewed Americans from all walks of life, including such historical figures as John Quincy Adams, Daniel Webster, and President Andrew Jackson. He was struck by the equality that was basic to the American lifestyle. "This equality of condition," he wrote, "is the fundamental fact from which all others seem to be derived, and the central point at which all my observations constantly terminated." Equality allowed for the success of freedom and democracy in de Tocqueville's America.

De Tocqueville's most important realization was the way Americans, armed with their equality, helped each other in time of need. He saw volunteerism as a way of life that was typically American. He said, "Americans combine to give fetes, found seminars, build churches, distribute books, and send missionaries to the antipode ...I have come across several types of associations in America of which, I confess, I had not previously the slightest conception, and I have often admired the extreme skills they show in proposing a common object for the exertions of very many and in inducing them voluntarily to pursue it."

Alexis de Tocqueville was the name chosen by the United Way when forming a very special group to honor individuals who give $10,000 or more to their local United Way. They selected the name because of de Tocqueville's admiration of the spirit of voluntary association he discovered in America.

The Alexis de Tocqueville Society Program is designed to create a partnership between community philanthropic leaders and United Way, the nation's most recognized human service organization. By unifying the philanthropic generosity in local communities with the most dynamic organization meeting human needs, the Alexis de Tocqueville Society Program is addressing concerns nationwide that can change the very fabric of American society.

The Alexis de Tocqueville Society:

- Unites the community's high net-worth leaders.
- Demonstrates new approaches to solving human care problems.
- Shares philanthropic dollars with those most in need.
- Recognizes the outstanding community service leadership efforts of individuals.

THE ALEXIS DE TOCQUEVILLE SOCIETY PROGRAM
NATIONAL PROGRAM HIGHLIGHTS

1972 The Alexis de Tocqueville Society was created by United Way of America to nationally recognize volunteers for outstanding service and to foster greater voluntary community service.

1973 The first national award recipient was Bob Hope. A national award has been presented in each consecutive year as part of United Way's Volunteer Leaders Conference.

1981 Thomas Frist, Jr., M.D., chairman and chief executive officer of Hospital Corporation of America, attended the Volunteer Leaders Conference and was so impressed with the Alexis de Tocqueville story and award presentation that he requested permission to establish a local philanthropic program in Nashville, Tennessee. This program linked entrepreneurs, supporters of higher education, the arts, and other social service-minded individuals to the United Way, in generous involvement by $10,000, $25,000, and $50,000 gifts.

1983 Dr. Frist presented the Nashville success story of the Alexis de Tocqueville Society to other communities represented at the annual Volunteer Leaders Conference. The United Way of America Board of Governors asked Dr. Frist to chair a committee to provide guidance to the Alexis de Tocqueville Society Leadership and Recognition Program.

1984 Standardized materials and guidelines for local programs were developed. Six metropolitan areas founded Alexis de Tocqueville Society affiliations. The National Alexis de Tocqueville Society was established to recognize donors of annual gifts of $100,000 or more. Overall results: $3,600,000 raised.

1985 Nineteen cities became Alexis de Tocqueville Society affiliates. 728 individuals made gifts of $10,000 or more. Fourteen individuals became National Society members. Overall results: $12,200,000 raised.

1986 Thirty-four local Alexis de Tocqueville Society affiliates, 1,358 members nationwide, 28 National Society members. Two individuals joined the $1,000,000 Roundtable. Overall results: $24,000,000 raised.

1987   Sixty-four local Alexis de Tocqueville Society affiliates, 2,100 members nationwide, 30 National Society members, three $1,000,000 Roundtable members. Overall results: $31,200,000 raised.

1988   Currently, there are 82 local Alexis de Tocqueville Society affiliates, 42 National Society members, four $1,000,000 Roundtable members. 1988 membership and overall results will be announced in January, 1989.

RECOGNITION OF OUTSTANDING SERVICE VOLUNTEERS

The national Alexis de Tocqueville Society Program was created by United Way of America to recognize individuals who have rendered outstanding service as volunteers within their own community or on a national scale. The program also exists to foster and promote voluntary service and to recognize the value and importance of such service to our nation.

The national Alexis de Tocqueville Society Award, cast in bronze, depicts a family: the essential ingredient in creating a strong, caring community. The community, in turn, grows and develops to ensure a strong future for its children. The tradition of volunteerism noted by de Tocqueville in his treatise *Democracy In America* cannot be better represented than by the family.

A replica of the national award, in lead crystal, is available for presentation to local Alexis de Tocqueville Society award recipients.

Local Alexis de Tocqueville Society members serve as the selection committee for recognizing outstanding service volunteers.

Local Society award recipients include community service volunteers, social service agency leaders, and local philanthropists.

LOCAL ALEXIS DE TOCQUEVILLE AWARD RECIPIENTS (52) 1985–1988

Ann Arbor, Michigan
Margaret Dow Towsley
and
Harry Albert Towsley, M.D.

Atlanta, Georgia
John A. Sibley, III
Theodora Fisher James
John Ackerman Conant

Birmingham, Alabama
Joseph S. Bruno

Boston, Massachusetts
David R. Pokross, Sr.
Edward B. Hanify
Helen Chin Schlichte

FRIST DEVELOPS CONCEPT FOR THE
ALEXIS DE TOCQUEVILLE SOCIETY

Thomas F. Frist, Jr., M.D., chairman and chief executive officer of Hospital Corporation of America, pioneered the first local

Alexis de Tocqueville Society in Nashville, Tennessee in 1981.

His dream to spread the Alexis de Tocqueville Society concept nationally has become a reality. Through his outstanding leadership and dedication, and personal visits to United Ways all over the country, there are now 82 local Alexis de Tocqueville Society affiliates across the nation.

In 1987, over $31 million was contributed in $10,000 plus annual gifts by 2,100 members of these societies. Local Alexis de Tocqueville Society awards have been presented to over 50 outstanding community service volunteers to date.

Dr. Frist has served as chairman since 1983 of the United Way of America Board of Governors committee that has guided the Alexis de Tocqueville Society Program. He is a recipient of the 1987 United Way of America's national Alexis de Tocqueville Society Award, as well as the local Alexis de Tocqueville Society Award of Nashville, Tennessee.

THERE ARE NOW 82 CITIES ACROSS THE COUNTRY THAT HAVE THE ALEXIS DE TOCQUEVILLE SOCIETY PROGRAM

Ann Arbor, MI	Kalamazoo, MI	Reading, PA
Atlanta, GA	Kansas City, MO	Richmond, VA
Baltimore, MD	Knoxville, TN	Rochester, NY
Baton Rouge, LA	Lakeland, FL	St. Louis, MO
Bergen County, NJ	Lima, OH	St. Petersburg, FL
Birmingham, AL	Little Rock, AR	Sacramento, CA
Boston, MA	Long Island, NY	Salt Lake City, UT
Cedar Rapids, IA	Los Angeles, CA	San Antonio, TX
Charlotte, NC	Memphis, TN	San Diego, CA
Charleston, WV	Midland, TX	San Francisco, CA
Chattanooga, TN	Milwaukee, WI	Santa Barbara, CA
Chicago, IL	Minneapolis, MN	Santa Clara, CA
Cincinnati, OH	Montgomery, AL	Sarasota, FL
Cleveland, OH	Morristown, NJ	Savannah, GA
Dallas, TX	Nashville, TN	Seattle, WA
Dayton, OH	New Orleans, LA	Somerville, NJ
Denver, CO	New York City, NY	South Palm Beach Co., FL
Des Moines, IA	Norfolk, VA	Tri-State, NY
Erie, PA	Omaha, NE	Tulsa, OK
Fort Worth, TX	Orange County, CA	Ventura, CA
Grand Rapids, MI	Palm Beach, FL	West Palm Beach, FL
Greensboro, NC	Philadelphia, PA	White Plains, NY
Hampton, VA	Phoenix, AZ	Wichita, KS
Harrisburg, PA	Pittsburgh, PA	Winston-Salem, NC
Honolulu, HI	Pittsfield, MA	Worcester, MA
Houston, TX	Portland, OR	York, PA
Indianapolis, IN	Providence, RI	
Jacksonville, FL	Raleigh, NC	

THE TOP 12 CITIES IN THE COUNTRY THIS YEAR—IN TOTAL NUMBER OF MEMBERS AND TOTAL AMOUNT GIVEN TO THE ALEXIS DE TOCQUEVILLE SOCIETY PROGRAM

City	Rank by Population	Members	$
1) Los Angeles	2	182	$3,400,000
2) Cleveland	23	216	$3,200,000
3) Philadelphia	5	140	$3,200,000
4) Pittsburgh	33	90	$2,400,000
5) San Francisco	13	146	$2,300,000
6) Columbus	21	128	$1,300,000
7) Minneapolis	42	88	$1,230,000
8) Dallas	7	82	$1,070,000
9) Nashville	27	69	$1,030,000
10) New York, Tri-State	1	79	$ 947,000
11) Cincinnati	38	75	$ 900,000
12) San Antonio	10	69	$ 750,000

SUSTAINING MEMBERSHIP (ANNUAL CONTRIBUTION) REVENUE TO THE 10 LARGEST METROPOLITAN BOY SCOUT COUNCILS IN THE COUNTRY

City/State	Annual Fund Contributions	Percentage of Annual Contributions to Total Annual Budget
1) Detroit, MI	$1,157,792	30.0
2) Salt Lake City, UT	987,139	39.6
3) Houston, TX	943,629	22.0
4) St. Louis, MO	920,385	30.2
5) Dallas, TX	919,826	28.1
6) Costa Mesa, CA	796,957	21.6
7) New York, NY	708,462	9.8
8) Bethesda, MD	539,488	18.7
9) Sherman Oaks, CA	405,073	15.0
10) Los Angeles, CA	394,214	7.8

ONE OF THE MIGHTY HAS PROBLEMS, TOO

Officials at Princeton University announced that they would close 1988 with a deficit that could be more than $1 million. It is the first time they have faced red ink since the 1977–78 fiscal year. The problem is attributed in a major way to the October stock-market bust. Donations are also down 4.5 percent from the $17.5 million raised the year before.

UNITED WAY REVENUE TO THE 10 LARGEST METROPOLITAN BOY SCOUT COUNCILS IN THE COUNTRY

City/State	United Way Revenue	Percentage of United Way Grants to Total Annual Budget
1) Houston, TX	$1,230,556	28.7
2) Detroit, MI	1,125,264	29.2
3) Dallas, TX	1,077,433	32.9
4) Los Angeles, CA	987,259	19.6
5) St. Louis, MO	924,812	30.3
6) Costa Mesa, CA	702,401	19.0
7) Bethesda, MD	586,793	20.3
8) Sherman Oaks, CA	431,483	16.0
9) Salt Lake City, UT	221,568	8.9
10) New York, NY	–0–	–0–

SPECIAL EVENTS REVENUE TO THE 10 LARGEST METROPOLITAN BOY SCOUT COUNCILS IN THE COUNTRY

City/State	Special Events Revenue	Percentage of Special Events Revenue to Total Annual Budget
1) New York, NY	$4,079,322	56.6
2) Los Angeles, CA	1,074,044	21.3
3) Costa Mesa, CA	399,665	10.8
4) Bethesda, MD	273,662	9.5
5) Detroit, MI	206,742	5.3
6) Sherman Oaks, CA	173,133	6.4
7) Dallas, TX	67,929	2.0
8) Salt Lake City, UT	–0–	–0–
9) Houston, TX	–0–	–0–
10) St. Louis, MO	–0–	–0–

ENDOWMENT FUNDS OF THE 10 LARGEST METROPOLITAN BOY SCOUT COUNCILS IN THE COUNTRY

City/State	Endowment
1) Dallas, TX	$10,207,898
2) Houston, TX	9,851,403
3) St. Louis, MO	6,538,188
4) Los Angeles, CA	4,088,675
5) Sherman Oaks, CA	3,803,854
6) Costa Mesa, CA	2,426,264
7) Bethesda, MD	1,735,850
8) New York, NY	1,731,778
9) Salt Lake City, UT	342,473
10) Detroit, MI	138,167

GIRL SCOUTS

Council	Contributions $000	Contributed per Member $
1) Los Angeles	472	55.74
2) Cumberland Valley, Nashville	450	30.09
3) Chicago	444	22.68
4) Greater New York	385	15.07
5) San Francisco Bay Area	329	16.13
6) Orange County	320	15.19
7) Michigan Metro	311	13.66
8) Kentuckiana, Louisville	260	13.61
9) Greater Minneapolis	250	14.78
10) Patriots' Trails, Boston	233	10.49
11) San Jacinto, Houston	229	6.85
12) Great Rivers, Cincinnati	221	10.09
13) San Gorgonio	218	17.25
14) San Diego–Imperial	213	9.70
15) Nation's Capital, Wash., D.C.	179	6.16
16) Greater St. Louis	149	4.31

Note: Some figures are estimates and unofficial

GIRL SCOUTS

Council	Membership	Rank of City by Population
1) Greater St. Louis	34,574	30
2) San Jacinto, Houston	33,436	4
3) Nation's Capital, Wash., D.C.	29,057	17
4) Greater New York	25,549	1
5) Michigan Metro**	22,762	6
6) Patriots' Trails, Boston	22,203	20
7) San Diego–Imperial	21,966	8
8) Great Rivers, Cincinnati	21,904	38
9) Orange County	21,067	*
10) San Francisco Bay Area	20,390	13
11) Chicago	19,578	3
12) Kentuckiana, Louisville	19,101	*
13) Los Angeles	18,336	2
14) Greater Minneapolis	16,917	42
15) Cumberland Valley, Nashville	15,119	27
16) San Gorgonio	12,634	*

*not among top 50 most populous cities
**rank refers to Detroit

Note: Some figures are estimates and unofficial

GIRL SCOUTS

Council	Current Fund Income $000	Expenses per Member $
1) San Jacinto, Houston	4,616	138.05
2) Greater St. Louis	4,258	123.16
3) Orange County	3,999	189.82
4) Nation's Capital, Wash., D.C.	3,658	125.89
5) Patriots' Trails, Boston	3,194	143.85
6) Michigan Metro	3,135	137.73
7) San Francisco Bay Area	3,121	153.06
8) Greater New York	3,011	117.85
9) San Diego–Imperial	2,983	135.80
10) Greater Minneapolis	2,441	144.29
11) Great Rivers, Cincinnati	2,054	93.77
12) Kentuckiana, Louisville	1,795	93.97
13) Los Angeles	1,559	85.02
14) San Gorgonio	1,559	123.40
15) Cumberland Valley, Nashville	1,513	100.07
16) Chicago	1,484	75.80

Note: Some figures are estimates and unofficial

FIFTH EDITION OF "GIVING IS CARING" CALENDAR WILL REACH OVER 50,000

The *Giving is Caring* Page-A-Day Calendar was first published in 1986, when 22,000 copies were distributed; the distribution has increased each year since. The calendar is published by Philanthropic Service for Institutions (PSI), a division of the Adventist World Headquarters. Dr. Milton Murray, who conceived the idea, is Director of the PSI.

Each year's calendar features 365 different quotations on topics relating to philanthropy and volunteerism. Since it was first published, it has presented nearly 1800 different quotations, each of great consequence and relevance to our field.

The calendar is printed using the name of an institution or organization and is sent to a variety of important groups: donors, prospective donors, Trustees and Directors, volunteers, alumni, foundations and corporations, state senators and representatives, and so forth.

The calendars are $6.50 each with sizeable reductions for quantity orders. **For more information: Giving Calendar, Philanthropic GIFT, P.O. Box 10214, Silver Spring, MD 20904.**

GIVING TO THE 15 LARGEST JUNIOR ACHIEVEMENT PROGRAMS

Junior Achievement was founded in 1919 as an after-school program to provide young people with the knowledge and skills needed in a manufacturing age. It is the largest program of its type among high school youth—this last year reaching over one million students in a single school year for the first time in its history. No other school program is as large or as effective in teaching incentive and profit motivation. It is a hands-on program where young people have an opportunity to become involved in simulating corporate and professional life.

Following is the top giving among the largest Junior Achievement programs. The giving is almost entirely from corporate philanthropy.

Area Name	Total Annual Revenue*
1) Chicago, IL	$1,356,500
2) Los Angeles, CA	1,224,490
3) St. Louis, MO	1,112,750
4) Detroit, MI	1,078,000
5) New York, NY	1,006,785
6) Twin Cities, MN	1,001,960
7) Milwaukee, WI	973,000
8) Houston, TX	701,000
9) Pittsburgh, PA	679,100
10) Dallas, TX	625,647
11) Seattle, WA	613,980
12) Denver, CO	609,507
13) Atlanta, GA	540,976
14) Fort Wayne, IN	490,000
15) Charlotte, NC	330,448

*Figures are for fiscal year 1986–87

Source: Junior Achievement Inc., Colorado Springs, CO

SIGNIFICANT DATES IN AMERICAN PHILANTHROPY

Historic Landmarks

1630   John Winthrop preaches "A Model of Christian Charity" to Puritans bound for New England.

1638   John Harvard bequeaths library and half of his estate to newly-founded school at Cambridge, Massachusetts.

1715   Elihu Yale sends gifts to Collegiate School of Connecticut (chartered 1701); school changes name to Yale College.

1729   First orphan home in present boundaries of United States established in Ursuline Convent, New Orleans, Louisiana.

1751   Benjamin Franklin challenged the Pennsylvania Assembly to award £2,000 on condition that Philadelphia citizens contribute £2,000 to build Pennsylvania Hospital, the first general hospital in the United States.

1774 Parliamentary act closing Boston Port creates greatest relief problem in colonial period; other towns and colonies send money, grain and livestock to aid Boston.

1790 Death of Benjamin Franklin; his will establishes Franklin Funds in Boston and Philadelphia to lend money to "young married artificers of good character."

1817 Thomas Hopkins Gallaudet establishes in Hartford, Connecticut, America's first free school for deaf.

1833 Washington National Monument Society organized to bring philanthropic support to memorialize nation's first president. Of $1 million cost, citizens contributed $300,000.

1846 Large American contributions for Irish famine relief.

1851 First YMCA organized in the United States, in Boston.

1861 United States Sanitary Commission, forerunner of American Red Cross, organized.

1881 Booker T. Washington organizes Tuskegee Institute for Negroes in Tuskegee, Alabama.

1887 Three clergymen start United Way in Denver, Colorado . . . launching America's annual community philanthropy effort. In 1987, $2.6 billion was raised to support 37,000 agencies.

1889 John D. Rockefeller gives $600,000 to help found new University of Chicago.
Jane Addams establishes Hull House in Chicago, Illinois.

1890 Yale University alumni launch first Annual Fund efforts—an idea that now generates $2 billion annually for higher education.

1910 Boy Scouts of America founded (Campfire Girls, 1910; Girl Scouts, 1912).

1913 American Cancer Society founded.

1914 American Jewish Joint Distribution Committee organized to coordinate Jewish war relief activities.

1919 Death of Andrew Carnegie; contributions total $350 million.

1927 Restoration of Williamsburg, Virginia, financed by John D. Rockefeller, Jr., begins.

1931 United States Postal Service issues stamp honoring 50th Anniversary of American Red Cross, first of scores of issues honoring not-for-profits.

1937 Congress accepts Andrew Mellon's offer to give art collection and National Gallery building in Washington, DC, to public.

1953 New Jersey Supreme Court upholds gift of $1,500 by A.P. Smith Manufacturing Co. to Princeton University, striking down stockholders' objections and affirming right and obligation of corporations to support higher education.

1955 Development of Salk vaccine against paralytic polio climaxes 17 years of work by National Foundation for Infantile Paralysis.

1961 Peace Corps established by the U.S. government, providing volunteers to needy countries.

1966   Jerry Lewis begins annual Muscular Dystrophy Association telethon, marking the arrival of major media as means of obtaining philanthropic support.

1976   Philanthropy reaches $32 billion annually on occasion of nations' 200th anniversary.

1985   Bob Geldolf organizes Live Aid, a music extravaganza, which raised $40 million for international hunger relief.

1986   National Philanthropy Day celebration, first for the nation, sparks events in 50 cities.

1987   INDEPENDENT SECTOR launches "Daring Goals for a Caring Society" to double annual giving by 1991.

Source: Philanthropic Service for Institutions General Conference of Seventh-Day Adventists

OLD BEN WAS FIRST!

Benjamin Franklin was the first fundraiser in the United States. Wouldn't you know!

The cause was for his beloved Pennsylvania Hospital. The hospital still operates, and is the oldest institution in the country.

The need for proper healthcare in the growing young Philadelphia became quite evident—and Ben Franklin decided that something had to be done about it. He tried to persuade the city and the state government to put up the funds but they declined.

He decided then that he would ask for gifts for the project from leading citizens. The concept was unknown at the time. He couldn't do it all by himself, so he began enlisting assistance from key community leaders. Franklin's 200-year-old formula for success is as relevant today as it was then: "My practice," explained Franklin, "is to go first to those who may be counted upon to be favorable, who know the cause and believe in it, and ask them to give as generously as possible. When they have done so, I go next to those who may be presumed to have a favorable opinion and to be disposed to listening, and I secure their adherence.

"Lastly, I go to those who know little of the matter or have no known predilection for it and influence them by presentation of the names of those who have already given."

Organizations and institutions still follow this sage advice. But now they structure their program so that the very first people contacted are not only the closest to the cause—but also the most likely to contribute at the highest level.

The campaign for Pennsylvania Hospital was a huge success and the goal was over-subscribed. The city was so impressed with the results that they made a matching grant. In soliciting a gift, Benjamin Franklin knew what he was talking about: "If you would persuade, you must appeal to interest, rather than the intellect."

HEALTH ORGANIZATIONS

CORPORATE SUPPORT TO HOSPITALS LAGGING

In 1987, Americans donated $93 billion to not-for-profit organizations and institutions. Of this amount, only $13 billion went to healthcare institutions. And hospitals only had a $3 billion share of that.

Corporate donations decreased in 1987 to $199 million, a drop of 3.3 percent. By contrast, total contributions to hospitals increased 25 percent to $1.56 billion.

There's a serious problem! The rationale from corporations on cutting their philanthropic support is that managers believe the expensive care they purchase through high priced benefit programs is enough of a contribution. It is possible, too, that hospitals are facing stiffer competition today for the corporate dollar from universities and local social agencies.

Increasingly, hospitals will be soliciting corporate donations to fund charitable services and care for the indigent. There will be less emphasis on gifts for capital projects.

As few as five years ago, more than 90 percent of all funds raised by hospitals were used for capital projects. This percentage has decreased measurably, down to about 10 percent in 1988. It will continue to decline.

NATIONAL HEALTH AGENCIES CONTINUE AMAZING GROWTH IN DOLLARS

In the past ten years, there has been surprisingly little change in the ranking of the top 15 gift-receiving agencies. The American Cancer Society and the American Heart Association have remained in the top two positions during this entire period. The Cancer Society continues to widen its lead over the Heart Association, and received more than $300 million last year in total contributions, including bequests.

Planned Parenthood took over the number 7 position in 1979 from the National Association for Retarded Citizens, and has continued to increase its fundraising revenue. The National Association for Retarded Citizens had a continued decline and went from number 10 to number 12, to number 14, and then finally off the list.

The National Kidney Foundation and the American Lung Association did not make the list in 1987.

Joining the list in 1985 was the ALSAC St. Jude Children's Research Hospital. It went from eighth place to sixth in 1988. The Juvenile Diabetes Foundation and the Epilepsy Foundation of America also made the list in 1985 and have remained on it.

NATIONAL HEALTH AGENCIES
TOP 15 IN CONTRIBUTIONS EACH YEAR—1978–1987

Agencies	1978 Contributions
1) American Cancer Society	$95,927,848
2) The National Foundation	63,151,030
3) Muscular Dystrophy Association, Inc.	56,807,754
4) American Heart Association	56,002,264
5) American Lung Association	42,102,000
6) National Easter Seal Society	40,000,000
7) National Association for Retarded Citizens	35,957,450
8) National Multiple Sclerosis Society	24,399,275
9) Planned Parenthood Federation of America, Inc.	24,150,000
10) United Cerebral Palsy Association, Inc.	19,723,100
11) Mental Health Association	16,092,000
12) The Arthritis Foundation	14,500,000
13) Cystic Fibrosis Foundation	13,540,000
14) Leukemia Society of America, Inc.	10,435,581
15) American Diabetes Association, Inc.	8,000,000

Agencies	1979 Contributions
1) American Cancer Society, Inc.	$102,778,011
2) The National Foundation	63,765,738
3) Muscular Dystrophy Association, Inc.	62,765,738
4) American Heart Association	59,594,573
5) American Lung Association	45,500,000
6) National Easter Seal Society	46,323,000
7) Planned Parenthood Federation of America, Inc.	34,500,000
8) National Association for Retarded Citizens	33,851,235
9) National Multiple Sclerosis Society	26,052,627
10) United Cerebral Palsy Association, Inc.	24,274,853
11) Mental Health Association	14,640,000
12) Cystic Fibrosis Foundation	14,450,000
13) The Arthritis Foundation	14,000,000
14) American Diabetes Association, Inc.	11,433,379
15) Leukemia Society of America, Inc.	10,330,156

Agencies	1980 Contributions
1) American Cancer Society, Inc.	$113,325,055
2) Muscular Dystrophy Association, Inc.	65,804,499
3) American Heart Association	64,620,688
4) The National Foundation	63,535,783
5) American Lung Association	53,000,000
6) National Easter Seal Society	52,750,000
7) National Multiple Sclerosis Society	28,674,260
8) National Association for Retarded Citizens	28,066,290
9) United Cerebral Palsy Association, Inc.	27,142,080
10) Planned Parenthood Federation of America, Inc.	24,000,000
11) The Arthritis Foundation	18,000,000
12) Mental Health Association	16,883,441
13) Cystic Fibrosis Foundation	15,330,000
14) American Diabetes Association, Inc.	14,235,452
15) Leukemia Society of America, Inc.	11,580,643

Agencies	1981 Contributions
1) American Cancer Society, Inc.	$124,615,571
2) American Heart Association	75,844,453
3) Muscular Dystrophy Association, Inc.	72,200,000
4) March of Dimes Birth Defects Foundation	68,186,001
5) American Lung Association	57,750,000
6) National Easter Seal Society	56,125,000
7) Planned Parenthood Federation of America, Inc.	44,248,000
8) National Association for Retarded Citizens	30,691,332
9) United Cerebral Palsy Association, Inc.	29,589,999
10) National Multiple Sclerosis Society	29,400,000
11) Mental Health Association	17,700,000
12) The Arthritis Foundation	17,200,000
13) Cystic Fibrosis Foundation	15,681,000
14) American Diabetes Association, Inc.	15,392,227
15) Leukemia Society of America, Inc.	13,081,687

Agencies	1982 Contributions
1) American Cancer Society, Inc.	$135,197,106
2) American Heart Association	83,354,528
3) March of Dimes Birth Defects Foundation	74,063,361
4) Muscular Dystrophy Association, Inc.	72,300,000
5) American Lung Association	63,500,000
6) National Easter Seal Society	60,100,000
7) Planned Parenthood Federation of America, Inc.	42,200,000
8) United Cerebral Palsy Association, Inc.	32,083,108
9) National Multiple Sclerosis Society	42,200,000
10) National Association for Retarded Citizens	25,052,884
11) American Diabetes Association, Inc.	18,899,897
12) The Arthritis Foundation	18,300,000
13) Cystic Fibrosis Foundation	15,799,126
14) Leukemia Society of America, Inc.	14,829,556
15) Mental Health Association	800,000

Agencies	1983 Contributions
1) American Cancer Society, Inc.	$151,181,758
2) American Heart Association	89,403,066
3) March of Dimes Birth Defects Foundation	79,665,000
4) Muscular Dystrophy Association, Inc.	74,515,000
5) American Lung Association	72,000,000
6) National Easter Seal Society	64,500,000
7) Planned Parenthood Federation of America, Inc.	44,000,000
8) United Cerebral Palsy Association, Inc.	33,449,000
9) National Multiple Sclerosis Society	32,449,000
10) National Association for Retarded Citizens	28,007,680
11) American Diabetes Association, Inc.	21,445,413
12) The Arthritis Foundation	19,900,000
13) National Mental Health Association	19,000,000
14) Leukemia Society of America, Inc.	17,073,876
15) Cystic Fibrosis Foundation	16,553,322

Agencies	1984 Contributions
1) American Cancer Society, Inc.	$166,998,926
2) American Heart Association	95,730,981
3) March of Dimes Birth Defects Foundation	90,177,000
4) Muscular Dystrophy Association, Inc.	79,983,925
5) National Easter Seal Society	70,000,000
6) American Lung Association	69,205,905
7) Planned Parenthood Federation of America, Inc.	50,500,000
8) United Cerebral Palsy Association, Inc.	34,899,923
9) National Multiple Sclerosis Society	33,244,341
10) American Diabetes Association, Inc.	28,904,038
11) National Association for Retarded Citizens	28,520,500
12) The Arthritis Foundation	25,400,000
13) National Mental Health Association	20,000,000
14) Leukemia Society of America, Inc.	18,755,636
15) Cystic Fibrosis Foundation	18,062,225

Agencies	1985 Contributions
1) American Cancer Society, Inc.	$185,477,642
2) American Heart Association	103,395,805
3) March of Dimes Birth Defects Foundation	97,716,000
4) Muscular Dystrophy Association, Inc.	87,300,000
5) American Lung Association	72,229,933
6) National Easter Seal Society	69,959,504
7) Planned Parenthood Federation of America, Inc.	51,000,000
8) ALSAC St. Jude Children's Research Hospital	44,570,050
9) National Multiple Sclerosis Society	38,585,199
10) United Cerebral Palsy Association, Inc.	37,370,190
11) The Arthritis Foundation	29,400,000
12) National Mental Health Association	29,558,256
13) American Diabetes Association, Inc.	29,215,061
14) National Association for Retarded Citizens	24,800,000
15) Leukemia Society of America, Inc.	19,983,169

Agencies	1986 Contributions
1) American Cancer Society, Inc.	$199,553,646
2) American Heart Association	111,772,000
3) March of Dimes Birth Defects Foundation	104,333,000
4) Muscular Dystrophy Association, Inc.	91,800,000
5) American Lung Association	74,673,134
6) National Easter Seal Society	73,100,000
7) Planned Parenthood Federation of America, Inc.	58,000,000
8) ALSAC St. Jude Children's Research Hospital	51,831,379
9) National Multiple Sclerosis Society	45,618,069
10) United Cerebral Palsy Association, Inc.	42,307,960
11) American Diabetes Association, Inc.	32,848,616
12) National Mental Health Association	32,223,269
13) Leukemia Society of America, Inc.	21,650,777
14) National Kidney Foundation	13,627,187
15) Juvenile Diabetes Foundation	13,000,000

Agencies	1987 Contributions
1) American Cancer Society, Inc.	$211,644,900
2) American Heart Association	121,669,000
3) March of Dimes Birth Defects Foundation	105,187,000
4) Muscular Dystrophy Association, Inc.	101,787,009
5) National Easter Seal Society	78,000,000
6) ALSAC St. Jude Children's Research Hospital	63,699,699
7) Planned Parenthood Federation of America, Inc.	63,000,000
8) National Multiple Sclerosis Society	49,800,000
9) The Arthritis Foundation	47,364,529
10) United Cerebral Palsy Association, Inc.	43,899,201
11) National Mental Health Association	34,219,000
12) Leukemia Society of America, Inc.	23,402,000
13) American Diabetes Association, Inc.	21,583,006
14) Juvenile Diabetes Foundation	21,561,942
15) Epilepsy Foundation of America	7,219,951

NATIONAL HEALTH AGENCIES
TOP 15 IN TOTAL BEQUESTS FOR EACH
YEAR—1978–1987

Agencies	1978 Bequests
1. American Cancer Society, Inc.	$30,178,722
2. American Heart Association	17,799,458
3. National Easter Seal Society	6,500,000
4. The Arthritis Foundation	3,500,000
5. American Lung Association	1,895,000
6. The National Foundation	1,541,911
7. Muscular Dystrophy Association, Inc	828,242
8. National Multiple Sclerosis Society	807,194
9. United Cerebral Palsy Association, Inc.	621,319
10. American Diabetes Association, Inc.	600,000
11. National Association for Retarded Citizens	521,791
12. National Mental Health Association	360,000

13. Planned Parenthood Federation of America, Inc.	350,000
14. Leukemia Society of America, Inc.	321,442
15. Cystic Fibrosis Foundation	60,000

Agencies	1979 Bequests
1. American Cancer Society, Inc.	$39,360,721
2. American Heart Association	23,343,575
3. National Easter Seal Society	5,677,000
4. The Arthritis Foundation	4,000,000
5. Muscular Dystrophy Association, Inc.	2,280,241
6. National Multiple Sclerosis Society	1,189,272
7. American Lung Association	1,500,000
8. The National Foundation	1,404,902
9. National Association for Retarded Citizens	614,103
10. United Cerebral Palsy Association, Inc.	562,664
11. American Diabetes Association, Inc.	500,000
12. Planned Parenthood Federation of America, Inc.	464,471
13. Leukemia Society of America, Inc.	360,000
14. National Mental Health Association	50,000
15. Cystic Fibrosis Foundation	

Agencies	1980 Bequests
1. American Cancer Society, Inc.	$41,366,087
2. American Heart Association	27,370,476
3. American Lung Association	7,000,000
4. National Easter Seal Society	6,200,000
5. The Arthritis Foundation	5,000,000
6. The National Foundation	1,358,935
7. United Cerebral Palsy Association, Inc.	1,294,070
8. Muscular Dystrophy Association	1,046,765
9. National Multiple Sclerosis Society	966,767
10. National Mental Health Association	600,000
11. Planned Parenthood Federation of America, Inc.	500,000
12. National Association for Retarded Citizens	495,910
13. Cystic Fibrosis Foundation	470,000
14. American Diabetes Association, Inc.	453,163
15. Leukemia Society of America, Inc.	346,606

Agencies	1981 Bequests
1. American Cancer Society, Inc.	$45,792,632
2. American Heart Association	18,773,754
3. National Easter Seal Society	8,500,000
4. The Arthritis Foundation	6,600,000
5. Muscular Dystrophy Association	2,300,000
6. American Lung Association	2,250,000
7. March of Dimes Birth Defects Foundation	1,839,297
8. American Diabetes Association, Inc.	1,828,522
9. Leukemia Society of America, Inc.	1,173,155
10. National Multiple Sclerosis Society	1,000,000
11. National Mental Health Association	800,000
12. United Cerebral Palsy Association, Inc.	708,782
13. Cystic Fibrosis Foundation	490,000

14. Planned Parenthood Federation of America, Inc.   255,000
15. National Association for Retarded Citizens   215,668

Agencies	1982 Bequests
1. American Cancer Society, Inc.	$47,799,594
2. American Heart Association	26,563,289
3. National Mental Health Association	19,700,000
4. National Easter Seal Society	7,900,000
5. The Arthritis Foundation	6,900,000
6. American Lung Association	3,000,000
7. Muscular Dystrophy Association, Inc.	2,300,000
8. March of Dimes Birth Defects Foundation	1,900,582
9. American Diabetes Association, Inc.	1,397,984
10. Cystic Fibrosis Foundation	1,325,000
11. United Cerebral Palsy Association, Inc.	1,304,533
12. Leukemia Society of America, Inc.	867,648
13. Planned Parenthood Federation of America, Inc.	800,000
14. National Association for Retarded Citizens	239,000
15. National Multiple Sclerosis Society	177,663

Agencies	1983 Bequests
1. American Cancer Society, Inc.	$51,907,532
2. American Heart Association	35,777,965
3. The Arthritis Foundation	7,700,000
4. National Easter Seal Society	7,500,000
5. National Mental Health Association	4,000,000
6. American Diabetes Association, Inc.	2,358,571
7. Muscular Dystrophy Association	2,085,000
8. National Multiple Sclerosis Society	1,853,000
9. March of Dimes Birth Defects Foundation	1,804,000
10. Leukemia Society of America, Inc.	1,115,456
11. Planned Parenthood Federation of America, Inc.	1,000,000
12. National Mental Health Association	1,000,000
13. United Cerebral Palsy Association, Inc.	972,351
14. National Association for Retarded Citizens	443,791
15. Cystic Fibrosis Foundation	310,957

Agencies	1984 Bequests
1. American Cancer Society, Inc.	$53,529,242
2. American Heart Association	32,287,860
3. The Arthritis Foundation	9,900,000
4. National Easter Seal Society	7,400,000
5. National Mental Health Association	4,000,000
6. American Lung Association	3,568,002
7. National Multiple Sclerosis Society	2,681,659
8. Muscular Dystrophy Association	1,948,191
9. American Diabetes Association, Inc.	1,904,946
10. March of Dimes Birth Defects Foundation	1,799,000
11. Planned Parenthood Federation of America, Inc.	1,500,000
12. Leukemia Society of America, Inc.	1,416,763
13. United Cerebral Palsy Association, Inc.	939,763

14. National Association for Retarded Citizens	500,000
15. Cystic Fibrosis Foundation	118,486

Agencies	1985 Bequests
1. American Cancer Society, Inc.	$57,366,540
2. American Heart Association	36,774,639
3. The Arthritis Foundation	11,300,000
4. National Easter Seal Society	8,534,690
5. ALSAC St. Jude Children's Research Hospital	4,503,942
6. American Lung Association	3,763,992
7. March of Dimes Birth Defects Foundation	3,711,000
8. Muscular Dystrophy Association, Inc.	3,200,000
9. American Diabetes Association, Inc.	2,286,611
10. National Multiple Sclerosis Society	1,045,682
11. Planned Parenthood Federation of America, Inc.	2,000,000
12. National Mental Health Association	1,216,539
13. United Cerebral Palsy Association, Inc.	1,087,190
14. Leukemia Society of America, Inc.	999,897
15. National Association for Retarded Citizens	500,000

Agencies	1986 Bequests
1. American Cancer Society, Inc.	$71,363,646
2. American Heart Association	39,666,000
3. National Easter Seal Society	9,000,000
4. ALSAC St. Jude Children's Research Hospital	5,105,293
5. American Lung Association	4,415,519
6. American Diabetes Association	3,354,158
7. National Multiple Sclerosis Society	3,344,191
8. Planned Parenthood Federation of America, Inc.	3,000,000
9. Muscular Dystrophy Association, Inc.	2,900,000
10. March of Dimes Birth Defects Foundation	1,627,000
11. United Cerebral Palsy Association, Inc.	1,147,586
12. Leukemia Society of America, Inc.	1,112,169
13. National Kidney Foundation	1,101,084
14. National Mental Health Association	1,000,000
15. Juvenile Diabetes Foundation	100,000

Agencies	1987 Bequests
1. American Cancer Society, Inc.	$97,617,064
2. American Heart Association	41,985,000
3. ALSAC St. Jude Children's Research Hospital	12,277,874
4. National Easter Seal Society	8,000,000
5. National Multiple Sclerosis Society	5,200,000
6. Muscular Dystrophy Association, Inc.	4,790,412
7. American Diabetes Association, Inc.	3,370,062
8. March of Dimes Birth Defects Foundation	3,317,000
9. Planned Parenthood Federation of America, Inc.	2,200,000
10. The Arthritis Foundation	1,474,533
11. Leukemia Society of America, Inc.	1,336,000
12. United Cerebral Palsy Association, Inc.	1,143,689
13. National Mental Health Association	530,000
14. Epilepsy Foundation of America	511,023
15. Juvenile Diabetes Foundation	5,482

GIVING TO CLINICS—1988

Of the thousands of clinics in the nation, there are nine considered to be the largest, the most visible, and the most highly regarded. There are, of course, hundreds of fine regional and community clinics—but these nine have a national platform and are the best known. Of this small group, the Mayo Clinic raises the most funds. The Henry Ford Hospital refused to provide information. The numbers listed do not include any government grants. However, giving in all categories during the year (not pledges) from foundations, corporations, and individuals is included.

GIVING TO CLINICS—1988

CLINIC	CONTRIBUTIONS (millions)
Mayo Clinic Eugene Mayberry Chairman of Development Rochester, MN	$26.7
Scripps Clinic David L. Mitchell V. P. for Development La Jolla, CA	25.0
Cleveland Clinic Hospital Howard B. Newman Director, Corporate & Foundation Relations Cleveland, OH	10.17
Virginia Mason Hospital Steven Harrison Executive Director of Foundation Seattle, WA	6.0
Lahey Clinic Hospital T. R. Miner Jr., FNAHD Director of Development Burlington, MA	5.38
Geisinger Medical Center H. W. Wieder Jr. Senior V. P. for Development Danville, PA	4.6
Scott & White Memorial Hospital Neil Haney Asst. to President, Development Temple, TX	4.47

Ochsner Foundation Hospital   3.5
Charles W. Heim, Jr. FNAHD
Vice President, Foundation
New Orleans, LA

Henry Ford Hospital   information refused
William J. Wildern
Vice President, The Fund for Henry Ford Hospital
Detroit, MI

EASTER SEAL TELETHON RAISES MORE
THAN EVER BEFORE

An estimated 60 million viewers watched and gave—as the National Easter Seal Society raised over $37 million in the 18th annual national telethon. The 1989 program surpassed its financial objective of $36 million and last year's total of $35.1 million.

This organization, through its telethon, has raised more money each year than the year before.

There were five corporations who each gave over $1 million: Amway Corporation, Century 21 Real Estate Corporation, Safeway Stores, Friendly Ice Cream Corporation, and Enesco Corporation. Total corporate giving amounted to over $13 million.

GIVING TO MUSCULAR DYSTROPHY—
VIRTUALLY A ONE MAN SHOW

Jerry Lewis has spent over 20 years raising funds for the Muscular Dystrophy Association, and in 1988 the annual Labor Day Telethon raised nearly $40 million. It surpassed the previous year's record by $5 million. In addition, a long list of corporate sponsors gave $34,306,197. The Telethon helped swell the total giving to the MDA to over $100 million—just behind donations for cancer, heart disease, and birth defects.

There is no other charity in which one individual has been involved for as long and is as identified as Jerry Lewis is with the Muscular Dystrophy Association.

AN INTERESTING BEQUEST

L.R. Hummel left Bethany College in Pennsylvania a bequest of $1.2 million. This is one of the largest Bethany has ever received.

There is nothing unusual about a bequest of this size. Countless colleges—even those much smaller than Bethany—have received larger bequests. What is unusual about this one is that Mr. Hummell was the groundskeeper at Bethany, a position he held with pride and love for many years.

CONTRIBUTIONS PER VICTIM

On the basis of contributions per victim, giving to Cystic Fibrosis places at the top of the contribution list for health causes.

Alcoholism, the national disease, continues to receive the least—a mere 10 cents per victim. This places it last among 17 other national health concerns.

The following chart shows charitable giving per victim for 18 major health issues.

Health Issue	Raised Per Victim
1. Cystic Fibrosis	$1,066.67
2. Leukemia	875.50
3. Muscular Dystrophy	473.50
4. Multiple Sclerosis	360.02
5. Kidney Disease	163.65
6. Cerebral Palsy	66.86
7. Cancer	66.06
8. Birth Defects	50.46
9. Venereal Disease	32.28
10. Blindness	24.20
11. Diabetes	8.50
12. Epilepsy	4.48
13. Lung Disease	3.95
14. Iletis and Colitis	3.39
15. Crippled, Handicapped	3.57
16. Cardiovascular	2.39
17. Mental Illness	1.13
18. Alcoholism	.10

HOSPITAL DEVELOPMENT SALARIES

Position	Median 1987 salary
Chief development officer	$54,125
Director of major gifts	$45,000
Director of planned giving	$40,000
Director of development	$35,000
Director of Corporate/ Foundation Giving	$35,000
Director of Annual Giving	$30,000
Director of Donor Research	$23,000

The highest chief development officer salary reported—$120,000. Lowest—$15,000.

Source: The Brakeley Hospital/Medical Center Development Office Compensation and Capital Campaign Survey, 1988

HOSPITAL ADMINISTRATION/DEVELOPMENT SALARIES

Position	Avg. 1988 Salary	Avg. 1988 Bonus
Administrator/Executive	$56,500	$4,000
Foundation Executive	$50,000	$4,000
Head of Department	$40,000	$4,000
Assistant/Associate Head of Department	$32,500	$1,000

Source: National Association for Hospital Development 1988 Salary and Benefits Report, USA

COMMUNITY HOSPITAL ANNOUNCES LARGEST CAMPAIGN IN HISTORY

In 1988, Scripps Memorial Hospitals launched a campaign for $100 million. This is believed to be the largest objective ever announced by an acute care community hospital. So far, $40 million has been pledged and given toward the project, called the Fund for Greatness.

The program is for a variety of capital and equipment needs. About half of the goal is to go toward endowment.

The program is to be completed in a ten year period, but officials feel confident that the goal will be exceeded within the next several years.

HEALTHCARE AWARENESS

The National Association for Hospital Development (NAHD) launched a media-blitz this year to help people become more aware of healthcare in this country, and the importance of giving to medical centers and hospitals.

Chairman of the campaign is Peter W. Ghiorse, Vice-President at St. Vincent's Hospital and Medical Center in New York. Through his efforts, and the efforts of the members of the NAHD, they have raised $2 million for television, radio, and newspaper advertising in an effort to spur giving to hospitals. The theme of their media campaign is "Give to Life. " The money is raised from not-for-profit hospitals that belong to the Association and companies that sell products to hospitals.

This is the first time that any program of this nature has been attempted by the NAHD.

GIVING TO HOSPITALS

According to a recent report, the most important reason people make contributions to hospitals is that they themselves or a loved one have benefited directly from the hospital service. The top 25 percent of contributors are individuals between 55 and 65 years of age. They are reported to be both generous and loyal, giving to a number of programs as well as participating in an annual gift program.

TOP 15 HOSPITALS IN THE ADVENTIST HEALTH SYSTEM/UNITED STATES
RANK BY TOTAL VOLUNTARY SUPPORT*
THE TOTAL AMOUNT RECEIVED DURING THE SIX YEARS OF 1982–1987

1) Florida Hospital Medical Center Orlando, FL	$9.7 million
2) Loma Linda University Medical Center Loma Linda, CA	$5.9 million
3) Kettering Medical Center Charles F. Kettering Memorial Hospital Kettering, OH	$5.35 million
4) Huguley Memorial Hospital Fort Worth, TX	$4.98 million
5) Glendale Adventist Medical Center Glendale, CA	$4.1 million
6) Porter Memorial Hospital Denver, CO	$4.0 million
7) St. Helena Hospital Deer Park, CA	$3.5 million
8) Hinsdale Hospital Hinsdale, IL	$3.1 million
9) Hackettstown Community Hospital Hackettstown, NJ	$2.54 million
10) White Memorial Medical Center Los Angeles, CA	$2.0 million
11) Shawnee Mission Medical Center Shawnee Mission, KS	$1.6 million
12) Castle Medical Center Kailua, HI	$1.58 million
13) Washington Adventist Hospital Takoma Park, MD	$1.56 million
14) Memorial Hospital, Boulder Boulder, CO	$1.5 million
15) Shady Grove Adventist Hospital Rockville, MD	$1.47 million

*Figures are for CASH ONLY (or cash value of gifts-in-kind); unpaid pledges are NOT included.

Source: General Conference of Seventh Day Adventists, Wash. DC

SOURCES OF CONTRIBUTIONS 1955–1987
($ IN BILLIONS)

	Corporations[1]	Foundations	Bequests[2]	Individuals
1955	$ .415	$ .300	$ .237	$ 6.75
1956	.418	.305	.239	7.33
1957	.419	.502	.450	7.89
1958	.395	.505	.451	8.15
1959	.482	.702	.512	8.68
1960	.482	.710	.574	9.16
1961	.412	.702	.650	9.50
1962	.595	.701	.701	9.89
1963	.657	.821	.880	10.86
1964	.729	.830	.951	11.19
1965	.785	1.13	1.02	11.82
1966	.805	1.25	1.31	12.44
1967	.830	1.40	1.40	13.41
1968	1.005	1.60	1.60	14.75
1969	1.055	1.80	2.00	15.93
1970	.797	1.90	2.00	16.19
1971	.865	1.95	3.00	17.62
1972	1.009	2.00	2.10	19.37
1973	1.174	2.00	2.00	20.53
1974	1.200	2.11	2.07	21.60
1975	1.202	1.65	2.23	23.53
1976	1.487	1.90	2.99	26.32
1977	1.791	2.00	2.99	29.55
1978	2.084	2.17	2.60	32.10
1979	2.288	2.42	2.23	36.59
1980	2.359	2.81	2.86	40.71
1981	2.514	3.07	3.49	46.42
1982	2.906	3.16	5.45	48.52
1983	3.300	3.60	4.52	53.54
1984	4.059	3.95	4.89	58.50
1985	4.400[e]	4.90	5.18	65.94[e]
1986	4.500[e]	5.90 [e]	5.57	72.03[e]
1987	4.500[e]	6.38 [e]	5.98	76.82[e]

[1]IRS-based data through 1984. IRS figures include giving by corporations to nonprofit organizations and to their own foundations. They do not include giving by corporate foundations to other nonprofits.

[2]Figures for certain years differ from bequest data released by the IRS, because the IRS excludes bequests on estates under $300,000 for 1983 and 1984, and under $500,000 for 1985. IRS bequests in 1983 totalled $2.55 billion, in 1984, $4.54 billion, and in 1985, $3.57 billion.

[e]Estimated.

Source: *Giving USA*

HOSPITAL GIVING

Giving to the nation's hospitals amounted to $13.65 billion in 1987, an increase of 11.3 percent over 1986. The $13.65 billion represents 14.57 percent of the total philanthropy during the year to all sources. Following is a list of eighteen hospitals—among the country's largest and most prestigious—and the amount of money they received in contributions in 1988. The figures include annual support, capital funds, and irrevocable planned giving.

Hospital	Contributions (millions)
Massachusetts General Hospital William E. Walch Vice President, Resource Development Boston, MA	$31.5
Baylor University Medical Center Gordon Caswell President, Foundation Dallas, TX	26.7
St. Vincent's Hospital & Medical Center Mark G. Ackerman Vice President New York, NY	16.35
Scripps Memorial Hospital James Lewis Bowers Executive Director La Jolla, CA	15.2
Rush-Presbyterian-St. Luke's Medical Center Jack R. Bohlen V. P. of Philanthropy and Community Relations Chicago, IL	15
Brigham & Women's Hospital Nancy Clark Administrative Assistant, Development Boston, MA	12
St. Joseph Medical Center Jon B. Olson, FNAHD President & CEO Burbank, CA	11.23
Children's Hospital Norman C. Myers, FNAHD Associate Director Columbus, OH	10.46

Eisenhower Medical Center   10.11
Joseph Tobin
Vice President Development
Rancho Mirage, CA

Morton F. Plant Hospital   7.5
David J. Rosser
Executive Director
Clearwater, FL

Beth Israel Medical Center   6.9
Jane Blumenfeld
Vice President/Development & Public Relations
New York, NY

Cedar Sinai Medical Center   6
Steven Klappholz
Senior Development Officer
Los Angeles, CA

Orthopaedic Hospital   6
Michael J. Pfaff
Sr. Vice President, Foundation
Los Angeles, CA

Lenox Hill Hospital   5.9
Peter Rude
Vice President
New York, NY

St. Joseph's Hospital   5.6
John R. Vitello, FNAHD
Executive Director
Houston, TX

New England Medical Center   5.2
John W. Thomas
Vice President Development
Boston, MA

Abbott-Northwestern Hospital   2.8
Glen Johnson
Vice President Development
Minneapolis, MN

Baptist Hospital   1.4
William S. Roth, FNAHD
President, Foundation
Birmingham, AL

HOSPITALS FACE TAX SCRUTINY

Not-for-profit hospitals are under close scrutiny regarding their tax-exempt status. Federal, state, and municipal authorities are questioning the charitable mission in the traditional role of hospitals.

Under closest attack is the question of charity patient care. And they also question the scope and depth of community health service.

In Vermont, the city of Burlington sought to put the Medical Center Hospital of Vermont on the property tax roles. Their contention was that the amount of charity patient care at the Hospital was insufficient to warrant tax exemption.

In Utah, local officials placed six hospitals on the property tax roles, relying on a state Supreme Court decision that charity care is one of six tests that can be used to determine the appropriateness of tax exemption.

In California, the Attorney General ruled that a hospital's net revenue in excess of 10 percent of gross revenue in any given year is insufficient reason for imposing property taxes on the institution. But he warned that the question will continue to be tested.

In Pittsburgh, three hospitals agreed to pay $11.1 million for city services over the next ten years. The agreement was interpreted as avoiding the issue of whether or not hospitals should be tax-exempt.

In Washington, the House Ways and Means Oversight Subcommittee drafted proposed rule changes that would tax more hospital revenues as unrelated business income. Of particular concern is the proposed taxation of sales of pharmaceuticals, durable medical goods and supplies, and some laboratory test patients.

Source: Roger Birdsell, Vice President, Memorial Health Foundation —South Bend, Indiana

SALARIES INCREASE FOR HOSPITAL DEVELOPMENT OFFICERS

As the pace and emphasis in hospital fundraising accelerates, salaries increase.

In a survey of 1987 salaries, the average salary for Chief Development Officers in hospitals was $56,668. The high salary was $120,000, and since that survey, several salaries have increased beyond that number.

Hospital development pay continues to lag behind college and university development salaries, but each year the gap is less.

In hospitals, the larger the institution, the more the development person is paid.

Academic medical centers pay the highest salaries.

The pay is highest in the west. The southwest pays next highest, followed by the east and mid-west. Salaries in the south are considerably lower than those in the rest of the country.

A considerable gap still exists between the salaries of men and women development officers, the average difference being about $13,000.

SIX CITED FOR PHILANTHROPY

Six men and organizations received philanthropy awards at the 1989 NSFRE International Conference. The awards are given each year to individuals and organizations that demonstrate outstanding and continuing support of philanthropy. It is the highest honor conferred by the NSFRE.

O. Wayne Rollins was honored as the **Outstanding Philanthropist.** He is Founder and Chairman of the Board of Rollins, Inc. of Atlanta—and has contributed more than $18 million to educational and charitable institutions in Georgia.

Harvey Meyerhoff of Baltimore has been Campaign Chairman of the United Way of Central Maryland, Chairman of the United States Holocaust Memorial Council, and is Chairman of both the Johns Hopkins Hospital and Health System. He was named **Outstanding Volunteer Fund-Raiser.**

Ernest W. Wood, Ed.D., of Pasadena was named **Outstanding Fund-Raising Executive.** He has been a professional development officer since 1965 and is currently vice-president of a Pasadena advertising agency.

Rotary International, Evanston received the award for **Outstanding Philanthropic Organization.** In 1988, it raised $219 million to provide the resources to offer all of the polio vaccines necessary for the next five years for any approved program of a national or regional health agency.

The Lilly Endowment, Indianapolis, received the award for **Outstanding Foundation.** The endowment is particularly recognized for its support of professional development and its efforts to elevate the professionalism and public accountability of charitable organizations.

The award for **Outstanding Corporation** was given to **The Dayton Hudson Corporation of Minneapolis.** For years, it has been considered one of the nation's leading corporate citizens and donors and has led the way in encouraging other businesses to contribute 5 percent of their profits to philanthropy.

NATIONAL ASSOCIATION FOR HOSPITAL DEVELOPMENT

NAHD is perhaps the fastest growing Association for Directors of Development. It was organized in 1967 by a few people who were related, in one way or another, to fundraising in their hospital. At the first meeting, there were fewer than a dozen people present. The group continued to flourish, and gained great respect among those engaged in fundraising in hospitals. Today, there are nearly 2,000 members of the NAHD.

The purpose of the organization is to enhance the performance of professionals engaged in the advancement of philanthropy, and other resource development in all healthcare institutions. Its mission is to strengthen the ability of the member institutions to provide and promote healthcare for the people they serve.

Quoted from the organization's mission statement, the purposes of the NAHD follow.

a) To foster a better understanding of the financial requirements of healthcare institutions;

b) To encourage the establishment of organized resource development programs in healthcare institutions;

c) To foster ethical standards in the professional practice of resource development;

d) To advance the members' professionalism; and

e) To communicate the association's annual programs and priorities to the membership and to others.

The Chief Executive Officer of the NAHD is Dr. William C. McGinly. Before joining NAHD, he was Assistant Executive Director of the National School Boards Association—representing more than 95,000 local school board members in 50 states. Prior to that, he was Director of Education for the American Healthcare Association, representing nursing home facilities and administrators.

For more information: National Association for Hospital Development, 112-B East Broad Street, Falls Church, VA 22046 (703) 532-6243.

CHAIRMEN OF THE NATIONAL ASSOCIATION FOR HOSPITAL DEVELOPMENT

1967–68
W. B. Harris, Jr., FNAHD

1966–70
R. Graham Nash

1968–69
Jack G. Bryan, FNAHD

1971–72
I. J. Mnookin, FNAHD

1972–73
Seymour Leon

1973–74
Robert C. Alexander, FNAHD

1974–75
John R. Vitello, FNAHD

1975–76
William S. Roth, FNAHD

1976–77
Lynn E. Kandel

1977–78
I. Brewster Terry, FNAHD

1978–79
Jack Herman, FNAHD

1979–80
Marilyn F. Erickson

1980–81
William D. Seeyle, FNAHD

1981–82
Joseph L. Kunec

1982–83
David B. Hanaman, FNAHD

1984
Winthrop B. Wilson, FNAHD

1985
Jerry A. Linzy

1986
Jon B. Olson, FNAHD

1987
Mary D. Poole, FNAHD

1988
Peter W. Ghiorse, FNAHD

1989
Charles W. Heim, FNAHD

BOARD OF DIRECTORS—1988
NATIONAL ASSOCIATION FOR HOSPITAL
DEVELOPMENT

The NAHD Board of Directors is made up of the Executive Committee, listed first, and the thirteen Regional Directors.

Chairman
Peter W. Ghiorse, FNAHD
Vice President
St. Vincent's Hospital & Medical Center
New York, New York

Chairman Elect
Charles W. Heim, Jr., FNAHD
Vice President
Alton Ochsner Medical Foundation
New Orleans, Louisiana

Past Chairman
Mary D. Poole, FNAHD
Vice President

Southwest Community Health Services

National Director, Education
T. Richardson Miner, Jr., FNAHD
Director of Development
Lahey Clinic Foundation
Boston, Massachusetts

National Director, Membership
Joan M. Lilly
Vice President
Northridge Hospital Medical Center
Northridge, California

RED CROSS WISHES TO TERMINATE PENSION FUND

One of the nation's largest not-for-profit organizations, the American Red Cross, wants to terminate its $740 million pension fund to capture the surplus. Officials at the Red Cross claim that they have $400 million in excess.

William Rose, the Director of Treasury Operations, says that the behemoth organization wishes to fund projects that could not otherwise by undertaken. The Red Cross would use some of the excess funds to create new health benefits for workers and some $260 million will stay in the pension fund to cover obligations for the next ten years.

As for the $100 million left, the money will fund projects, such as blood collection, that are digging dangerously deep into the charity's $1 billion in annual revenues.

This move comes just in time. The extra cost of testing blood donations for the AIDS virus has caused the Red Cross operating surplus to shrink from $95 million to $8 million for the year just ended.

FUNNY MONEY!

A book on the lighter side of philanthropy is available for the first time. *Accent on Humor* is a lively little book—filled with cartoons and witticisms about philanthropy. Published in 1988, single copies are $5.50, and quantity discounts are available.

For more information: PSI, 12501 Old Columbia Pike, Silver Spring, MD 20904 (202) 722-6131.

NAHD AWARDS

Each year, the National Association for Hospital Development (NAHD) recognizes and awards prizes for writing at its Annual Conference.

First and second prizes are given for the best article appearing the prior year in the *NAHD JOURNAL*.

A prize is also awarded to the winner of the Professional Papers Competition.

Members of the *NAHD JOURNAL* Committee judge both the articles in the *NAHD JOURNAL* and the entries in the papers competition.

Former Award Winners follow.

First Place	JOURNAL AWARDS	Second Place
	1988	
Roger Birdsell		Frank Hall, FNAHD
	1987	
Jeffrey N. Elliott		John E. Walsh, Ph.D.
	1986	
Jerold Panas		Don Bresnahan
	1985	
Edward F. Kenney, FNAHD		Steven T. Ast
	1984	
Sandra Hellman, Ph. D.		Peter C. Barnard
Nick G. Costa		Jack Shakely
	1983	
Henry V. Lione, FNAHD		Sister M. Therese Gottschalk
Dr. Eva Schindler-Rainman		Phyllis A. Allen, FNAHD
	1982	
James M. Carmen		Herbert A. Segawa
Mervin G. Morris		Robert M. Ellis, FNAHD
	1981	
Sherwin L. Memel		Sister Margaret Vincent Blandford

THE HAROLD J. (SI) SEYMOUR AWARD
MOST PRESTIGIOUS RECOGNITION
CONFERRED BY NAHD

The National Association for Hospital Development presents annually to one of its members the Harold J. (Si) Seymour Award. It is the highest honor the profession confers.

A panel of judges determines which member's achievements have most aided the cause of hospital philanthropy. The award is presented to the person felt to bring the highest prominence and honor to the individual and the profession.

The Seymour Award is now in its nineteenth year. It commemorates the life and professional work of Si Seymour, who launched a career at Harvard University in fundraising that lasted fifty distinguished years.

He was awarded the Order of Knights of Sylvester, the highest honor conferred on protestants by the Catholic Church, by Pope Paul VI.

Award Winners, 1970–1988

1970—R. Graham Nash
1971—Barbara B. Janes, FNAHD
1972—Alfred Wardley

1973—Ted Rowe
1974—John C. Shimer, FNAHD
1975—Henry V. Lione, FNAHD
1976—David B. Hanaman, FNAHD
1977—Jack G. Bryan, FNAHD
1978—John R. Vitello, FNAHD
1979—Paul M. Ireland, FNAHD
1980—Milton J. Murray, FNAHD
1981—I. Brewster Terry, FNAHD
1982—Marilyn F. Erickson and Jack Herman, FNAHD
1983—William S. Roth, FNAHD
1984—Frank R. Hall, FNAHD
1985—John W. Dolan, FNAHD
1986—Don L. Albertson, FNAHD
1987—James G. Marshall, FNAHD
1988—William D. Seelye, FNAHD

ONE OF THE MOST EFFECTIVE RECORDS IN FUNDRAISING

Over the years, philanthropy at Memorial Sloan-Kettering has continued to grow, more than doubling in the past eight years. In 1980, $33,687,000 was given to the institution. In 1987, the amount was nearly $70 million. The audited report for 1988 has not yet been completed, but it is anticipated that giving will be about the same or more than 1987. It is an extraordinary record.

The totals are remarkable. First of all, this very likely represents the most funds given to any medical institution in the nation. Secondly, compared with other major institutions and the Ivy League universities, the Memorial Sloan-Kettering totals probably represent the most cost-effective expenditure for fundraising and the fewest professional staff in relationship to the amount raised.

The record follows.

PRIVATE PHILANTHROPY RECEIVED BY MEMORIAL SLOAN-KETTERING

	1980	1981	1982	1983	1984	1985	1986	1987
Unrestricted Contributions and Bequests	$15,397	$18,585	$16,989	$17,924	$14,671	$18,864	$19,981	$20,490
Restricted Contributions and Bequests	6,722	9,112	12,938	14,027	16,056	13,456	17,870	33,340
Plant Expansion Contributions and Bequests	1,747	679	1,403	195	6,147	15,178	4,366	8,190
Endowment Contributions and Bequests	10,001	4,608	1,831	3,481	5,451	5,089	9,364	7,630
Total Philanthropy	$33,867	$32,984	$33,161	$35,627	$42,325	$52,587	$51,581	$69,650

Philanthropic income by category in millions. Government grants not included.

THE SPIRIT OF PHILANTHROPY

Every President in our nation's history has reinforced the spirit and works of philanthropy. Each has called attention to the important value of individual Americans helping one another and their community. Philanthropy's essential role in our democratic society is illustrated in the following Presidential statements.

RONALD REAGAN

"You meet heroes across the counter—and they're on both sides of that counter.... They are individuals and families whose taxes support the government and whose voluntary gifts support church, charity, culture, art and education. Their patriotism is quiet but deep. Their values sustain our national life."

JOHN F. KENNEDY

"The raising of extraordinarily large sums of money, given voluntarily and freely by millions of our fellow Americans, is a unique American tradition, it represents the best trend of American tradition, the private, voluntary giving, a helping hand to those who need it, who are our neighbors and friends...."

DWIGHT D. EISENHOWER

"The true slogan of a true democracy is not "Let the Government do it." The true slogan is, "Let's do it ourselves." In this spirit, citizens from all walks of life, of all religious faiths and racial backgrounds, unite annually to work and to give together. This is the spirit of a people dedicated to helping themselves—and one another."

HARRY S. TRUMAN

"...so in generous giving, we will affirm before the world our nation's faith in the inalienable right of every man to a life of freedom and justice and decent security...."

FRANKLIN D. ROOSEVELT

"Charity literally translated from the original means love, the love that understands, that does not merely share the wealth of the giver, but in true sympathy and wisdom helps men to help themselves."

CALVIN COOLIDGE

"To place your name by gift or bequest in the keeping of an active educational institution is to be sure that the name and project with which it is associated will continue down the centuries to quicken the minds and hearts of youth and thus make a permanent contribution to the welfare of humanity."

THEODORE ROOSEVELT

"The friends of property...must realize that the surest way to provoke an explosion of wrong and injustice is to be greedy and arrogant, and to fail to show in actual work that here in this republic it is peculiarly incumbent upon the man with whom things have prospered to be in a certain sense the keeper of the brother with whom life has gone hard."

THOMAS JEFFERSON
"I deem it the duty of every man to devote a certain portion of his income for charitable purposes; and that it is his further duty to see it so applied and to do the most good for which it is capable. This I believe to be best insured by keeping within the circle of his own inquiry and information the subject of distress to whose relief his contribution should be applied."

Source: Philanthropic Service for Institutions General Conference of Seventh-Day Adventists

THE GROWTH OF PHILANTHROPY 1955–1987
($ IN BILLIONS)

	Total Giving	Percent Change	GNP	Giving as % of GNP
1955	$ 7.70		$ 405.9	1.90
1956	8.33	8.18	428.2	1.95
1957	9.26	11.16	451.0	2.05
1958	9.50	2.59	456.8	2.08
1959	10.37	9.16	495.8	2.09
1960	10.92	5.30	515.3	2.12
1961	11.36	4.03	533.8	2.13
1962	11.88	4.58	574.6	2.07
1963	13.21	11.20	606.9	2.18
1964	13.70	3.71	649.8	2.11
1965	14.75	7.66	705.1	2.09
1966	15.80	7.12	772.0	2.06
1967	17.04	7.85	816.4	2.09
1968	18.95	11.21	892.7	2.12
1969	20.79	9.71	963.9	2.16
1970	20.89	0.49	1,015.5	2.07
1971	23.44	11.51	1,102.7	2.13
1972	24.48	4.44	1,212.8	2.02
1973	25.70	4.99	1,359.3	1.89
1974	26.98	4.98	1,472.8	1.83
1975	28.61	6.04	1,598.4	1.79
1976	32.70	14.30	1,782.8	1.80
1977	36.34	13.35	1,990.5	1.83
1978	38.95	7.18	2,249.7	1.73
1979	43.69	12.17	2,508.2	1.74
1980	48.74	11.56	2,732.0	1.78
1981	55.49	13.85	3,052.6	1.82
1982	60.04	8.20	3,166.0	1.90
1983	65.78	9.56	3,405.7	1.93
1984	71.35	8.47	3,772.2	1.89
1985	80.42	12.71	4,010.3	2.01
1986	88.00	9.43	4,235.0	2.08
1987	93.68	6.45	4,486.2	2.09

Source: Giving USA

ARTS

It was not a good year for culture!

The stage went dark in New Orleans. The professional theatre went into bankruptcy. Proctor Theatre in Schenectady was one minute away from closing permanently—until a small group of community leaders raised $2 million from a handful of gifts. But these weren't exceptions. Nearly half the professional theatres in the country ended 1988 in the red. Of the nearly 200 not-for-profit professional theatres in 37 states, there was an aggregate deficit of $1.4 million.

The New Orleans Symphony declared Chapter 11: so did the Denver Symphony, and a number of others. The San Diego and Phoenix Symphonies face horrendous financial problems. Many of the nation's orchestras dipped into modest endowments in order to make payroll. The manager of the Phoenix Symphony resigned unexpectedly, vowing "to leave the field for good."

Giving increased nearly ten percent over 1987 to the arts and culture. But this represented less than seven cents out of every philanthropic dollar. And the increase in giving for the year was offset by accelerating salaries, increased costs for productions, and the escalating expense of just staying in business.

In San Francisco, "years of stagnant and non-existent fundraising have brought the 118-year-old Historical Society to near-bankruptcy." The New York City Historical Society faced the same problem, but received considerable national media coverage, which did not enhance the image of either the board or the Society.

In spite of high hopes and expectations, Miss Tallchief's Ballet Company in Chicago folded—because "board members refused to work or to give." Giving to dance increased by nearly 9 percent over 1987, but this only helped giving keep pace with inflation.

Of all the categories, this is the one for which it was the most difficult to get information.

FIFTEEN LARGEST GIFTS TO ARTS, CULTURE, AND HUMANITIES

The arts, culture and humanities includes giving to theatres, museums, arts organizations, public television and radio, and symphony orchestras. These organizations received 6.84 percent of the total giving to not-for-profits last year, or $6.41 billion.

FIFTEEN LARGEST GIFTS TO ARTS, CULTURE, AND HUMANITIES FOR LAST YEAR REPORTED

The Lillian B. Disney Foundation and Lillian B. Disney
$50 million to Los Angeles Music Center, Los Angeles, CA

Carl and Lilly Pforzheimer Foundation
$23 million to New York Public Library, New York, NY
(collection of 19th century English literature)

Andy Warhol
$15 million to the Andy Warhol Foundation for the Visual Arts, New York, NY

Tisch Foundation
$10 million to the Metropolitan Museum of Art, New York, NY

Paul Mellon & Andrew Mellon
$10 million to Choate Rosemary Hall, Wallingford, CT

Henry R. Kravis
$10 million to the Metropolitan Museum of Art, New York, NY

Iris and Gerald B. Kantor
$7 million to the Metropolitan Museum of Art, New York, NY

The Family of Joseph Meyerhoff
$6 million to Baltimore Symphony Orchestra, Baltimore, MD

Skirball Foundation
$5 million to the Hebrew Union College-Jewish Institute of Religion, Cincinnati, OH

David Mugar
$4 million to the Mugar Omni Theater at the Museum of Science, Boston, MA

David and Mary Ann Cofrin
$4 million to the University of Wisconsin at Green Bay, Green Bay, WI

Urbanch
$3.5 million to the Performing Arts Center, Ft. Lauderdale, FL

Helena Rubinstein Foundation
$3 million to the United States Holocaust Memorial Museum, Washington, DC

Roy and Patty Disney and the Disney Family Foundation
$3 million to the Contemporary Arts Training Institution, Valencia, CA

J. Paul Getty Trust Fund
$3 million to the California Community Foundation, Los Angeles, CA

Source: *Giving USA*

NATIONAL PUBLIC RADIO

National Public Radio (NPR) provides award-winning news and cultural programs to more than 350 public radio stations throughout America. It has a large and grateful following among its listeners and is a recognized force in broadcasting and in the not-for-profit community.

The President and Chief Executive Officer of NPR is Douglas J. Bennet, who has headed the organization since 1983. He served as President and CEO of the Roosevelt Center for American Policy Studies, a privately operated foundation. For two years, he was head of the United States Agency for International Development, where he managed the U.S. economic assistance program for 70 developing countries.

The work and coordinating of the public radio stations is done through the national office. **For more information: National Public Radio, 2025 M Street, N.W., Washington, DC 20036 (202) 822-2000.**

THE TEN PUBLIC RADIO STATIONS RECEIVING THE LARGEST SUBSCRIBER GIFT INCOME

Station	Subscriber Gift Income (millions)
1) KSJN Minneapolis, MN	$1.78
2) KUSC Los Angeles, CA	1.60
3) WNYC New York, NY	1.46
4) WETA Washington, DC	1.27
5) WGBH Boston, MA	1.19
6) KCRW Santa Monica, CA	1.16
7) WHYY Philadelphia, PA	.98
8) WERN Madison, WI	.883
9) WBUR Boston, MA	.881
10) KPFA Berkeley, CA	.79

Source: Development Exchange, Washington, DC

IN NEW ORLEANS...IT WAS THE WORST OF TIMES, IT WAS THE BEST OF TIMES

As 1988 came to a close, New Orleans faced the most financially depressed and crippling time in its history. The state of Louisiana announced it was days away from declaring bankruptcy, and New Orleans was fast cutting back on all services. The famed trolley was bankrupt and the utilities were not far behind.

Louisiana was the only state in the union that reduced spending on drug treatment and drug related funding from 1985 to 1987, and then reduced it further from 1987 to 1989—a total reduction of over 50 percent. The state now has 400 fewer state patrolmen than five years ago. The state has the highest rate of unemployment in the country; if you include underemployed, some say the figure goes to 30 percent.

All of this is aggravated by a petroleum industry which was once the pride of the state. Today, there is no new land exploration and only mild activity in off-shore drilling. Several of the major corporations have moved corporate headquarters out of the state. Office space goes begging—two years free if you take a five-year lease.

Now, with all of this going on—New Orleans leadership succeeded in raising an extraordinary $10 million for the Metropolitan Arts Fund. This represents the most ever raised in a city for a fund of this sort. The Fund will pay off the debt of the New Orleans Symphony which went bankrupt two years ago. It will also help assure the financial base of the ballet and the opera—both of which are near bankruptcy. The $10 million was raised mostly through the efforts of a few community leaders. Most of the gifts came from major businesses and corporations.

All things considered, it was a remarkable achievement. Surely, in no other major city does the sense of civic responsibility and community spirit glow as brightly.

ART MUSEUMS

Position	Average 1988 Salary	Average 1987 Salary
Director	$75,679	$69,510
Administrator	$47,448	$44,623
Development Officer	$46,484	$43,700
Marketing Director	$35,805	$36,535
Public Relations Officer	$29,269	$28,073
Membership Secretary	$22,432	$21,379

Highest salary for a director 1988—$180,000. Lowest salary—$37,853.

Source: The Association of Art Museum Directors 1988 Salary Survey.

PUBLIC BROADCASTING SERVICE

The Public Broadcasting Service (PBS) is the national office which represents all public television stations.

In virtually all cities, public television stations raise their operating and programming funds from a variety of sources: individual and annual giving from on-air pledge drives, direct mail, and telemarketing. Corporations are another major funding source—they make either unrestricted grants or grants to cover the acquisition costs of public television programs. Other major sources are the on-air auctions and special events, major giving, planned giving, and other miscellaneous sources.

The core of the public television schedule programs includes "MYSTERY!", "Masterpiece Theater," "Nova," "Nature," "Great Performances," "American Playhouse," "MacNeil-Lehrer Newshour," "Firing Line," and many others. These programs are produced by public television stations which secure corporate dollars—in the minimum $500,000 grant range—to produce the programs. These programs are then distributed to local stations. Some of them, such as "Masterpiece Theater," are funded fully by one corporation and are sent to local stations at no charge. "Masterpiece Theater" is funded entirely by Mobil Corporation. Others, which may be only partially funded, cost the stations an amount based on their audience size and funding base—and these stations then seek local corporate dollars to help them cover the cost.

Bruce L. Christensen is President and Chief Executive Officer of PBS, the third president in its sixteen year history. Christensen administers the national office of PBS which represents public television's legislative, regulatory, and planning interests on behalf of member stations. He holds degrees in journalism from the University of Utah and Medill School of Journalism at Northwestern University.

For more information: Public Broadcasting Service, 1320 Braddock Place, Alexandria, VA 22314-1698 (703) 739-5000.

GIVING FROM THE PRIVATE SECTOR TO THE TOP EIGHT U.S. SYMPHONY ORCHESTRAS
($000's)

	Corporate	Foundations	Individuals	Total
1) Chicago Symphony	1,290	738	2,808	5,316
2) Minnesota Symphony	1,775	490	1,980	4,245
3) New York Philharmonic	845	735	2,290	3,870
4) Boston Symphony	1,390	280	2,159	3,829
5) Los Angeles Philharmonic	580	580	1,750	2,910
6) Philadelphia Symphony	1,062	413	1,151	2,626
7) San Francisco Symphony	731	195	1,645	2,571
8) Cleveland Symphony	812	495	957	2,264

PUBLIC TELEVISION STATIONS
FUNDRAISING PRODUCTION
FY'88 (July 1, 1987–June 30, 1988)

WNET/New York	$54,847,235
WGBH/Boston	$36,037,103
WETA/Washington, DC	$27,362,778
KCET/Los Angeles	$26,047,900**
KQED/San Francisco	$20,549,900
WQED/Pittsburgh	$16,767,673
WTTW/Chicago	$15,865,316**
KTCA/St. Paul	$10,896,172
WHYY/Philadelphia	$ 8,830,275
WTVS/Detroit	$ 8,287,439

Based on FY'87 figures; stations did not report in FY'88. The figures listed do not include any federal funds. Source: Public Broadcasting Service as voluntarily reported by each station.

GIVING FROM THE PRIVATE SECTOR TO THE TOP EIGHT U.S. SYMPHONY ORCHESTRAS AS A PERCENTAGE OF THE GROSS ANNUAL EXPENSE BUDGET

	Total $ Raised	Gross Annual Budget Expense	$ Raised as Percentage Annual Expense Budget
1) Minnesota Symphony	4,245	15,577	27.2
2) Chicago Symphony	5,316	21,489	24.7
3) New York Philharmonic	3,870	19,693	19.7
4) Philadelphia Symphony	2,626	16,640	15.8
5) Boston Symphony	3,829	27,974	13.7
6) San Francisco Symphony	2,571	21,400	12.0
7) Los Angeles Philharmonic	2,910	24,649	11.8
8) Cleveland Symphony	2,264	22,319	10.1

TAX NOT A FACTOR

The severe 1986 Tax Reform Act initially caused philanthropy-watchers great concern. It made deductions much less valuable and limited tax-exemptions for charity for those who itemized their annual returns. Thus far, there has been no cause for concern. Giving has continued at an accelerated pace through 1988 and a recent study shows that 80 to 90 percent of the non-itemizers intend to continue and increase their donations.

ENDOWMENT OF THE TOP EIGHT U.S. SYMPHONY ORCHESTRAS

	Market Value of Endowment Fund	Income From Endowment for Annual Operations
1) Boston Symphony	$62,962,000	$1,949,000
2) New York Philharmonic	56,171,000	3,569,000
3) Minnesota Symphony	46,000,000	2,487,000
4) Cleveland Symphony	43,000,000	2,126,000
5) San Francisco Symphony	37,500,000	1,716,000
6) Philadelphia Symphony	36,057,000	2,030,000
7) Chicago Symphony	34,511,000	2,251,000
8) Los Angeles Philharmonic	13,100,000	678,000

GIVING TO THE OPERA—1988

The twelve opera companies that raised the most money from the private sector.

	Total Amount of Contributions
Metropolitan Opera Robert De Micco Associate Director of Development Lincoln Center New York, NY 10023	$26,780,000
Lyric Opera of Chicago Farrell Frentress Director of Development 20 North Wacker Drive Chicago, IL 60606	10,780,123
San Francisco Opera Julie H. LeVay Director of Development War Memorial Opera House San Francisco, CA 94102	8,955,303
New York City Opera Barbara Zarlengo Director of Development New York State Theatre Lincoln Center 63rd & Columbus New York, NY 10023	8,605,000

Opera Colorado   7,750,000
Rebecca Reynolds
Director of Development
695 S. Colorado Blvd.
Suite 20
Denver, CO 80222

Houston Grand Opera   4,646,900
Marsha James
Director of Development
510 Preston
Houston, TX 77002

San Diego Opera Association   2,415,589
Domenick Ietto
Director of Development
San Diego, CA 92112-0988

Opera Guild of Greater Miami   1,939,093
William J. Conner
Director of Development
1200 Coral Way
Miami, FL 33145

Opera Theatre of St. Louis   1,781,286
Davis Allen
Director of Development
P.O. Box 13148
St. Louis, MO 63119

The Minnesota Opera   1,280,556
Daniel L. Berg
Development Director
400 Sibley Street
Suite 20
St. Paul, MN 55101

Central City Opera   893,691
Barbara Arko
Director of Development
621 17th Street
Denver, CO 80293

Lyric Opera of Kansas City   864,918
Martha E. Lawrence
Development Associate
1029 Central
Kansas City, MO 64105-1677

Cleveland Opera   740,055
JoAnn Boscia
Director of Development
1438 Euclid Avenue
Cleveland, OH 44115-1806

CONTRIBUTIONS TO MUSEUMS

	Total Contributions
The Henry Francis du Pont Winterthur Museum Marilyn D. Stetson Assistant Director of Development Winterthur, DE 19735	$1,846,662
The Museum of Modern Art Daniel Vecchitto Director of Development 11 East 53 Street New York, NY 10019	$15,623,500
The St. Louis Art Museum Kathryn J. Rybolt White Director of Development Forest Park St. Louis, MO 63110-1380	$4,328,533
Whitney Museum of American Art Deborah W. Addison Associate Development Officer 945 Madison Avenue at 75th Street New York, NY 10021	$7,508,672
The Metropolitan Museum of Art Emily Kernan Rafferty Vice President for Development Fifth Avenue at 82nd Street New York, NY 10028	$31,776,265
The Art Institute of Chicago Christine O'Neill Assistant Vice President for Development and Public Affairs Michigan Avenue at Adams Street Chicago, IL 60603	$32,639,203
The Detroit Institute of Arts Marianne L. DePalma Associate Director 5200 Woodward Avenue Detroit, MI 48202	$7,703,168
Philadelphia Museum of Art Maria T. Giliotti Development Director P.O. Box 7646 Philadelphia, PA 19101	$10,233,389

National Gallery of Art	$6,619,747
Laura E. Smith	
Development Officer	
Washington, DC 20565	

The Brooklyn Museum	$1,711,863
Horace S. Solomon	
Vice-Director for Development	
200 Eastern Parkway	
Brooklyn, NY 11238	

The Cleveland Museum of Art	$4,466,469
Lawrence J. Wheeler	
Assistant Director for Development	
11150 East Boulevard	
Cleveland, OH 44106	

Where applicable, figures include gifts, grants, membership income, bequests and endowment and other investment income.

NATIONAL FUND RAISER

The *National Fund Raiser* was first published in November, 1974. It is now in its 15th year of publication. The one-year subscription rate is $79, which includes 12 monthly issues, supplements each month, a complimentary copy of their publication *How to Meet Today's Fund Raising Challenges,* and free "Hot Line" consulting services. Individuals or organizations may receive a free sample of the *National Fund Raiser* and subscription information by writing to: **National Fund Raiser, 603 Douglas Boulevard, Roseville, CA 95678-3244   (916) 786-7471.**

Currently, there are 2,300 not-for-profit organizations subscribing to the *National Fund Raiser.* Subscribers are located in all 50 states and in 20 foreign nations. They include trustees, executive directors, directors of development, development staff members and many of the nation's leading fundraising consultants.

BEQUESTS REACH AN ALL-TIME HIGH

In 1988 giving through bequests reached an all-time high, doubling in a ten year period.

Bequests to not-for-profit organizations and institutions reached nearly $6 billion. The major portion of that, more than 70 percent, went to education.

Although this remains an unpredictable source of income, many feel that this area represents the highest potential for most philanthropic institutions. And in the case of most organizations, it receives the least attention.

RECOGNITION PAYS OFF

Philanthropic Service for Institutions (PSI) publishes a very handy booklet replete with recognition ideas, techniques, and examples of how to select who your organization will recognize. Being able to say "thank you" in a very special way paves the way for repeat gifts. **For a copy:** *Accent on Recognition: Saying Thank You to Donors and Volunteers,* **PSI, 12501 Old Columbia Pike, Silver Spring, MD 20904.** The first copy is free.

Here is our own source of suppliers and vendors for recognition materials. The list does not constitute an endorsement and we apologize to any which have been omitted.

MEDALLIONS

Ashworth International
Douglas R. Ashworth
President
753 East Washington Street
North Attleboro, MA 02760
(617) 695-1900

Awardcraft, Inc.
Pete Chubb
11311 Hampshire Avenue, South
Minneapolis, MN 55438
(612) 829-0400

Honorcraft Incorporated
James J. Rapoport
90 River Street
Braintree, MA 02184
(617) 848-6013

W. & E. Baum Bronze Tablet Corp.
Richard Baum
Vice President
200 60th Street
Brooklyn, NY 11220
(718) 439-3311

MISCELLANEOUS

Achievement Products, Inc.
Philip Van Rooyen
294 Route 10–
P.O. Box 388
East Hanover, NJ 07936
(201) 887-5090

Ashworth Associates
Douglas R. Ashworth
President
753 East Washington Street
North Attleboro, MA 02760
(617) 695-1900

Benedeck & Fey Engravers
Ms. Melody Maier
7005 Ogden Avenue
Berwyn, IL 60402
(312) 484-3606

Jardine Associates
Leonard Jardine
President
97 Cottage St.
Pawtucket, RI 02860
(401) 724-1880

William Chelsea Ltd.
F. David Wessel
P.O. Box 159
Scarsdale, NY 10583
(914) 725-2040
(neckties)

RECOGNITION WALL UNITS

Adelphia Graphic Systems
Josh Jacobson
302 Commerce Drive
Exton, PA 19341
(215) 363-8150

Ames & Rollinson, Inc.
Paul Barmoski
President
215 Park Avenue, South
New York, NY 10003
(212) 473-7000

Ashworth International
Douglas R. Ashworth
President
753 East Washington Street
North Attleboro, MA 02760
(617) 695-1900

Awardcraft, Inc.
Pete Chubb
11311 Hampshire Avenue South
Minneapolis, MN 55438
(612) 829-0400

Bruce Fox, Inc.
Mack Phillips
President
1909 McDonald Lane
New Albany, IN 47150
(812) 945-3511

Forsythe-French, Inc.
Robert W. Forsythe
Executive Vice President
108 North Scott Avenue
P.O. Box 538
Belton, MO 64012
(816) 322-2580

Gabel & Schubert
Richard Robe
4500 North Ravenswood Avenue
Chicago, IL 60640
1-800-692-4547

Honorcraft Incorporated
James J. Rapoport
90 River Street
Braintree, MA 02184
(617) 848-6013

Metal Decor
Charles Patterson
National Sales Manager
P.O. Box 3606
2731 North Dirksen Parkway
Springfield, IL 62708
(217) 523-4565

Mitchell Associates
Lou Rosenberg
President
One Avenue of the Arts
Wilmington, DE 19801
(302) 594-9400

Sanford Werfel—Artist
Sanford Werfel
302 Old Georges Road
North Brunswick, NJ 08902
(201) 297-1166

W. & E. Baum Bronze Tablet Corp.
Richard Baum
Vice President
200 60th Street
Brooklyn, NY 11220
(718) 439-3311

PLAQUES AND PYLONS

Achievement Products, Inc.
Philip Ban Rooyen
294 Route 10—P.O. Box 388
East Hanover, NJ 07936
(201) 887-5090

Benedeck & Fey Engravers
Ms. Melody Maier
7005 Ogden Avenue
Berwyn, IL 60402
(312) 484-3606

Adelphia Graphic Systems
Josh Jacobson
302 Commerce Drive
Exton, PA 19341
(215) 363-8150

Ames & Rollinson, Inc.
Paul Barmoski
President
215 Park Avenue, South
New York, NY 10003
(212) 473-7000

Awardcraft, Inc.
Pete Chubb
11311 Hampshire Avenue, South
Minneapolis, MN 55438
(612) 829-0400

Meierjohan-Wengler, Inc.
Ernie Winkler
President
10330 Wayne Avenue
Cincinnati, OH 45215
(513) 771-6074

Metal Decor
Charles Patterson
National Sales Manager
P.O. Box 3606
2731 N. Dirksen Parkway
Springfield, IL 62708
(217) 523-4565

Bruce Fox, Inc.
Mack Phillips
President
1909 McDonald Lane
New Albany, IN 47150
(812) 945-3511

Gabel & Schubert
Richard Robe
4500 North Ravenswood Avenue
Chicago, IL 60640
1-800-692-4547

Honorcraft Incorporated
James J. Rapoport
90 River Street
Braintree, MA 02184
(617) 848-6013

The Massiollon Plaque Company
David L. Rosborough
VP, Sales and Marketing
5757 Mayfair Road
P.O. Box 2539
North Canton, OH 44720
(216) 494-4199

W. & E. Baum Bronze Tablet Corp.
Richard Baum—Vice President
200 60th Street
Brooklyn, NY 11220
(718) 439-3311

CERTIFICATES

Ames & Rollinson, Inc.
Paul Barmoski
President
215 Park Avenue, South
New York, NY 10003
(212) 473-7000

Awardcraft, Inc.
Pete Chubb
11311 Hampshire Avenue, South
Minneapolis, MN 55438
(612) 829-0400

Bruce Fox, Inc.
Mack Phillips
President
1909 McDonald Lane
New Albany, IN 47150
(812) 945-3511

W. & E. Baum Bronze Tablet Corp.
Richard Baum—Vice President
200 60th Street
Brooklyn, NY 11220
(718) 439-3311

HAROLD J. (SI) SEYMOUR

He never headed a fundraising firm, he was never in charge of a Development Office of an organization—yet Si Seymour is perhaps the most important and the most highly recognized man in the field. He served with distinction a wide range of organizations and institutions which covered virtually the entire spectrum of philanthropy.

He began his career in 1919, on the staff of the Harvard Endowment Fund Campaign. He continued in fundraising in one form or another until his death in 1968. He is certainly the most quoted man in the field. His book, *Elements Of Fund Raising*, is the best selling of any in the field. It has gone through seven printings by McGraw-Hill, the original publishers. In 1989, the Fund-Raising Institute published a new version.

Mr. Seymour served as Executive Vice-President of the John Price Jones Corporation, one of the charter firms in the American Association of Fund-Raising Counsel. The firm, particularly during Mr. Seymour's tenure, dominated the field.

For three years, during World War II, he was General Manager of the War Fund, raising $321 million. It conducted appeals nationally for 22 war-related agencies.

He served as a consultant for institutional public relations and finance for colleges, universities, and national health and welfare organizations. There were few organizations at the time that did not feel the impact of his work. Every organization in the field today has been influenced, directly or indirectly, by his life and work.

Si Seymour is one of the founders, a past President, and was for years an honorary member of the American Association of Fund-Raising Counsel.

He was involved with almost every major charity, including the YMCA, YWCA, Salvation Army, Girls Scouts of America, American Cancer Society, and the United Negro College Fund.

SEYMOURISMS—AS RELEVANT TODAY AS THEY WERE 50 YEARS AGO

"Every cause needs people more than money for when the people are with you and are giving your cause attention, interest, confidence, advocacy and service, financial support should just about take care of itself. Whereas, without them—and the right quality and quantity, and the right places and states of mind and spirit—you might as well go and get lost. So you had better know as much about people as you can, keep it ever in mind, and always let it light your way."

In talking about the importance of proper and sustained cultivation, Seymour said: "You don't make a pickle by taking a cucumber and sprinkling a little vinegar over it. You have to immerse it."

"These are exciting days ahead of us, in which much of what we consider to be grave problems will be most likely solved when seen as exciting opportunities. What it will take, I think, as in the past, will be mostly perspective, imagination, faith, and healthy glands."

"The late Daniel Willard used to say to me when importuned to move faster on fundraising: 'You can get two or three crops a year if you want to raise alfalfa. But you have to allow a lot more time than that, if you're raising an oak.'"

"It is not enough for the President and Trustees merely to approve building and endowment projects; just to stand waving on the pier while the good little ships set sail...the rule of experience is that while no President should directly ask for money, nearly all big gifts are made with the President directly in the picture."

Writing about Case Statements, Seymour said: "Those who know most about the project are usually the least qualified to write about it. Their point of view is apt to be too institutional, or too narrow ...they know too much to distinguish the significant from the unimportant detail...their writing habits are related more to dissertation than to the arts of persuasion and promotion."

"The general tendency, in special gifts efforts, is to include in the prospect list far too many names. It is also a general tendency to ask for too little. Big prospects always think in big terms, and in many celebrated cases have thought in bigger terms than those seeking the aid. Special gift donors rarely use a standard subscription blank. The legal aspects of important contributions are usually covered by an exchange of letters."

In terms of copy for fundraising material, Seymour said: "Keep it simple, say it often, and be sure it's true."

"Certainly the words that sent Paul on his most fateful trip were as simple as possible: 'Come over into Macedonia and help us.' It's fun to speculate on what Paul would have done if he had been urged to 'cooperate in the implementation of a program of outreach on the Macedonian local level.'"

"Let's not be apologetic about the goals and deadlines that make for pressure. On the contrary, let's advocate all the pressure that can be brought to bear. It's pressure that makes a campaign a success."

Speaking of what he called the Law of Minor Concessions, *Seymour said*: "To win wars, you don't have to win all the battles. Fund-raisers may fatten their own egos by insisting on having everything go their own way, and may rationalize such attitudes as being in the best interest of the cause's concern. But there is no easier way to lose friends. To yield on minor points actually makes it easier to gain major decisions. This also has a bearing on that always dangerous subject of 'credit.' It is worth repeating, I think, that the layman takes the credit, and the professional takes the rap—that to seek credit is to lose it, and that to avoid credit usually results in getting more than you really deserve."

"Two popular and persistent fallacies are 1) That publicity in itself can raise substantial sums of money; and 2) That the easy way to raise money is by simple application of the multiplication table."

When Seymour spoke about recruiting, he said: "All the old-timers know that it is far easier to get someone 'to see a few important and influential people' than it is to get the same person 'to join the Special Gifts Committee.'"

In some of his rules for a fundraiser (Development Officer), Seymour said: "Be on the phone when you call, and when the layman calls you, never be 'in conference.' Be on time, and start meetings on time—particularly the first of a series. In your work, don't swoop in and out, like a seagull; stay there until you see action. Never try to emulate Atlas, Ajax, or Alexander. Remember that two-thirds of Promotion is Motion. And, nothing worthwhile ever gets done all at once."

"Don't be an Expert. Whatever you do, don't try to pose as omniscient. If you don't know (which is probably most of the time), say so frankly, but add quickly that you'll try to find out."

"The word 'assume' should be stricken from the professional vocabulary. 'Check it—verify it—look it up—confirm it'—these are the thoughts to live with, and to live with openly, in order to foster and retain lay confidence."

Seymour called these his Five Essential Elements Of Fundraising:

1) A strong and timely case.

2) Active and influential leadership.

3) An adequate number of informed and enthusiastic volunteer workers.

4) A field of support in which the known giving potential is commensurate with the campaign goal. And

5) Dynamics.

"No one should participate on any level of any campaign until he has been fully indoctrinated on the appeal. In fact, the most successful campaigns are those in which no worker is permitted to take a single prospect unless he has attended one or meetings for training and indoctrination."

Seymour said that it is appropriate to admire excellence, but to suspect perfection!

Seymour lists Ten Basic Laws And Principles. Here are some that continue to have penetrating importance today:

1) No organization is ever stronger than the quality of its leadership, or ever extends its constituency beyond the degree to which the leadership is representative.

2) The case must be bigger than the institution.

3) Duly proportionate quotas or goals, whether for dollars or units of work, should be established and accepted for every part of the total campaign structure; for every division, every team, every worker, and every prospective contributor.

4) The effectiveness of a campaign organization is limited by a law of diminishing returns; the wider its periphery, the lower the returns and the greater the proportionate costs.

5) To paraphrase Shakespeare, if a campaign were to be done, it were done quickly; in communities as in kindergartens, attention periods have their limits.

6) You can't raise money without spending money; within reasonable limits the return is likely to be commensurate with the investment.

7) Campaigns are best conducted in an atmosphere of optimism and universality.

"I believe that even the wisest of the old pros have trouble with perspective—that participation comes more readily when people know the background and the reason for the task they are asked to assume, and that most of the troubles in organized fundraising are due either to ignored or misunderstood laws and principles or to proceeding in the wrong order at the wrong times."

"The vineyards of philanthropy are pleasant places, and I would hope many more good men and women will be drawn there. Most of all, I would hope that it would be better understood that if these vineyards are to thrive and bear their best fruits, they must always have first-class attention."

"In any field of human activity, not just in fundraising, leaders are indeed rare—never more than 5 percent of any group of constituency, and usually less. These are the creative citizens, with what Harry Emerson Fosdick has called 'a sense of privilege.' They light the way, originate action, take the responsibility, establish the standards, create the confidence, sustain the mood, and keep things moving."

"For any major type of campaign, some weird rule of three seems to be involved which should be heeded even though it is hard indeed to understand. For it has long been customary to say, at the upper levels of fundraising, that a third of the money has to come from the top ten gifts, the next third from the next 100 gifts, and the last third from everybody else. Similarly, with most of the workers in most campaigns, it is usual to say that a third will perform as asked (the responsible ones), a third group will respond under pressure and prodding, and the last third, no matter what you or anyone else does, will turn out to be mostly dead wood; there will just be time, if all goes well, to reassign their unfinished work to the performing top third, God bless 'em, who meanwhile have finished their jobs."

About deadlines and pressure, Seymour said: "One fact of life we usually find it convenient to ignore is that whatever we have plenty of time to do is often the thing that never gets done. It seems to be popular to decry pressure. Nobody likes the words, 'do it now,' but on the other hand, one of the greatest soporifics since Rip van Winkle is the line, 'at your convenience.' Whether the deadlines are genuine or merely plausible, there has be a fairly imminent time limit on whatever you wish to persuade people to do."

"Seymour discusses the Seven Deadly Sins of Fundraising:

1) *Ad-libbing*. (No study, no planning, no preparation, no consultation, no concurrence...)

2) *Panhandling*. ('Any amount will be welcome' cheapens the cause...)

3) *Automation*. (Human equation gives way to mechanics ...)

4) *Groupism*.

5) *Averaging*. (Accent on averages leads to lower standards ...)

6) *Pessimism*. (Whenever you let them know it isn't going well, the chances are everything will stop right there.)

7) *Parsimony*. (The good omelette needs enough broken

eggs. More often than not, fundraising costs are set too low.)"

"Honest job descriptions are indeed important, but I have always felt that in the honeymoon stage of incoming leadership the switch from orange blossoms to dishpans shouldn't be too abrupt. Requests for initial service should begin with something relatively easy; let them lick a stamp before you ask them to lick an army."

Regarding development staff, Seymour said: " 'Hire them slowly, and fire them fast' is a good rule, remembering that careful and dependable mediocrity is much to be preferred to the kind of easy affability or occasional brilliance that too often is sustained either by the Martini Crutch or by hopeless addiction to the needs of a starving ego."

"The well-loved Pope John XXIII is said to have squirmed at the very mention of 'infallibility'...and I like to remember too when Columbia's Professor Montague said...'if you want to persuade anyone, you can afford to be more than 85 percent right.' It is certain that the very word 'perfect,' either as a verb or as an adjective, should be used sparingly, if at all."

"That people love winters is part of our folk lore. And by now it should be one of the accepted legends of fundraising that support flows to promising programs rather than to needy institutions. You may think, as too many often do, that people will rally around if you tell them that things are going badly. But they won't. You have to whistle the happy tune and keep on the sunny side of the street, where success lies just around the corner."

"A cause today should have a clear image of importance. It should have importance both in its own field and within its own sphere of influence. Otherwise, with all the myriad pleas clamoring daily for attention, the agency will probably find it too difficult and far too costly to do what every cause must ultimately do—catch the eye, warm the heart, and stir the mind."

"All glory to tithers and to those who give as much or almost as much as the income tax regulations permit them to deduct. Theirs is a godly and goodly company—but a small one."

"People seldom give serious sums without being directly asked to do so. And this goes for even Trustees and all others at the very heart of causes. They give because people at their own or higher level asked them to give—usually more thoughtfully when asked with good reasons, more proportionately when the giving requirements are explained and the worker himself has helped set the standards, and more regularly and dependably when the contact is personal and influential."

"Pre-campaign procedures are paramount. It is what you do ahead of time and how it is done that usually decides whether you win or lose. So many shrewd laymen have observed this to be true that it is a common thing to say to a professional that if his services could be had for only one period, before or during the campaign, the preference would be for pre-campaign time."

"Where to list the step of selecting leadership is often puzzling. For sheer importance, it belongs in first place. But the case for fundraising usually wins that spot merely because you need the best possible case in order to enlist the best possible leadership. And if there is any one thing you really have to have in successful fundraising, that is it: Exciting leadership, many would say—the kind that knows you can't hope to borrow their ears if you're merely going to lend your name."

"People are asked to serve on campaign committees instead of joining a group to help solve some relevant and urgent problem. They are asked 'to take a few names,' with such a palpable effort to make the task sound easy that the end effect is to make it seem trivial and of no great importance either way. The trouble is, you see, that fundraising is put ahead of program, instead of the other way around."

"Causes don't need 'workers' so much as they need 'informed and dedicated advocates.' "

"The two most important things to bear in mind about timing are that whatever anyone has plenty of time to do is what rarely gets done, and that if you wait for just the right time to launch your fundraising campaign, it will never get off the ground."

NO LONGER NECESSARY TO DISCLOSE FUNDRAISING COSTS

In 23 states, a law requires the disclosure of information and provides clear limitations on the use of the funds raised. One of these states is North Carolina, and the decision made by the Supreme Court on June 29, 1988, in the case of Riley versus The National Federation of the Blind of North Carolina provided a sweeping decision in the matter.

The North Carolina statute stipulated that paid fundraisers must disclose to potential donors the average percentage of the prior year's funds that were actually turned over to the charity. These lengthy disclosures were to be made "at the point of solicitation." The court ruled that the provision was unconstitutional "because mandating that speech that a speaker would not otherwise make, necessarily alters the speech's content." The court concluded this constitutes a violation of rights guaranteed by the First Amendment. It added that "the state's interest in informing donors how the money they contribute is spent...is not sufficiently weighty, and the means chosen to accomplish it are unduly burdensome and not narrowly tailored."

Fundraisers and organizations argued that the legal responsibility for making lengthy disclosures during a verbal request for donations was not only burdensome, but would seriously detract from the fundraising appeal itself.

The court also ruled against the North Carolina provision which limits fundraisers' fees to a certain percentage of the total amount raised. The statute stipulates that "a fee of 20–35 percent or above is unreasonable." The Court said this regulation was "not narrowly tailored to the state's interest in preventing fraud."

The Supreme Court decision probably will impact on state statutes across the nation. A major result of the decision: it will no longer be necessary for charities to limit their fundraising expenses. It will be necessary for not-for-profits to respond to this issue with their donors in a responsible and appropriate way.

> *"I was trained from the beginning to work, to save, and to give."*
> *John D. Rockefeller, Jr. (1874-1960)*

FOUNDATIONS
AND
CORPORATIONS

CORPORATE GIVING IS FLAT

It is now the second consecutive year that charitable contributions from corporations showed virtually no growth. Expectations for the future are not encouraging. It is projected that in the next few years, corporate contributions will continue to grow, but at a very slow pace. Real growth in corporate contributions this past year was almost non-existent. This is in dramatic contrast to the extraordinary growth rate of the years between 1976 and 1985.

In 1988, there was some reordering of priorities in corporate giving—a shifting of funds among major classifications and beneficiaries.

Contributions reached $4.5 billion, an increase of less than 1 percent over 1987. It also represented the smallest increase since 1975.

One of the major changes in corporate giving is the surge in giving to education. Education is now the chief beneficiary of corporate giving, representing 43 percent of total contributions, compared to 38 percent in 1987. This was mainly donations to higher education, which traditionally receive the major share of educational gifts.

According to the reputable "Survey of Corporate Contributions," 1988 Edition: "Corporate giving to health and human services organizations, including federated campaigns, such as United Way, continue to slip in share of total contributions. With the exception of 1985, corporate grant making in this category has been in steady decline for over a decade, falling from a high of 42 percent of total contributions in 1972 to only 28 percent in 1986."

The business community now accounts for about 5 percent of all philanthropy. Although profits are rising, gifts are not. And corporations are now scrutinizing their gifts more closely, seeking a direct return. Because of take-over fears, many corporations are forced to think more carefully about their bottom line than they are about civic responsibility and consciousness.

ANNUAL "GENEROUS AMERICAN AWARD" GOES TO SYBIL HARRINGTON

The publisher of *Town & Country* named Sybil Harrington the recipient of its coveted "Generous American Award," represented by the Extended Blue Ark designed by Harvey Littleton. Mrs. Harrington was featured in the December 1988 issue of the magazine. The nomination celebrates the vision of an exceptional American philanthropist.

This is the third year *Town & Country* has made the tribute. The recipient of the first award in 1986 was Anthony Drexel Duke, who has worked a lifetime to extend the opportunities of inner-city young people. Curtis L. Carlson was honored in 1987. He was instrumental in encouraging hundreds of corporations to commit a high percentage of their profits to philanthropy.

Mrs. Harrington is considered one of the most magnanimous individual benefactors in the history of the Metropolitan Opera. Through the Harrington Foundation, she has benefited the people of her native Amarillo, and people of the Texas Panhandle, with needed books, medical centers, and a planetarium.

According to *Town & Country,* Mrs. Harrington is a fierce champion of private philanthropy. "We've got to have free enterprise," she says. "It's important in charitable institutions as well as in business. Art has to have freedom."

Her list of generosities is near-endless. The Phoenix Art Museum, the Amarillo-Panhandle Humane Society, the National Cowgirl Hall of Fame, the Western Heritage Center, the Amarillo Speech and Hearing Center, the New York Ballet, West Texas State University, the Amarillo Ballet...the list goes on.

Sybil Buckingham Harrington was born and reared in Amarillo. The President and Medical Director of the Harrington Cancer Center—founded and funded by Mrs. Harrington—says that: "Independence of mind is a Panhandle trait. The people who came here were risk-takers. Sybil doesn't do anything the way anyone else does. She's a woman of immense intelligence and perception and she has a great sense of humor."

FOUNDATION DIRECTORIES

Most states publish directories of foundations and grant makers both at the state and local level. These are often more complete and detailed than a national compilation.

Individuals and organizations looking for project funding can refer to these directories for specific information on the number and amounts of grants given by foundations, corporations, and other grant making agencies as well as the types of organizations funded. A list of available directories of state and local grant makers follows.

DIRECTORIES OF STATE AND LOCAL GRANTMAKERS

Alabama (184 foundations).
Alabama Foundation Directory.
Reference Department
Birmingham Public Library
2100 Park Place
Birmingham, Alabama 35203.
$39.95 prepaid.

Alabama (212 foundations).
*Foundation Profiles of the
Southeast: Alabama, Arkansas,
Louisiana, Mississippi.*
James H. Taylor Associates, Inc.
804 Main Street
Williamsburg, Kentucky 40769
$39.95 prepaid.

Arizona. Private, corporate and
community foundations in
Arizona.
Junior League of Phoenix
1949 Camelback Road
P.O. Box 10377
Phoenix, Arizona 85064.

Arkansas (148 foundations). See
Alabama.

Arkansas (120 grantmakers).
*Guide to Arkansas Funding
Sources.*
Independent Community
Consultants
P.O. Box 1673
West Memphis, Arkansas 72301.
$13.50 plus $1.50 postage and
handling.

California (approximately 749
foundations). *Guide to
California Foundations.*
Northern California
Grantmakers
334 Kearny Street
San Francisco, California 94108.
$17.00 plus $2.00 tax and
postage, prepaid.

California (620 corporations).
*National Directory of Corporate
Charity: California Edition.*
Regional Young Adult Project
330 Ellis Street
Room 506
San Francisco, California 94102.
$14.95 plus $2.00 shipping and
$.97 sales tax for California
residents.

California (67 foundations and
56 corporations). *San Diego
County Foundation Directory.*
San Diego Community
Foundation
625 Broadway, Suite 1015
San Diego, California 92101.
$20.00 includes postage.

California (45 Bay Area
foundations). *Small Change
from Big Bucks: A Report and
Recommendations on Bay Area
Foundation and Social Change.*
Regional Young Adult Project
330 Ellis Street, Room 506
San Francisco, California 94102.
Make check payable to: Regional
Young Adult Project.
$3.00 plus $1.50 postage.

California (525 foundations).
*Where the Money's At, How to
Reach Over 500 California
Grant-Making Foundations.*
Irving R. Warner
3235 Berry Drive
Studio City, California 91604.
$17.00.

Colorado (approximately 250
foundations). *Colorado
Foundation Directory.*
Junior League of Denver, Inc.
6300 East Yale Avenue
Denver, Colorado 80222
Make check payable to:
Colorado Foundation Directory.
$10.00 prepaid.

Connecticut (61 foundations).
*Directory of the Major
Connecticut Foundations.*
Logos, Inc.
7 Park Street, Room 212
Attleboro, Massachusetts 02703.
$19.95 prepaid.

Connecticut (approximately 865
foundations). *Connecticut
Foundation Directory.*
DATA
880 Asylum Avenue
Hartford, Connecticut 06105
$25.00 prepaid.

Connecticut (approximately 890
corporations). *Guide to
Corporate Giving in
Connecticut.*
DATA
880 Asylum Avenue
Hartford, Connecticut 06105

Delaware (154 foundations).
Delaware Foundations.
United Way of Delaware, Inc.,
701 Shipley Street
Wilmington, Delaware 19801.
$14.50 prepaid.

District of Columbia
(approximately 500 foundations).
*The Directory of Foundations of
the Greater Washington Area.*
Community Foundation of
Greater Washington
3221 M Street, N.W.
Washington, DC 20007
        or
College University Research
Institute, Inc.
1707 K Street, N.W.
Washington, DC 20006.
$10.00 plus $1.50 postage.

Florida (954 foundations). *The
Complete Guide to Florida
Foundations.*
Adams and Co., Inc.
Publications Department
P.O. Box 561565
Miami, Florida 33156.
$55.00.

Florida (780 foundations).
*Foundations Profiles of the
Southeast: Florida.*
James H. Taylor Associates, Inc.
804 Main Street
Williamsburg, Kentucky 40769.
$39.95 prepaid.

Georgia (457 foundations).
*Foundation Profiles of the
Southeast: Georgia.*
James H. Taylor Associates, Inc.
804 Main Street
Williamsburg, Kentucky 40769.
$39.95 prepaid.

Georgia (530 foundations).
*Guide to Foundations in
Georgia.*
Atlanta-Fulton Public Library
#1 Margaret Mitchell Square
Atlanta, Georgia 30303.
Free.

Hawaii (143 foundations, 25 local
service organizations, 13 church
funding sources). *A Guide to
Charitable Trusts and
Foundations in the State of
Hawaii.*
Alu Like, Inc.
401 Kamakee Street, 3rd floor
Honolulu, Hawaii 96814.
$35.00 ($30.00 for nonprofits).

Idaho (89 foundations).
Directory of Idaho Foundations.
Caldwell Public Library
1010 Dearborn
Caldwell, Idaho 83605.
$3.00 prepaid.

A man wrapped up in himself makes a very small bundle.
Benjamin Franklin

Illinois (approximately 200 corporations). *The Chicago Corporate Connection: A Directory of Chicago Area Corporate Contributors, Including Downstate Illinois and Northern Indiana.*
Donors Forum of Chicago
208 South LaSalle Street
Chicago, Illinois 60604.
$18.50 plus $1.50 postage and handling, prepaid.

Illinois (approximately 103 grantmakers). *Donors Forum Member Grants List.*
Donors Forum of Chicago
208 South LaSalle Street
Chicago, Illinois 60604.
$35.00 plus $2.00 postage and handling.

Illinois (approximately 1900 foundations). *Illinois Foundation Directory.*
Foundation Data Center
Kenmar Center
401 Kenmar Circle
Minnetonka, Minnesota 55343.
(612) 542-8582.
$275 (includes annual seminar).
Update service by annual subscription, $210.

Indiana (288 foundations). *Indiana Foundations: A Directory.*
Central Research Systems
320 North Meridian, Suite 515
Indianapolis, Indiana 46204.
$24.75 prepaid.

Iowa (247 foundations). *Iowa Directory of Foundations.*
Trumpet Associates, Inc.
P.O. Box 172
Dubuque, Iowa 52001.
$19.75 plus $2.00 postage and handling.

Kansas (approximately 255 foundations). *Directory of Kansas Foundations.*
Association of Community Arts Agencies of Kansas
P.O. Box 62
Oberlin, Kansas 67749.
$5.80 prepaid.

Kentucky (117 foundations). *Foundation Profiles of the Southeast: Kentucky, Tennessee, Virginia.*
James H. Taylor Associates, Inc.
804 Main Street
Williamsburg, Kentucky 40769.
$39.95 prepaid.

Kentucky (101 foundations). *A Guide to Kentucky Grantmakers.*
Louisville Community Foundations, Inc.
Three Riverfront Plaza
Louisville, Kentucky 40202.
$6.00 prepaid.

Louisiana (229 foundations). See Alabama.

Maine (74 foundations). *A Directory of Foundations in the State of Maine.*
Center for Research and Advanced Study
University of Southern Maine
246 Deering Avenue
Portland, Maine 04102.
$3.50 prepaid.

Maine (approximately 75 corporations). *Maine Corporate Funding Directory.*
Center for Research and Advanced Study
University of Southern Maine
246 Deering Avenue
Portland, Maine 04102.
$5.50 prepaid.

The only gift is a portion of thyself.
Ralph Waldo Emerson

Maine (218 corporations). *Guide to Corporate Giving in Maine.* OUA/DATA 81 Saltonstall Avenue New Haven, Connecticut 06513. $15.00.

Maryland (approximately 380 foundations). *Annual Index Foundation Reports.* Office of the Attorney General 7 North Calvert Street Baltimore, Maryland 21202. Attention: Sharon Sullivan. $35.00 prepaid.

Massachusetts (385 foundations and corporations). *Massachusetts Grantmakers.* Associated Grantmakers of Massachusetts, Inc. 294 Washington St., Suite 501 Boston, Massachusetts 02108. $25.00 plus $3.00 handling.

Massachusetts (737 corporations). *Guide to Corporate Giving in Massachusetts.* OUA/DATA 81 Saltonstall Avenue New Haven, Connecticut 06513. $30.00 plus $1.50 postage and handling.

Massachusetts (56 Boston area foundations). *Directory of the Major Greater Boston Foundations.* Logos Associates 12 Gustin Attleboro, Massachusetts 02703. $19.95 prepaid.

Massachusetts (approximately 150 foundations). *Private Sector Giving: Greater Worcester Area.* The Social Service Planning Corporation 340 Main Street Suite 329 Worcester, Massachusetts 01608. $12.50 plus $2.25 postage and handling for photocopy (printed edition depleted).

Michigan (859 foundations). *The Michigan Foundation Directory.* Michigan League for Human Services 300 North Washington Square, Suite 401 Lansing, Michigan 48933. $15.00 for members, $18.00 for nonmembers.

Minnesota (approximately 700 foundations). *Minnesota Foundations Directory.* Foundation Data Center Kenmar Center 401 Kenmar Circle Minnetonka, Minnesota 55343. (612) 542-8582. $275 (includes annual seminar). Update service by annual subscription, $210.

Minnesota (420+ grantmakers). *Guide to Minnesota Foundations and Corporate Giving Programs.* University of Minnesota Press 2037 University Avenue S.E. Minneapolis, Minnesota 55414. $14.95 plus 6% sales tax or tax exempt number for Minnesota residents.

Mississippi (54 foundations). See Alabama.

Missouri (788 foundations). *The Directory of Missouri Foundations.* Swift Associates P.O. Box 28033 St. Louis, Missouri 63119. $15.00 plus $2.10 shipping.

Montana (65+ Montana and 20+ Wyoming foundations). *The Montana and Wyoming Foundation Directory.* Grant Assistance Eastern Montana College Library 1500 North 30th Street Billings, Montana 59101. $6.00 prepaid.

Nebraska (approximately 200 foundations). *Nebraska Foundations Directory.*
Junior League of Omaha
808 South 74th Plaza
Omaha, Nebraska 68114.
$6.00.

Nevada (41 foundations). *Nevada Foundation Directory.*
Community Relations Department
Las Vegas-Clark County Library District
1401 East Flamingo Road
Las Vegas, Nevada 89109.
$10.00 plus $2.00 postage.

New Hampshire (239 corporations). *Guide to Corporate Giving in New Hampshire.*
OUA/DATA
81 Saltonstall Avenue,
New Haven, Connecticut 06513.
$15.00.

New Hampshire (approximately 400 foundations). *Directory of Charitable Funds in New Hampshire.*
Division of Charitable Trusts
400 State House Annex
Concord, New Hampshire 03301-6397.
$2.00.
Annual supplement, which includes changes, deletions, and additions, available from the same address for $2.00 prepaid. Make check payable to "State of N.H."

New Jersey (approximately 116 foundations and approximately 500 corporations). *The New Jersey Mitchell Guide: Foundations, Corporations, and Their Managers.*
The Mitchell Guide
P.O. Box 413
Princeton, New Jersey 08542.
$65.00 prepaid.

New Jersey (approximately 66 foundations). *The Directory of the Major New Jersey Foundations.*
Logos Associates
Room 212
7 Park Street
Attleboro, Massachusetts 02703.
$19.95.

New Mexico (approximately 41 foundations). *New Mexico Private Foundations Directory.*
New Moon Consultants
P.O. Box 532
Tijeras, New Mexico 87059.
$10.00 plus $1.00 postage.

New York (approximately 125 organizations). *Guide to Grantmakers: Rochester Area.*
Published by Reynolds Information Center, Monroe County Library System. May be used in libraries of Monroe County Library System.

New York (62 foundations and 125 corporations). *The Mitchell Guide to Foundations, Corporations and Their Managers: Central New York State* (includes Binghamton, Corning, Elmira, Geneva, Ithaca, Oswego, Syracuse and Utica).
The Mitchell Guide
P.O. Box 413
Princeton, New Jersey 08542.
$25.00 prepaid.

New York (149 foundations and 125 corporations). *The Mitchell Guide to Foundations, Corporations and Their Managers: Long Island* (includes Nassau and Suffolk Counties).
The Mitchell Guide
P.O. Box 413
Princeton, New Jersey 08542.
$30.00 prepaid.

New York (61 foundations and 125 corporations). *The Mitchell Guide to Foundations, Corporations and Their Managers: Upper Hudson Valley* (includes the Capital Area, Glenns Falls, Newburgh, Plattsburgh, Poughkeepsie and Schenectady).
The Mitchell Guide
P.O. Box 413
Princeton, New Jersey 08542.
$25.00 prepaid.

New York (148 foundations and 58 corporations). *The Mitchell Guide to Foundations, Corporations and Their Managers: Westchester* (includes Putnam, Rockland and parts of Orange Counties).
The Mitchell Guide
P.O. Box 413
Princeton, New Jersey 08542.
$30.00 prepaid.

New York (125 foundations and 132 corporations). *The Mitchell Guide to Foundations, Corporations and Their Managers: Western New York State* (includes Buffalo, Jamestown, Niagara Falls and Rochester).
The Mitchell Guide
P.O. Box 413
Princeton, New Jersey 08542
$30.00 prepaid.

New York (1,832 foundations and 750 corporations). *The New York City Mitchell Guide: Foundations, Corporations and Their Managers.*
The Mitchell Guide
P.O. Box 413
Princeton, New Jersey 08542.
$75.00 prepaid.

North Carolina (492 foundations). *Foundations Profiles of the Southeast: North Carolina, South Carolina.*
James H. Taylor Associates, Inc.
804 Main Street
Williamsburg, Kentucky 70769.
$39.95 prepaid.

North Carolina (589 foundations and 362 corporations). *Grant-seeking in North Carolina: A Guide to Foundation and Corporate Giving.*
North Carolina Center for Public Policy Research
P.O. Box 430
Raleigh, North Carolina 27602.
$35.00 plus $2.50 postage and handling.

Ohio (1800 foundations). *Charitable Foundations Directory of Ohio.*
Charitable Foundations Directory
Attention: Faye Sebert
Attorney General Celebrezze's Office
30 Broad Street, 15th floor
Columbus, Ohio 43215.
$6.00 prepaid.

Ohio (38 foundations). *Guide to Charitable Foundations in the Greater Akron Area.*
Grants Department
United Way of Summit County
P.O. Box 1260
90 North Prospect Street
Akron, Ohio 44304.
$7.50

Ohio (22 foundations). *Directory of Dayton Area Grantmakers.*
Belinda Hogue
449 Patterson Road, Apt. A
Dayton, Ohio 45419.
Free plus $1.25 postage and handling.

The surest way to be happy is to seek happiness for others.
Martin Luther King, Jr.

Ohio (259 foundations). *The Source: A Directory of Cincinnati Foundations.* Junior League of Cincinnati Grantsmanship Committee Regency Square 2334 Dana Avenue Cincinnati, Ohio 45208. $9.85 ($10.32 Ohio residents).

Oklahoma (approximately 150 foundations). *Directory of Oklahoma Foundations.* University of Oklahoma Press 1005 Asp Avenue Norman, Oklahoma 73019. $22.50 plus $.86 postage.

Oregon (approximately 300 foundations). *The Guide to Oregon Foundations.* Bonnie Smith United Way of the Columbia-Willamette 718 West Burnside Portland, Oregon 97209. $15.00 prepaid.

Pennsylvania (2300 + foundations). *Directory of Pennsylvania Foundations.* Make check payable to "Directory of Pa. Foundations" P.O. Box 336 Springfield, Pennsylvania 19064. $37.50 prepaid (plus Pa. sales tax of $2.25, unless exempt).

Rhode Island (91 foundations). *Directory of Grant-Making Foundations in Rhode Island.* Council for Community Services 229 Waterman Street Providence, Rhode Island 02906. $8.00 prepaid.

Rhode Island (188 corporations). *Guide to Corporate Giving in Rhode Island.* OUA/DATA 81 Saltonstall Avenue New Haven, Connecticut 06513. $15.00.

South Carolina (174 foundations). *South Carolina Foundation Directory.* Out of Print. Available on inter-library loan from South Carolina State Library, Columbia, South Carolina.

South Carolina (49 foundations). See North Carolina.

Tennessee (58 foundations; 21 corporations and corporate foundations). *Tennessee Directory of Foundations and Corporate Philanthropy.* Executive and Management Services Room 508, City Hall 125 North Mid-America Mall Memphis, Tennessee 38103. $30.00 plus $2.50 postage and handling. Diskette available ($30.00).

Tennessee (202 foundations). See Kentucky.

Texas (approximately 1232 foundations). *The Hooper Directory of Texas Foundations.* Funding Information Center of Texas 507 Brooklyn San Antonio, Texas 78215. $30.00. Companion supplement listing 267 foundations also available. $20.00 ($45.00 for both publications).

Texas (268 foundations). *Directory of Dallas County Foundations.* Urban Information Center Dallas Public Library 1515 Young St. Dallas, Texas 75201. $14.75 plus $2.35 postage and handling.

Texas (approximately 115 foundations). *Directory of Tarrant County Foundations* Funding Information Center Texas Christian University Library P.O. Box 32904 Fort Worth, Texas 76129. $6.00 plus $1.00 postage and handling.

Utah (163 foundations). *A Directory of Foundations in Utah.* University of Utah Press 101 University Services Building Salt Lake City, Utah 84112. $50.00.

Utah (200 foundations). *The Directory of Utah Foundations.* MG Enterprises 839 East South Temple #107 Salt Lake City, Utah 84102. $35.00 plus $2.50 postage and handling.

Vermont (132 corporations and 56 foundations). *OUA/ATA's Guide to Corporate and Foundation Giving in Vermont.* OUA/DATA 81 Saltonstall Avenue New Haven, Connecticut 06513

Source: *Foundation Fundamentals* **The Foundation Center**

Virginia (approximately 500 foundations). *Virginia Foundations.* Sharen Sinclair Grants Resources Library Hampton City Hall, 9th floor 22 Lincoln Street Hampton, Virginia 23669. $16.00 prepaid.

Virginia (326 foundations). See Kentucky.

Washington (approximately 968 organizations). *Charitable Trust Directory.* Office of the Attorney General Temple of Justice Olympia, Washington 98504. $4.00 prepaid.

Wisconsin (626 foundations). *Foundation in Wisconsin: A Directory.* The Foundation Collection Marquette University Memorial Library 1415 West Wisconsin Avenue Milwaukee, Wisconsin 53233. $16.00 prepaid plus $2.00 shipping.

Wyoming (45 foundations). *Wyoming Foundations Directory.* Laramie County Community College Library 1400 East College Drive Cheyenne, Wyoming 82007. Free. $1.00 postage for out-of-state orders.

Wyoming (20 foundations). See Montana.

> *"When an American asks for the cooperation of his fellow citizens, it is seldom refused; and, I have often seen it afforded spontaneously, and with great goodwill."*
> —*Alexis de Tocqueville*
> *Democracy in America*
> *1832*

FOUNDATION GIVING IS TOP-HEAVY

The most current *Foundation Directory* reports that there are 36,615 active foundations. Of this group, 5,148 foundations are listed with either assets of over $1 million or annual giving of over $100,000. This represents 14 percent of the total number of foundations. This group covers 97 percent of all foundation assets and 92 percent of foundation giving in America.

FOUNDATIONS WITH ASSETS OVER
$100 MILLION—1988

For the current year, there were 146 foundations with assets in excess of $100 million. Of this group, four states (New York, California, Texas, and Pennsylvania) had over half the total.

	FOUNDATION	STATE	ASSET AMOUNT	TOTAL GIVING	NO. OF GRANTS
1	The Ford Foundation	NY	5,509,053,000	219,403,872	1,710
2	J. Paul Getty Trust	CA	4,140,834,871	134,108,773	86
3	W. K. Kellogg Foundation	MI	3,581,473,230	88,979,208	684
4	The Pew Charitable Trusts	PA	2,396,543,807	102,895,490	915
5	John D. and Catherine T. MacArthur Foundation	IL	2,271,000,000	100,500,000	
6	Lilly Endowment Inc.	IN	1,983,317,615	71,356,902	683
7	The Robert Wood Johnson Foundation	NJ	1,908,243,386	90,660,928	
8	The Rockefeller Foundation	NY	1,676,015,284	70,866,814	613
9	The Andrew W. Mellon Foundation	NY	1,478,000,000	67,356,663	
10	The Kresge Foundation	MI	1,045,631,114	39,195,000	144
11	Carnegie Corporation of New York	NY	807,142,249	34,443,031	341
12	The Duke Endowment	NC	771,871,787	41,417,157	873
13	The McKnight Foundation	MN	764,354,998	37,292,318	195
14	Charles Stewart Mott Foundation	MI	749,512,063	33,038,681	
15	The William and Flora Hewlett Foundation	CA	661,185,000	32,236,759	286
16	W. M. Keck Foundation	CA	640,481,151	38,122,500	51
17	Otto Bremer Foundation	MN	628,000,000	3,416,175	491
18	Gannett Foundation, Inc.	NY	608,202,145	28,839,238	2,816
19	Houston Endowment, Inc.	TX	595,723,714	10,874,517	278
20	The New York Community Trust	NY	541,000,000	38,860,600	4,971
21	Alfred P. Sloan Foundation	NY	482,920,715	20,837,718	
22	The Moody Foundation	TX	462,058,620	12,106,057	73
23	The Starr Foundation	NY	460,546,892	16,333,449	262
24	The Cleveland Foundation	OH	459,051,318	20,999,671	
25	Knight Foundation	OH	435,132,256	15,503,167	298
26	Marin Community Foundation	CA	430,000,000	12,400,000	
27	The James Irvine Foundation	CA	423,008,466	17,302,736	230
28	Meadows Foundation, Inc.	TX	413,248,176	20,989,992	283
29	The William Penn Foundation	PA	412,597,281	21,109,802	387
30	The Brown Foundation, Inc.	TX	410,634,817	16,843,127	175
31	Robert R. McCormick Charitable Trust	IL	400,787,000	8,487,546	237
32	Howard Heinz Endowment	PA	390,112,066	7,845,940	138
33	The Edna McConnell Clark Foundation	NY	384,509,809	16,046,445	253
34	The Annie E. Casey Foundation	CT	375,202,555	5,278,052	7
35	Weingart Foundation	CA	368,002,381	12,294,501	124
36	The Henry J. Kaiser Family Foundation	CA	359,265,215	8,735,345	93
37	The Ahmanson Foundation	CA	350,400,000	16,343,720	422
38	Arthur S. DeMoss Foundation	PA	345,408,930	33,678,358	75
39	Surdna Foundation, Inc.	NY	343,997,992	17,636,977	103
40	The J. E. and L. E. Mabee Foundation, Inc.	OK	338,821,450	16,573,984	85
41	The Lynde and Harry Bradley Foundation, Inc.	WI	336,543,703	18,393,379	265
42	The Bush Foundation	MN	332,263,000	13,889,666	187
43	The Commonwealth Fund	NY	299,156,099	9,680,987	83
44	The Whitaker Foundation	PA	292,018,330	12,886,722	185
45	The Norton Simon Foundation	CA	288,429,821	752,131	
46	The Samuel Roberts Noble Foundation, Inc.	OK	285,836,668	13,611,249	160
47	Stratford Foundation	MA	283,677,525	5,789,406	45
48	The Chicago Community Trust	IL	278,024,000	22,613,367	450
49	The Joyce Foundation	IL	262,308,265	11,524,811	

50	The Robert A. Welch Foundation	TX	259,179,000	11,921,000	
51	Fred Meyer Charitable Trust	OR	252,412,500	9,242,728	100
52	The William K. Warren Foundation	OK	251,396,993	1,181,550	21
53	The Henry Luce Foundation, Inc.	NY	245,094,357	12,884,250	205
54	The Skillman Foundation	MI	238,072,990	10,128,616	149
55	The George Gund Foundation	OH	236,000,000	7,621,885	310
56	Longwood Foundation, Inc.	DE	235,600,181	8,168,350	
57	William Randolph Hearst Foundation	NY	232,920,685	6,805,554	280
58	McCune Foundation	PA	231,520,988	11,234,258	68
59	Amherst H. Wilder Foundation	MN	226,511,103	26,228,456	5
60	Rockefeller Brothers Fund	NY	220,733,767	6,872,250	148
61	Conrad N. Hilton Foundation	CA	220,306,295	6,914,240	65
62	The Spencer Foundation	IL	219,558,357	4,698,296	89
63	F. W. Olin Foundation, Inc.	NY	218,670,318	13,801,300	12
64	William R. Kenan, Jr. Charitable Trust	NC	218,234,000	8,457,000	
65	Smith Richardson Foundation, Inc.	NY	215,880,190	10,741,794	165
66	Hall Family Foundations	MO	215,321,156	5,688,122	72
67	Public Welfare Foundation, Inc.	DC	213,755,000	9,496,000	
68	Horace W. Goldsmith Foundation	NY	211,162,643	7,310,797	139
69	The Clark Foundation	NY	210,106,662	7,164,612	102
70	Sid W. Richardson Foundation	TX	206,125,000	10,078,581	100
71	The John A. Hartford Foundation, Inc.	NY	205,848,848	6,802,727	299
72	The Champlin Foundations	RI	200,606,411	7,141,056	112
73	Alcoa Foundation	PA	198,592,557	10,507,005	1,430
74	M. J. Murdock Charitable Trust	WA	197,817,219	10,409,431	154
75	Peter Kiewit Foundation	NE	196,132,258	6,731,892	68
76	Northwest Area Foundation	MN	196,049,298	6,872,789	203
77	The Boston Foundation, Inc.	MA	194,375,685	12,846,816	958
78	General Motors Foundation, Inc.	MI	192,989,188	22,693,143	642
79	The Sherman Fairchild Foundation, Inc.	CT	190,945,087	11,296,166	34
80	The Herbert H. and Grace A. Dow Foundation	MI	189,091,293	7,016,445	128
81	Vira I. Heinz Endowment	PA	185,966,202	3,068,519	61
82	Joseph B. Whitehead Foundation	CA	184,142,403	7,164,250	36
83	Andersen Foundation	MN	177,010,012	3,851,098	78
84	James Graham Brown Foundation, Inc.	KY	175,559,631	6,990,103	68
85	Bat Hanadiv Foundation, No. 3	NY	173,933,578	4,253,829	44
86	Herrick Foundation	MI	173,886,324	7,454,400	199
87	T. L. L. Temple Foundation	TX	172,265,826	5,705,623	122
88	Koret Foundation	CA	171,733,466	6,001,985	176
89	The San Francisco Foundation	CA	170,898,950	12,800,135	662
90	Norton Simon Art Foundation	CA	170,703,496	2,060,000	
91	Kate B. Reynolds Charitable Trust	NC	169,851,010	3,854,856	97
92	Sarah Scaife Foundation, Inc.	PA	168,357,340	8,295,500	86
93	Amon G. Carter Foundation	TX	160,000,000	8,856,042	111
94	Connelly Foundation	PA	159,942,673	3,758,113	188
95	W. Alton Jones Foundation, Inc.	VA	159,232,806	9,788,601	201
96	Anne Burnett and Charles D. Tandy Foundation	TX	158,937,882	8,715,992	52
97	Communities Foundation of Texas, Inc.	TX	157,966,678	17,242,732	1,040
98	The Morris and Gwendolyn Cafritz Foundation	DC	157,775,120	6,137,741	112
99	The Danforth Foundation	MO	153,054,107	76,774,922	112
100	Dan Murphy Foundation	CA	152,134,409	5,513,083	111
101	AT&T Foundation	NY	152,000,000	30,308,282	1,057
102	El Pomar Foundation	CO	151,000,000	6,494,008	54
103	The Charles A. Dana Foundation, Inc.	NY	149,178,828	10,054,480	119
104	Z. Smith Reynolds Foundation, Inc.	NC	146,949,656	6,866,891	203
105	F. M. Kirby Foundation, Inc.	NJ	145,763,608	7,459,870	480
106	Charles Hayden Foundation	NY	145,693,479	5,386,987	135
107	Claude Worthington Benedum Foundation	PA	145,275,000	6,678,214	74
108	The Wunsch Americana Foundation	DE	141,544,007	126,920	2
109	Lettie Pate Whitehead Foundation, Inc.	GA	138,661,201	5,194,000	192
110	The Ralph M. Parsons Foundation	CA	138,105,500	5,770,765	108
111	Timken Foundation of Canton	OH	137,750,000	4,811,000	26
112	Callaway Foundation, Inc.	CA	135,403,142	4,555,121	77
113	The Aaron Diamond Foundation, Inc.	NY	133,443,185	8,907,978	108
114	The Wortham Foundation	TX	132,719,639	7,404,921	44
115	The David and Lucile Packard Foundation	CA	132,612,000	11,588,110	335
116	William T. Grant Foundation	NY	131,258,000	4,628,883	125
117	DeWitt Wallace-Reader's Digest Fund, Inc.	NY	128,639,950	2,558,500	47
118	Ford Motor Company Fund	MI	125,525,839	16,336,928	1,352
119	Geraldine R. Dodge Foundation, Inc.	NJ	125,372,300	7,665,000	307
120	Fritz B. Burns Foundation	CA	122,596,020	3,791,000	65
121	Roy J. Carver Charitable Trust	IA	121,524,450	610,749	1
122	The GAR Foundation	OH	121,147,462	4,728,661	159
123	The Columbus Foundation	OH	119,000,000	7,880,000	1,600
124	The Cullen Foundation	TX	118,166,677	6,400,000	33
125	John Simon Guggenheim Memorial Foundation	NY	116,595,296	7,041,000	

126 Charles E. Culpeper Foundation, Inc.	NY	115,751,939	5,216,100	186
127 Hartford Foundation for Public Giving	CT	114,692,423	6,272,075	215
128 Mary Flagler Cary Charitable Trust	NY	113,833,904	6,047,794	72
129 Lyndhurst Foundation	TN	112,402,088	11,028,897	70
130 Jessie Ball duPont Religious Charitable and Educational Fund	FL	112,273,807	6,145,181	71
131 The Prudential Foundation	NJ	111,488,000	11,646,519	817
132 The Schubert Foundation, Inc.	NY	109,995,000	2,783,900	142
133 The John G. and Marie Stella Kenedy Memorial Foundation	TX	109,437,338	4,803,086	75
134 G. Harold & Leila Y. Mathers Charitable Foundation	NY	109,229,832	5,073,597	50
135 Lannan Foundation	CA	108,210,017		
136 China Medical Board of New York, Inc.	NY	108,056,592	5,342,939	33
137 The Hearst Foundation, Inc.	NY	106,009,560	3,577,000	273
138 The Abell Foundation, Inc.	MD	105,022,416	3,108,649	158
139 The Saint Paul Foundation	MN	104,131,705	6,766,846	405
140 The Flinn Foundation	AZ	104,075,276	5,022,503	102
141 S. H. Cowell Foundation	CA	104,000,000	4,979,005	122
142 Charles F. Kettering Foundation	OH	103,714,370	6,908,660	4
143 Russell Sage Foundation	NY	103,022,217	4,050,390	31
144 The Pittsburgh Foundation	PA	101,427,129	4,788,195	550
145 Dr. Scholl Foundation	IL	101,072,753	7,328,675	297
146 Booth Ferris Foundation	NY	100,984,048	4,893,434	88

TOTAL NUMBER OF FOUNDATIONS WITH ASSETS OVER $100 MILLION BY STATE—1988

Foundation State	No. of Foundations	Foundation State	No. of Foundations
Alabama	—	Nevada	—
Alaska	—	New Hampshire	—
Arizona	1	New Jersey	4
Arkansas	—	New Mexico	—
California	19	New York	36
Colorado	1	North Carolina	4
Connecticut	3	North Dakota	—
Delaware	2	Ohio	7
District of Columbia	2	Oklahoma	3
Florida	1	Oregon	1
Georgia	3	Pennsylvania	12
Hawaii	—	Rhode Island	1
Idaho	—	South Carolina	—
Illinois	6	South Dakota	—
Indiana	1	Tennessee	1
Iowa	1	Texas	13
Kansas	—	Utah	—
Kentucky	1	Vermont	—
Louisiana	—	Virginia	1
Maine	—	Washington	1
Maryland	1	West Virginia	—
Massachusetts	2	Wisconsin	1
Michigan	8	Wyoming	—
Minnesota	7	Total number of foundations	
Mississippi	—	with assets over	
Missouri	2	$100 million	146
Montana	—		
Nebraska	1		

In 1988, foundations provided a smaller share of the private funding for all not-for-profit activities, approximately 6 percent. In 1970, it was 10 percent.

NATIONAL FOUNDATIONS NOT A GOOD SOURCE FOR INDEPENDENT SCHOOLS

There are only four national foundations which consistently support independent schools. And they support only at the secondary level. Each of the four foundations is specific in its parameters.

The Edward E. Ford Foundation provides grants in the range of $15,000 to $35,000. These are most often matching grants for capital purposes for endowment and buildings. There are some funds provided for equipment, special program awards, and scholarships.

The Geraldine R. Dodge Foundation supports projects which lead to major and significant development in secondary education. The funds are provided mostly for secondary independent schools in the New England and middle Atlantic states.

The William R. Kenan, Jr. Charitable Trust limits its funding to secondary schools in the eastern states.

The Independence Foundation concentrates most of its funding in the area of student financial aid. This takes the form of student loan funds ranging from $2,000 to $100,000.

TRY, TRY AGAIN!

Don't be discouraged. Many organizations and agencies are turned down—but the acceptance rates are encouraging. Try your proposal again or try another foundation.

ACCEPTANCE RATES AT FOUNDATIONS

Meadows Foundation, Dallas TX
2,000 proposals received
200 proposals granted
10% acceptance rate

Kresge Foundation, Troy MI
676 proposals received
172 approved
25.4% acceptance rate

Bush Foundation, St. Paul MN
237 proposals received
123 approved
51.8% acceptance rate

Ford Foundation, New York NY
17,000 proposals received
1900 approved
11.1% acceptance rate

Parker Foundation, San Diego CA
180 proposals received
52 approved
28.8% acceptance rate

Lilly Endowment, Indianapolis IN
3,485 proposals received
685 approved
19.6% acceptance rate

Hearst Foundation, New York NY
3,000 proposals received
547 approved
18.2% acceptance rate

Irvine Foundation, San Francisco CA
870 eligible proposals received
169 approved
19.4% acceptance rate

Rockefeller Brothers Fund, New York NY
1,570 proposals received
110 approved
7% acceptance rate

WHERE FOUNDATION MONEY GOES

There are over 25,000 foundations registered in the United States. In the last year reported, they gave away a total of $2,216,647,033. The pie chart shows the percentage for each major type and category of grant awarded.

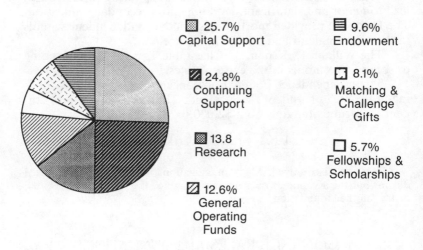

■ 25.7%
Capital Support

▨ 24.8%
Continuing
Support

▨ 13.8
Research

▨ 12.6%
General
Operating
Funds

☰ 9.6%
Endowment

▫ 8.1%
Matching &
Challenge
Gifts

☐ 5.7%
Fellowships &
Scholarships

A number of grants are included in more than one category, so the total percentages amount to more than 100 percent.

Source: adapted from *Foundation Grants Index*.

THE NON-PROFIT TIMES

The *Non-Profit Times* is a news publication servicing the not-for-profit sector. The publication is geared toward management level executives of not-for-profit corporations. Subscriptions are offered free to management level full-time employees of not-for-profit organizations. Proof of not-for-profit status must be shown by completing a free-subscription order form. Regular subscription price is $39 per year. The *Non-Profit Times* was first published in April, 1987 and has a total of 30,000 subscribers. Any subscription questions can be directed to: **The Non-Profit Times, P.O. Box 870, Wantagh, NY 11793-0870   (516) 781-7032.**

FIFTEEN LARGEST FOUNDATIONS FOR
THE PAST SIX YEARS BY TOTAL ASSETS

Giving USA reports that last year, a total of $93.68 billion was given from all sources for philanthropic endeavors. Of this amount, $6.38 billion came from foundations. This represents an increase of 6.45 percent over the year before, and nearly 7 percent of the total philanthropic pie. It is anticipated that the total dollars from foundations will continue to rise.

	Foundation Name	Asset Amount
1988	1) The Ford Foundation	5,509,053,000
	2) J. Paul Getty Trust	4,140,834,871
	3) W. K. Kellogg Foundation	3,581,473,230
	4) The Pew Charitable Trusts	2,396,543,807
	5) John D. and Catherine T. MacArthur Foundation	2,271,000,000
	6) Lilly Endowment, Inc.	1,983,317,615
	7) The Robert Wood Johnson Foundation	1,908,243,386
	8) The Rockefeller Foundation	1,676,015,284
	9) The Andrew W. Mellon Foundation	1,478,000,000
	10) The Kresge Foundation	1,045,631,114
	11) Carnegie Corporation of New York	807,142,249
	12) The Duke Endowment	771,871,787
	13) The McKnight Foundation	764,354,998
	14) Charles Stewart Mott Foundation	749,512,063
	15) The William and Flora Hewlett Foundation	661,185,000
1987	1) The Ford Foundation	4,758,862,000
	2) J. Paul Getty Trust	3,690,833,873
	3) W. K. Kellogg Foundation	3,108,333,370
	4) John D. and Catherine T. MacArthur Foundation	2,271,000,000
	5) Lilly Endowment, Inc.	1,912,593,072
	6) The Robert Wood Johnson Foundation	1,803,866,438
	7) The Rockefeller Foundation	1,605,602,953
	8) The Pew Memorial Trust	1,550,025,174
	9) The Andrew W. Mellon Foundation	1,477,000,000
	10) The Kresge Foundation	1,047,073,511
	11) The Duke Endowment	797,524,573
	12) Charles Stewart Mott Foundation	733,290,217
	13) Carnegie Corporation of New York	715,333,222
	14) The McKnight Foundation	711,300,000
	15) The Richard King Mellon Foundation	684,366,808
1986	1) The Ford Foundation	3,897,258,000
	2) J. Paul Getty Trust	3,414,666,464
	3) John D. and Catherine T. MacArthur Foundation	2,045,238,000
	4) W. K. Kellogg Foundation	1,908,481,661
	5) The Robert Wood Johnson Foundation	1,544,830,998
	6) Lilly Endowment, Inc.	1,466,766,867
	7) The Pew Memorial Trust	1,233,226,633
	8) The Rockefeller Foundation	1,101,856,013
	9) The Andrew W. Mellon Foundation	1,016,625,922
	10) The Kresge Foundation	813,648,263
	11) The Duke Endowment	654,811,771

	12) The McKnight Foundation	629,293,513
	13) Charles Stewart Mott Foundation	572,341,683
	14) Carnegie Corporation of New York	565,019,130
	15) The Richard King Mellon Foundation	564,826,800
1985	1) The Ford Foundation	3,497,800,000
	2) J. Paul Getty Trust	2,684,185,155
	3) John D. and Catherine T. MacArthur Foundation	1,920,260,560
	4) W. K. Kellogg Foundation	1,291,843,298
	5) The Robert Wood Johnson Foundation	1,173,836,335
	6) The Pew Memorial Trust	1,171,419,665
	7) The Rockefeller Foundation	1,101,856,013
	8) The Andrew W. Mellon Foundation	997,174,164
	9) Lilly Endowment, Inc.	889,437,000
	10) The Kresge Foundation	813,648,263
	11) Charles Stewart Mott Foundation	569,037,725
	12) The Duke Endowment	551,459,647
	13) The McKnight Foundation	509,422,638
	14) Carnegie Corporation of New York	503,942,991
	15) W. M. Keck Foundation	500,000,000
1984	1) The Ford Foundation	3,529,188,000
	2) The Robert Wood Johnson Foundation	1,238,203,255
	3) The Rockefeller Foundation	1,119,363,698
	4) W. K. Kellogg Foundation	1,052,493,408
	5) John D. and Catherine T. MacArthur Foundation	990,326,359
	6) Andrew W. Mellon Foundation	935,399,569
	7) Pew Memorial Trust	908,994,894
	8) Kresge Foundation	792,086,846
	9) Lilly Endowment, Inc.	774,746,001
	10) William and Flora Hewlett Foundation	576,604,594
	11) Carnegie Corporation of New York	517,264,406
	12) Duke Endowment	497,933,182
	13) San Francisco Foundation	488,963,756
	14) Richard King Mellon Foundation	482,889,700
	15) Charles Stewart Mott Foundation	471,298,929
1983	1) Ford Foundation	2,565,572,000
	2) Robert Wood Johnson Foundation	1,421,084,994
	3) W.K. Kellogg Foundation	1,046,224,366
	4) John D. and Catherine T. MacArthur Foundation	927,967,952
	5) Pew Memorial Trust	903,469,881
	6) Rockefeller Foundation	883,200,092
	7) Andrew W. Mellon Foundation	816,855,412
	8) Lilly Endowment, Inc.	779,036,055
	9) Kresge Foundation	681,467,736
	10) William and Flora Hewlett Foundation	531,528,674
	11) Charles Stewart Mott Foundation	471,298,929
	12) Duke Endowment	462,658,021
	13) W. M. Keck Foundation	460,037,974
	14) Carnegie Corporation of New York	381,668,694
	15) San Francisco Foundation	377,540,812

THE OLDER, THE BETTER

By the end of 1989, nearly one-quarter of America's population will be 55 years of age and over. Americans over 50 now control more than half of the nation's assets and discretionary income.

Seniors are more likely than the rest of the population to own their own homes and to have paid off their mortgages. Over 60 percent of those 65 and over live mortgage-free and rent-free. Two out of three American homes which are mortgage-free belong to persons over age 65. It is estimated that over two out of every five senior home owners have no financial burden. The wealthiest 1 percent of those in the 65 and over population have 28 percent of the total wealth of the group—and the top 10 percent own nearly two-thirds of the total wealth.

According to Age Wave, Inc., headed by Dr. Ken Diquald—a leading authority on seniors—"seniors have disposable income greater than any other segment of our population." He says that they spend money to satisfy a range of personal as well as practical needs. "They want to have fun, enjoy life, they want to feel a part of a community, they may want to leave a legacy to show they were here and like the rest of us, many feel like they are going to live forever."

Diquald points out that for the fundraiser, the approach to seniors must be that the institution offers something of value and prestige just for them. "In general, the idea is to stress how important the senior is to you. Give the targeted seniors a vehicle for fulfilling their need for community participation, involvement and desire for enjoyment. If possible, give them a way to showcase their involvement with others who are important to them..."

LENGTH OF TIME AS A FUNDRAISER

	Less than 3 years	3–4 years	5–9 years	10–19 years	20 or more years
Educational institution	16.3	12.1	32.9	32.6	6.2
Hospital/medical center	15.5	8.3	30.6	36.9	8.7
National health agency	17.3	9.9	32.1	24.7	16.0
National social agency	18.8	7.2	34.8	29.0	10.1
Regional/local service agency	31.1	13.6	31.1	17.5	6.8
Youth organization	15.1	7.5	33.3	33.3	10.8
Cultural organization	18.2	11.7	36.4	32.5	1.3
Religious organization	7.3	16.4	36.4	25.5	14.5
Retirement community	31.3	15.6	37.5	6.3	9.4
Conservation/wildlife	27.3	18.2	27.3	18.2	9.1
Environmental	11.1	0.0	33.3	44.4	11.1
Member of small consulting firm	6.5	2.2	21.7	32.6	37.0
Member of large consulting firm	0.0	2.9	22.9	37.1	37.1
Independent consultant	3.3	10.0	21.7	36.7	28.3

Source: NSFRE, 1988

25 LARGEST COMPANY SPONSORED FOUNDATIONS
BY TOTAL ASSETS

Name	State	Assets	Gifts Received	Total Giving	Fiscal Date
Alcoa Foundation	PA	$198,593		$10,507	12/31/86
General Motors Foundation, Inc.	MI	192,989	$20,000	22,693	12/31/86
AT&T Foundation	NY	125,000	456	29,789	12/31/86
Ford Motor Company Fund	MI	124,109	70,009	12,296	12/31/86
Prudential Foundation, The	NJ	117,410	35,000	10,494	12/31/86
Amoco Foundation, Inc.	IL	78,619		23,825	12/31/86
Metropolitan Life Foundation	NY	74,095		7,389	12/31/86
Exxon Education Foundation	NJ	67,909	26,933	21,986	12/31/86
McDonnell Douglas Foundation	MO	57,629		7,109	6/30/86
General Electric Foundation	CT	57,581	8,200	18,395	12/31/86
Hoover Foundation, The	OH	37,071		1,387	12/31/86
UPS Foundation, Inc., The	CT	34,890	6,884	3,718	12/31/85
Ameritech Foundation	IL	33,920		1,626	12/31/86
Rockwell International Corporation Trust	PA	31,536	20,000	10,789	9/30/86
Texaco Philanthropic Foundation Inc.	NY	30,340		7,394	12/31/85
Cargill Foundation, The	MN	29,487	1,000	2,015	12/31/86
Pacific Telesis Foundation	CA	28,657	10,673	5,103	12/31/86
Eastman Kodak Charitable Trust	NY	28,219	4,500	7,755	12/31/86
Southwestern Bell Foundation	MO	28,056	24,690	11,929	12/31/86
Federated Department Stores Foundation	OH	28,006		5,417	1/31/87
Massey Foundation	VA	27,749		1,039	11/30/86
USX Foundation, Inc.	PA	27,399		8,437	11/30/86
Steelcase Foundation	MI	26,242	5,000	1,938	11/30/86
May Stores Foundation, Inc., The	MO	25,969	2,200	4,495	12/31/85
Burlington Northern Foundation	WA	25,600	13,550	14,532	12/31/85

SOURCE: The Foundation Center Database

FIVE MAJOR FOUNDATIONS AND THEIR STAFFS

There is no common denominator between the assets of a foundation and the size of their professional and program staff. Among major foundations, for instance, the Ford Foundation has the largest staff and the highest staff-to-asset ratio. Following are five major foundations and the staff-assets ratio for each.

Foundation	Assets (billions)		Total Staff	$ per Staff Member (millions)
Ford Foundation	$5.3		560	$9.5
Carnegie Corporation	63.7	(million)	53	12
Robert Wood Johnson Foundation	1.9		103	18.4
Pew Charitable Trusts	2.3		50	46
Lilly Endowment, Inc.	1.7		21	81

Source: *Foundation Directory*

THE FOUNDATION CENTER

The Foundation Center is an independent national service organization established by foundations to provide an authoritative source of information on private philanthropic giving. In fulfilling its mission, The Center disseminates information on private giving through public service programs, publications and through a national network of library reference collections for free public use. The New York, Washington DC, Cleveland and San Francisco reference collections operated by The Foundation Center offer a wide variety of services and comprehensive collections of information on foundations and grants. The Cooperating Collections are libraries, community foundations and other nonprofit agencies that provide a core collection of Foundation Center publications and a variety of supplementary materials and services in subject areas useful to grantseekers.

Over 100 of the network members have sets of private foundation information returns (IRS Form 990-PF) for their states or regions which are available for public use. A complete set of U.S. foundation returns can be found at the New York and Washington, DC offices of The Foundation Center. The Cleveland and San Francisco offices contain IRS returns for those foundations in the midwestern and western states, respectively.

Because the collections vary in their hours, materials and services, IT IS RECOMMENDED THAT YOU CALL EACH COLLECTION IN ADVANCE. To check on new locations or current information, call toll-free 1(800)424-9836.

Those collections marked with a bullet(•) have sets of private foundation information returns (IRS Form 990-PF) for their states or regions, available for public reference.

Reference collections operated by The Foundation Center are in boldface.

Alabama

• Birmingham Public Library
2100 Park Place
Birmingham 35203
(205) 226-3600

Huntsville-Madison County
Public Library
108 Fountain Circle
P.O. Box 443
Huntsville 35804
(205) 532-5940

University of South Alabama
Library Building
Reference Department
Mobile 36688
(205) 460-7025

• Auburn University at
Montgomery Library
Montgomery 36193-0401
(205) 271-9649

Alaska

• University of Alaska,
Anchorage Library
3211 Providence Drive
Anchorage 99508
(907) 786-1848

Arizona

• Phoenix Public Library
Business and Sciences
Department
12 East McDowell Road
Phoenix 85004
(602) 262-4636

- Tucson Public Library
Main Library
200 South Sixth Avenue
Tucson 85701
(602) 791-4393

Arkansas

- Westark Community College
Library
Grand Avenue at Waldron Road
Fort Smith 72913
(501) 785-7000

- Little Rock Public Library
Reference Department
700 Louisiana Street
Little Rock 72201
(501) 370-5950

California

- California Community
Foundation Funding Information
Center
3580 Wilshire Blvd., Suite 1660
Los Angeles 90010
(213) 413-4042

- Community Foundation for
Monterey County
420 Pacific Street
Monterey 93940
(408) 375-9712

California Community
Foundation
4050 Metropolitan Drive #300
Orange 92668
(714) 937-9077

Riverside Public Library
3581 7th Street
Riverside 92501
(714) 782-5201

California State Library
Reference Services, Rm 309
914 Capital Mall
Sacramento 95814
(916) 322-4570

- San Diego Community
Foundation
525 "B" Street, Suite 410
San Diego 92101
(619) 239-8815

- **The Foundation Center**
312 Sutter Street, Room 312
San Francisco 94108
(415) 397-0902

- Grantsmanship Resource
Center
Junior League of San Jose, Inc.
Community Foundation of Santa
Clara County
1762 Technology Dr., Suite 225
San Jose 95110
(408) 452-8181

- Orange County Community
Developmental Council
1695 MacArthur Blvd.
Costa Mesa 92626
(714) 540-9293

- Peninsula Community
Foundation
1204 Burlingame Avenue
Burlingame 94011-0627
(415) 342-2505

- Santa Barbara Public Library
Reference Section
40 East Anapamu
P.O. Box 1019
Santa Barbara 93102
(805) 962-7653

Santa Monica Public Library
1343 Sixth Street
Santa Monica 90401-1603
(213) 458-8603

Tuolomne County Library
465 S. Washington Street
Sonora 95370
(209) 533-5707

*"Only a life lived for others
is a life worthwhile."*
Albert Einstein (1879–1955)

Colorado

Pikes Peak Library District
20 North Cascade Avenue
Colorado Springs 80901
(303) 473-2780

• Denver Public Library
Sociology Division
1357 Broadway
Denver 80203
(303) 571-2190

Connecticut

Danbury Public Library
170 Main Street
Danbury 06810
(203) 797-4527

• Hartford Public Library
Reference Department
500 Main Street
Hartford 06103
(203) 525-9121

D.A.T.A.
30 Arbor Street
Hartford 06106
(203) 232-6619

D.A.T.A.
25 Science Park
Suite 502
New Haven 06511
(203) 786-5225

Delaware

• Hugh Morris Library
University of Delaware
Newark 19717-5267
(302) 451-2965

District of Columbia

• **The Foundation Center**
1001 Connecticut Avenue, NW
Washington 20036
(202) 331-1400

*"What you get is a living—
what you give is a life."
Lillian Gish (1896–)*

Florida

Volusia County Public Library
City Island
Daytona Beach 32014
(904) 252-8374

• Jacksonville Public Library
Business, Science, and Industry
Department
122 North Ocean Street
Jacksonville 32202
(904) 633-3926

• Miami-Dade Public Library
Humanities Department
101 W. Flagler St.
Miami 33132
(305) 375-2665

• Orange County Library
System
101 E. Central Blvd.
Orlando 32801
(305) 425-4694

Selby Public Library
1001 Boulevard of the Arts
Sarasota 33577
(813) 366-7303

• Leon County Public Library
Community Funding Resources
Center
1940 North Monroe Street
Tallahassee 32303
(904) 487-2665

Palm Beach County Community
Foundation
324 Datura Street, Suite 340
West Palm Beach 33401
(305) 659-6800

Georgia

• Atlanta-Fulton Public Library
Ivan Allen Department
1 Margaret Mitchell Square
Atlanta 30303
(404) 688-4636

Hawaii

• Thomas Hale Hamilton
Library
General Reference
University of Hawaii
2550 The Mall
Honolulu 96822
(808) 948-7214

The Hawaiian Foundation
Resource Room
130 Merchant Street
Bancorp Tower, Suite 901
Honolulu 96813
(808) 538-4540

Idaho

• Caldwell Public Library
1010 Dearborn Street
Caldwell 83605
(208) 459-3242

Illinois

Belleville Public Library
121 East Washington Street
Belleville 62220
(618) 234-0441

DuPage Township
300 Briarcilff Road
Bolingbrook 60439
(312) 759-1317

• Donors Forum of Chicago
53 W. Jackson Blvd., Rm. 430
Chicago 60604
(312) 431-0265

• Evanston Public Library
1703 Orrington Avenue
Evanston 60201
(312) 866-0305

• Sangamon State University
Library
Shepherd Road
Springfield 62708
(217) 786-6633

Indiana

Allen County Public Library
900 Webster Street
Fort Wayne 46802
(219) 424-7241

Indiana University Northwest
Library
3400 Broadway
Gary 46408
(219) 980-6580

• Indianapolis-Marion County
Public Library
40 East St. Clair Street
Indianapolis 46204
(317) 269-1733

Iowa

• Public Library of Des Moines
100 Locust Street
Des Moines 50308
(515) 283-4259

Kansas

• Topeka Public Library
Adult Services Department
1515 West Tenth Street
Topeka 66604
(913) 233-2040

• Wichita Public Library
223 South Main
Wichita 67202
(316) 262-0611

Kentucky

Western Kentucky University
Division of Library Service
Helm-Cravens Library
Bowling Green 42101
(502) 745-3951

• Louisville Free Public Library
Fourth and York Streets
Louisville 40203
(502) 561-8600

Louisiana

• East Baton Rouge Parish
Library
Centroplex Library
120 St. Louis Street
Baton Rouge 70821
(504) 389-4960

• New Orleans Public Library
Business and Science Division
219 Loyola Avenue
New Orleans 70140
(504) 596-2583

• Shreve Memorial Library
424 Texas Street
Shreveport 71101
(318) 226-5894

Maine

• University of Southern Maine
Office of Sponsored Research
96 Falmouth Street
Portland 04103
(207) 780-4411

Maryland

• Enoch Pratt Free Library
Social Science and History
Department
400 Cathedral Street
Baltimore 21201
(301) 396-5320

Massachusetts

• Associated Grantmakers of
Massachusetts
294 Washington Street
Suite 501
Boston 02108
(617) 426-2608

• Boston Public Library
Copley Square
Boston 02117
(617) 536-5400

Walpole Public Library
Common Street
Walpole 02081
(617) 668-5497 ext. 340

• Western Massachusetts
Funding Resource Center
Campaign for Human
Development
Chancery Annex
73 Chestnut Street
Springfield 01103
(413) 732-3175 ext. 67

• Grants Resource Center
Worcester Public Library
Salem Square
Worcester 01608
(617) 799-1655

Michigan

• Alpena County Library
211 North First Avenue
Alpena 49707
(517) 356-6188

University of Michigan-Ann
Arbor
Reference Department
209 Hatcher Graduate Library
Ann Arbor 48109-1205
(313) 764-1149

• Henry Ford Centennial
Library
16301 Michigan Avenue
Dearborn 48126
(313) 943-2337

• Purdy Library
Wayne State University
Detroit 48202
(313) 577-4040

• Michigan State University
Libraries
Reference Library
East Lansing 48824
(517) 353-8818

They who give have all things. They who withhold have nothing.
Hindu Proverb

- Farmington Community
Library
32737 West 12 Mile Road
Farmington Hills 48018
(313) 553-0300

- University of Michigan-Flint
Library
Reference Department
Flint 48503
(313) 762-3408

- Grand Rapids Public Library
Business Dept.
60 Library Plaza
Grand Rapids 49503
(616) 456-3600

- Michigan Technological
University Library
Highway U.S. 41
Houghton 49931
(906) 487-2507

Minnesota

- Duluth Public Library
520 Superior Street
Duluth 55802
(218) 723-3802

- Southwest State University
Library
Marshall 56258
(507) 537-7278

- Minneapolis Public Library
Sociology Department
300 Nicollet Mall
Minneapolis 55401
(612) 372-6555

Rochester Public Library
Broadway at First Street, SE
Rochester 55901
(507) 285-8002

Saint Paul Public Library
90 West Fourth Street
Saint Paul 55102
(612) 292-6311

Mississippi

Jackson Metropolitan Library
301 North State Street
Jackson 39201
(601) 944-1120

Missouri

- Clearinghouse for
Midcontinent Foundations
P.O. Box 22680
Univ. of Missouri, Kansas City
Law School, Suite 1-300
52nd Street and Oak
Kansas City 64113
(816) 276-1176

- Kansas City Public Library
311 East 12th Street
Kansas City 64106
(816) 221-2685

- Metropolitan Association for
Philanthropy, Inc.
5585 Pershing Avenue
Suite 150
St. Louis 63112
(314) 361-3900

- Springfield-Greene County
Library
397 East Central Street
Springfield 65801
(417) 866-4636

Montana

- Eastern Montana College
Library
Reference Department
1500 N. 30th Street
Billings 59101-0298
(406) 657-2262

- Montana State Library
Reference Department
1515 E. 6th Avenue
Helena 59620
(406) 444-3004

Nebraska

• University of Nebraska,
Lincoln
106 Love Library
Lincoln 68588-0410
(402) 472-2848

• W. Dale Clark Library
Social Sciences Department
215 South 15th Street
Omaha 68102
(402) 444-4826

Nevada

• Las Vegas-Clark County
Library District
1401 East Flamingo Road
Las Vegas 89119
(702) 733-7810

• Washoe County Library
301 South Center Street
Reno 89505
(702) 785-4012

New Hampshire

• The New Hampshire
Charitable Fund
One South Street
Concord 03301
(603) 225-6641

Littleton Public Library
109 Main Street
Littleton 03561
(603) 444-5741

New Jersey

Cumberland County Library
800 E. Commerce Street
Bridgeton 08302
(609) 453-2216

The Support Center
17 Academy Street, Suite 1101
Newark 07102
(201) 643-5774

County College of Morris
Masten Learning Resource
Center
Route 10 and Center Grove Rd.
Randolph 07869
(201) 361-5000 ext. 470

• New Jersey State Library
Governmental Reference
185 West State Street
Trenton 08625
(609) 292-6220

New Mexico

Albuquerque Community
Foundation
6400 Uptown Boulevard N.E.
Suite 500-W
Albuquerque 87110
(505) 883-6240

• New Mexico State Library
325 Don Gaspar Street
Santa Fe 87503
(505) 827-3824

New York

• New York State Library
Cultural Education Center
Humanities Section
Empire State Plaza
Albany 12230
(518) 474-7645

Bronx Reference Center
New York Public Library
2556 Bainbridge Avenue
Bronx 10458
(212) 220-6575

Brooklyn in Touch
101 Willoughby Street
Room 1508
Brooklyn 11201
(718) 237-9300

• Buffalo and Erie County
Public Library
Lafayette Square
Buffalo 14203
(716) 856-7525

Huntington Public Library
338 Main Street
Huntington 11743
(516) 427-5165

• Levittown Public Library
Reference Department
One Bluegrass Lane
Levittown 11756
(516) 731-5728

• **The Foundation Center**
79 Fifth Avenue
New York 10003
(212) 620-4230

SUNY/College at Old Westbury
Library
223 Store Hill Road
Old Westbury 11568
(516) 876-3156

• Plattsburgh Public Library
Adult Service Department
15 Oak Street
Plattsburgh 12901
(518) 563-0921

Adriance Memorial Library
93 Market Street
Poughkeepsie 12601
(914) 485-3445

Queens Borough Public Library
89-11 Merrick Boulevard
Jamaica 11432
(718) 990-0700

• Rochester Public Library
Business and Social Sciences
Division
115 South Avenue
Rochester 14604
(716) 428-7328

Staten Island Council on the
Arts
One Edgewater Plaza Rm. 311
Staten Island 10305
(718) 447-4485

*"When people are serving, life is
no longer meaningless."
John W. Gardner (1912–)*

• Onondaga County Public
Library at the Galleries
447 S. Salina Street
Syracuse 13202-2494
(315) 448-4636

• White Plains Public Library
100 Martine Avenue
White Plains 10601
(914) 682-4488

• Suffolk Cooperative Library
System
627 North Sunrise Service Road
Bellport 11713
(516) 286-1600

North Carolina

• The Duke Endowment
200 S. Tryon Street, Ste. 1100
Charlotte 28202
(704) 376-0291

Durham County Library
300 N. Roxboro Street
Durham 27701
(919) 683-2626

• North Carolina State Library
109 East Jones Street
Raleigh 27611
(919) 733-3270

• The Winston-Salem
Foundation
229 First Union National Bank
Building
Winston-Salem 27101
(919) 725-2382

North Dakota

Western Dakota Grants Resource
Center
Bismarck Junior College Library
Bismarck 58501
(701) 224-5450

• The Library
North Dakota State University
Fargo 58105
(701) 237-8876

Ohio

• Public Library of Cincinnati
and Hamilton County
Education Department
800 Vine Street
Cincinnati 45202
(513) 369-6940

• **The Foundation Center**
Kent H. Smith Library
1442 Hanna Building
1422 Euclid Avenue
Cleveland 44115
(216) 861-1933

The Public Library of Columbus
and Franklin County
Main Library
96 S. Grant Avenue
Columbus 43215
(614) 222-7180

• Dayton and Montgomery
County Public Library
Grants Information Center
215 E. Third Street
Dayton 45402-2103
(513) 227-9500 ext. 211

• Toledo-Lucas County Public
Library
Social Science Department
325 Michigan Street
Toledo 43624
(414) 255-7055 ext. 221

Ohio University-Zanesville
Community Education and
Development
1425 Newark Road
Zanesville 43701
(614) 453-0762

Stark County District Library
715 Market Avenue North
Canton 44702-1080
(216) 452-0665

*"Philanthropy is almost
the only virtue which is
sufficiently appreciated by
mankind."*
Henry David Thoreau (1817–1862)

Oklahoma

• Oklahoma City University
Library
NW 23rd at North Blackwelder
Oklahoma City 73106
(405) 521-5072

• Tulsa City-County Library
System
400 Civic Center
Tulsa 74103
(918) 592-7944

Oregon

• Library Association of
Portland
Government Documents Room
801 S.W. Tenth Avenue
Portland 97205
(503) 223-7201

Oregon State Library
State Library Building
Salem 97310
(503) 378-4274

Pennsylvania

Northhampton County Area
Community College
Learning Resources Center
3835 Green Pond Road
Bethlehem 18017
(215) 865-5358

• Erie County Public Library
3 South Perry Square
Erie 16501
(814) 452-2333 ext. 54

• Dauphin County Library
System
Central Library
101 Walnut Street
Harrisburg 17101
(717) 234-4961

Lancaster County Public Library
125 North Duke Street
Lancaster 17602
(717) 394-2651

- The Free Library of
Philadelphia
Logan Square
Philadelphia 19103
(215) 686-5423

- Hillman Library
University of Pittsburgh
Pittsburgh 15260
(412) 624-4423

Economic Development Counsel
of Northeastern Pennsylvania
1151 Oak Street
Pittston 18640
(717) 655-5581

James V. Brown Library
12 E. 4th Street
Williamsport 17701
(717) 326-0536

Rhode Island

- Providence Public Library
Reference Department
150 Empire Street
Providence 02903
(401) 521-7722

South Carolina

- Charleston County Public
Library
404 King Street
Charleston 29403
(803) 723-1645

- South Carolina State Library
Reader Services Department
1500 Senate Street
Columbia 29201
(803) 734-8666

South Dakota

- South Dakota State Library
State Library Building
800 North Illinois Street
Pierre 57501
(605) 773-3131

Sioux Falls Area Foundation
404 Boyce Greeley Building
321 South Phillips Avenue
Sioux Falls 57102-0781
(605) 336-7055

Tennessee

- Knoxville-Knox County Public
Library
500 West Church Avenue
Knoxville 37902
(615) 523-0781

- Memphis Shelby County
Library
1850 Peabody Avenue
Memphis 38104
(901) 725-8876

- Public Library of Nashville
and Davidson County
8th Avenue, North and Union
Street
Nashville 37203
(615) 244-4700

Texas

Amarillo Area Foundation
1000 Polk
P.O. Box 25569
Amarillo 79105-269
(806) 376-4521

- The Hogg Foundation for
Mental Health
The University of Texas
Austin 78712
(512) 471-5041

- Corpus Christi State University
Library
6300 Ocean Drive
Corpus Christi 78412
(512) 991-6810

- El Paso Community
Foundation
El Paso National Bank Building
Suite 1616
El Paso 79901
(915) 533-4020

• Funding Information Center
Texas Christian University
Library
Ft. Worth 76129
(817) 921-7664

• Houston Public Library
Bibliographic & Information
Center
500 McKinney Avenue
Houston 77002
(713) 236-1313

• Lubbock Area Foundation
502 Commerce Bank Building
Lubbock 79401
(806) 762-8061

• Funding Information Library
507 Brooklyn
San Antonio 78215
(512) 227-4333

• Dallas Public Library
Grants Information Service
1515 Young Street
Dallas 75201
(214) 670-1487

• Pan American University
Learning Resource Center
1201 W. University Drive
Edinburgh 78539
(512) 381-3304

Utah

• Salt Lake City Public Library
Business and Science Department
209 East Fifth South
Salt Lake City 84111
(801) 363-5733

Vermont

• State of Vermont Department
of Libraries
Reference Services Unit
111 State Street
Montpelier 05602
(802) 828-3261

Virginia

• Grants Resources Collection
Hampton Public Library
4207 Victoria Blvd.
Hampton 23669
(804) 727-6234

• Richmond Public Library
Business, Science, & Technology
Department
101 East Franklin Street
Richmond 23219
(804) 780-8223

Washington

• Seattle Public Library
1000 Fourth Avenue
Seattle 98104
(206) 386-4620

• Spokane Public Library
Funding Information Center
West 906 Main Avenue
Spokane 99201
(509) 838-3364

West Virginia

• Kanawha County Public
Library
123 Capital Street
Charleston 25301
(304) 343-4646

Wisconsin

• Marquette University
Memorial Library
1415 West Wisconsin Avenue
Milwaukee 53233
(414) 224-1515

• University of
Wisconsin-Madison Memorial
Library
728 State Street
Madison 53706
(608) 262-3647

Wyoming

• Laramie County Community
College Library
1400 East College Drive
Cheyenne 82007
(307) 634-5853

Australia

Victorian Community
Foundation
94 Queen Street
Melbourne Vic 3000
(607) 5922

Canada

Canadian Center for
Philanthropy
74 Victoria Street
Suite 920
Toronto, Ontario M5C 2A5
(416) 368-1138

England

Charities Aid Foundation
18 Doughty Street
London W1N 2 PL
01-831-7798

Japan

Foundation Center Library of
Japan
Elements Shinjuku Bldg. 3F
2-1-14 Shinjuku, Shinjuku-ku
Tokyo
03-350-1857

Mexico

Biblioteca Benjamin Franklin
Londres 16
Mexico City 6,D.F.
(525) 591-0244

Puerto Rico

Universidad Del Sagrado
Corazon
M.M.T. Guevarra Library
Correo Calle Loiza
Santurce 00914
(809) 728-1515 ext. 357

Virgin Islands

University of the Virgin Islands
Library
Saint Thomas
U.S. Virgin Islands 00802
(809) 776-9200 ext. 1487

WHAT'S IN A NAME?

For three major institutions, 1988 posed an interesting question
and created some problems.

At the Columbia University's New York Hospital, university
Trustees were pondering what to do with the medical tower which
had just been named the year before in honor of Harry and Leona
Helmsley as the result of a $33 million gift. The Helmsleys have
been charged with tax fraud, and insiders bet they will be found
guilty and that the penalty will be stiff. The hospital may change
the name.

Princeton University made certain that Ivan Boesky cancelled
his $1.5 million check for their new student center just before he was
indicted for insider trading. And just in the nick of time.

At Duke University, David Bloom was charged with operating
a fraudulent multi-million dollar investment racket. They returned
several paintings of his (valued in the millions) and $20,000 in cash.

GIFT LEVEL CLUB CATEGORIES: THE EVOLUTION OF A PHILANTHROPIST

Kiddie Kar Klub	$10
Scooter Club	$25
Tricycle Club	$50
Bicycle Club	$100
Skateboard Club	$500
Motor Bike Club	$1000
Motorcycle Club	$2500
Van Club	$5000
Golf Cart Club	$10,000
Mercedes Club	$25,000
Private Plane Club	$100,000
World Class Yacht Club	$1,000,000

Source: Arthur C. Frantzreb

WHERE THE MONEY COMES FROM

In 1988, there were approximately 821,000 not-for-profit organizations and institutions on record in the United States with 501(c)(3) status—official recognition and approval by the Internal Revenue Service. That group reported $253 billion in revenue. Here's where the money comes from.

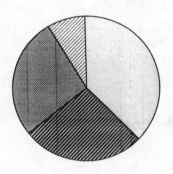

37.8%
Dues, fees, charges, participant and member charges

26.9%
Contributions...gifts from individuals, corporations, foundations, etc.

26.9%
Government sources & grants

8.4%
Other revenue, including mostly endowment and investment income

SOURCES OF CONTRIBUTIONS ($ IN BILLIONS)

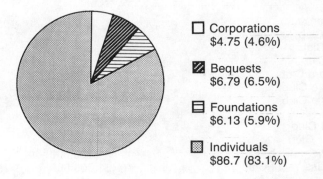

☐ Corporations
$4.75 (4.6%)

▨ Bequests
$6.79 (6.5%)

▤ Foundations
$6.13 (5.9%)

▨ Individuals
$86.7 (83.1%)

Source: *Giving USA* 1989

USES OF CONTRIBUTIONS ($ IN BILLIONS)

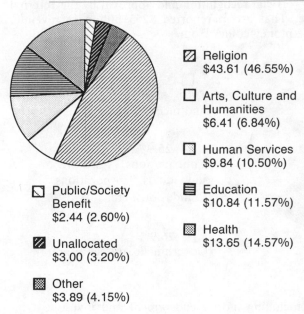

▨ Religion
$43.61 (46.55%)

☐ Arts, Culture and
Humanities
$6.41 (6.84%)

▢ Human Services
$9.84 (10.50%)

▤ Education
$10.84 (11.57%)

▨ Health
$13.65 (14.57%)

◪ Public/Society
Benefit
$2.44 (2.60%)

▨ Unallocated
$3.00 (3.20%)

▨ Other
$3.89 (4.15%)

THE FOUNDATION CENTER AFFILIATES PROGRAM

As participants in the cooperating collection network, affiliates are libraries or nonprofit agencies that provide fundraising information or other funding-related technical assistance in their communities. Affiliates agree to provide free public access to a basic collection of Foundation Center publications during a regular schedule of hours, offering free funding research guidance to all visitors. Many also provide a variety of special services for local nonprofit organizations using staff or volunteers to prepare special materials, organize workshops, or conduct library orientations.

The affiliates program began in 1981 to continue the expansion of The Foundation Center's funding information network of 90 funding information collections. Since its inception, over 80 organizations have been designated Foundation Center affiliates. Affiliate collections have been established in a wide variety of host organizations, including public and university libraries, technical assistance agencies, and community foundations.

For more information, please write to: The Foundation Center, 79 Fifth Avenue, New York, NY 10003.

SMALLEST COMPANIES MAKE LARGEST GIFTS

Companies with under 1,000 employees traditionally make the highest contribution to philanthropy per employee. According to the latest data that is available, this group gives more than twice the median per employee for all other size corporations.

Number of Employees	Median Gift—$
Below 1000	$396
1000–2499	$193
2500–4999	$204
5000–9999	$164
10,000–14,999	$126
15,000–24,999	$159
25,000–49,999	$176
50,000 & Over	$104

"The duty of every man is to devote a certain portion of his income for charitable purposes and...his further duty is to see it applied as to do the most good."
Thomas Jefferson

A Guide to Charitable Giving by 137 Corporations

The Council on Economic Priorities, a non-profit group that conducts research on the role and responsibilities of corporations, has released a guide for "socially responsible" consumers that rates companies on the basis of various criteria, including charitable giving.

Called *Shopping for a Better World: A Quick and Easy Guide to Socially Responsible Supermarket Shopping,* the 128-page book was published with the help of a grant from the Cook Brothers Educational Fund. Copies of the guide, which cost $4.95 plus $1 for postage, may be obtained from the council, 30 Irving Place, New York 10003.

Following are the ratings of charitable giving by various companies, which provided information to the council during the spring and summer of 1988. Company officials were allowed to review their ratings before the guide was published. Figures for charitable giving were calculated as a percentage of the average of pre-tax worldwide earnings over a three-year period.

Gave 2 per cent or more of net pre-tax earnings to charity:

Anheuser-Busch Companies Inc.
Ben & Jerry's Homemade Inc.
Colgate-Palmolive Company
Curtice-Burns Foods Inc.
Dow Chemical Company
General Mills Inc.
Newman's Own Inc.
Pennwalt Corporation
Pillsbury Company
Polaroid Corporation
Tom's of Maine Inc.

Gave between 1 and 2 per cent of net pre-tax earnings:

American Cyanamid Company
Atlantic Richfield Company
Bristol-Myers Company
Clorox Company
Eastman Kodak Company

General Electric Company
Gerber Products Company
Gillette Company
Hershey Foods Corporation
S.C. Johnson & Son Inc.
Kellogg Company
Kraft Inc.
McCormick & Company Inc., Consumer Products Group
Mead Corporation
Mobil Corporation
Noxell Corporation
PepsiCo Inc.
Procter & Gamble Company
Quaker Oats Company
RJR Nabisco Inc.
Rorer Group Inc.
Sara Lee Corporation
Scott Paper Company
Shell Oil Company
Sun Company
Upjohn Company
Warner-Lambert Company

Gave between 0.6 per cent to 1 per cent:

Abbott Laboratories
Amoco Corporation
Campbell Soup Company
Chevron Corporation
ConAgra Inc.
Exxon Corporation
GTE Corporation
H. J. Heinz Company
IC Industries Inc.
Johnson & Johnson
Miles Inc.
Minnesota Mining & Manufacturing Company
Pfizer Inc.
Schering-Plough Corporation
J. M. Smucker Company

Gave 0.6 per cent or less:

American Brands Inc.
Aura Cacia Inc.
Autumn Harp Inc.
Borden Inc.
Caesar Cardini Foods Inc.
Cherry Hill Cooperative Cannery Inc.
Coca-Cola Company
CPC International Inc.
Cream of the Bean Inc.
D&P Products Inc.
DoleFam Corporation
Georgia-Pacific Corporation
Great Eastern Sun Trading Company Inc.
Homestyle Foods
Kimberly-Clark Corporation
Naturade Products Inc.
Occidental Petroleum Corporation
Philip Morris Companies Inc.
Rachel Perry Inc.
Phillips Petroleum Company
Ralston Purina Company
Reynolds Metals Company

21st Century Foods Inc.
Tenneco Inc.
Texaco Inc.
Unilever United States Inc.
Wm. Wrigley, Jr., Company

Did not disclose giving

Alacer Corp.
Alberto-Culver Company
American Health Plus Corporation
American Home Products Corporation
American Natural Beverage Inc.
Apple & Eve Inc.
Aroma Vera Inc.
Associated Cooperatives Inc.
Aubrey Organics
Barbara's Bakery Inc.
BP America Inc.
Brown Cow West Corporation
Carmè Inc.
Carter-Wallace Inc.
Castle & Cooke Inc.
Chiquita Brands Inc.
Church & Dwight Company Inc.
Dean Foods Company
Deer Valley Farm
Eden Foods Inc.
Falcon Trading Company Inc.
Flowers Industries Inc.
Garden of Eatin' Inc.
Greyhound Corporation
Holly Farms Corporation
Geo. A. Hormel & Company
Ida Grae Cosmetics Inc.
International Protein Industries Inc.
Iroquois Brands Ltd.
James River Corporation
Johnson Products
Klaire Laboratories Inc.
Le Sueur Isolates Inc.
Lifetone International Inc.
Loma Linda Foods Inc.
Mars Inc.
Mayacamas Fine Foods Inc.
Modern Products Inc.
Mountain Ocean Ltd.
Natura Inc.
Nature's Herbs Inc.
Nature's Way Products Inc.
Nestle Foods Corporation
Orjene Cosmetic Company Inc.
Rapid-American Corporation
Reviva Labs Inc.
John B. Sanfilippo & Son Inc.
Solgar Vitamin Company
Squibb Corporation
Tasty Baking Company
Tillamook County Creamery Association
Topps Company Inc.
Twin Laboratories Inc.
Universal Laboratories Inc.
USX Corporation
Vegetarian Health Society
Vita Mix Corporation

Source: The Council on Economic Priorities, *Chronicle of Philanthropy.*

The Philanthropy Monthly is a hard-hitting and irreverent newsletter that strips off the outside layers and gets to some of the very critical issues of fundraising. It is published eleven times a year (July and August are combined). **For a sample copy write to: Henry C. Suhrke, Editor, *The Philanthropy Monthly*, P.O. Box 989, New Milford, CT 06776.**

CORPORATE CONTRIBUTIONS REACH WATERSHED

According to the 1988 edition of the Survey of Corporate Contributions "charitable contribution activities by the nation's leading corporations have reached a watershed." The survey points out that the extraordinary growth rate that during the 1970s and early 1980s often reached growth in double digits, has "eroded steadily since 1985." There was no real growth in 1986 and 1987.

The Conference Board—a business information service designed to assist senior executives and other leaders in management in arriving at sound decisions—calls for creative approaches which will maximize the benefits of every contribution's dollar. It was founded in 1916, and during those years has created a close personal networking of leaders who exchange experience and judgment on significant issues. More than 3,600 organizations participate in the work of The Conference Board. It is a not-for-profit corporation with the greatest share of its support coming from business concerns. The President is James T. Mills.

The 1988 Survey of Corporate Contributions is the twenty-first edition. It provides executives and the entire giving community with a detailed and comprehensive overview of contributions practices based on information provided by 372 firms. The major corporations and corporate foundations use the document as a budgeting and planning tool to assist them in their own programs.

For more information: The Conference Board, 845 Third Avenue, New York, NY, 10022 (212) 759-0900.

CARVING YOUR NAME IN STONE

In 1988, Lincoln Center distributed an opulent, over-sized four-color brochure for its new $85 million facility, inviting potential patrons to, "Make an indelible mark on the future."

For one of the large museums in New York, the glossy brochure stated: "We did not write our names in sand...rather we carved them in granite...always with the hope that they will have significance and beauty for those who follow."

The concept of honoring the living in tributes or memorializing the dead is not new. But in 1988, the idea received even greater emphasis.

For $25 million, the new 625 bed pavilion at Mount Sinai Hospital could be yours. A seat at Carnegie Hall goes for just $5,000! At Carnegie Hall in the recent renovation, they created the Joan and Sanford I. Weill Recital Hall ($2.5 million), the Carl Icahn Parquet Terrace ($500,000), and the Lester S. Morse, Jr. Lobby ($2 million). At Lincoln Center, you can have the dressing room for

$75,000, but the education center will cost more—$5 million.

Not all naming opportunities are glamorous and glitzy! Take, for instance, Lenox Hill Hospital in New York, where they have the $500,000 Sol Goldman Renal Therapy Center and the $450,000 Abram and Irma Croll Endoscopy Suite.

Major memorial gifts do not necessarily follow religious lines. Paul and Seymour Milstein and their sister, Gloria Flanzer—a prominent New York Jewish family, gave $25 million to Presbyterian Hospital last year. They issued the following statement: "We made the gift because four generations of our family received devoted and outstanding medical care at Presbyterian." This confirms the fundraising verity that people give because they believe in the work and the mission of the institution. Nothing else is as important.

And for most donors, there is the undeniable desire that their name live on in perpetuity. When Leonard N. Stern gave $30 million to New York University to name their School of Business, the publishing and pet-products magnate told his children: "You'll bring your children here, and they won't know me, but they'll see this and see what I believed in."

Following is a list of institutions and the names and categories they use for donor recognition, designed to help suggest names for one of your own groups should you be starting or modifying the recognition program in your organization.

The list comes from the valuable book: *Accent On Recognition*. In this section, the editor points out that it is important for each organization to structure giving levels according to the donors' giving history and potential. The dollar amounts represent annual contributions.

Education

Columbia Union College
Takoma Park, Maryland

Centurion	$100 +
Investor	$250 +
Patron	$500 +

President's Round Table

Associate	$1,000 + cumulative
Benefactor	$5,000 + cumulative
Founder	$10,000 + cumulative

Grand Canyon College
Phoenix, Arizona

Canyon Friends	$1–$99
Arizona Club	$100–$500
University Club	$501–$999
Dean's Club	$1,000 +

Green Mountain College
Poultney, Vermont

2nd Century Club	$100–$249
1834 Club (year founded)	$250–$499
Green & Gold Club (school colors)	$500–$999

Silver Circle	$1,000–$4,999
President's Circle	$5,000 +

Pacific Union College
Angwin, California

GEM Club (Gift Every Month)	$60–$106
Founders Club (based on age of college)	$107–$259
DEW Club (Donation Every Week)	$260–$499
Committee of 100	$500–$999
President's Circle	$1,000 +

United States Merchant Marine Academy
Long Island, New York

Leadership Club	$100–$499
Mariners Club	$500–$999
Admirals Club	$1,000 +

Health
Florida Hospital
Orlando, Florida

Centurion	$100–$499
Patrons	$500–$999
President's Council	$1,000–$4,999
Chairman's Council	$5,000–$9,999
Benefactor	$10,000–$24,999
Founder	$25,000–$49,999
Humanitarian	$50,000–$99,999
Philanthropist	$100,000 +

Henry Ford Hospital
Detroit, Michigan

Associate	$25–$49
Partner	$50–$99
Centurion	$100–$499
Fellow	$500–$999
Leadership	$1,000 +

Glendale Adventist Medical Center
Glendale, California
(Cumulative amounts for donor wall.)

Patron	$1,000–$4,999
Sponsor	$5,000–$9,999
Golden Sponsor	$10,000–$24,999
Associate	$25,000–$49,999
Ambassador	$50,000–$99,999
Founder	$100,000–$999,999
Benefactor	$1,000,000 +

Leland Memorial Hospital
Riverdale, Maryland
(Cumulative amounts for donor wall.)

Contributor	$250
Supporter	$500
Friend	$2,500
Guardian	$5,000
Good Samaritan	$10,000
Humanitarian	$20,000
Benefactor	$50,000 +

White Memorial Medical Center
Los Angeles, California
(Cumulative amounts for donor wall.)

Friend	$2,500–$9,999
Sponsor	$10,000–$24,999
Builder	$25,000–$49,999
Patron	$50,000–$99,999
Benefactor	$100,000 +

Club Names

Advocate	Contributor	Investor	Sponsor
Ambassador	Fellow	Leader	Steward
Associate	Founder	Medalist	Supporter
Benefactor	Friend	Pacesetter	Trailblazer
Builder	Good Samaritan	Partner	Visionary
Centurion	Guardian	Patron	_____ Club
Circle of Friends	Humanitarian	Philanthropist	_____ Council
Committee of 100	Innovator	Pioneer	_____ Round Table

Adjectives

Bronze	Distinguished	Golden	President's
Chairman's	Founding	Honorary	Silver
Dean's	Gold	Major	Sustaining

Other
Canvasback Missions, Inc.
Benicia, California

Crew Member	$1–$299 (sporadic gifts)
Seaman	$1–$299 (regular annual gifts)
Voting Member	$300–$999
Yeoman	$1,000 cumulative
First Mate	$5,000 cumulative
Captain	$10,000 cumulative
Admiral	$50,000 cumulative
Commander-In-Chief	$100,000 cumulative

Milton Murray Foundation for Philanthropy
Washington, DC

Friend	$100 cumulative
Advocate	$500 cumulative
Builder	$1,000 cumulative
Pacesetter	$10,000 cumulative
Visionary	$25,000 cumulative

"The reason people do not give is because they are not asked."
From a study conducted by the Gallup Organization.

COMPANY-SPONSORED FOUNDATIONS BY TOTAL GIVING CATEGORIES
(All dollar figures expressed in thousands)

Total Giving Category	No. of Foundations	Percent	Total Giving¹	Percent	Grants	Percent	Assets	Percent	Gifts Received	Percent
$10 million and over	17	2.2	$272,091	27.9	$238,878	27.6	$1,137,015	28.0	$293,057	31.0
$5 million–under $10 million	22	2.9	148,127	15.2	132,121	15.2	397,124	9.8	119,448	12.7
$1 million–under $5 million	167	21.7	354,697	36.3	311,617	36.0	1,185,240	29.2	310,901	32.9
$500,000–under $1 million	143	18.5	99,911	10.2	91,521	10.6	539,628	13.3	111,335	11.8
$300,000–under $500,000	131	17.0	50,480	5.2	45,758	5.3	332,499	8.2	56,117	5.9
$200,000–under $300,000	107	13.9	26,480	2.7	24,234	2.8	174,336	4.3	21,334	2.3
$100,000–under $200,000	149	19.3	22,167	2.3	19,716	2.3	199,097	4.9	21,849	2.3
Under $100,000	35	4.5	2,165	0.2	1,685	0.2	92,828	2.3	9,794	1.1
Total	771	100.0	$976,118	100.0	$865,530	100.0	$4,057,767	100.0	$943,835	100.0

Company-sponsored foundations with assets of $1 million or more or annual giving of $100,000 or more.

SOURCE: The Foundation Center Database.

COMPANY-SPONSORED FOUNDATIONS BY ASSET CATEGORIES
(All dollar figures expressed in thousands)

Asset Category	No. of Foundations	Percent	Assets	Percent	Gifts Received	Percent	Total Giving	Percent	Grants	Percent
$100 million and over	5	0.6	$ 758,101	18.7	$125,466	13.3	$ 85,779	8.8	$ 77,694	9.0
$50 million–under $100 million	5	0.6	335,833	8.3	35,133	3.7	78,704	8.1	63,918	7.4
$25 million–under $50 million	16	2.1	468,639	11.5	98,466	10.4	105,011	10.8	99,563	11.5
$10 million–under $25 million	67	8.7	1,025,190	25.3	218,304	23.1	184,897	18.9	167,382	19.3
$5 million–under $10 million	98	12.7	702,333	17.3	106,096	11.3	126,085	12.9	106,159	12.3
$1 million–under $5 million	271	35.2	667,141	16.4	201,716	21.4	207,888	21.3	182,358	21.1
Under $1 million	309	40.1	100,530	2.5	158,654	16.8	187,754	19.2	168,456	19.4
Total	771	100.0	$4,057,767	100.0	$943,835	100.0	$976,118	100.0	$865,530	100.0

Company-sponsored foundations with assets of $1 million or more or annual giving of $100,000 or more.

SOURCE: The Foundation Center Database.

COMPANY-SPONSORED FOUNDATIONS BY REGION AND STATE
(Dollar figures expressed in thousands)

Region	No. of Foundations	Percent	Total Giving	Percent	Assets	Percent	Gifts Received	Percent
Middle Atlantic	**180**	**23.3**	**$303,961**	**31.2**	**$1,228,073**	**30.3**	**$256,014**	**27.1**
New Jersey	27		64,184		257,341		89,637	
New York	105		166,175		605,472		116,839	
Pennsylvania	48		73,602		365,260		49,538	
East North Central	**216**	**28.0**	**248,205**	**25.4**	**1,209,447**	**29.8**	**266,193**	**28.2**
Illinois	76		99,516		316,754		63,718	
Indiana	19		10,138		40,187		3,610	
Michigan	22		55,901		426,075		128,931	
Ohio	61		63,214		290,719		54,026	
Wisconsin	38		19,436		135,712		15,908	
Pacific	**74**	**9.6**	**104,700**	**10.7**	**359,637**	**8.9**	**111,579**	**11.8**
Alaska	1		151		43		159	
California	53		77,658		259,190		64,747	
Hawaii	2		666		3,161		0	
Oregon	5		3,867		11,156		3,530	
Washington	13		22,358		86,087		43,143	
West South Central	**34**	**4.4**	**43,075**	**4.4**	**176,870**	**4.4**	**24,023**	**2.5**
Arkansas	2		544		7,355		1,888	
Louisiana	1		570		3,895		19	
Oklahoma	5		7,584		18,894		6,455	
Texas	26		34,377		146,726		15,661	
South Atlantic	**87**	**11.3**	**47,106**	**4.8**	**274,080**	**6.7**	**53,499**	**5.7**
Delaware	3		1,448		18,029		755	
District of Columbia	1		525		14,959		14,100	
Florida	13		7,184		22,990		7,594	
Georgia	15		7,480		44,586		8,307	

	No.	%		%		%		%
Maryland	12		9,207		9,598		8,596	
North Carolina	18		10,011		93,389		7,135	
South Carolina	10		3,832		25,125		2,839	
Virginia	14		7,340		44,254		4,173	
West Virginia	1		79		1,150		0	
West North Central	**81**	**10.5**	**116,009**	**11.9**	**424,990**	**10.5**	**132,098**	**14.0**
Iowa	8		4,676		21,732		4,721	
Kansas	6		1,894		15,870		320	
Minnesota	29		48,749		124,396		61,116	
Missouri	27		51,530		230,375		58,263	
Nebraska	10		9,021		31,900		7,665	
South Dakota	1		139		717		13	
New England	**69**	**9.0**	**92,605**	**9.5**	**296,902**	**7.3**	**84,814**	**9.0**
Connecticut	30		69,457		183,332		55,325	
Maine	5		1,531		11,188		2,744	
Massachusetts	25		17,867		73,545		22,153	
New Hampshire	1		139		2,038		0	
Rhode Island	8		3,611		26,799		4,592	
Mountain	**12**	**1.6**	**9,985**	**1.0**	**33,180**	**0.8**	**10,216**	**1.1**
Arizona	5		3,521		14,248		2,700	
Colorado	4		5,572		12,779		7,276	
New Mexico	1		151		2,166		0	
Nevada	2		741		3,987		240	
East South Central	**18**	**2.3**	**10,472**	**1.1**	**54,587**	**1.3**	**5,399**	**0.6**
Alabama	5		2,596		13,323		320	
Kentucky	4		3,819		7,782		2,475	
Mississippi	2		865		1,030		528	
Tennessee	7		3,192		32,452		2,076	
Total	**771**	**100.0**	**$976,118**	**100.0**	**$4,057,767**	**100.0**	**$943,835**	**100.0**

*Company-sponsored foundations with assets of $1 million or more or annual giving of $100,000 or more.
SOURCE: The Foundation Center Database.

25 LARGEST COMPANY SPONSORED FOUNDATIONS
BY TOTAL GIVING

Name	State	Total Giving	Gifts Received	Assets	Fiscal Date
AT&T Foundations	NY	$29,789	$ 456	$125,000	12/31/86
Amoco Foundation, Inc.	IL	23,825		78,619	12/31/86
General Motors Foundation, Inc.	MI	22,693	20,000	192,989	12/31/86
Exxon Education Foundation	NJ	21,986	26,933	67,909	12/31/86
General Electric Foundation	CT	18,395	8,200	57,581	12/31/86
Shell Companies Foundation, Incorporated	TX	17,437	9,967	25,496	12/31/86
ARCO Foundation	CA	15,238	14,000	6,126	12/31/86
Dayton Hudson Foundation	MN	14,540	13,043	12,758	1/31/86
Burlington Northern Foundation	WA	14,532	13,550	25,600	12/31/85
Mobil Foundation, Inc.	NY	13,747	13,186	15,202	12/31/86
Procter & Gamble Fund, The	OH	12,710	13,000	15,027	6/30/86
Ford Motor Company Fund	MI	12,296	70,010	124,109	12/31/86
Southwestern Bell Foundation	MO	11,929	24,691	28,056	12/31/86
GTE Foundation	CT	11,184	11,022	15,004	12/31/86
Rockwell International Corporation Trust	PA	10,789	20,000	31,536	9/30/86
Alcoa Foundation	PA	10,507		198,593	12/31/86
Prudential Foundation, The	NJ	10,494	35,000	117,410	12/31/86
Xerox Foundation, The	CT	9,700	5,000	9,700	12/31/85
American Express Foundation	NY	9,459	9,290	472	12/31/85
USX Foundation, Inc.	PA	8,437		27,399	11/30/86
Eastman Kodak Charitable Trust	NY	7,755	4,500	28,219	12/31/86
Kraft Foundation	IL	7,470	12,005	17,534	12/28/85
Texaco Philanthropic Foundation Inc.	NY	7,394		30,340	12/31/85
Metropolitan Life Foundation	NY	7,389		74,095	12/31/86
Monsanto Fund	MO	7,373	8,285	2,647	12/31/85

SOURCE: The Foundation Center Database.

THE CASE FOR CORPORATE GIVING

According to Brian O'Connell, President of Independent Sector, a business corporation should target its charitable activity and its public service "at the crossroads where company and public interest intersect."

One of the most compelling responses as to whether it is the business of business to give anything away was provided by James Burke, Chairman of Johnson & Johnson. As described in Independent Sector's *Corporate Philanthropy*, Burke said: "Those companies that organize their business around the broad concept of public service, over the long run provide superior performance for their stockholders."

This extraordinary justification for corporate giving was the result of a survey of companies that received special awards for their giving and for service. Burke noted: "These companies showed an annual 11 percent growth in profits, compounded over 30 years! That happens to be better than three times the growth of the Gross National Product."

Burke concluded: "I have long harbored the belief that most successful corporations in this country—the ones that have delivered outstanding results over a long period of time—were driven by a simple moral imperative—serving the public in the broadest possible sense—better than their competition...we as businessmen and

women have extraordinary leverage on our most important asset...
good will...the good will of the public...if we make sure our enterprises are managed in terms of their obligations to society...
that is also the best way to defend this democratic, capitalistic system that means so much to all of us.

There is clear and irrefutable evidence that companies that are
generous in their philanthropic support and service do better financially, are more profitable, and generate greater dividends for their
stockholders.

Source: Independent Sector

CHIEF OF CHEROKEE NATION OF OKLAHOMA IS 1988 GARDNER WINNER

In 1988, Wilma Mankiller was the recipient of the John W.
Gardner Leadership Award. Mankiller is Principal Chief of the
Cherokee Nation of Oklahoma. The award is given by Independent
Sector, and honors an outstanding American who most exemplifies
the leadership and ideals of John W. Gardner—and recognizes the
man or woman who has done the most during the year to build,
mobilize, and unify people, and provide the funding for institutions
or causes.

A former Secretary of Health, Education, and Welfare, Dr.
Gardner is one of the nation's most distinguished participants in educational, philanthropic, and political life.

In 1987, the award was given to James W. Rouse, Chairman,
Enterprise Foundation and the Enterprise Development Committee; and Faye Wattleton, President, Planned Parenthood Federation of America.

FOUNDING OF AAFRC

The records aren't clear, but there is some evidence that the
idea for the American Association of Fund-Raising Council
(AAFRC) was first proposed over lunch at the Royal Restaurant at
Fifth Avenue and 43rd Street in New York. Present were: Carlton G.
Ketchum (Ketchum, Inc.), Christian H. Dreshman (Ward,
Dreshman, & Reinhardt), and Cornelius M. Smith (Will, Folsom &
Smith). The first meeting of record was held October 8, 1934, at the
Advertising Club in New York. Ten firms were represented. They in-
cluded the original and founding members of the Association.
Most still exist, either as a direct descendant of the original firm or
in merged versions. Represented that day more than fifty-five years
ago at the Advertising Club were: American City Bureau; John
Price Jones Corp.; Ketchum, Inc.; Marts & Lundy, Inc.; MacArt &
Campbell; Pierce & Hedrick; Tamblyn & Brown; Tamblyn &
Tamblyn; Ward, Wells, & Dreshman; and Will, Folsom, & Smith.

NEW FUNDRAISING TABLOID IS LAUNCHED

The *Chronicle of Philanthropy* had its inaugural issue late in 1988. It has a five column tabloid format and will be published every other week. It will quickly gain an important share of the readership and advertising market. The introduction of the *Chronicle* is one of the most significant fundraising publication events of the year.

Its frequency will allow it to publish more current news. There will be fewer feature articles, but the *Chronicle of Philanthropy* will be able to provide news of the latest trends in fundraising.

In addition, it plans to feature:

- In-depth profiles of foundations and corporate grant-makers.

- The latest ideas in fundraising, marketing and recruiting volunteers.

- Lists of new grants.

- Updates on tax rulings, postal policies, and other government regulations affecting charities.

- Reports on the latest court rulings.

- Key statistics on giving, volunteers, salaries, and expenditures.

- The latest information on training and professional development.

- Extensive calendars of upcoming events and conferences.

- Summaries and reviews of professional books.

- News of appointments and promotions.

The editor and publisher of the new tabloid is Philip W. Semas. The annual subscription price will be $57.50.

For more information: Chronicle of Philanthropy, 1255 Twenty-third Street N.W., Washington, DC 20037 (202) 466-1200.

COMPANIES WHICH PUBLISH BOOKS RELATING TO FUNDRAISING AND PHILANTHROPY

American Association of Fund Raising Council (AAFRC)
25 West 43rd Street
New York, NY 10036
(212) 354-5799

Continuing Education Publications
Portland State University
P.O. Box 1394
Portland, OR 97207

Council on Foundations
1828 L Street N.W., Suite 1200
Washington, DC 20036
(202) 466-6512

The Foundation Center
79 5th Avenue
New York, NY 10003
(212) 620-4230

Fund-Raising Institute
Box 365
Ambler, PA 19002-0365
(215) 975-1120

Greenwood Press, Inc.
88 Post Rd., W.
P.O. Box 5007
Westport, CT 06881
(203) 226-3571

Hoke Communications, Inc.
224 Seventh Street
Garden City, NY 11530
1 (800) 645-6132

Independent Sector
1828 L Street, N.W.
Washington, DC 20036
(202) 223-8100

Jossey-Bass, Inc.
433 California Street
San Francisco, CA 94104
(415) 433-1740

Macmillan Publishing Company
866 Third Avenue
New York, NY 10022
(212) 702-2000

National Society of Fund Raising
Executives
1101 King Street, Suite 3000
Alexandria, VA 22314
(703) 684-0410

Pluribus Press, Inc.
160 E. Illinois Street
Chicago, IL 60611
(312) 467-0424

Public Management Institute
358 Brannan St.
San Francisco, CA 94107
(415) 896-1900

Public Services Materials Center
111 North Central Avenue
Hartsdale, NY 10530
(914) 949-2242

Seven Locks Press
Box 27
Cabin John, MD 20818
(201) 320-2130

The Taft Group
5130 MacArthur Blvd., N.W.
Washington, DC 20016-3316
(202) 966-7086

Third Sector Press
2000 Euclid Avenue
P.O. Box 18044
Cleveland, OH 44118
(216) 831-9300

Transaction Books
Rutgers University
New Brunswick, NJ 08903
(201) 932-2280

THE AMERICAN ASSOCIATION OF FUND-RAISING COUNSEL

The AAFRC was founded in 1935 to advance the philanthropic cause and establish an ethical approach to fundraising.

It was an attempt to bring a level of understanding and confidence to a field that was too often disorganized and mistrusted. A Fair Practice Code was developed. It is still accepted as the standard for professional conduct for professional counsel.

The Association is also committed to promoting the philanthropic cause, which led to the formation of its Trust for Philanthropy.

Each member firm is expected to adhere to the tenets of the Fair Practice Code. In addition, they must have a record of continuity and of successful campaigns. Member firms and their major headquarters follow.

Alford, Ver Schave & Associates, Inc.
9501 West Devon Avenue
Rosemont, IL 60018
(312) 823-5775
Comprehensive resource development consultation services. Serves a range of institutions, including higher and secondary education, cultural, civic, health and social agencies. No geographic limitations.

American City Bureau
Poplar Creek Office Plaza
1721 Moon Lake Boulevard

Hoffman Estates, IL 60194
(312) 490-5858
Serves a wide range of organizations in health and health care,
education, youth development, religion, and the arts. No geographic
limitations.

Paul Blanshard Associates, Inc.
645 East Butler Avenue
P.O. Box 99
New Britain, PA 18901
(215) 345-4616
Consultants to health, education, social welfare and international
organizations on a continuing basis. Service centers normally in
mid-Atlantic region of the country.

Brakeley, John Price Jones Inc.
1600 Summer Street
Stamford, CT 06905
(203) 348-8100
FAX: 203/978-0114
A full-service organization in providing fund-raising consulting,
planning, and management services in the fields of education, health,
culture and the arts, community and civic organizations, and national
associations throughout the United States and abroad.

Caesar & Washburn, Incorporated
1841 Broadway
New York, NY 10023
(212) 362-2774
A full-service fund-raising and management consulting firm serving
health and welfare agencies, educational and cultural institutions, civic,
public policy and advocacy organizations, religious institutions and
international programs. No geographic limitations.

Donald A. Campbell and Company, Inc.
One East Wacker Drive
Chicago, IL 60601
(312) 644-7100
A full-service philanthropic development firm, specializing in counsel
and management of capital, annual, and planned giving programs;
campaign feasibility studies, marketing and development audits and
plans; capital-by-phone and telemarketing programs; market research;
and a full spectrum of communications services.

Community Counselling Service Co., Inc.
Empire State Building
350 Fifth Avenue, Suite 7210
New York, NY 10118
(212) 695-1175
Comprehensive capital fund-raising campaigns, public relations, and
long-range programs for colleges, universities, hospitals, religious
communities, retreat houses, homes for the aged, schools for exceptional
children, social and cultural agencies, political organizations, annual

giving programs, alumni cultivation, trustee development, student recruitment, management placement, membership drives. Serves entire United States, Canada, Great Britain, Ireland, Europe, South America, Bahamas, and Africa.

Community Service Bureau, Inc.
3500 Oak Lawn, Suite 180
Dallas, TX 75219
(214) 526-5252
Offers the spectrum of fund development management and counseling services to meet the unique needs of its clients. CSB provides specific services appropriate to a component of a fund development program or of a development office.

Cosgriff Company
One Continental Building
Omaha, NE 68102
(402) 344-7220
Fund-raising counsel for community, religious and educational institutions. Services include full-time resident campaign management and part-time consultation for operating fund and capital fund projects. Serves entire United States.

John B. Cummings Co., Inc.
350 Fifth Avenue, 64th Floor
New York, NY 10118-0001
(212) 988-8162
A full-service, consulting firm specializing in long-range development for schools, colleges, universities, religious organizations, health care agencies, civic and cultural organizations. Serves entire United States and Europe.

Development Management Associates
249 East Ocean Boulevard, Suite 712
Long Beach, CA 90802
(213) 436-2221
Provides development and fund-raising feasibility and planning studies; capital campaign management; counsel on long-range planning, planned giving, and leadership development. Serves the United States and selected international clients.

R. F. Dini & Associates, Inc.
600 Jefferson, Suite 630
Houston, TX 77002
(713) 654-9210
Capital campaigns, annual support campaigns, foundation planning, institutional master planning and fund-raising studies. Multi-million dollar capital and endowment campaign direction and management, development program planning, institutional long-range planning and fund-raising feasibility studies.

J. Donovan Associates, Inc.
One Derby Square

Salem, MA 01970
(508) 744-8558 (in Mass.)
An international, professional, fund-raising consulting firm, serves
health care, cultural, social service, religious and educational institutions.

Holland Estill and Company, Inc.
217 First Street
Hohokus, NJ 07423
(201) 444-0665
Capital projects, development programs and annual budget campaigns
for educational institutions, health causes and hospitals, cultural and
civic organizations, welfare agencies and religious bodies. Serves entire
United States.

Charles R. Feldstein & Company, Inc.
135 South LaSalle Street, Suite 1260
Chicago, IL 60603
(312) 558-1800
Education, medicine, social welfare, culture—annual development
programs, capital campaigns, institutional public relations. Serves entire
United States.

Fitzgerald, Graves & Company
1737 Union Street
San Francisco, CA 94123
(415) 346-1800
Management consultants to gift-supported institutions for capital fund
raising. Focus on major gift counseling, capital campaign direction,
institutional planning, and feasibility and planning studies. No
geographic limitations.

Fund Consultants, Inc.
One Richmond Square
Providence, RI 02906
(401) 751-4300
Firm plans, manages, advises and assists national and international
charitable organizations to raise private/public funds in capital and
annual giving campaigns. No geographic limitations.

J. C. Geever, Inc.
417 Canal Street
New York, NY 10013
(212) 925-5800
Fund-raising, development and management services provided for the
entire spectrum of nonprofit agencies. Campaign services include:
feasibility studies; pre-campaign planning; leadership development;
individual, corporate, and foundation prospect research; grant proposals;
solicitor and volunteer training; creative materials development and
cultivation events. No geographic limitations.

Goodale Associates
3 West 51st Street, Suite 601

New York, NY 10019
(212) 586-1466
A fund-raising consulting firm serving the boards of trustees and
development offices of a variety of nonprofit organizations, independent
schools, colleges and universities. Emphasis on: feasibility studies and
fund-raising audits; capital campaigns; major donor programs; and
annual fund-raising campaigns. No geographic limitations.

John Grenzebach & Associates, Inc.
211 West Wacker Drive, Suite 500
Chicago, IL 60606
(312) 372-4040
Counsel in philanthropic planning and management; feasibility/planning
studies; resident campaign management and campaign consultation;
program audit and planning services, alumni program audit and counsel;
full range of high technology consultation including data processing,
office automation, and computerized prospect screening; executive
search; and specialized writing, market research and public relations
services. Serves entire United States.

The Bill Heim Company
133 East College Street
Granville, OH 43023
(614) 587-2137
Management and fund-raising counsel for trustees, presidents, vice
presidents, executive directors, and directors of development. Serves
private and public colleges and universities, independent schools,
hospitals, historical and historic preservation societies, chambers of
commerce, sports and athletic organizations, and professional and
specialized business associations. Serves entire United States.

IDC
Corporate Headquarters
1260 Broad Street
Bloomfield, NJ 07003
(201) 338-6300
Creators of PHONE/MAIL® brand telecommunications program for
educational, medical, and cultural institutions.

Ketchum, Inc.
1030 Fifth Avenue
Pittsburgh, PA 15219
(412) 281-1481
Direction of fund-raising campaigns, planning studies, internal and
external surveys, and fund-raising counsel for: educational institutions;
health care institutions; youth agencies; churches and temples and other
church-related institutions; cultural organizations; service organizations;
United Ways; and other gift-supported institutions. Counsel in annual
and planned giving programs.

Marts & Lundy, Inc.
1280 Wall Street West

Lyndhurst, NJ 07071
(201) 460-1660
Full range of services and techniques—full-time resident management or
part-time counseling with client staff— including studies,
ELECTRONIC SCREENING Prospect Identification Process, prospect
research, direction of capital fund-raising programs, counseling on
development programs, annual funds, writing services and training of
new development officers. No geographic limitations.

The Martin J. Moran Company, Inc.
One Penn Plaza
Suite 2134
New York, NY 10119
(212) 736-9550
A full-service firm providing both personal visitation and direct mail
programs to raise funds for dioceses, churches, hospitals and health
agencies, private schools, colleges and universities, religious
communities, retreat houses, homes for aged, social and cultural
agencies. Serves entire United States, Canada, Ireland, Great Britain,
Europe and Latin America.

Newtel Associates, Inc.
172 Lincoln Street
Worcester, MA 01605
(617) 791-8403
Professional counsel for fund-raising feasibility and planning studies and
management of capital fund drives. Services for nonprofit organizations,
particularly private schools and colleges, hospital and health agencies,
social service institutions and cultural organizations. Serves New
England area exclusively.

Sumner Rahr & Company, Inc.
One North LaSalle Street, Suite 3600
Chicago, IL 60602
(312) 899-0977
Institutional planning, marketing, fund-raising counsel and program
management. Serves colleges and universities, secondary schools,
hospitals and health agencies, cultural and social service agencies and
other not-for-profit institutions.

Arthur D. Raybin Associates, Inc.
P.O. Box 67
Chappaqua, NY 10514
(914) 238-8157
Fund-raising and strategic planning counseling for colleges, independent
schools, cultural organizations, social service agencies, hospitals, and
other gift-supported institutions. No geographic limitations.

Ruotolo Associates
50 East Palisade Avenue, Suite 304/306
Englewood, NJ 07631
(201) 568-3898

Provides professional fund-raising/development and public relations counsel to nonprofit organizations and institutions throughout the United States and Caribbean.

Robert F. Semple Associates
One Edgewood Avenue
Nutley, NJ 07110
(201) 284-0444
Fund-raising counsel for annual and capital campaigns; planning studies, public attitude surveys and geo-demographic mapping, training workshops for board and staff; executive recruitment. Serves all gift-supported organizations and institutions. Serves United States, Latin America and Caribbean.

Staley/Robeson/Ryan/St. Lawrence, Inc.
388 Westchester Avenue
Port Chester, NY 10573
(914) 939-3167
Services include management of capital fund-raising campaigns, campaign feasibility studies, counseling for annual fund and deferred giving programs, institutional planning, staff training and recruitment, records and research system analysis, evaluation of ongoing development and public relations programs, and writing and design services. No geographical limitations.

Ward, Dreshman & Reinhardt, Inc.
6660 North High Street
P.O. Box 448
Worthington, OH 43085
(614) 888-5376
Fund-raising direction for church and church related institutions and causes. Emphasis also on hospitals and other health agencies, colleges and universities, secondary schools, youth agencies, Red Cross and blood banks, art centers, symphony orchestras, chambers of commerce, united funds and museums, historical societies and industrial developments. Feasibility studies, leader cultivation programs, and fund-raising counseling. Full range of service in planned giving and endowment building.

Milton Hood Ward & Co., Inc.
The Waldorf-Astoria
301 Park Avenue, Suite 1875
New York, NY 10022
(212) 753-7680
Capital and budget campaigns for hospitals, colleges, secondary schools, homes, the arts, "Y"'s, JCCs, and synagogues. Serves entire United States and Canada.

Note: There are a number of firms that serve a national and international group of clients—some of the firms are actually larger than the AAFRC. And most of these operate under a code of principles and ethics as stringent as those of the AAFRC.

THE TRUST FOR PHILANTHROPY

In 1985, the American Association of Fund-Raising Counsel (AAFRC) established the Trust for Philanthropy. Its purpose is to advance understanding of philanthropy and its contribution to the American people. The trust conducts symposia, undertakes research, and publishes the highly recognized and reputable *Annual Report on Philanthropic Giving in the USA*. The trust is a grant-making foundation as well as a catalyst for initiating programs undertaken by other agencies.

The trust is responsible for having introduced philanthropy into the curricula of 16 colleges and universities. It is a step toward the larger goal of including philanthropy in all university and college curricula.

It commissioned an in-depth study of critical issues affecting philanthropy, to be published in book form.

The trust's initial funding of $200,000 was contributed by AAFRC member-firms. Since then, more than $600,000 has been raised in gifts and pledges. Maurice G. Gurin is the current Chairman of the trust. **For more information: American Association of Fund-Raising Counsel Trust for Philanthropy, 25 West 43rd Street, New York, NY 10036   (212) 354-5799.**

THE END OF AN ERA...THE START OF AN ERA

When John J. Schwartz retired in 1987 as President of the American Association of Fund-Raising Counsel, it marked a major milestone—fundraising had truly come of age. Mr. Schwartz served with great distinction as Chief Executive Officer of the AAFRC for twenty-one years.

During his tenure, the organization became one of the nation's most significant voices for philanthropy. It also became a major force for overseeing the ethical standards of fundraising firms.

He has been privileged to work closely with some of the giants in the field: John Price Jones, Carlton Ketchum, Dr. Arnaud C. Marts, Robert F. Duncan, David M. Church, Harold J. Seymour, and Basil O'Connor. Schwartz joins this elite group as one of the field's top people.

He begins a new career as consultant to the Indiana University Center on Philanthropy, and as President of National Philanthropy Day.

The American Association of Fund-Raising Council completed a one-year search in April, 1988—naming JoAnne Hayes as the new President of the organization. Ms. Hayes leaves her post as

President of Women & Foundations to accept her new position.

Ms. Hayes is 54 years old, and brings to her position major experience and background in association and philanthropic work. She heads the AAFRC at a time when the group is developing major long-range plans to assure its mission and increase its work with state legislatures on laws affecting fundraising. The group is also considering the development of a formal certification program for fundraising consultants.

The AAFRC represents many of the large consulting firms in the fundraising field. Ms. Hayes will become one of the most prominent and visible women in fundraising and as president, will be spokesperson for the field.

PEROT WANTS HIS MONEY BACK

H. Ross Perot has a great deal of money. And he gives a great deal away. Now he wants some of it back!

Several years ago, Perot donated $2 million and pledged $6 million more to develop an arboretum and botanical exhibit at a Dallas park.

Voters approved a bond issue to raise additional money for the facility. The problem is, few bonds were sold. This was the result of a depleted and sagging Texas economy.

Perot decided that the arboretum would never become a world-class facility. For that reason, he wanted to withdraw his gift.

"We can't afford to spend money on things like this now," he said. "There are no villains. It's the economic period we're going through."

Officials at the Dallas Arboretum and Botanical Society said that Perot's contribution has not been spent. The Board would meet to decide whether or not to return it. As of now, the decision has not been made.

Perot said if the money is returned, he will give it away again to worthy people.

EXTRAORDINARY SUCCESS IN RESPONSE MAIL PROGRAM

In direct mail programs for local Animal Welfare agencies, one firm dominates the field—Grizzard Advertising of Atlanta, Georgia. They have an outstanding record. Of particular interest; if Grizzard undertakes a project, the firm will write off the difference between the actual cost of the mailings and the direct attributable income should there be a short-fall in the results. For more information: (404) 622-1501.

The results from 34 local Animal Welfare Agency appeal mailings follow.

RESULTS ACHIEVED FROM LOCAL ANIMAL WELFARE AGENCY FUND APPEAL MAILINGS

ANIMAL HUMANE ASS'N. OF N.M.
Albuquerque, New Mexico
(Beginning Base of 1,423 Contributors; Initial Prospect Mailing of 50,000 Pieces....
Increased to 65,000 in 1982...
Increased to 70,000 in 1986)

	YEAR ONE	YEAR TWO	YEAR THREE	YEAR FOUR	YEAR FIVE	YEAR SIX	YEAR SEVEN	YEAR EIGHT
	1978	1979	1980	1981	1982	1983	1984	1985
Gross:	$29,431	$39,048	$49,991	$55,255	$68,543	$74,922	$75,811	$84,801
Profit:	$15,023	$23,228	$32,670	$35,817	$43,147	$51,039	$52,740	$61,458

	YEAR NINE	YEAR TEN
	1986	1987
Gross:	$89,224	$94,849
Profit:	$63,461	$66,695

ANIMAL H.S. OF HENNEPIN COUNTY
Minneapolis, Minnesota
(Beginning Base of 7,691 Contributors; Initial Prospect Mailing of 237,000 Pieces....
Increased to 240,000 in 1987)

	YEAR ONE	YEAR TWO	YEAR THREE	YEAR FOUR	YEAR FIVE	YEAR SIX
	1982–83	1983–84	1984–85	1985–86	1986–87	1987–88
Gross:	$198,065	$192,287	$200,565	$235,857	$269,972	$256,812
Profit:	$131,637	$128,457	$134,586	$165,197	$185,001	$165,838

ANIMAL PROTECTIVE LEAGUE
Cleveland, Ohio
(Beginning Base of 1,662 Contributors; Initial Prospect Mailing of 200,000 Pieces....
Increased to 300,000 in 1983...
Increased to 343,000 in 1984...
Decreased to 300,000 in 1985)

	YEAR ONE	YEAR TWO	YEAR THREE	YEAR FOUR	YEAR FIVE	YEAR SIX	YEAR SEVEN	YEAR EIGHT
	1980	1981	1982	1983	1984	1985	1986	1987
Gross:	$101,270	$116,004	$142,800	$205,805	$222,696	$249,969	$264,478	$268,253
Profit:	$57,802	$66,203	$82,041	$124,422	$131,222	$161,890	$170,871	$167,869

ANIMAL RESCUE LEAGUE OF IOWA, INC.
Des Moines, Iowa
(Beginning base of 817 Contributors; Initial Prospect Mailing of 82,000 Pieces)

	YEAR ONE
	1987–88
Gross:	$41,993
Profit:	$16,432

ANIMAL RESCUE LEAGUE OF WESTERN PENNSYLVANIA
Pittsburgh, Pennsylvania
(Beginning Base of 2,703 Contributors; Initial Prospect Mailing of 200,000 Pieces....
Increased to 250,000 in 1984)

	YEAR ONE	YEAR TWO	YEAR THREE	YEAR FOUR	YEAR FIVE
	1983	1984	1985	1986	1987
Gross:	$112,482	$129,352	$151,751	$182,447	$198,588
Profit:	$60,485	$65,634	$83,988	$106,876	$117,009

THE ARLINGTON HUMANE SOCIETY
Arlington, Texas
(Beginning Base of 1,638 Contributors; Initial Prospect Mailing of 100,000 Pieces... Decreased to 50,000 in 1988)

	1987-88
Gross:	$ 15,942
Profit:	$-0-

ATLANTA HUMANE SOCIETY
Atlanta, Georgia
(Beginning Base of 6,061 Contributors; Initial Prospect Mailing of 100,000 Pieces... Increased Over a Several Year Period to Current 280,000 Pieces)

	1975-76	1976-77	1977-78	1978-79	1979-80	1980-81	1981-82	1982-83
Gross:	$136,496	$118,795	$127,247	$144,569	$139,018	$130,223	$150,502	$168,752
Profit:	$110,016	$ 87,955	$ 96,434	$111,992	$104,075	$ 93,546	$102,193	$112,414

	YEAR NINE 1983-84	YEAR TEN 1984-85	YEAR ELEVEN 1985-86	YEAR TWELVE 1986-87	YEAR THIRTEEN 1987-88
Gross:	$178,929	$180,811	$183,630	$207,046	$214,928
Profit:	$122,398	$122,149	$122,133	$135,454	$122,029

Capital fund raising campaigns in 1977–78 to rebuild a major retaining wall that collapsed and in 1979–1982 for construction of a $500,000 clinic facility had a negative impact on direct mail results during those periods. A third capital fund raising campaign with a goal of $2,300,000 + for construction of a new shelter and administrative offices was implemented in the fall of 1984 and undoubtedly had a negative impact on direct mail results in subsequent years.

BIDE-A-WEE HOME ASSOCIATION
New York, New York
(Beginning Base of 24,976 Contributors; Initial Prospect Mailing of 350,000 Pieces... Increased to 425,000 in 1988)

	1987-88
Gross:	$346,223
Profit:	$188,074

BOULDER COUNTY HUMANE SOCIETY
Boulder, Colorado
(Beginning Base of 730 Contributors; Initial Prospect Mailing of 55,017 Pieces)

	1984-85	1985-86
Gross:	$ 31,815	$ 30,989
Profit:	$13,332	$19,523

COLORADO HUMANE SOCIETY
Henderson, Colorado
(Beginning Base of 700 Contributors; Initial Prospect Mailing of 350,000 Pieces)

	1987-88
Gross:	$93,534
Profit:	$ -0-

Grizzard Advertising Program Implemented Fall, 1987

CONNECTICUT HUMANE SOCIETY
Hartford, Connecticut
(Beginning Base of 12,261 Contributors; Initial Prospect Mailing of 200,000 Pieces . . . Increased to 400,000 in 1985 . . . Decreased to 200,000 in 1986)

	1982	1983	1984	1985	1986	1987
Gross:	$103,666	$138,460	$155,126	$206,798	$202,950	$205,977
Profit:	$ 40,699	$ 80,323	$ 98,548	$104,318	$135,424	$133,198

DENVER DUMB FRIENDS LEAGUE
Denver, Colorado
(NO Beginning Contributor Base; Initial Prospect Mailing of 200,000 Pieces . . . Increased to 275,000 in 1983)

	1981	1982	1983	1984	1985*	1986	1987
Gross:	$ 93,289	$180,577	$286,553	$307,912	$319,805	$312,400	$286,590
Profit:	$ 50,199	$124,894	$215,058	$234,767	$240,252	$217,619	$184,646

*The names of donors of $100 or more were deleted from the League's donor file effective with the spring, 1985 mailing cycle. These contributors are receiving special handling internally at the Denver Dumb Friends League but the deletion of this group of major donors from the file has understandably had an adverse impact on the response to the direct mail appeals. An additional negative impact on donations has resulted from the severely depressed economy in the Denver area for the past several years. A "January" test mailing was released in late December of 1985 in an effort to determine the potential profitability of adding a fourth mailing cycle to the mailing schedule. The January mailing proved to be very productive and has become a permanent part of the League's program.

GREATER ANOKA COUNTY HUMANE SOCIETY
Anoka, Minnesota
(Beginning Base of 525 Contributors; Initial Prospect Mailing of 47,000 Pieces . . . Increased to 75,000 in 1988)

	1987–1988
Gross:	$ 13,157
Profit:	$ -0-

HAMILTON COUNTY S.P.C.A.
Cincinnati, Ohio
(Beginning Base of 3,875 Contributors; Initial Prospect Mailing of 150,000 Pieces . . . Increased to 165,000 in 1988)

	1982–83	1983–84	1984–85	1985–86	1986–87**
Gross:	$ 76,828	$ 61,435	$ 61,906	$ 70,341	$105,555
Profit:	$ 37,031	$ 20,163	$ 20,634	$ 27,087	$ 52,243

**Due to a shift in the prospecting mailing cycle from fall to year-end, the results of four contributor mailing cycles (rather than three in prior years) are included in the 1986–1987 fund year computations.

HOUSTON-FT. BEND S.P.C.A.
Houston, Texas
(Beginning Base of 1,119 Contributors; Initial Prospect Mailing of 200,000 Pieces . . . Increased to 330,000 in 1982 . . . Increased to 450,000 in 1985)

	1979–80	1980–81	1981–82	1982–83	1983–84	1984–85	1985–86*	1986–87*
Gross:	$116,739	$131,431	$176,485	$228,444	$263,806	$282,467	$299,527	$288,296
Profit:	$ 74,624	$ 84,880	$121,260	$143,163	$180,079	$193,743	$184,650	$158,208

*The severe impact on the Houston area economy resulted in a decrease in direct mail donations during the 1985–1986 and 1986–1987 fund years.

THE HUMANE SOCIETY
Grand Rapids, Michigan
(Beginning Base of 3,494 Contributors; Initial Prospect Mailing of 115,000 Pieces...Increased to 165,000 in 1986...Decreased to 126,000 in 1988...Increased to 137,000 in 1989)

	1982–83	1983–84	1984–85	1985–86	1986–87
Gross:	$ 92,491	$109,341	$106,627	$113,957	$135,666
Profit:	$ 56,652	$ 72,846	$ 68,063	$ 73,741	$ 81,530

HUMANE SOCIETY FOR PREVENTION OF CRUELTY TO ANIMALS
Columbia, South Carolina
(Beginning Base of 725 Contributors; Initial Prospect Mailing of 75,000 Pieces...Increased to 85,000 in 1988)

	1982–83	1983–84	1984–85	1985–86	1986–87
Gross:	$ 48,284	$ 47,525	$ 49,578	$ 49,806	$ 57,218
Profit:	$ 23,630	$ 24,512	$ 26,190	$ 24,736	$ 29,090

H.S. OF AUSTIN & TRAVIS COUNTY
Austin, Texas
(Beginning Base of 1,490 Contributors; Initial Prospect Mailing of 115,000 Pieces...Increased to 126,000 in 1987...Increased to 140,000 in 1988)

	1983–84	1984–85	1985–86*	1986–87*
Gross:	$ 85,352	$ 99,930	$100,112	$106,235
Profit:	$ 53,872	$ 66,361	$ 62,679	$ 63,731

*The impact on the Austin area economy caused by depressed oil prices and a depressed real estate market had a negative impact on the direct mail results for the 1985–1986 and 1986–1987 fund years.

HUMANE SOCIETY OF CHARLOTTE
Charlotte, North Carolina
(Beginning Base of 378 Contributors; Initial Prospect Mailing of 85,000 Pieces...Increased to 156,000 in 1988...Decreased to 100,000 in 1989)

	1983	1984	1985	1986	1987
Gross:	$ 43,462	$ 50,036	$ 59,586	$ 79,221	$ 75,447
Profit:	$ 20,305	$ 26,531	$ 34,430	$ 48,663	$ 42,433

H.S. OF CHATHAM-SAVANNAH
Savannah, Georgia
(Beginning Base of 883 Contributors; Initial Prospect mailing of 40,000 Pieces)

	1986–87
Gross:	$ 40,247
Profit:	$ 22,888

H.S. OF GREATER AKRON
Akron, Ohio
(NO Beginning Contributor Base; Initial Prospect Mailing of 120,000 Pieces)

	1984–85	1985–86	1986–87	1987–88
Gross:	$ 43,852	$ 56,588	$ 89,363	$ 98,708
Profit:	$ 10,894	$ 21,910	$ 47,451	$ 53,128

H.S. OF GREATER MIAMI
Miami, Florida
(Beginning Base of 18,284 Contributors; Initial Prospect Mailing of 200,000 Pieces...Increased to 350,000 in 1985...Increased to 450,000 in 1987...Decreased to 350,000 in 1988)

	1981–82*	1982–83	1983–84	1984–85	1985–86	1986–87	1987–88
Gross:	$ 76,968	$112,954	$136,124	$139,049	$167,010	$205,060	$207,144
Profit:	$ 24,912	$ 48,973	$ 62,855	$ 76,880	$ 78,228	$101,305	$ 77,166

*The 1981–82 fund year results include only two contributor mailings as the client produced one contributor mailing internally during that fund year.

HUMANE SOCIETY OF MACOMB
Utica, Michigan
(Beginning Base of 979 Contributors; Initial Prospect Mailing of 212,000 Pieces... Increased to 225,000 in 1986)

	1983-84	1984-85	1985-86	1986-87
Gross:	$126,217	$144,271	$171,646	$205,383
Profit:	$ 72,705	$ 85,871	$108,980	$128,762

H.S. OF SANTA CLARA VALLEY
Santa Clara, California
(Beginning Base of 690 Contributors; Initial Prospect Mailing of 200,000 Pieces... Increased to 275,000 in 1985)

	1981-82	1982-83	1983-84	1984-85	1985-86	1986-87*
Gross:	$72,594	$102,024	$117,389	$156,987	$200,815	$286,443
Profit:	$27,553	$ 49,054	$ 64,852	$101,578	$127,142	$192,933

*Due to a shift in the prospecting mailing cycle from fall to year-end, the results of four contributor mailing cycles (rather than three in prior years) are included in the 1986–1987 fund year computations.

HUMANE SOCIETY OF S.E. TEXAS
Beaumont, Texas
(Beginning Base of 1,901 Contributors; Initial Prospect Mailing of 62,000 Pieces... Increased to 70,000 in 1988)

	1984-85	1986	1987*
Gross:	$ 60,515	$ 57,444	$ 21,951
Profit:	$ 38,058	$ 33,144	$ 15,445

*Due to the shift in the prospecting mailing cycle from spring to year-end, the results of only two contributor mailings (rather than three contributor mailings and a prospecting mailing in prior years) are included in the 1987 fund year computations. The impact on the Beaumont area economy caused by depressed oil prices had a negative impact on 1986 and 1987 direct mail donations.

KANSAS HUMANE SOCIETY
Wichita, Kansas
(Beginning Base of 450 Contributors; Initial Prospect Mailing of 75,000 Pieces... Increased to 87,000 in 1982... Decreased to 75,000 in 1985... Increased to 89,000 in 1987)

	1980-81	1981-82	1982-83	1983-84	1984-85	1985-86	1986-87	1987-88
Gross:	$ 25,871	$ 34,956	$ 50,150	$ 48,444	$ 50,439	$ 52,919	$ 55,245	$ 56,822
Profit:	$ 4,621	$ 12,624	$ 24,441	$ 22,131	$ 23,056	$ 27,781	$ 27,153	$ 23,777

LEXINGTON HUMANE SOCIETY
Lexington, Kentucky
(Beginning Base of 2,319 Contributors; Initial Prospect Mailing of 36,000 Pieces... Increased to 40,000 in 1988)

	1982	1983	1984	1985	1986	1987
Gross:	$ 42,426	$ 42,138	$ 41,694	$ 42,850	$ 48,676	$ 41,544
Profit:	$ 23,545	$ 24,427	$ 24,975	$ 25,700	$ 30,131	$ 22,557

LORAIN COUNTY ANIMAL PROTECTIVE LEAGUE
Elyria, Ohio
(Beginning Base of 1,174 Contributors; Initial Prospect Mailing of 65,000 Pieces)

	1986-87	1987-88
Gross:	$ 47,269	$ 44,146
Profit:	$ 24,335	$ 19,544

NORFOLK S.P.C.A.
Norfolk, Virginia
(Beginning Base of 905 Contributors; Initial Prospect Mailing of 100,000 Pieces... Increased to 128,000 in 1987)

	1979–80	1980–81	1981–82	1982–83	1983–84	1984–85	1985–86	1986–87
Gross:	$ 43,751	$ 46,292	$ 56,955	$ 59,583	$ 67,888	$ 68,769	$ 74,135	$ 75,284
Profit:	$ 16,248	$ 17,204	$ 24,937	$ 28,225	$ 35,760	$ 36,176	$ 39,659	$ 37,168

RIVERSIDE HUMANE S.P.C.A.
Riverside, California
(Beginning Base of 571 Contributors; Initial Prospect Mailing of 200,000 Pieces... Decreased to 100,000 in 1982... Increased to 140,000 in 1986... Increased to 150,000 in 1988)

	1981–82	1982–83	1983–84	1984–85	1985–86	1986–87	1987*
Gross:	$ 36,032	$ 39,406	$ 38,327	$ 46,270	$ 54,148	$ 64,024	$ 31,612
Profit:	$ -0-	$ 8,846	$ 9,195	$ 16,475	$ 23,176	$ 19,774	$ 24,401

*Due to a shift in the prospecting mailing cycle from fall to spring, the results of only two contributor mailing cycles (rather than three contributor mailing cycles and one prospect mailing cycle in prior years) are included in the 1987 fund year computations.

ST. CROIX ANIMAL SHELTER
Afton, Minnesota
(Beginning Base of 894 Contributors; Initial Prospect Mailing of 62,000 Pieces... Increased to 70,000 in 1987)

	1983–84	1984–85	1985–86	1986–87
Gross:	$ 35,319	$ 37,707	$ 40,850	$ 55,570
Profit:	$ 14,591	$ 16,224	$ 17,615	$ 29,838

SAN DIEGO HUMANE SOCIETY
San Diego, California
(Beginning Base of 2,127 Contributors; Initial Prospect Mailing of 200,000 Pieces... Increased to 250,000 in 1984... Increased to 325,000 in 1986... Increased to 400,000 in 1987... Decreased to 350,000 in 1988)

	1982–83	1983–84	1984–85	1985–86	1986–87	1987–88
Gross:	$249,759	$190,955	$274,128	$271,214	$420,304	$305,991
Profit:	$194,693	$136,848	$202,765	$197,586	$316,581	$181,008

Two gifts totalling $70,000 were received from a single donor (who was previously unidentified) during the 1982–1983 fund year; two gifts totalling $30,000 were received during the 1983–1984 fund year; three gifts totalling $55,000 were received during the 1984–1985 fund year; five gifts totalling $29,000 were received during the 1985–1986 fund year; and two gifts totalling $125,000 were received during the 1986–1987 fund year. These unusually large "windfall" gifts distorted the income and profit figures for all five of the fund years summarized above.

SANTA CRUZ S.P.C.A.
Santa Cruz, California
(Beginning Base of 449 Contributors; Initial Prospect Mailing of 38,000 Pieces... Increased to 50,000 in 1988)

	1984–85	1985–86	1986–87
Gross:	$ 26,452	$ 30,999	$ 39,236
Profit:	$ 11,286	$ 14,560	$ 20,530

TOLEDO HUMANE SOCIETY
Toledo, Ohio
(Beginning Base of 4,705 Contributors; Initial Prospect Mailing of 132,000 Pieces)

	1987–88
Gross:	$ 71,494
Profit:	$ 23,923

EDUCATIONAL
INSTITUTIONS

THE EARLY COLLEGE YEARS

The 1920s ushered in the true beginning of college and university campaigning as we know it today. At that time, the fundraising and public relations firm of John Price Jones Corp. dominated the field. Between 1919 and 1925, the company managed 14 college and university campaigns which raised nearly $68 million. Of special note is that the average cost of raising the money was 2.34 percent. These earliest university and college campaigns follow.

Institution	Amount sought	Amount obtained	Percent-age of goal
Harvard University	$15,250,000	$13,931,780.69	90.7
Northwestern University	5,050,000	9,599,243.27	190.0
Hampton and Tuskegee	5,000,000	9,269,840.49	185.4
University of Chicago	17,500,000	8,664,797.50	49.3
University of Pennsylvania	5,000,000	5,344,366.00	106.8
Johns Hopkins University and Hospital	10,890,000	4,505,395.45	42.0
Smith College	4,000,000	4,021,893.91	100.5
Wellesley College	2,700,000	2,740,779.10	101.5
Lehigh University	4,000,000	2,625,000.00	65.6
Bryn Mawr College	2,000,000	2,204,412.39	110.0
Pennsylvania State College	2,000,000	1,612,442.60	80.6
Ohio State University	1,000,000	1,040,000.00	104.0
Trinity College	1,500,000	1,030,000.00	68.6
Tufts College	750,000	700,000.00	93.3

Source: *FUND RAISING IN THE UNITED STATES*, Scott M. Cutlip.

NEW DATA AVAILABLE ON SUPPORT FOR WOMEN'S COLLEGES

A study released in 1988 by the Women's College Coalition demonstrated that alumni of women's colleges give in greater numbers and in greater amounts than women alumni of co-educational colleges. This is in contrast to past years, when women had less discretion over individual and family resources. Today, the study indicated, women are more aware of the financial needs of women's colleges.

The study noted that bequests had quadrupled at women's colleges in the past ten years, and that giving to women's colleges had more than tripled for the same period.

Copies of the study cost $9.50 each and are available from: Women's College Coalition, Suite #1001, 1101 17th Street, N.W., Washington, DC 20036.

MATCHING GIFTS BY TYPE OF INSTITUTION, 1986–87

Matching-gift programs send more money to private-sector institutions than to public, and are particularly important to the private baccalaureate institutions, where such gifts make up 27 percent of all direct corporate gifts. Support received from employee matching-gift programs has increased from $4.2 million to $129 million since 1966.

Type of Institution	Matching Gifts				
	Total Received (000)	As Percent of Corporate Support	Number of Colleges Reporting	Average per Institution	Average Match*
Doctoral					
Private (56)	$ 35,527	7.0	52	$683,213	$299
Public (98)	30,907	5.2	88	351,212	224
Comprehensive					
Private (133)	17,385	11.8	126	137,977	286
Public (130)	3,924	5.5	114	34,419	161
General Baccalaureate					
Private (402)	32,913	27.4	390	84,392	320
Public (40)	570	8.1	35	16,276	236
Specialized					
Private (125)	5,094	9.1	115	44,293	273
Public (21)	2,055	4.7	16	128,416	280
Total Four-Year					
Private (716)	$ 90,919	10.9	683	$133,117	$302
Public (289)	37,456	5.2	253	148,043	218
Two-Year					
Private (30)	411	11.9	29	14,194	181
Public (124)	255	1.4	79	3,238	204
All Private (746)	$ 91,330	10.9	712	$128,273	$301
All Public (413)	37,711	5.1	332	113,586	218
Grand Total (1,159)	$129,041	8.2	1,044	$123,602	$270

(Numbers in parentheses show the number of colleges and universities reporting corporate support.)
*Because many companies match gifts at ratio of $2 or sometimes $3 for every employee dollar, the average match is estimated to be about one third more than the employee's gift.

Source: Council For Aid to Education (CFAE)

COUNCIL FOR ADVANCEMENT AND SUPPORT OF EDUCATION

The most highly recognized and respected name in educational philanthropy is CASE—the Council for Advancement and Support of Education.

In 1974, the American Alumni Council (founded in 1913) and the American College Public Relations Association (founded in 1917) merged to become CASE.

Nearly 3,000 colleges, universities, and independent elementary and secondary schools make up the membership. More institutions belong to it than any other not-for-profit educational association.

CASE is organized into eight geographic districts around the country, with a Board of Trustees of up to 40 members. The board employs the President, who is supported by a staff of 60 men and women.

Gary H. Quehl is President of CASE. Before that, he served for 12 years as President of the Council of Independent Colleges. His telephone number is: (202) 328-5925.

CASE produces a Membership Directory which is distributed free to members. Non-members may purchase a copy by calling (202) 328-5973.

To help member institutions fill professional staff vacancies and to help individuals find suitable positions, CASE publishes a monthly newsletter. Member institutions are encouraged to submit their position announcements free of charge. For information about the placement services: (202) 328-5958.

For more information: the Council for Advancement and Supportive Education, 11 DuPont Circle, Suite #400, Washington, DC 20036 (202) 328-5900.

CASE OFFICES

CASE Main Number
                        (202) 328-5900

Dial (202) 328- and the number below to reach the departments/individuals listed.

Office of the President

Gary H. Quehl, President   5925
Charles Michael Helmken,
    Special Assistant to the
    President   5916

Liaisons to Two-year Institutions:
Jefferson G. Burnett,
    Executive Assistant to the
    President   5925
Sarah Spradlin, Program
    Assistant   5966

Recognition Awards Program:
Joanne Catlett, Coordinator 5915

Resource Development:
Anne Carman, Vice
    President   5976

Professional Services:
*Conferences, Workshops,
Matching Gifts*

Richard A. Edwards, Senior
    Vice President   5938

*Alumni Administration
Programs:*
Paul Chewning, Vice
    President   5924

172

Educational Fund Raising
Programs:
**Mary Joan McCarthy, Interim
Vice President** 5950
Norma Walker, Director 5935

Institutional Relations,
Periodicals, and Publications
Programs:
**Nancy S. Raley, Vice
President** 5940

Management Programs:
**Vivienne M. Lee, Vice
President** 5922

Matching Gift Programs:
Elizabeth Hall, Director 5934

Student Recruitment Programs:
Joan Paschal, Director 5921

**Institutional, Senior, and
Independent School Services**

**Eric Wentworth, Senior Vice
President** 5920

CASE on Your Campus:
Cary Bowdich, Director 5975

Independent School Programs:
**Carol Ramsey, Vice
President** 5971

Public Affairs

**Ron Eisenberg, Senior Vice
President** 5981

Communications/Media
Relations:
Sarah Hardesty, Director 5983

Public Affairs Programs:
Donna Orem, Director 5917

Operations

**Virginia Carter Smith, Senior
Vice President** 5930

Assembly:
**Sandra Kidd, Executive
Assistant** 5931

CURRENTS:
**Karla Taylor, Executive
Editor** 5948

Marketing and Publications:
Julie Landes, Director 5929

District Services:
Cynthia Snyder, Director 5918

Membership Services:
Anne Randazzo, Manager 5936

Reference Center:
Bob Vittel, Manager 5942

Research:
Judy Grace, Director 5985

**Financial and Administrative
Services**

**Wilson (Bill) Korpi, Chief
Financial Officer and
Controller** 5947

Accounting Services:
Margie Joyner 5937

To order CASE books, CURRENTS
issues, and matching gift
materials, call the CASE
Publications Order Department
at (703) 823-6966.

ORGANIZATIONS WITH IRS
TAX-EXEMPT STATUS

Currently, the Internal Revenue Service (IRS) has listed 881,
019 organizations as having tax-exempt status. This general category includes all organizations that are not established to make a
profit and that are recognized by the IRS to be exempt from federal
income taxes. While this category includes organizations with
501(c)(3) charitable tax-exempt status, it also includes trade associa-

tions, labor unions, political parties, public interest groups, and advocacy groups.

As of January 1988, a total of 400,160 organizations have been granted 501(c)(3) status as charitable, educational, or religious organizations. (The actual number is higher since religious organizations are free not to report, and other organizations, such as the Red Cross, are listed only once, despite their local units.) Eligibility for *charitable* status is much more narrow than eligibility for general 501(c)(3) status. Charitable organizations are defined as those organized and operated for purposes beneficial to the public interest.

1989 DEFERRED MAINTENANCE DEFICIT A "TICKING TIME BOMB" FOR COLLEGES AND UNIVERSITIES

This year, colleges and universities in the United States face $20 billion in necessary repairs to their facilities and campus. Some situations are considered desperate.

The data and the projected funding need are the results of a study sponsored by the National Association of College and University Business Officers and the Association of Physical Plant Administrators.

The report—titled "The Decaying American Campus: A Ticking Time Bomb"—indicates that total capital renewal and replacements costs could reach as much as $70 billion.

The study shows that:

1. The most common construction and renovation priorities for colleges and universities are laboratories, classrooms, and libraries.

2. Based on this year's priority needs and funding, colleges and universities will defer $4 of needed maintenance for every dollar that is spent.

3. Of the $20 billion which is urgently needed to repair or replace buildings, only $1.2 billion is actually allocated.

4. The older the campus and the institution, the lower the level of routine maintenance funding, and the higher the level of deferred maintenance.

The study imposes a great responsibility on college and university trustees for careful strategic planning and a program of philanthropy which would require quantum increases for most institutions. Without question, fundraising will be a more significant issue on most of the nation's campuses in 1989 than ever before.

GIVING TO SEVENTH-DAY ADVENTIST COLLEGES AND UNIVERSITIES

Institution	Total Support (Dollars)	Alumni Giving (Dollars)	Property, Buildings & Equipment (Dollars)	Enrollment
1) Andrews University Berrien Springs, MI	8,683,011	375,936	1,856,123	3,053
2) Oakwood College Huntsville, AL	4,431,478	200,000	350,000	1,003
3) Pacific Union College Angwin, CA	3,627,495	795,273	760,172	1,499
4) Walla Walla College College Place, WA	2,902,214	544,659	774,153	1,456
5) Columbia Union College Takoma Park, MD	2,772,808	289,955	218,588	1,031
6) Southern College of Seventh-Day Adventists Collegedale, TN	2,210,341	287,543	107,255	1,325
7) Atlantic Union South Lancaster, MO	2,036,229	216,209	373,749	750
8) Union College Lincoln, NE	2,030,342	602,064	198,742	677
9) Southwestern Adventist Keene, TX	1,177,312	342,605	52,018	795
10) Antillian College Mayaguez, PR	107,448	18,173	98,998	728

Source: Council for Aid to Education (CFAE)

AN EXTRAORDINARY GROUP OF MEN

The Christian Brothers are a Roman Catholic congregation. They are laymen who do not aspire to become priests but do take vows of poverty, chastity, obedience, and service to others through education.

In the United States, they operate seven colleges. In addition, they operate and staff over 100 elementary and high schools, teacher education schools, orphan and reform schools, military institutes, and institutions dedicated to the development of professional and technical services.

The official name for the Christian Brothers is the Congregation of the Brothers of the Christian Schools. It was founded in 1681 by a French priest, Saint John Baptist De La Salle. Much of what we know today as education was instituted by De La Salle: the grading of students according to ability and achievement, the simultaneous method of teaching, and teaching in the vernacular, not in Latin.

The Brothers are engaged in all phases of education through-out the world, in over 80 countries. An extraordinary group, the Christian Brothers are the largest non-clerical, male religious group in the Catholic Church, numbering over 9,000. Their slogan is: "The sign of God is that we will be led where we did not plan to go."

THE CHRISTIAN BROTHERS' COLLEGES ALUMNI GIVING

Institution	Alumni Giving (Dollars)	Total no. of Alumni	Total Support (Dollars)
1) Manhattan College Bronx, NY	1,900,000	31,000	3,700,000
2) Saint Mary's College Moraga, CA	1,380,052	10,967	6,885,459
3) La Salle College Philadelphia, PA	943,189	29,156	1,809,385
4) Saint Mary's College Winona, MN	529,128	10,993	1,456,526
5) Christian Brothers College Memphis, TN	115,505	4,810	4,049,281
6) Lewis University Romeoville, IL	84,958	12,000	771,356

Figures were unavailable for the College of Santa Fe

Source: Council For Aid to Education (CFAE) and other research

THE CHRISTIAN BROTHERS' COLLEGES TOTAL CONTRIBUTED SUPPORT

Institution	Total Dollars
1) Saint Mary's College Moraga, CA	$6,885,459
2) Christian Brothers College Memphis, TN	$4,049,281
3) Manhattan College Bronx, NY	$3,700,000
4) La Salle College Philadelphia, PA	$1,809,385
5) Saint Mary's College Winona, MN	$1,456,526
6) Lewis University Romeoville, IL	$ 771,356

Figures were unavailable for the College of Santa Fe

Source: Council For Aid to Education (CFAE) and other research.

I feel that the greatest reward for doing is the opportunity to do more.
Jonas Salk

THE CHRISTIAN BROTHERS' COLLEGES PER CAPITA ALUMNI GIVING

Institution	Per Capita Alumni Support (Dollars)	Total no. of Alumni	Total Support (Dollars)
1) Saint Mary's College Moraga, CA	125.84	10,967	6,885,459
2) Manhattan College Bronx, NY	61.29	31,000	3,700,000
3) Saint Mary's College Winona, MN	48.13	10,993	1,456,526
4) La Salle College Philadelphia, PA	32.35	29,156	1,809,385
5) Christian Brothers College Memphis, TN	24.01	4,810	4,049,281
6) Lewis University Romeoville, IL	7.08	12,000	771,356

Figures were unavailable for the College of Santa Fe

Source: Council for Aid to Education (CFAE) and other research.

ALUMNI GIFTS FOR CURRENT OPERATIONS FOR INSTITUTIONS REPORTING IN BOTH 1985–86 AND 1986–87*

Most institutions conduct annual campaigns to raise funds for ongoing operations. This table shows alumni gifts for support of current operations in both 1985–86 and 1986–87. The average gift ranged from $256 for the private doctoral institutions to $28 for the public two-year colleges.

Type of Institution	1985–86			1986–87		
	Number	Amount (000)	Average	Number	Amount (000)	Average
Doctoral	1,303,905	$230,556	$177	1,590,814	$297,640	$187
Private	641,057	128,806	201	642,741	164,666	256
Public	662,848	101,750	154	948,073	132,974	140
Comprehensive	621,867	71,814	115	742,929	89,800	121
Private	411,199	61,070	149	444,783	72,701	163
Public	210,668	10,744	51	298,146	17,099	57
General Baccalaureate	813,195	120,335	148	916,984	157,422	172
Private	762,326	117,478	154	877,156	154,316	176
Public	50,869	2,857	56	39,828	3,106	78
Specialized	135,200	25,265	187	146,917	28,548	194
Private	100,072	16,131	161	112,160	17,289	154
Public	35,128	9,134	260	34,757	11,259	324
Total Four-Year	2,874,167	$447,970	$156	3,397,644	$573,410	$169
Private	1,914,654	323,485	169	2,076,840	408,972	197
Public	959,513	124,485	130	1,320,804	164,438	124
Two-Year	50,347	1,734	34	36,367	2,225	61
Private	20,029	1,415	71	21,783	1,818	83
Public	30,318	319	11	14,584	407	28
Grand Total	2,924,514	$449,704	$154	3,434,011	$575,635	$168
Private	1,934,683	324,900	168	2,098,623	410,790	196
Public	989,831	124,804	126	1,335,388	164,845	123

*These data reflect the amounts reported only for those institutions providing complete answers.

Source: Council For Aid to Education (CFAE)

A COMMEMORATIVE STAMP FOR PHILANTHROPY...BUT NOT QUITE YET!

Dr. Milton J. Murray conceived the idea of a commemorative stamp to honor philanthropy in 1981. For the next five years, he worked almost single-handedly for the issuance of such a stamp. He made contact with dozens of officials in the United States Postal Services through hundreds of letters and phone calls, and almost as many personal visits.

Networking began. In one of his telephone calls about the stamp, he learned of a lawyer on the West Coast who was lobbying Congress for a National Philanthropy Day. This man was Douglas Freeman, and Dr. Murray was in contact with him by early 1986. The two discussed their mutual interest in philanthropy and exchanged notes about lobbying the government.

A committee was formed to develop the plans for National Philanthropy Day. Dr. Murray was asked to be a member of that group and to direct the subcommittee for the issuance of a stamp for philanthropy.

Efforts increased. Through Dr. Murray's efforts, thousands of letters were written to the Postmaster General, senators, and representatives; a number of letters were also sent to the White House. Four different persons have served as Postmaster General in the past few years, but that has not diminished Dr. Murray's enthusiasm or interest.

A decision has not been made, but the prospects look good! The stamp has been on the agenda, for the past three years, of the Advisory Committee that determines which commemorative stamps will be issued. Even when the Committee decides in favor of a proposal, it still could be several years before the stamp is completed. But the effort continues, and with renewed vigor.

The following message was sent to the Advisory Committee in an effort to win acceptance for the stamp.

- Philanthropy is essential to a strong democratic society. For this reason, our government tax policy has always recognized and reinforced voluntary giving and financial support by individuals and corporations.

- 850,000 not-for-profit organizations in America rely on philanthropy. Together, these institutions account for approximately 10 percent of our national economy.

- Philanthropy is more important than ever in helping to meet needs.

- From 1952 to 1987, Americans gave $1 trillion to support causes in the United States and throughout the world.

- By recognizing the American tradition of philanthropy with a commemorative stamp, the United States Postal Service will be honoring the millions of citizens and thousands of companies and foundations who give to help their community each year.

- Through joint marketing and local stamp commemorative activities, the Postal Service will be building a partnership with not-for-profit organizations in every community throughout the world. At the same time, the commemorative stamp will serve to reinforce the concept of philanthropy as an important cultural value.

INDEPENDENT SCHOOLS

Position	Median 1988 salary
Head	$60,000
President	$56,719
Business Officer	$37,422
Development Officer	$33,808
Admission Officer	$30,484
Alumni Officer	$24,700

Highest 1988 salary for president—$130,000. Lowest—$18,600.

Source: National Association of Independent Schools Fall Statistics.

COMPARISON OF 1986 TO 1988 CONTRIBUTIONS USE

	1986	1987	1988
Uses of Contributions			
Religion	$41.68	$43.61	$48.21
Education	10.08	10.84	9.78
Health	12.26	13.65	9.52
Human Services	9.13	9.84	10.49
Arts, Culture & Humanities	5.83	6.41	6.82
Public/Society Benefit	2.38	2.44	3.02
Other	7.54	15.37	16.53

*"Gain all you can,
save all you can,
give all you can."*
John Wesley (1703–1791)

*"When you stop giving
and offering something to
the rest of the world, it's time
to turn out the lights."*
George Burns (1896–)

JESUIT COLLEGES AND UNIVERSITIES
ALUMNI GIVING

Institution	Total Alumni Giving	No. of Alumni	Per Capita Alumni Giving
1) Georgetown University Washington, DC	$10,428,093	70,097	$148.77
2) Boston College Chestnut Hill, MA	6,913,574	78,008	88.63
3) College of the Holy Cross Worcester, MA	4,941,294	21,610	228.66
4) Marquette University Milwaukee, WI	4,797,934	77,445	61.95
5) St. Louis University St. Louis, MO	3,756,200	10,419	50.00
6) Fordham University Bronx, NY	3,077,442	95,809	32.12
7) Santa Clara University Santa Clara, CA	2,401,073	38,000	63.19
8) Creighton University Omaha, NE	1,752,261	32,837	53.36
9) Loyola Marymount University Los Angeles, CA	1,691,638	24,193	69.92
10) University of Detroit Detroit, MI	1,654,733	36,200	45.46
11) Loyola University of Chicago Chicago, IL	1,488,569	80,263	18.55
12) Canisius College Buffalo, NY	1,364,348	24,150	56.49
13) University of San Francisco San Francisco, CA	1,361,697	49,376	27.58
14) University of Scranton Scranton, PA	1,101,121	18,949	58.11
15) Xavier University Cincinnati, OH	1,075,087	40,963	26.25
16) St. Joseph's University Philadelphia, PA	1,022,202	24,500	41.72
17) John Carroll University Cleveland, OH	1,005,076	22,745	44.19
18) Gonzaga University Spokane, WA	958,597	15,587	61.50
19) Fairfield University Fairfield, CT	826,696	19,747	41.86
20) Loyola College Baltimore, MD	717,601	24,915	28.80
21) Seattle University Seattle, WA	596,328	23,798	25.06
22) Loyola University of New Orleans New Orleans, LA	577,611	25,823	22.37
23) St. Peter's College Jersey City, MO	507,969	16,463	30.86
24) Rockhurst College Kansas City, MO	458,846	10,064	45.59
25) Regis College Denver, CO	448,515	12,791	35.06
26) Spring Hill College Mobile, AL	411,271	7,921	51.92

27) Le Moyne College   335,434   12,381   27.09
    Syracuse, NY

Source: Council For Aid to Education (CFAE)

Note: Wheeling Jesuit College in Wheeling, West Virginia did not respond to the CFAE survey.

COLLEGE & UNIVERSITY DEVELOPMENT OFFICERS LEAD IN ANNUAL SALARY

While the average salary for hospital development officials reached $56,668 this year, those heading the development departments of higher education earned a record median salary of $64,832.

DEVELOPMENT WHERE THE MONEY IS

Sector	Avg. annual 1988 salary for chief development officer
Colleges and universities	$64,832
National health and welfare agencies	$61,900
Hospitals	$56,668
Art museums	$46,484
Independent schools	$33,808**

**Median

Source: Compiled from various surveys of the sector conducted by Brakeley, John Price Jones

MORE WOMEN IN FUNDRAISING THAN MEN

A study completed in 1988 by the National Society of Fund Raising Executives (NSFRE) shows that 52 percent of the members are women. That is an increase from 49 percent in a similar study done in 1985.

The results represent only a sampling of the 10,000 member organization—but it seems women are now dominant in the profession.

The study also found that women make less money on the average than men and receive fewer benefits, however, the margin between the two has narrowed measurably in the past few years. The study also shows that the women are generally younger than the men, and tend to work for organizations that are often lower paying, with smaller budgets.

Recently, *Cosmopolitan* listed fundraising as one of the most promising and rewarding professions for females.

TOTAL VOLUNTARY SUPPORT TO JESUIT
COLLEGES AND UNIVERSITIES

Institution	Total Support
1) Georgetown University Washington, DC	$30,515,905
2) Loyola University of Chicago Chicago, IL	29,002,966
3) St. Louis University St. Louis, MO	15,311,059
4) Marquette University Milwaukee, WI	12,798,622
5) Boston College Chestnut Hill, MA	11,794,426
6) Santa Clara University Santa Clara, CA	11,585,083
7) Loyola Marymount University Los Angeles, CA	10,912,141
8) University of San Francisco San Francisco, CA	10,297,292
9) Xavier University Cincinnati, OH	9,174,810
10) Creighton University Omaha, NE	9,164,403
11) Gonzaga University Spokane, WA	6,708,988
12) Fordham University Bronx, NY	6,629,314
13) University of Detroit Detroit, MI	6,189,003
14) College of the Holy Cross Worcester, MA	6,157,436
15) University of Scranton Scranton, PA	5,726,449
16) Seattle University Seattle, WA	5,526,449
17) John Carroll University Cleveland, OH	5,264,337
18) Canisius College Buffalo, NY	4,270,147
19) Fairfield University Fairfield, CT	4,262,287
20) Rockhurst College Kansas City, MO	3,869,906
21) Regis College Denver, CO	3,247,064
22) Loyola College of Maryland Baltimore, MD	3,093,623
23) St. Joseph's University Philadelphia, PA	3,043,386
24) Loyola University of New Orleans New Orleans, LA	2,093,938

25) St. Peter's College			1,600,127
Jersey City, MO			
26) Le Moyne College			1,418,697
Syracuse, NY			
27) Spring Hill College			959,068
Mobile, AL			

Source: Council For Aid to Education (CFAE)

Note: Wheeling Jesuit College in Wheeling, West Virginia did not respond to the CFAE survey.

COLLEGES AND UNIVERSITIES OF THE UNITED METHODIST CHURCH U.S.A.
TOP 15 IN PER CAPITA ALUMNI GIVING

Institutions	Total No. of Alumni	Per Capita Alumni Support (Dollars)	Total Support (Dollars)
1) DePauw University Greencastle, IN	27,864	316.33	12,520,267
2) Birmingham-Southern College Birmingham, AL	9,902	206.43	9,164,574
3) Willamette University Salem, OR	14,703	187.18	7,305,374
4) Millsaps College Jackson, MS	12,513	185.43	8,721,172
5) Duke University Durham, NC	74,366	177.16	73,563,708
6) University of Evansville Evansville, IN	24,642	118.40	5,280,072
7) Southern Methodist University Dallas, TX	69,072	103.11	20,860,651
8) Meharry Medical College Nashville, TN	5,252	101.30	10,973,504
9) Boston University Boston, MA	144,309	90.26	35,672,003
10) Emory University Atlanta, GA	52,214	74.62	29,508,863
11) Syracuse University Syracuse, NY	125,600	60.65	22,687,510
12) Southwestern University Georgetown, TX	9,853	42.09	5,785,281
13) University of the Pacific Stockton, CA	33,199	40.06	5,569,101
14) University of Denver Denver, CO	82,666	36.13	7,225,163
15) Drew University Madison, NJ	12,601	35.09	5,738,365

Source: Council For Aid to Education (CFAE)

> *You raise money when you ask for it*
> Irving Warner, *The Art of Fund Raising.*

GIVING TO UNITED METHODIST COLLEGES AND UNIVERSITIES

There are 105 United Methodist colleges and universities in the United States. These institutions have a collective revenue of $3 billion and collective expenditures of $2.9 billion. Private gifts make up 14-15 percent of revenue.

Source: United Methodist Board for Higher Education; Nashville, TN

COLLEGES AND UNIVERSITIES OF THE UNITED METHODIST CHURCH U.S.A. TOP 15 IN TOTAL SUPPORT

Institution	Total Support (Dollars)	Alumni Giving (Dollars)	Property, Buildings & Equipment (Dollars)	Enrollment
1) Duke University Durham, NC	73,563,708	13,174,513	7,601,100	10,434
2) Boston University Boston, MA	35,672,003	13,025,994	1,497,826	27,147
3) Emory University Atlanta, GA	29,508,863	3,896,183	7,856,469	8,791
4) Syracuse University Syracuse, NY	22,687,510	7,617,995	7,744,828	20,275
5) Southern Methodist University Dallas, TX	20,860,651	7,121,973	5,559,366	9,019
6) DePauw University Greencastle, IN	12,520,267	8,814,317	2,467,018	2,368
7) Meharry Medical College Nashville, TN	10,973,504	532,042	59,252	725
8) Birmingham-Southern College Birmingham, AL	9,164,574	2,044,075	5,178,961	1,725
9) Millsaps College Jackson, MS	8,721,172	2,320,228	NA	1,385
10) Willamette University Salem, OR	7,305,374	2,752,154	4,086,814	2,041
11) University of Denver Denver, CO	7,225,163	2,986,597	56,211	7,044
12) Southwestern University Georgetown, TX	5,785,281	414,681	1,130,144	1,119
13) Drew University Madison, NJ	5,738,365	442,205	1,372,893	5,844
14) University of the Pacific Stockton, CA	5,569,101	1,330,108	1,403,546	5,599
15) University of Evansville Evansville, IN	5,280,072	2,917,801	2,475,365	5,844

Source: Council for Aid to Education (CFAE)

I believe that every human mind
feels pleasure in doing good to another.
Thomas Jefferson

FUND RAISING INSTITUTE
MONTHLY PORTFOLIO

The *FRI Monthly Portfolio* is an eight-page monthly newsletter that specializes in providing "million-dollar" ideas to fundraising executives for virtually all types and sizes of not-for-profit causes. For many fundraisers it is *the* source of those one or two really imaginative ideas that they depend on to spark their gift programs to higher levels each year. Each issue contains an average of ten articles. They are extremely easy to read—packed with how-to facts, and short on adjectives and fluff. The writers and sources of information are almost all fundraising executives. The editor, an NSFRE Certified Fund-Raising Executive, is a nationally recognized newswriter. The *Portfolio* is sold under a no-questions-asked, money-back guarantee. And each new subscriber also receives a packet of "most valuable" articles pulled from previous issues of the Portfolio. The packet is called the "FRI Idea Pack," and it sells separately for $12.50. The *FRI Monthly Portfolio* was first published in 1962 and now has a readership of 12,000. The cost of subscription is $59 and questions can be directed to: **The FRI Monthly Portfolio, P.O. Box 365, Ambler, PA 19002.**

BAPTIST UNIVERSITIES AND COLLEGES
TOP 15 IN TOTAL SUPPORT

Institution	Total Support (Dollars)	Alumni Giving (Dollars)	Property, Buildings & Equipment (Dollars)	Enrollment
1) Wake Forest University Winston-Salem, NC	66,255,408	5,919,579	52,565,630	5,049
2) Baylor University Waco, TX	21,637,613	7,463,665	4,327,371	11,556
3) Samford University Birmingham, AL	15,643,199	548,826	2,161,089	3,835
4) Stetson University Deland, FL	11,143,068	7,714,923	4,406,215	2,841
5) Hardin-Simmons University Abilene,TX	8,155,425	4,478,857	328,928	1,804
6) University of Richmond Richmond, VA	6,804,078	3,320,934	607,287	4,705
7) Mercer University Macon, CA	6,511,333	990,820	317,599	5,773
8) Furman University Greenville, SC	6,504,003	1,774,638	951,175	2,960
9) Kalamazoo College Kalamazoo, MI	6,283,668	775,810	1,047,960	1,219
10) Union University Jackson, TN	4,918,399	975,956	495,217	1,546
11) Carson-Newman College Jefferson City, TN	4,765,161	614,038	511,781	1,681
12) Ouachita Baptist University Arkadelphia, AR	4,665,590	537,335	1,501,259	1,403
13) Mississippi College Clinton, MS	4,624,788	1,399,879	369,964	3,598
14) Campbell University Buies Creek, NC	4,250,708	731,384		3,647
15) Bethel College and Theological Seminary St. Paul, MN	4,159,980	412,626	758,795	2,144

Source: Council for Aid to Education (CFAE)

BAPTIST UNIVERSITIES AND COLLEGES
TOP 15 IN PER CAPITA ALUMNI GIVING

Institution	Total No. of Alumni	Per Capita Alumni Support (Dollars)	Total Support (Dollars)
1) Stetson University Deland, FL	20,267	380.66	11,143,068
2) Hardin-Simmons University Abilene, TX	20,164	222.12	8,155,425
3) Wake Forest University Winston-Salem, NC	34,422	171.97	66,255,408
4) University of Richmond Richmond, VA	24,508	135.50	6,804,078
5) Baylor University Waco, TX	68,011	109.74	21,637,613
6) Union University Jackson, TX	11,283	86.50	4,918,399
7) Kalamazoo College Kalamazoo, MI	10,778	71.98	6,283,668
8) Furman University Greenville, SC	24,143	73.51	6,504,003
9) Mississippi College Clinton, MS	20,113	69.60	4,624,788
10) Mercer University Macon, CA	20,377	48.62	6,511,333
11) Campbell University Buies Creek, NC	15,507	47.16	4,250,708
12) Carson-Newman College Jefferson City, TN	14,247	43.10	4,765,161
13) Ouachita Baptist University Arkadelphia, AR	15,620	34.40	4,665,590
14) Bethel College and Theological Seminary St. Paul, MN	18,272	22.58	4,159,980
15) Samford University Birmingham, AL	27,255	20.14	15,643,199

Source: Council For Aid to Education (CFAE)

501(C)(3) MONTHLY LETTER

The *501(c)(3) Monthly Letter* offers information, news and advice to not-for-profit organizations nationwide. Some of the most respected names in the not-for-profit community contribute articles on fundraising, volunteer development, membership recruitment, communications, fiscal management, taxation and legislation. The *Monthly Letter* was first published by Margaret Stewart Carr in 1985. It was purchased by Great Oaks Communication Services, Inc. in December, 1988 and is now published by them. Subscribing organizations cover the entire spectrum: arts; culture; education; environment; health; human services; international, private & community foundations; public and societal benefits; religion; and youth development. An annual subscription is $42. Circulation totals 6,500 in all 50 states & Guam. **For more information or a sample: 501(c)(3) Monthly Letter, P.O. Box 17040, Des Moines, IA 50317.**

THE 20 LUTHERAN COLLEGES AND UNIVERSITIES
REPORTING THE HIGHEST TOTAL SUPPORT

1) St. Olaf College Northfield, MN	$8,144,991
2) Valparaiso University Valparaiso, IN	6,347,005
3) Gettysburg College Gettysburg, PA	6,244,502
4) Concordia College at Moorhead Moorhead, MN	6,197,944
5) Gustavus Adolphus College St. Peter, MN	5,996,641
6) Texas Lutheran College Seguin, TX	5,145,994
7) Wittenberg University Springfield, OH	4,183,861
8) Capital University Columbus, OH	3,780,307
9) California Lutheran University Thousand Oaks, CA	3,617,308
10) Roanoke College Salem, VA	3,420,525
11) Augsburg College Minneapolis, MN	3,330,017
12) Pacific Lutheran University Tacoma, WA	3,147,651
13) Luther College Decorah, IA	3,093,308
14) Susquehanna University Selinsgrove, PA	3,087,609
15) Augustana College Rock Island, IL	2,976,361
16) Muhlenberg College Allentown, PA	2,559,160
17) Augustana College Sioux Falls, SD	2,352,137
18) Newberry College Newberry, SC	2,073,637
19) Wartburg College Waverly, IA	1,816,876
20) Dana College Blair, NE	1,739,896

Source: Council For Aid to Education (CFAE)

"It is high time the ideal of success should be replaced with the ideal of service."
Albert Einstein (1879–1955)

"The highest service we can perform for others is to help them help themselves."
Horace Mann (1796–1859)

LUTHERAN COLLEGES AND UNIVERSITIES
TOP 20 IN TOTAL ALUMNI GIVING

1) St. Olaf College Northfield, MN	$3,662,645
2) Wittenberg University Springfield, OH	2,431,499
3) Valparaiso University Valparaiso, IN	2,405,263
4) Gettysburg College Gettysburg, PA	2,048,042
5) Capital University Columbus, OH	1,320,604
6) Concordia College Moorhead, MN	1,314,884
7) Augsburg College Minneapolis, MN	1,284,887
8) Gustavus Adolphus College St. Peter, MN	1,181,285
9) Luther College Decorah, IA	1,099,252
10) Augustana College Rock Island, IL	1,080,612
11) Susquehanna University Selinsgrove, PA	829,778
12) Muhlenberg College Allentown, PA	773,823
13) Augustana College Sioux Falls, SD	735,836
14) Pacific Lutheran University Tacoma, WA	671,159
15) Thiel College Greenville, PA	546,280
16) Roanoke College Salem, VA	501,836
17) Bethany College Lindsborg, KS	463,311
18) Midland Lutheran College Fremont, NE	456,677
19) Texas Lutheran College Seguin, TX	451,317
20) Wartburg College Waverly, IA	402,545

Source: Council For Aid to Education (CFAE)

LUTHERAN COLLEGES AND UNIVERSITIES
TOP 20 IN PER CAPITA ALUMNI GIVING

Institution	Per Capita Alumni Support (Dollars)	Total No. of Alumni	Total Support (Dollars)
1) St. Olaf College Northfield, MN	152.85	23,653	8,144,911

2) Augsburg College Minneapolis, MN	115.25	11,149	3,330,017
3) Gettysburg College Gettysburg, PA	114.72	17,852	6,244,502
4) Wittenberg University Springfield, OH	113.70	21,385	4,183,861
5) Susquehanna University Selinsgrove, PA	79.64	10,419	3,087,609
6) Gustavus Adolphus College St. Peter, MN	76.00	15,545	5,996,641
7) Bethany College Lindsborg, KS	75.53	6,134	1,548,399
8) Capital University Columbus, OH	67.38	19,598	3,780,307
9) Valparaiso University Valparaiso, IN	66.54	36,149	6,347,005
10) Muhlenberg College Allentown, PA	59.52	13,000	2,559,160
11) Luther College Decorah, IA	59.48	18,482	3,093,308
12) Concordia College Moorhead, MN	54.64	24,064	6,197,944
13) Augustana College Rock Island, IL	48.30	22,373	2,976,361
14) Texas Lutheran College Seguin, TX	45.26	9,971	5,145,994
15) Midland Lutheran College Fremont, NE	42.43	10,762	1,534,517
16) Roanoke College Salem, VA	38.69	12,970	3,420,525
17) Thiel College Greenville, PA	37.22	14,678	1,579,480
18) Newberry College Newberry, SC	33.54	8,596	2,073,637
19) Pacific Lutheran University Tacoma, WA	33.38	20,106	3,147,651
20) Wartburg College Waverly, IA	33.29	12,093	1,816,876

Source: Council For Aid to Education (CFAE)

HIGHER EDUCATION AND AMERICAN PHILANTHROPY (HEAP)

Contributions to 71 of the nation's leading colleges and universities—representing the most prominent large institutions, and the most distinguished smaller schools and women's colleges—amounted to $2.77 billion during fiscal 1986–87, an increase of more than 17 percent over the previous fiscal year. The HEAP survey has been conducted annually by Brakeley, John Price Jones for the past 67 years.

Most of the giving reported in the HEAP survey, as in the CFAE survey, came from individuals: $1.2 billion, representing 44.5

percent of the total and an increase of 39 percent over the amount individuals gave the previous fiscal year.

Corporations gave over $586 million, up 1.5 percent, and foundations gave $475 million, up 17 percent. Religious and other organizations gave $186 million, down 4 percent.

GIVING TO HIGHER EDUCATION BY MAJOR SOURCES—1987*

Alumni

1979–80	.23.9%
1980–81	.24.8%
1981–82	.25.5%
1982–83	.24.0%
1983–84	.23.3%
1984–85	.23.1%
1985–86	.24.7%
1986–87	.27.6%

Business

1979–80	.18.3%
1980–81	.18.4%
1981–82	.20.1%
1982–83	.21.5%
1983–84	.22.7%
1984–85	.24.9%
1985–86	.23.0%
1986–87	.21.4%

Non-Alumni

1979–80	.22.3%
1980–81	.23.8%
1981–82	.22.6%
1982–83	.23.1%
1983–84	.23.5%
1984–85	.22.4%
1985–86	.24.1%
1986–87	.24.3%

Religion

1979–80	4.1%
1980–81	3.3%
1981–82	3.6%
1982–83	4.0%
1983–84	3.4%
1984–85	3.3%
1985–86	2.8%
1986–87	2.4%

Foundations

1979–80	.23.8%
1980–81	.21.8%
1981–82	.20.6%
1982–83	.19.7%
1983–84	.19.3%
1984–85	.18.6%
1985–86	.18.4%
1986–87	.17.8%

Other

1979–80	7.6%
1980–81	7.9%
1981–82	7.6%
1982–83	7.7%
1983–84	7.8%
1984–85	7.7%
1985–86	7.0%
1986–87	6.8%

Source: Council for Aid to Education

*Last year reported

*It is every man's obligation to put back into
the world at least the equivalent of what he takes out of it.*
Albert Einstein

DISTRIBUTION OF CORPORATE GIVING TO EDUCATION

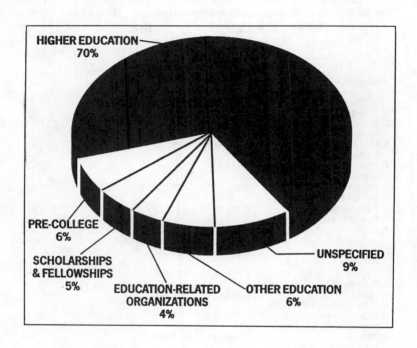

HIGHER EDUCATION
70%

PRE-COLLEGE
6%

SCHOLARSHIPS
& FELLOWSHIPS
5%

EDUCATION-RELATED
ORGANIZATIONS
4%

OTHER EDUCATION
6%

UNSPECIFIED
9%

CONTRIBUTIONS TO THE UNITED NEGRO COLLEGE FUND—BY SOURCES
1983–1988

Individuals make the difference. Since 1983, the fund has grown from $29.6 million to $46.2 million—an increase of $16.6 million. Of this amount $12.2 million came from the increase in giving from individuals. Corporate giving has been flat for the past three years and grants from foundations have also decreased in that period.

	1983	1984	1985/6	1986/7	1987/8
Corporations	$ 8,697,181	$ 9,681,525	$11,003,211	$11,785,362	$11,785,362
Foundations	3,220,654	4,120,894	5,263,149	4,930,273	4,174,322
Individuals	4,984,512	10,619,850	9,272,782	13,064,103	17,231,453
Organizations	4,507,944	1,969,153	1,324,288	5,428,518	5,500,446
Other Sources*	8,204,857	6,639,625	11,461,674	4,610,133	7,484,643
Total	29,615,148	33,031,047	38,325,104	39,818,389	46,176,226

*Other sources include investment earnings, gain on sale of securities, and capital campaign contributions.

Source: A compilation from the Annual Reports of the United Negro College Fund.

BLACK COLLEGES
TOP 15 IN DONATIONS—1987

There are a number of colleges and universities in the United States that serve a predominately black student enrollment. Here are the top 15 institutions of that group that generated the greatest gift income last year.

Institution	Total Support (Dollars)	Alumni Giving (Dollars)	Property, Buildings & Equipment (Dollars)	Enrollment
1) St. Augustine's College Raleigh, NC 27611	6,400,833	98,163	228,670	1,653
2) Oakwood College Huntsville, AL 35896	4,431,478	200,000	350,000	1,003
3) Fisk University Nashville, TN 37203	4,074,989	319,123	*	538
4) Florida Memorial College Miami, FL 33054	3,944,807	9,641	126,349	2,172
5) Bethune Cookman College Dayton Beach, FL 32015	3,863,743	77,036	970,535	1,708
6) Xavier University New Orleans, LA 70125	3,635,860	290,167	988,310	2,071
7) Clark College Atlanta, GA 30314	3,465,870	178,478	450,000	1,885
8) Wilberforce University Wilberforce, OH 45384	2,644,045	193,947	691,178	720
9) Virginia University Richmond, VA 23220	2,549,381	286,596	265,704	1,108
10) Rust College Holly Springs, MS 38635	2,548,914	118,948		810
11) Dillard University New Orleans, LA 70122	2,306,345	53,189	245,557	1,316
12) Wiley College Marshall, TX 75670	2,008,141	112,502		443
13) Claflin College Orangeburg, SC 29115	1,822,089	132,020	395,626	800
14) Stillman College Tuscaloosa, AL 35403	1,788,635	19,926	367,540	792
15) Paine College Augusta, GA 30910	1,718,756	113,049		790

*If the column is blank, school did not provide information. Blanks can be interpreted as either information is not available or no support was reported.

THE NATIONAL URBAN LEAGUE

The National Urban League (NUL) is an interracial, not-for-profit community service organization that uses the tools and methods of education, social work, economics, law, business management and other disciplines to secure equal opportunities in all sectors of our society for black Americans and other minorities.

The NUL, which has 112 affiliates in 34 states and the District of Columbia, accomplishes its mission through programs of direct services, research, advocacy, and the building of understanding and partnerships among different groups. For over three quarters of a century, the National Urban League has existed to make the system work better for black America.

GIVING TO THE NATIONAL URBAN LEAGUE

Type of Public Support	1985	1986	1987
Contributions	$10,341,006	$6,213,890	6,833,317
Legacies and bequests	68,060	20,596	133,145
Special events	327,725	413,199	383,869
Allocated by federated fundraising agencies	13,267	14,392	8,681
Grants and contracts from government agencies	10,413,060	11,485,812	11,615,719
Direct mail campaign	58,432	114,730	50,868
In-kind contributions	2,351,733	2,094,160	1,922,475
Total Public Support	23,573,283	20,356,779	20,998,074

Source: The National Urban League, Inc.

LARGEST GIFT TO A BLACK SCHOOL

This year, Bill Cosby and his wife, Camille, donated $20 million to Spelman College in Atlanta. It is considered to be among the elite black women's colleges.

It is the largest single contribution ever made to a black college, and one of the largest donations in recent years to any school. The gift was announced at the inauguration celebration of Johnetta B. Cole, the college's first woman President.

Referring to President Cole at the inauguration banquet, Bill Cosby announced to an amazed and applauding audience that: "Mrs. Cosby and I wanted this woman to know how much we love this school." Mr. and Mrs. Cosby considered the donation not only an expression of their support for Spelman, but also a challenge to other black Americans to support black colleges.

The announcement was greeted by "gasps of wonder, foot-stomping, shouts of jubilation, and prolonged applause." In accepting the gift, President Cole said, "Either we support these institutions, or they will die."

Mr. Cosby graduated from Temple University in Philadelphia, and has earned a Doctorate in Education from the University of Massachusetts at Amherst. One of his daughters recently graduated from Spelman.

There are 117 historically black colleges and universities in the United States.

GIVING TO UNITED NEGRO COLLEGE FUND

Since 1983, contributions to the United Negro College Fund have grown from $29.6 million to $46.2 million. Adjusted for inflation, the growth becomes only $33.8 million. This still represents an important increase, but not as much as is necessary to sustain the significant work of this group.

RELATIONSHIP OF TOTAL CONTRIBUTIONS TO THE UNITED NEGRO COLLEGE FUND TO THE U.S. ALL-ITEMS CONSUMER PRICE INDEX 1983–1987

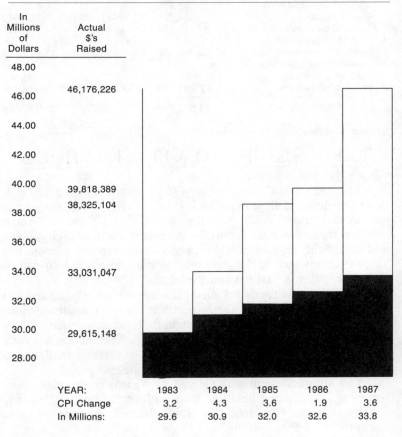

In Millions of Dollars	Actual $'s Raised
48.00	
46.00	46,176,226
44.00	
42.00	
40.00	39,818,389
38.00	38,325,104
36.00	
34.00	33,031,047
32.00	
30.00	29,615,148
28.00	

YEAR:	1983	1984	1985	1986	1987
CPI Change	3.2	4.3	3.6	1.9	3.6
In Millions:	29.6	30.9	32.0	32.6	33.8

☐ Total Contributions
■ "Real Dollars" adjusted for inflation

MICHIGAN STATE UNIVERSITY ANNOUNCES FIRST CAMPUS-WIDE CAPITAL CAMPAIGN

Michigan State University announced its first major capital campaign. The objective is $160 million, to be raised by 1993. Sixty million dollars contribution has been pledged so far.

The largest gift thus far is a $5 million from General Motors

Corporation for a new building for the College of Business, and for laboratories for the College of Engineering.

BUSINESS SCHOOLS ARE GOING THROUGH NAME CHANGES; UC BERKELEY RECOGNIZES THE LARGEST GIFT IN ITS HISTORY

The new $40 million School of Business building at the University of California at Berkeley will be renamed the Walter A. Haas School of Business. The University just received a $15 million gift from the Haas family, principle owners of Levi Strauss & Company. It is the largest gift ever made to the institution. The gift was presented by Peter Haas, Walter's son, who said the family gave the money to Berkeley "because of the love affair my dad had with the University."

The gift is one of a series of business school renamings. Last year, the UCLA Business School was renamed the John E. Anderson Graduate School of Management to honor the lawyer who gave them $15 million. And then there is the Fuqua School of Business at Duke University, the William E. Simon Graduate School of Business Administration at the University of Rochester, and the Samuel C. Johnson School of Management at Cornell University. The largest donation was a $30 million gift last fall to the business school at New York University from Leonard Stern.

Berkeley, by the way, has other naming opportunities available: classrooms start at $50,000, outdoor terraces are $250,000, the cafe is $500,000, the courtyard and computer center are $2 million each, and the library is $5 million.

FUNDRAISERS NOW ALLOWED TO ACCEPT COMMISSIONS

At the 1989 meeting of the National Society of Fund Raising Executives, the Board of Directors gave approval for its members to work on a commission basis. This is a major departure from the long-standing accepted policy which required members and all others in the profession to work for a fixed salary or fee. The decision was and continues to be fiercely contested, and the divisions in thinking are deep. The new provision was adopted at a closed-door meeting of the NSFRE Board.

Accepting a commission has long been thought to lead potential donors to question whether the fundraiser was trying to raise major funds or increase the size of a gift for the benefit of the charity or for personal financial gain.

PROFESSIONAL AND SPECIALIZED INSTITUTIONS

Professional and Specialized Institutions are baccalaureate and postbaccalaureate institutions with an emphasis in one area, usually a professional field such as business, engineering, law, medicine, theology, or art.

THE 20 PROFESSIONAL AND SPECIALIZED INSTITUTIONS REPORTING THE HIGHEST ENDOWMENTS

1) Princeton Theological Seminary Princeton, NJ	$322,089,738
2) Harvard Law School Cambridge, MA	164,381,868
3) Thomas Jefferson University Philadelphia, PA	160,724,200
4) Georgia Institute of Technology Atlanta, GA	100,777,380
5) Juilliard School New York, NY	99,521,063
6) Rush University Chicago, IL	97,713,000
7) Worcester Polytechnic Institute Worcester, MA	79,028,149
8) Stevens Institute of Technology Hoboken, NJ	67,485,245
9) Oregon Health Sciences University Portland, OR	61,626,009
10) Rose-Hulman Institute of Technology Terre Haute, IN	59,900,000
11) Texas, University of-System Cancer Center Austin, TX	59,487,877
12) Rhode Island School of Design Providence, RI	51,599,707
13) Harvey Mudd College Claremont, CA	50,747,466
14) Columbia University Teachers College New York, NY	50,214,695
15) Philadelphia College of Pharmacy and Science Philadelphia, PA	49,978,500
16) Protestant Theological Seminary Alexandria, VA	44,943,749
17) Union Theological Seminary New York, NY	42,353,892
18) Bentley College Waltham, MA	39,336,520
19) Clarkson University Potsdam, NY	37,325,408
20) Wentworth Institute of Technology Boston, MA	35,776,725

Source: Council For Aid to Education (CFAE)

On my honor, I will try to serve God and my country, to help people at all times, and to live by the Girl Scout Law.
Scout Law, Girl Scouts of America

PEOPLE WHO GIVE THEIR TIME,
GIVE THEIR MONEY

The Independent Sector is a coalition of nearly 700 not-for-profit groups. In a recent study, they confirmed what those involved in fundraising already know: people who are generous with their time are also generous with their money. The most generous givers of both time and money are the two-thirds of American adults who go to church or synagogue.

"The pathway to success is in serving humanity."
Albert Hubbard (1856–1915)

"Success in life has nothing to do with what you gain in life or accomplish for yourself. It's what you do for others."
Danny Thomas (1914–)

TOP 15 PUBLIC PROFESSIONAL AND SPECIALIZED INSTITUTIONS IN TOTAL SUPPORT

Institution	Total Support (Dollars)	Alumni Giving (Dollars)	Property, Buildings & Equipment (Dollars)	Enrollment
1) University of California, San Francisco, San Francisco, CA 94143	35,851,141	1,042,673	5,897,847	3,556
2) Oregon Health Science University, Portland, OR 97201	30,254,017	128,704		1,200
3) University of Texas Medical Branch – Galveston, Galveston, TX 77550	29,557,101	449,472	16,566,578	2,148
4) Georgia Institute of Technology, Atlanta, GA 30332	24,303,925	10,674,033	4,415,505	11,494
5) University of Texas System Cancer Center, Houston, TX 77225	17,159,294			1,519
6) University of Texas, Health Center, Dallas, Dallas, TX 75235	16,466,980	157,678	2,761,016	1,519
7) University of Texas, Health Center, San Antonio, San Antonio, TX 78284	11,027,282		637,096	2,174
8) University of Texas, Health Center, Houston, Houston, TX 77225	8,387,569	121,123	921,700	2,664
9) Colorado School of Mines, Golden, CO 80401	7,408,727	1,517,768	2,229,025	2,882
10) New Jersey Institute of Technology, Newark, NJ 07102	7,355,296	821,416	5,025,265	7,591
11) Medical College of Georgia, Augusta, GA 30912	4,250,067	648,054	116,000	2,300
12) Medical University of South Carolina, Charleston, SC 29425	4,224,814	441,649	449,237	2,066
13) Michigan Technical University, Houghton, MI 49931	3,400,489	1,349,051	593,380	6,326
14) Maine Maritime Academy, Castine, ME 04420	2,236,059	121,484	1,786,903	436
15) SUNY – Health Science Center, Syracuse, NY	1,179,501	68,342		250

THE 20 PROFESSIONAL AND SPECIALIZED INSTITUTIONS REPORTING THE HIGHEST TOTAL ALUMNI CONTRIBUTIONS

1) Georgia Institute of Technology Atlanta, Ga	$10,674,033
2) Harvard Law School Cambridge, MA	7,290,551
3) Loma Linda University Loma Linda, CA	3,094,498
4) Stevens Institute of Technology Hoboken, NJ	2,073,916
5) Rose-Hulman Institute of Technology Terre Haute, IN	2,065,614
6) Thomas Jefferson University Philadelphia, PA	1,896,768
7) Worcester Polytechnic Institute Worcester, MA	1,893,708
8) Polytechnic University Brooklyn, NY	1,822,095
9) Wheelock College Boston, MA	1,712,407
10) Medical College of Wisconsin Milwaukee, WI	1,660,387
11) Colorado School of Mines Golden, CO	1,517,768
12) University of Redlands Redlands, CA	1,460,160
13) Albany Law School of Union University Albany, NY	1,443,192
14) American College Bryn Mawr, PA	1,400,961
15) Michigan Technical University Houghton, MI	1,249,051
16) Columbia University Teachers College New York, NY	1,210,046
17) Kirksville College of Osteopathic Medicine Kirksville, MO	1,133,269
18) Clarkson University Potsdam, NY	1,087,865
19) University of California–San Francisco San Francisco, CA	1,042,673
20) Babson College Babson Park, MA	1,020,991

Source: Council For Aid to Education (CFAE)

THE 20 PROFESSIONAL AND SPECIALIZED INSTITUTIONS REPORTING THE HIGHEST CORPORATE SUPPORT

1) Georgia Institute of Technology Atlanta, GA	$9,574,453
2) New Jersey Institute of Technology Newark, NJ	5,655,002
3) University of Texas Health Center-San Antonio San Antonio, TX	5,605,735
4) GMI Engineering and Management Institute Flint, MI	4,004,466
5) University of California – San Francisco San Francisco, CA	3,950,995
6) Colorado School of Mines Golden, CO	3,748,897

7) Clarkson University	3,498,918
Potsdam, NY	
8) Gordon-Conwell Theological Seminary	3,114,165
South Hamilton, MA	
9) Polytechnic University	2,860,497
Brooklyn, NY	
10) Rush University	2,857,576
Chicago, IL	
11) University of Texas Medical Branch at Galveston	2,791,182
Galveston, TX	
12) Worcester Polytechnic Institute	2,696,341
Worcester, MA	
13) University of Texas Health Center-Houston	2,578,642
Houston, TX	
14) Baylor College of Medicine	2,487,485
Houston, TX	
15) Westworth Institute of Technology	2,439,757
Boston, MA	
16) American College	2,395,347
Bryn Mawr, PA	
17) Milwaukee School of Engineering	2,277,901
Milwaukee, WI	
18) University of Texas System Cancer Center	2,200,007
Austin, TX	
19) Meharry Medical College	2,147,052
Nashville, TN	
20) Medical College of Wisconsin	2,050,337
Milwaukee, WI	

Source: Council For Aid to Education (CFAE)

VOLUNTARY SUPPORT BY SOURCE, 1985–86 TO 1986–87

Perhaps the most interesting aspect of this table is the surge in alumni support in 1986–87 over the preceding year, an increase of 32.1 percent. Donations from religious organizations, on the other hand, declined in 1986–87 and have been steadily falling since the late 1950s.

	All Institutions Reporting					Core Group
	1985–86		1986–87			
	Amount (000)	Average per Institution	Amount (000)	Average per Institution	% Change in Average	% Change
Alumni	$1,555,641 (24.6)	$1,302,882	$2,020,207 (27.6)	$1,720,790	+ 32.1	+ 29.0
Nonalumni Individuals	1,518,828 (24.0)	1,272,050	1,775,491 (24.2)	1,512,344	+ 18.9	+ 14.9
Foundations	1,179,270 (18.6)	987,664	1,302,300 (17.8)	1,109,284	+ 12.3	+ 9.3
Corporations	1,456,044 (23.0)	1,219,468	1,568,792 (21.4)	1,336,279	+ 9.6	+ 7.8
Religious Organizations	180,271 (2.8)	150,981	175,799 (2.4)	149,744	– 0.8	+ 0.6
Other	441,633 (7.0)	369,877	480,467 (6.6)	409,256	+ 10.6	+ 7.8
GRAND TOTAL	$6,331,687 (100.0)	$5,302,922	$7,323,056 (100.0)	$6,237,697	+ 17.6	+ 14.9
No. Institutions Reporting	1,194		1,174			1,015

(Figures in parentheses show percent of total in each column.)

Source: Council For Aid to Education (CFAE)

TOP 15 PRIVATE PROFESSIONAL AND SPECIALIZED INSTITUTIONS IN TOTAL SUPPORT
TOP 15 IN DONATIONS—1987

Institution	Total Support (Dollars)	Alumni Giving (Dollars)	Property, Buildings & Equipment (Dollars)	Enrollment
1) Mayo Medical School Rochester, MN 55905	26,221,811	683,880	2,097,745	1,482
2) Baylor College of Medicine Houston, TX 77030	15,393,778	229,915	1,333,384	2,081
3) Loma Linda University Loma Linda, CA 92350	15,016,261	3,094,498	294,115	4,390
4) Rush University Chicago, IL 60612	11,251,358	446,735	675,336	1,540
5) Meharry Medical School Nashville, TN 37206	10,973,504	532,042	59,252	725
6) Thomas Jefferson University Philadelphia PA 19107	10,038,225	1,896,768	1,057,919	1,973
7) New York Medical College Valhalla, NY 10595	9,314,113	651,549	5,837,449	1,308
8) Medical College of Wisconsin Milwaukee, WI 53226	8,315,326	1,660,387	2,730,356	850
9) Harvard Law School Cambridge, MA 02138	8,274,984	7,290,551	189,050	1,812
10) Harvey Mudd College Claremont, CA 91711	7,483,888	197,455	734,329	560
11) Julliard School of Music New York, NY 10023	6,958,920	124,085	629,501	1,565
12) Fuller Theological Seminary Pasadena, CA 91182	6,472,047	188,541	1,847,535	2,679
13) GMI Engineering & Management Institute Flint, MI 48502	6,293,434	354,672	361,806	3,092
14) Worcester Polytechnic Institute Worcester, MA 01609	6,144,250	1,893,708	240,853	4,032
15) Polytechnic University Brooklyn, NY 11201	6,003,219	1,822,095	*	5,161

Source: Council for Aid to Education (CFAE)

*If the column is blank, school did not provide information. Blanks can be interpreted as either information is not available or no support was reported.

THE 20 COLLEGES AND UNIVERSITIES REPORTING THE MOST VOLUNTARY SUPPORT

Stanford University	$198,534,823
Harvard University	177,976,000
Cornell University	149,702,435
Yale University	120,063,734
Minnesota, University of	116,328,173
Washington University (St. Louis)	110,427,402
Columbia University	104,645,815
Massachusetts Inst. of Tech.	101,421,830
Johns Hopkins University	92,646,994
Southern California, University of	91,203,534
Princeton University	90,808,608
Wisconsin, University of – Madison	88,148,459
Pennsylvania, University of	87,241,444
Illinois, University of	84,075,515
California Inst. of Tech.	80,349,037
Washington, University of	77,687,223
Chicago, University of	74,965,280

Duke University	73,563,708
Wake Forest University	66,255,408
Ohio State University	64,769,998

Source: Council For Aid to Education (CFAE)

THE 20 COLLEGES AND UNIVERSITIES REPORTING THE HIGHEST TOTAL ALUMNI CONTRIBUTIONS

1) Stanford University Stanford, CA	$79,238,413
2) Harvard University Cambridge, MA	71,238,000
3) Cornell University Ithaca, NY	65,656,963
4) Yale University New Haven, CT	51,905,213
5) Princeton University Princeton, NJ	48,495,793
6) University of Illinois Urbana, IL	36,801,228
7) Massachusetts Institute of Technology Cambridge, MA	29,700,141
8) Dartmouth College Hanover, NH	29,199,558
9) Columbia University New York, NY	28,453,833
10) Brown University Providence, RI	28,183,227
11) University of North Carolina Chapel Hill, NC	26,596,942
12) University of Pennsylvania Philadelphia, PA	22,434,989
13) University of Michigan Ann Arbor, MI	20,562,129
14) Northwestern University Evanston, IL	20,358,125
15) Virginia Polytechnic Institute & State University Blacksburg, VA	19,092,473
16) University of California – Berkeley Berkeley, CA	18,582,261
17) University of Notre Dame Notre Dame, IN	18,447,106
18) Lafayette College Easton, PA	18,085,409
19) Washington University St. Louis, MO	17,858,272
20) Wellesley College Wellesley, MA	17,619,694

Source: Council For Aid to Education (CFAE)

CONTRIBUTIONS INVOLVING A "PREMIUM" NOT DEDUCTIBLE

In June, 1988, 400,000 charitable organizations received a memorandum from Commissioner Lawrence Gibbs of the IRS.

Organizations were informed that current tax laws allowed donors to deduct from their taxable income only the amount of their actual gift. Substantial benefits such as dinner, books, presents, and other premiums they received in exchange for making a contribution are not deductible. Merchandise purchased in auction parties is not deductible.

It is the responsibility of the organizations to take the necessary steps to inform donors of what is deductible and what is not.

THE 20 COLLEGES AND UNIVERSITIES REPORTING THE HIGHEST CORPORATE SUPPORT

1) Wake Forest University Winston-Salem, NC	$51,183,428
2) Massachusetts Institute of Technology St. Louis, MA	49,754,376
3) Harvard University Cambridge, MA	33,954,000
4) Cornell University Ithaca, NY	33,657,722
5) Stanford, University Stanford, CA	33,572,316
6) University of Minnesota Minneapolis, MN	30,903,761
7) University of Washington Seattle, WA	29,360,316
8) University of California – Berkeley Berkeley, CA	28,256,688
9) University of California – Los Angeles Los Angeles, CA	23,117,081
10) Ohio State University Columbus, OH	22,418,197
11) University of Illinois Urbana, IL	22,108,747
12) Duke University Durham, NC	21,649,054
13) Texas A & M University College Station, TX	21,635,266
14) University of Wisconsin Madison, WI	21,587,872
15) Columbia University New York, NY	21,179,031
16) University of Pennsylvania Philadelphia, PA	20,424,497
17) Carnegie-Mellon University Pittsburgh, PA	18,392,194
18) Pennsylvania State University University Park, PA	18,100,906
19) University of Southern California Los Angeles, CA	17,961,137
20) Yale University New Haven, CT	16,800,058

Source: Council For Aid to Education (CFAE)

GENERAL BACCALAUREATE INSTITUTIONS

General Baccalaureate Institutions are those in which the primary emphasis is on general undergraduate and baccalaureate education. These college grant degrees in three or more baccalaureate programs or in interdisciplinary studies. Over 75 percent of their degrees are at the baccalaureate level or above, and fewer than 30 percent are for postbaccalaureate work.

THE 20 GENERAL BACCALAUREATE INSTITUTIONS REPORTING THE HIGHEST ENDOWMENTS

1) Wellesley College Wellesley, MA	297,958,120
2) Williams College Williamstown, MA	287,753,076
3) Swathmore College Swathmore, PA	277,516,000
4) Amherst College Amherst, MA	248,353,638
5) Pomona College Claremont, CA	232,675,167
6) Grinnell College Grinnell, IA	226,931,500
7) Berea College Berea, KY	225,938,100
8) Vassar College Poughkeepsie,NY	224,356,000
9) Oberlin College Oberlin, OH	217,951,931
10) Lafayette College Easton, PA	176,332,000
11) Mount Holyoke College South Hadley, MA	151,915,562
12) Carleton College Northfield, MN	144,190,176
13) Macalester College St. Paul, MN	137,501,000
14) Bowdoin College Brunswick, ME	127,123,000
15) Occidental College Los Angeles, CA	126,317,000
16) Wabash College Crawfordsville, IN	121,593,000
17) Colorado College Colorado Springs, CO	113,101,620
18) Earlham College Richmond, IN	111,304,133
19) Whitman College Walla Walla, WA	108,444,888
20) Hamilton College Clinton, NY	103,190,210

Source: Council For Aid to Education (CFAE)

TO BUILD FOR LIVES YET UNBORN

Therefore, when we build, let us think that we build forever. Let it not be for present use alone; let it be such work as our descendants will thank us for; and let us think as we lay stone on stone, that a time is to come when these stones will be held sacred because our hands have touched them, and that men will say as they look upon the labour and the wrought substance of them, "See, this our fathers did for us."
John Ruskin

PRIVATE GENERAL BACCALAUREATE INSTITUTIONS
TOP 15 IN DONATIONS—1987

Institution	Total Support (Dollars)	Alumni Giving (Dollars)	Property, Buildings & Equipment (Dollars)	Enrollment
1) Wellesley College Wellesley, MA 02181	22,938,229	17,619,694	1,475,332	2,114
2) Reed College Portland, OR 97202	22,619,577	13,496,396	6,268,458	1,142
3) Lafayette College Easton, PA 18042	21,479,977	18,085,409	9,104,238	2,032
4) Berea College Berea, KY 40404	18,293,879	1,348,976	2,307,877	1,587
5) Williams College Williamstown, MA 01267	18,224,363	11,389,703	1,168,411	2,157
6) Mount Holyoke College South Hadley, MA 01075	16,992,258	13,621,855	1,842,188	1,980
7) Pomona College Claremont, CA 91711	16,552,493	7,168,122	2,468,185	1,360
8) Hartwick College Oneonta, NY 13820	15,092,373	502,460	825,909	1,465
9) Bowdoin College Brunswick, ME 04011	15,059,461	7,452,485	1,258,682	1,413
10) Colorado College Colorado Springs, CO 80903	14,574,727	2,513,639	3,125,000	1,965
11) Grinnell College Grinnell, IA 51526	13,670,062	11,731,699	532,486	1,393
12) Hamilton College Clinton, NY 13323	13,523,699	9,036,965	2,558,475	1,692
13) Oberlin College Oberlin, OH 44074	13,310,194	7,713,692	2,991,125	2,850
14) Swathmore College Swathmore, PA 19081	12,071,748	9,278,956	847,439	1,358
15) Amherst, College Amherst, MA 01002	11,869,841	7,675,874	272,429	1,570

Source: Council for Aid to Education (CFAE)

PUBLIC GENERAL BACCALAUREATE INSTITUTIONS
IN TOTAL SUPPORT
TOP 15 IN DONATIONS—1987

Institution	Total Support (Dollars)	Alumni Giving (Dollars)	Property, Buildings & Equipment (Dollars)	Enrollment
1) Virginia Military Institute Lexington, VA 24450	7,897,918	5,585,307	*	1,338
2) State University of N.Y. College at Purchase Purchase, NY 10577	2,931,600	5,577		3,865
3) Washburn University of Topeka Topeka, KS 66621	2,294,641	756,509	179,334	6,110
4) St. Mary's College of Maryland St. Mary's City, MD 20686	1,436,315	63,826	644,920	1,396
5) Southern Colorado, University of Pueblo, CO 81001	1,148,921	1,700	83,332	3,693
6) Longwood College Farmville, VA 23901	1,005,394	249,300		2,884
7) Kentucky State University Frankfort, KY 40601	906,298	78,763		2,205
8) Eastern Montana College Billings, MT 59101	730,878	183,136		3,920
9) Missouri Western State College St. Joseph, MO 64507	728,740	68,886	112,114	3,936
10) Southern Arkansas University Magnolia, AR 71753	727,334	264,861		2,065

11) Cameron University Lawton, OK 73505	724,518			5,309
12) Southwest State University Marshall, MN 56258	654,241	56,488	241,465	2,450
13) Mary Washington College Fredericksburg, VA 22401	636,828	295,999		3,187
14) Evergreen St. College Olympia, WA 98505	631,785	51,453	398,955	2,965
15) N.C. at Asheville, University of Asheville, NC 28804	605,962	46,316	10,601	2,939

Source: Council for Aid to Education (CFAE)

*If the column is blank, school did not provide information. Blanks can be interpreted as either information is not available or no support was reported.

THE 20 GENERAL BACCALAUREATE INSTITUTIONS REPORTING THE HIGHEST TOTAL ALUMNI CONTRIBUTIONS

1) Lafayette College Easton, PA	$18,085,409
2) Wellesley College Wellesley, MA	17,619,694
3) Mount Holyoke College South Hadley, MA	13,621,855
4) Reed College Portland, OR	13,496,396
5) Grinnell College Grinnell, IA	11,731,699
6) Williams College Williamstown, MA	11,389,703
7) Swathmore College Swathmore, PA	9,279,956
8) Hamilton College Clinton, NY	9,036,965
9) Vassar College Poughkeepsie, NY	8,499,035
10) Oberlin College Oberlin, OH	7,713,692
11) Amherst College Amherst, MA	7,675,874
12) Bowdoin College Brunswick, ME	7,452,485
13) Pomona College Claremont, CA	7,168,122
14) Hobart and William Smith Colleges Geneva, NY	7,077,394
15) Davidson College Davidson, NC	5,604,473
16) Virginia Military Institute Lexington, VA	5,585,307
17) Scripps College Claremont, CA	5,044,014
18) Washington and Lee University Lexington, VA	4,757,716
19) Bates College Lewiston, ME	4,509,409
20) Carleton College Northfield, MN	4,397,116

Source: Council For Aid to Education (CFAE)

*Although the world is full of suffering, it is
also full of the overcoming of it.*
Helen Keller

THE 20 GENERAL BACCALAUREATE INSTITUTIONS
REPORTING THE HIGHEST CORPORATE SUPPORT

1) Christian Brothers College Memphis, TN	$2,614,857
2) Mount Vernon Nazarene College Mount Vernon, OH	1,822,297
3) State University of New York College at Purchase Purchase, NY	1,792,500
4) Birmingham Southern College Birmingham, AL	1,549,166
5) Lawrence University Appleton, WI	1,516,382
6) Willamette University Salem, OR	1,329,723
7) Lafayette College Easton, PA	1,329,690
8) Huntingdon College Montgomery, AL	1,279,569
9) Clark College Atlanta, GA	1,256,424
10) Mount Holyoke College South Hadley, MA	1,230,821
11) Davidson College Davidson, NC	1,220,622
12) Hobart and William Smith Colleges Geneva, NY	1,200,788
13) Bowdoin College Brunswick, ME	1,179,286
14) Oklahoma Christian College Oklahoma City, OK	1,048,600
15) Millikin University Decatur, IL	1,003,024
16) Hope College Holland, MI	971,332
17) Maharishi International University Fairfield, IA	971,277
18) Holy Cross, College of the Worcester, MA	956,974
19) Tri-State University Angola, IN	915,311
20) Williams College Williamstown, MA	908,204

Source: Council For Aid to Education (CFAE)

"The life worth living
is giving for the good
of others."
Booker T. Washington (1856–1915)

"When you cease to make a
contribution you begin to
die."
Eleanor Roosevelt (1884–1962)

TWO-YEAR INSTITUTIONS

Two-year institutions are those that confer more than 75 percent of their degrees or awards for 2 years of work and less than 25 percent at the baccalaureate or postbaccalaureate level. (Institutions with a two-year upper-division program do not fall in this category, since they grant baccalaureate degrees).

THE 20 TWO-YEAR INSTITUTIONS REPORTING THE HIGHEST ENDOWMENTS

1) Mott Community College Flint, MI	$18,547,247
2) Cazenovia College Cazenovia, NY	10,805,491
3) Lees-McRae College Banner Elk, NC	7,938,514
4) Bay Path Junior College Longmeadow, MA	7,067,385
5) Miami-Dade Community College Miami, FL	6,728,941
6) State Technical Institute at Knoxville Knoxville, TN	5,873,400
7) Dean Junior College Franklin, MA	5,094,978
8) Keystone-Junior College La Plume, PA	4,973,949
9) Lasell Junior College Newton, MA	4,771,899
10) State University of New York Jamestown Community College Jamestown, NY	4,725,050
11) Lees College Jackson, KY	4,162,552
12) Louisburg College Louisburg, NC	4,097,253
13) Montreat-Anderson College Montreat, NC	3,854,932
14) Edison Community College Fort Myers, FL	3,763,450
15) Peirce Junior College Philadelphia, PA	3,433,904
16) Spartanburg Methodist College Spartanburg, SC	3,295,128
17) Mount Olive College Mount Olive, NC	3,052,000
18) New Mexico Military Institute Roswell, NM	3,000,000
19) North Greenville College Tigerville, SC	2,638,459
20) Lorain County Community College Elyria, OH	2,621,120

Source: Council For Aid to Education (CFAE)

One man gives freely, yet grows all the richer;
another withholds what he should give, and only suffers want.
Proverbs 11:24

THE 20 TWO-YEAR INSTITUTIONS REPORTING THE
HIGHEST TOTAL ALUMNI CONTRIBUTIONS

1) New Mexico Military Institute Roswell, NM	$3,705,000
2) Lasell Junior College Newton, MA	485,897
3) Hesston College Hesston, KS	456,414
4) Central College McPherson, KS	384,110
5) Spartanburg Methodist College Spartanburg, SC	348,592
6) Edison Community College Fort Myers, FL	340,349
7) Dean Junior College Franklin, MA	297,119
8) Waldorf College Forest City, IA	277,623
9) North Greenville College Tigerville, SC	187,455
10) Lees College Jackson, KY	169,241
11) Louisburg College Louisburg, NC	121,937
12) Less-McRae College Banner Elk, NC	95,004
13) Keystone Junior College La Plume, PA	92,956
14) Montreat-Anderson College Montreat, NC	89,671
15) Wood Junior College Mathiston, MS	86,950
16) Peirce Junior College Philadelphia, PA	80,472
17) Southern Seminary Junior College Buena Vista, VA	69,334
18) State University of New York College of Agriculture & Technology Cobleskill, NY	68,643
19) Georgia Military College Milledgeville,GA	67,851
20) Cazenovia College Cazenovia, NY	65,858

Source: Council For Aid to Education (CFAE)

PRIVATE TWO-YEAR INSTITUTIONS
TOP 15 IN DONATIONS—1987

Institution	Total Support (Dollars)	Alumni Giving (Dollars)	Property, Buildings & Equipment (Dollars)	Enrollment
1) Hesston College Hesston, KS 67062	2,055,415	456,414	968,229	440
2) Waldorf College Forest City, IA 50436	2,002,634	277,623	656,584	397
3) Lees-McRae College Banner Elk, NC 28604	1,957,569	95,004	385,419	679
4) Spartanburg Methodist College Spartanburg, SC 29301	1,649,468	348,592	368,958	1,008
5) Louisburg College Louisburg, NC 27549	1,572,393	121,937	719,504	802
6) Montreat-Anderson College Montreat, NC 28757	1,488,366	89,671	146,235	367

	Total Support (Dollars)	Alumni Giving (Dollars)	Property, Buildings & Equipment (Dollars)	Enrollment
7) North Greenville College Tigerville, SC 29688	1,454,114	187,455	369,874	470
8) Mount Olive College Mount Olive, NC 29365	1,096,775	53,380	63,929	773
9) Lees College Jackson, KY 41339	1,093,339	169,241	*	389
10) Dean Junior College Franklin, MA 02038	938,344	297,119	738,110	2,458
11) Lasell Junior College Newton, MA 02166	810,570	485,897	619,818	479
12) Presentation College Aberdeen, SD 57401	794,939	30,874		447
13) Central College McPherson, KS 67460	781,129	384,110	291,585	248
14) Wood Junior College Mathiston, MS 39752	472,282	86,950	21,125	459
15) Champlain College Burlington, VT 05402	468,199	55,981	46,773	1,801

Source: Council for Aid to Education (CFAE)

*If the column is blank, school did not provide information. Blanks can be interpreted as either information is not available or no support was reported.

PUBLIC TWO-YEAR INSTITUTIONS
TOP 15 IN DONATIONS—1987

Institution	Total Support (Dollars)	Alumni Giving (Dollars)	Property, Buildings & Equipment (Dollars)	Enrollment
1) New Mexico Military Institute Roswell, NM 88201	4,618,900	3,705,000	1,485,000	925
2) Miami-Dade Community College Miami, FL 33132	3,718,365	46,625	*	47,501
3) Triton College River Grove, IL 60171	3,279,336		3,269,636	21,049
4) Dallas Co. Community College Dallas, TX 75202	1,903,096		10,350	46,342
5) Pasco Hernando Community College Dade City, FL 32802	1,298,699			2,997
6) Valencia Community College Orlando, FL 32802	936,871	6,039	569,571	47,000
7) State Univ. of New York Monroe Community College Monroe, NY	929,154	49,966	533,805	11,866
8) Harrisburg Area Community College Harrisburg, PA 17110	921,867	16,900	469,100	3,744
9) Washington State Community College District 17 Office Spokane, WA 99207	887,987	5,306		14,710
10) Edison Community College Fort Myers, FL 33907	848,164	340,349	205,500	6,483
11) City University of New York La Guardia Community College Long Island City, NY 11101	823,086	5,973	10,500	24,800
12) State University of New York Suffolk Co. Community College – Seldon Seldon, NY	752,534	16,215		12,542
13) Marin Community College Kentfield, CA 94904	750,729		61,854	7,106
14) Allegheny Co. Community College Cumberland, MD 21502	669,695		174,938	45,848
15) Grand Rapids Junior College Grand Rapids, MI	539,132	3,565	15,855	10,596

Source: Council for Aid to Education (CFAE)

*If the column is blank, school did not provide information. Blanks can be interpreted as either information is not available or no support was reported.

THE 20 TWO-YEAR INSTITUTIONS REPORTING THE HIGHEST TOTAL SUPPORT

1) Triton College River Grove, IL	$3,279,336
2) Dallas County Community College Dallas, TX	1,421,032
3) State University of New York Monroe Community College Rochester, NY	729,604
4) Miami-Dade Community College Miami, FL	694,982
5) Spartanburg Methodist College Spartanburg, SC	572,382
6) Des Moines Area Community College Ankeny, IA	552,857
7) Hesston College Hesston, KS	547,712
8) Louisburg College Louisburg, NC	532,072
9) Harrisburg Area Community College Harrisburg, PA	486,675
10) Allegheny County Community College Meadville, PA	476,459
11) Pikes Peak Community College Colorado Springs, CO	441,627
12) Gateway Technical Institute Kenosha, WI	414,000
13) Central Piedmont Community College Charlotte, NC	340,917
14) Washington State Community College District 17 Office Spokane, WA	340,370
15) State University of New York College of Technology – Delhi Delhi, NY	319,010
16) State University of New York Agricultural and Technical College at Farmingdale Farmingdale, NY	302,975
17) Texas State Technical Institute Waco, TX	302,353
18) State University of New York Hudson Valley Community College Troy, NY	286,124
19) Rock Valley College Rockford, IL	274,824
20) State Technical Institute at Knoxville Knoxville, TN	233,686

Source: Council For Aid to Education (CFAE)

A MOUTHFUL!

There's a word that you need to become acquainted with if you haven't already: eleemosynary. In our field, organizations and agencies are often referred to as eleemosynary institutions. That simply means that we are organizations supported by charity.

Now, here's more about the word than you probably ever cared to know. Eleemosynary comes from the Greek word for pity or compassion. The word was shortened in Latin to aelmesse, and then to almes (two syllables), and finally to alms. From six syllables to one!

Alms is relief given to the poor. It appears early in the Bible, in the Gospel of Luke, and again later in Acts.

The word alms is properly singular—and thus the expression "ask an alms."

WHERE TO FIND COLLEGE FUNDRAISING PROGRAMS

Departments devoted to not-for-profit organizations, fundraising and philanthropy are springing up at universities around the country. Following is a list of some of these centers and a description of the services they offer. Many of these universities are offering courses on not-for-profit management and fund raising, and some are beginning master's programs on the subject.

INSTITUTE FOR NONPROFIT ORGANIZATION MANAGEMENT

In 1983 the University of San Francisco inaugurated a master's degree program for nonprofit managers. The program is offered in San Francisco and Los Angeles, enrolling about 125 students. The university created the Institute for Nonprofit Organization Management in 1985 in order to add a research and publications component to the master's degree. The Master of Nonprofit Administration (M.N.A.) degree is a 36-unit, two-year program for working nonprofit managers. The curriculum includes five major areas of study: resource development skills • resource management skills • context studies • management and organization • analytical skills.

The institute gives priority to applied research on financial management, personnel management, fundraising, boards, and planning and evaluation in nonprofit organizations. **For more information: Michael O'Neill, Director, Department of Public Management, Institute for Nonprofit Organization Management, College of Professional Studies, University of San Francisco, Ignatian Heights, San Francisco, CA 94117-1080   (415) 666-6867.**

THE MANDEL CENTER FOR NON-PROFIT ORGANIZATIONS

The Mandel Center for Non-Profit Organizations is located at Case Western Reserve University in Cleveland and offers Certificate, Executive Education and other programs in Non-Profit Management. Lecture series, symposia, seminars, conferences and publications periodically address topical issues and disseminate results of the Center's wide-ranging scholarly research. In June of 1988, the Board of Trustees of Case Western Reserve University approved a new professional master's degree for managers and leaders of nonprofit organizations, to be administered by the Mandel Center. The degree, called a Master of Non-Profit Organizations (MNO), will be a 45-unit program that can be completed in 18–24 months. The first class of students will be accepted for the fall term of 1989. The list of classes which will be offered includes "Social History, Development and Context of Non-Profit Organizations" and "Legal Issues in Non-Profit Organizations."

For more information: **Mandel Center for Non-Profit Organizations, Case Western Reserve University, 2035 Abington Road, Cleveland, Ohio 44106 (216) 368-2275.**

THE INDIANA UNIVERSITY CENTER ON PHILANTHROPY

The Indiana University Center on Philanthropy was created on July 1, 1987 in cooperation with The Fund Raising School, the Lilly Endowment, Inc. and Indiana University.

The Fund Raising School was founded in 1973 by Henry A. Rosso. It is considered one of the best in the field for training and fundraising management. The Fund Raising School educates volunteers and staffs of the independent sector in fundraising and management principles and practices. It offers intensive three and five day courses, and one two week course.

The Center focuses on philanthropy as a vital part of the national and global economy and is dedicated to serving not-for-profit institutions. Included in the educational topics being explored by the Center are "Principles and Practices of Effective Fund Raising", "Legal Aspects of Philanthropy" and "Philanthropy in American Culture". An ongoing research program on the social, legal, cultural, economic and ethical aspects of philanthropy is of major concern to the Center. Those who wish to be added to the mailing list of the Indiana University Center on Philanthropy may direct their request to: **Director, Indiana University Center on Philanthropy, Conference Center, 850 W. Michigan St., Indianapolis, IN 46223 (317) 274-4200.**

THE CENTER FOR THE STUDY OF PHILANTHROPY AND VOLUNTARISM

The Center for the Study of Philanthropy and Voluntarism was established at Duke University to focus on the importance of philanthropy, the purpose it serves in American society, and the forces which shape its size and direction. Courses on philanthropy and voluntarism are major objectives for development by the Duke center. Classes include "Philanthropy and the Arts", "Federal Policy and the Nonprofit Sector" and "Philanthropy and American Society". The center makes working papers and course outlines available to individuals and institutions on its mailing list. To obtain working papers or other general information about the Center contact: **Center for the Study of Philanthropy and Voluntarism, Duke University, Box 4875 Duke Station, Durham, N.C. 27706 (919) 684-2672.**

THE INITIATIVE ON NONPROFIT ENTREPRENEURSHIP

The Initiative on Nonprofit Entrepreneurship (INE) is a program of the Center for Entrepreneurial Studies at New York University Graduate School of Business Administration. The program is committed to furthering the understanding of venturing and income—producing activities within nonprofit corporations through research, education, and publications. Included in the list of conferences and workshops given by INE are "Legal Structure and Tax Planning", "Business Planning" and "Marketing Income-Producing Ventures for Nonprofit Organizations." Members who pay an annual fee of $25 are entitled to receive all INE research reports and publications free, and to receive reduced rates on registration fees for conferences and workshops. If you would like to become a member, send your name, title, organization name, address and telephone number along with a check made payable to Initiative on Nonprofit Entrepreneurship to: **Initiative on Nonprofit Entrepreneurship, New York University, 90 Trinity Place, Room 421, New York, NY 10006 (212) 285-6548.**

THE CENTER FOR THE STUDY OF PHILANTHROPY

The Center for the Study of Philanthropy was founded in September of 1986 and serves as a base for scholarly research and interchange among scholars and practitioners in the field of philanthropy. The center is located in the Graduate School of the City University of New York. Its studies are interdisciplinary, including philanthropy and the welfare state, charity and philanthropy in New York City, and international dimensions, which looks at philanthropy in other cultures as well as American giving overseas. The center also offers other special programs. The Research Awards Program grants up to $1,000 to scholars engaged in philanthropy-related research. The International Fellows Program offers the opportunity for young people from less developed countries to learn about American philanthropy and not-for-profit organizations. For specific information about these programs or general information about the Center, contact: **Center for the Study of Philanthropy, Graduate School and University Center, City University of New York, 33 West 42nd Street, Room 1512, New York, NY 10036 (212) 642-2130.**

THE PROGRAM ON NON-PROFIT ORGANIZATIONS

The Program on Non-Profit Organizations was instituted in 1978 and is an interdisciplinary research program based at the Institution for Social and Policy Studies, Yale University. Scholars study the role, character, organization and impact of the American voluntary sector, generating research which will assist those involved with the voluntary sector. Research participants are Yale faculty members and students, and scholars based at other institutions. Approximately 300 papers and 30 books based on program-related research have been published or are under publication contracts. A copy of *WORK IN PROGRESS,* which lists research projects already completed, underway, or scheduled to begin in the future; and a list of *WORKING PAPERS* published by the Program, including information on how these may be ordered are available on request. You can also be placed on the mailing list for the program's occasional newsletter, *RESEARCH REPORTS.*

Contact: **Program on Non-Profit Organizations, Yale University, P.O. Box 154 Yale Station, 88 Trumbull Street, New Haven, CT 06520 (203) 436-0155.**

ALUMNI GIFTS FOR ALL PURPOSES FOR INSTITUTIONS REPORTING IN BOTH 1985–86 AND 1986–87*

Of 20.8 million graduates solicited in 1986–87 by colleges and universities, 4.8 million alumni made a gift. The percentage of those who gave (22.4) remained the same as the year before, but there was an increase in the average gift—from $329 to $399.

Type of Institution	1985–86			1986–87		
	Number of Alumni Donors	Solicitation Effectiveness**	Average Gift	Number of Alumni Donors	Solicitation Effectiveness**	Average Gift
Doctoral	1,794,213	21.7%	$376	2,148,588	22.1%	$459
Private	719,762	28.3	557	899,466	30.0	698
Public	1,074,451	18.8	242	1,249,122	18.5	279
Comprehensive	752,895	18.2	222	907,827	18.3	268
Private	502,347	23.6	306	552,648	23.7	377
Public	250,548	12.4	73	355,179	13.6	100
General						
Baccalaureate	959,102	30.2	331	1,064,126	31.1	416
Private	913,702	30.9	340	1,009,460	31.6	430
Public	45,400	21.6	137	54,666	24.4	157
Specialized	154,698	22.9	277	185,418	24.3	274
Private	116,012	22.9	245	137,813	24.2	242
Public	38,686	23.0	378	47,605	24.4	372

Total Four-Year	3,660,908	22.5%	$331	4,305,959	22.8%	$402
Private	2,251,823	27.6	406	2,599,387	28.6	507
Public	1,409,085	17.4	211	1,706,572	17.4	242
Two-Year	29,558	9.2	148	42,547	8.7	104
Private	20,617	16.0	192	25,462	17.0	138
Public	8,941	4.6	44	17,085	5.0	52
Grand Total	3,690,466	22.3%	$329	4,348,506	22.4%	$399
Private	2,272,440	27.4	404	2,624,849	28.4	504
Public	1,418,026	17.1	210	1,723,657	17.0	240

*These data reflect the amounts reported only for those institutions providing complete answers.
**Donors as a percent of alumni asked to give

Source: Council For Aid to Education (CFAE)

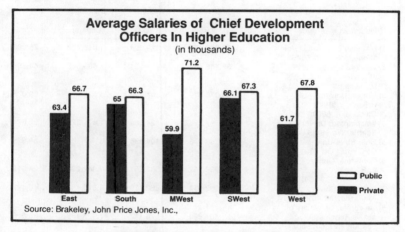

Average Salaries of Chief Development Officers In Higher Education (in thousands)

	East	South	MWest	SWest	West
Private	63.4	65	59.9	66.1	61.7
Public	66.7	66.3	71.2	67.3	67.8

Source: Brakeley, John Price Jones, Inc.,

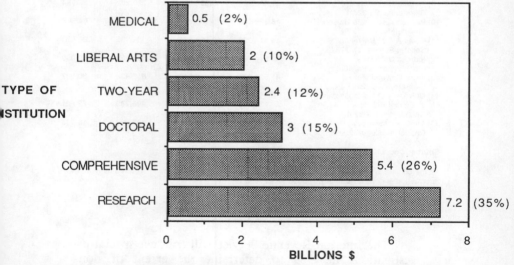

TYPE OF INSTITUTION

- MEDICAL — 0.5 (2%)
- LIBERAL ARTS — 2 (10%)
- TWO-YEAR — 2.4 (12%)
- DOCTORAL — 3 (15%)
- COMPREHENSIVE — 5.4 (26%)
- RESEARCH — 7.2 (35%)

BILLIONS $

COLLEGES AND UNIVERSITIES URGENTLY NEED $20.5 BILLION FOR PHYSICAL PLANT RENEWAL AND REPAIR PROJECTS

DOCTORAL UNIVERSITIES

*Doctoral Universities are defined as those that are active at the doctoral level, granting a minimum of 30 doctorates in 3 or more doctoral-level programs, including first-professional level medical studies.

PUBLIC DOCTORAL INSTITUTIONS
TOP 15 IN DONATIONS—1987

Institution	Total Support (Dollars)	Alumni Giving (Dollars)	Property, Buildings & Equipment (Dollars)	Enrollment
1) Minnesota, University of Minneapolis, MN 55455	116,328,173	12,819,394	1,018,172	75,083
2) Wisconsin University of, at Madison Madison, WI 53706	88,148,459	14,783,324	1,588,643	44,384
3) Illinois, University of Urbana, IL 61801 Chicago, IL 60680	84,075,515	36,801,228	26,623,277	60,036
4) Washington, University of Seattle, WA 98195	77,687,223	10,924,865	11,371,925	33,674
5) Ohio State University Columbus, OH 43210	64,769,998	15,404,496	*	58,838
6) California, University of, at Berkeley Berkeley, CA 94720	63,996,262	18,582,261	14,942,238	29,012
7) Michigan, University of Ann Arbor, MI 48109	612,002,654	20,562,129	8,810,453	48,192
8) California, University of, at Los Angeles Los Angeles, CA 90024	58,467,963	9,676,117	17,973,138	30,525
9) Florida, University of Gainesville, FL 32611	51,436,026	10,922,903	1,120,262	35,094
10) Pennsylvania State University Philadelphia, PA 19104	48,838,160	13,203,690	10,607,596	64,368
11) Texas A & M University College Station, TX 77843	46,514,598	10,522,676	7,805,396	36,570
12) Indiana University Bloomington, IN 47405	43,514,598	9,815,452	10,394,282	80,000
13) Iowa, University of Iowa City, IA 52242	41,539,801	14,870,245	818,836	30,867
14) University of North Carolina at Chapel Hill Chapel Hill, NC 27514	40,752,138	29,596,942	5,295,789	22,921
15) Virginia, University of Charlottesville, VA 22903	35,094,169	13,200,606	3,493,993	16,985

Source: Council for Aid to Education (CFAE)

*If the column is blank, school did not provide information. Blanks can be interpreted as either information is not available or no support was reported.

IRS CRACK DOWN

The Internal Revenue Service will conduct special investigations in 1989 to determine the extent of non-compliance regarding deductions allowed for fundraising events. The examination will be made of charities selected at random.

The IRS had written to over 100,000 charitable groups

discussing the widespread misunderstanding and misuse of the limitations on deductions of payments for special events, dances, and dinners.

In other words, you can't take a deduction—as some have—for payments for school tuition, personal vacation travel, valuable goods purchased at auctions, a dinner dance, or buying Christmas cards from your local hospital. Some charities have been accused of intentionally contributing to the problem of misleading donors, or not properly informing them of the extent to which contributions are or are not deductible.

The Independent Sector has an excellent free booklet entitled *How Much Really is Tax Deductible?* **For more information: Independent Sector, 1828 L Street, N.W., Washington, DC 20036 (202) 223-8100.**

PRIVATE DOCTORAL INSTITUTIONS TOP 15 IN DONATIONS – 1987

Institution	Total Support (Dollars)	Alumni Giving (Dollars)	Property, Buildings & Equipment (Dollars)	Enrollment
1) Stanford University Stanford, CA 94305	198,534,823	79,238,413	59,174,811	13,272
2) Harvard University Cambridge, MA 02138	177,976,000	71,238,000	NA	17,298
3) Cornell University Ithaca, NY 14853	149,702,435	65,656,963	33,858,984	18,807
4) Yale University New Haven, CT 06520	120,063,734	51,905,213	22,295,300	10,569
5) Washington University St. Louis, MO 63130	110,427,402	17,858,272	8,221,780	10,523
6) Columbia University New York, NY 10027	104,645,815	28,453,833	1,153,960	18,761
7) Massachusetts Institute of Technology Cambridge, MA 02139	101,421,830	29,700,141	27,331,818	9,756
8) Johns Hopkins University Baltimore, MD 21218	92,646,994	13,168,914	14,034,794	12,226
9) University of Southern California Los Angeles, CA 90089	91,203,534	14,805,324	18,844,685	30,831
10) Princeton University Princeton, NJ 08544	90,808,608	48,495,793	13,454,745	6,267
11) University of Pennsylvania Philadelphia, PA 19104	87,241,444	22,434,989	8,893,396	21,742
12) California Institute of Technology Pasadena, CA 91125	80,349,037	7,210,198	41,026,835	1,814
13) University of Chicago Chicago, IL 60637	74,965,280	16,237,793	14,259,608	8,933
14) Duke University Durham, NC 27706	73,563,708	13,174,513	7,601,100	10,434
15) University of Miami Coral Gables, FL 33124	58,437,240	4,053,857	6,957,541	13,383

Source: Council for Aid to Education (CFAE)

STUDY: MAJORITY DONATES LESS THAN 1% OF INCOME TO CHARITY

Independent Sector has launched a series of biennial surveys on giving and volunteering in the United States. In March, the Gallup Organization conducted in-home personal interviews with 2,775 Americans 18 years of age and older. Respondents were asked a series of questions about total giving in their households in 1987. Then, as individuals, they were asked about their own volunteering, personal goals, motivations for giving and volunteering, and opinions about charitable organizations and the roles and responsibilities of individuals and government to help others.

The purpose of this study and this new series of regular surveys is to provide accurate trend data about the patterns of and the motivation for giving and volunteering in the United States.

The study found that the average contribution for all households in 1987, including noncontributors, was $562, or 1.5 percent of income, and 71 percent of the respondents reported that their households contributed to charity.

Following is a breakdown of those contributions as a percentage of household income. The study showed that 51 percent of contributing households reported giving less than 1 percent of their household income to charity; 18 percent reported giving between 1 and 2 percent; 9 percent reported giving between 2 and 3 percent; 8 percent reported giving between 3 and 5 percent and 14 percent reported giving 5 percent or more.

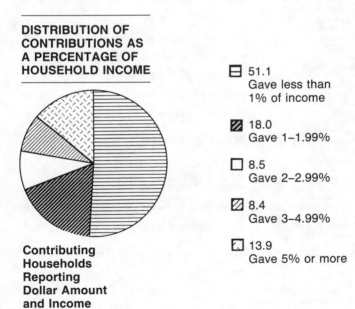

DISTRIBUTION OF CONTRIBUTIONS AS A PERCENTAGE OF HOUSEHOLD INCOME

Contributing Households Reporting Dollar Amount and Income (Percentage)

51.1
Gave less than 1% of income

18.0
Gave 1–1.99%

8.5
Gave 2–2.99%

8.4
Gave 3–4.99%

13.9
Gave 5% or more

Type of Respondent and % of Household Income Contributed	All Households (Percent)	Contributing Households (Percent)	Percentage of Respondents Who Volunteered
All	100.0*	NA	45.3
Noncontributors	28.9	NA	19.6
All contributors	71.0	NA	55.8
Contributors reporting dollar amount and income	62.8	100.0*	56.6
Gave less than 1 percent	32.1	51.1	49.2
Gave 1–1.99 percent	11.3	18.0	56.9
Gave 2–2.99 percent	5.3	8.5	57.0
Gave 3–4.99 percent	5.2	8.4	71.0
Gave 5 percent or more	8.7	13.9	74.8

*Totals may vary from 100 percent because of rounding.
NA–Not applicable.

VOLUNTARY SUPPORT OF INDEPENDENT SCHOOLS FOR CURRENT OPERATIONS AND CAPITAL PURPOSES BY SOURCE OF SUPPORT, 1986–87 (000 OMITTED)

The following table examines the purposes designated by specific donor groups. All types of individual donors — alumni, parents, and others — directed a larger share of their total contributions to capital needs. Foundations contributed almost four fifths of their gifts for capital purposes, while the other types of organizations designated a larger share for current operations.

Purpose	Individuals			Organizations			
	Alumni	Parents	Other Individuals	Foundations	Corporations	Religious Organizations	Other Sources
CURRENT OPERATIONS							
Unrestricted	$ 49,327	$ 53,083	$ 13,611	$ 5,121	$ 9,757	$ 1,587	$ 4,402
	(28.3)	(35.8)	(16.0)	(8.7)	(41.9)	(55.3)	(42.4)
Restricted	5,297	7,858	4,862	7,340	2,580	647	2,449
	(3.0)	(5.3)	(5.8)	(12.5)	(11.1)	(22.5)	(23.6)
TOTAL	$ 54,624	$ 60,941	$ 18,473	$ 12,461	$ 12,337	$ 2,234	$ 6,851
	(31.3)	(41.1)	(21.8)	(21.2)	(53.0)	(77.8)	(66.0)
CAPITAL PURPOSES							
Property, Buildings & Equipment	$ 55,980	$ 42,599	$ 30,498	$ 22,283	$ 6,342	$ 181	$ 950
	(32.2)	(28.7)	(36.1)	(38.0)	(27.3)	(6.3)	(9.1)
Endowment: Income Unrestricted	28,486	23,188	16,326	7,080	2,148	2	1,807
	(16.3)	(15.6)	(19.4)	(12.1)	(9.2)	(0.1)	(17.4)
Endowment: Income Restricted	35,288	21,336	19,057	15,688	2,346	456	781
	(20.2)	(14.4)	(22.5)	(26.7)	(10.1)	(15.8)	(7.5)
Loan Funds	81	335	201	1,178	90	—	—
	n.s.	(0.2)	(0.2)	(2.0)	(0.4)	—	—
TOTAL	$119,835	$ 87,458	$ 66,082	$ 46,229	$ 10,926	$ 639	$ 3,538
	(68.7)	(58.9)	(78.2)	(78.8)	(47.0)	(22.2)	(34.0)
GRAND TOTAL	$174,459	$148,399	$ 84,555	$ 58,690	$ 23,263	$ 2,873	$ 10,389
	(100.0)	(100.0)	(100.0)	(100.0)	(100.0)	(100.0)	(100.0)

(Figures in parentheses show percent of total in each column.)

Source: Council for Aid to Education (CFAE)

GIVING BY INDIVIDUALS

Gifts from individuals, including bequests, made up 88 percent of the total giving in 1987 or nearly $83 billion. The amount of money individuals give continues to rise each year. This increase represents real change, since growth in individual giving surpassed growth in inflation. It is also true that Americans not only give more money every year, but it represents a larger and larger percentage of their annual income.

FOR THOSE WHO COME AFTER ME
THE PARABLE OF THE CAROB TREE

One day when
Honi Ha-Ma 'Aggel
was traveling,
he saw an old man
planting a carob tree.
Puzzled by
what he saw, he
stopped
and asked the old man
when he
thought the
tree would bear fruit.
"After 70 years,"
the old man replied.
"Dost thou
expect to live 70 years
and eat the fruit
of thy labors?" asked
Honi Ha-Ma 'Aggel.
To this
the old man replied,
"I did not find
the world desolate
when I entered
it, and as
my father planted for me
before I was born, so I
plant for those who
come after me."

IMPORTANT FUNDRAISING
PUBLICATIONS

The following represents a list of some of the outstanding books published in the last 20 years for the field of fundraising.

CALL FOR HELP: How To Raise Philanthropic Funds With Phonothons, William F. Balthaser

AMERICA'S VOLUNTARY SPIRIT: A Book of Readings, Brian O'Connell

THE ART OF FUND RAISING, Irving R. Warner

THE BOARD MEMBER'S BOOK, Brian O'Connell

BORN TO RAISE: What Makes A Great Fundraiser, What Makes A Fundraiser Great, Jerold Panas

THE COSTS AND BENEFITS OF DEFERRED GIVING, Norman S. Fink and Howard C. Metzler

DEAR FRIEND: Mastering the Art of Direct Mail Fund Raising, Kay Partney Lautman and Henry Goldstein

DEFERRED GIFTS: How to Get Them, George V. King

DESIGNS FOR FUND RAISING: Principles/Patterns/Techniques, Harold J. Seymour

FUND RAISING: The Guide to Raising Money from Private Sources, Thomas E. Broce

FUND RAISING AND PUBLIC RELATIONS: A Critical Guide to Literature and Resources, Paul Dannelley

STRATEGIC MARKETING FOR NOT-FOR-PROFIT ORGANIZATIONS, Armand Lauffer

FUND RAISING LETTERS, Jerry Huntsinger

GIVING USA: Annual Report (Published Annually by the American Association of Fund Raising Counsel)

HOW TO RATE YOUR DEVELOPMENT DEPARTMENT, Robert J. Berendt and J. Richard Taft

HOW TO FIND PHILANTHROPIC PROSPECTS, Jeanne B. Jenkins and Marilyn Lucas

FRI PROSPECT-RESEARCH RESOURCE DIRECTORY, The Fund Raising Institute

MEGA GIFTS: Who Gives Them, Who Gets Them, Jerold Panas

PHILANTHROPY AND MARKETING, James Gregory Lord

PHILANTHROPY AND VOLUNTARISM: An Annotated Bibliography, Daphne Niobe Layton

RAISING FUNDS FROM AMERICA'S 2,000,000 OVERLOOKED CORPORATIONS, Aldo C. Podesta

STRATEGIC MARKETING FOR NON-PROFIT ORGANIZATIONS, Philip Kotler

TESTED WAYS TO SUCCESSFUL FUND RAISING, George A. Brakeley, Jr.

WHAT VOLUNTEERS SHOULD KNOW FOR SUCCESSFUL FUND RAISING, Maurice G. Gurin

BEYOND TIME MANAGEMENT: Organizing the Organization, Jane Elizabeth Allen

THE MARKETING IMAGINATION, Theodore Levitt

THE ORGANIZED EXECUTIVE, Stephanie Winston

"Philanthropist: a rich (and usually bald) old gentleman who has trained himself to grin while his conscience is picking his pocket."
Ambrose Bierce (1842-1914)

THE 20 DOCTORAL INSTITUTIONS REPORTING THE HIGHEST ENDOWMENTS

1) Harvard University Cambridge, MA	$4,515,980,673
2) Princeton University Princeton, NJ	2,147,000,000
3) Yale University New Haven, CT	2,111,082,000
4) Stanford University Stanford, CA	1,839,490,485
5) Columbia University New York, NY	1,402,667,000
6) Texas A & M University College Station, TX	1,358,184,371
7) Washington University St. Louis, MO	1,218,883,764
8) Massachusetts Institute of Technology Cambridge, MA	1,169,740,000
9) Northwestern University Evanston, IL	948,556,000
10) Chicago, University of Chicago, IL	914,100,000
11) Rice University Houston, TX	893,027,000

12) Emory University Atlanta, GA	849,247,023
13) Cornell University Ithaca, NY	777,100,000
14) Pennsylvania, University of Philadelphia, PA	648,528,000
15) Dartmouth College Hanover, NH	577,639,175
16) Rochester, University of Rochester, NY	564,300,000
17) Rockefeller University New York, NY	542,764,615
18) Johns Hopkins University Baltimore, MD	534,809,000
19) New York University New York, NY	502,000,000
20) Notre Dame, University of South Bend, IN	456,098,517

Source: Council For Aid to Education (CFAE)

THE 20 DOCTORAL INSTITUTIONS REPORTING THE HIGHEST TOTALS OF TOTAL ALUMNI CONTRIBUTIONS

1) Stanford University Stanford, CA	$79,238,413
2) Harvard University Cambridge, MA	71,238,000
3) Cornell University Ithaca, NY	65,656,963
4) Yale University New Haven, CT	51,905,213
5) Princeton University Princeton, NJ	48,495,793
6) Illinois, University of Urbana, IL	36,801,228
7) Massachusetts Institute of Technology Cambridge, MA	29,700,141
8) Dartmouth College Hanover, NH	29,199,558
9) Columbia University New York, NY	28,453,833
10) Brown University Providence, RI	28,183,227
11) North Carolina, University of Chapel Hill, NC	26,596,942
12) Pennsylvania, University of Philadelphia, PA	22,434,989
13) Michigan, University of Ann Arbor, MI	20,562,129
14) Northwestern University Evanston, IL	20,358,125
15) Virginia Polytechnic Institute & State University Blacksburg, VA	19,092,473
16) University of California – Berkeley Berkeley, CA	18,582,261
17) Notre Dame, University of South Bend, IN	18,447,106
18) Washington University St. Louis, MO	17,858,272
19) Chicago, University of Chicago, IL	16,237,793
20) Ohio State University Columbus, OH	15,404,496

Source: Council For Aid to Education (CFAE)

THE 20 DOCTORAL INSTITUTIONS REPORTING THE
HIGHEST CORPORATE SUPPORT

1) Massachusetts Institute of Technology Cambridge, MA	$49,754,376
2) Harvard University Cambridge, MA	33,954,000
3) Cornell University Ithaca, NY	33,657,722
4) Stanford University Stanford, CA	33,572,316
5) Minnesota, University of Minneapolis, MN	30,903,761
6) Washington, University of Seattle, WA	29,360,316
7) University of California – Berkeley Berkeley, CA	28,256,688
8) University of California – Los Angeles Los Angeles, CA	23,117,081
9) Ohio State University Columbus, OH	22,418,197
10) Illinois, University of Urbana, IL	22,108,747
11) Duke University Durham, NC	21,649,054
12) Texas A & M University College Station, TX	21,635,266
13) Wisconsin, University of Madison, WI	21,587,872
14) Columbia University New York, NY	21,179,031
15) Pennsylvania, University of Philadelphia, PA	20,424,497
16) Carnegie-Mellon University Pittsburgh, PA	18,392,194
17) Pennsylvania State University University Park, PA	18,100,906
18) Southern California, University of Los Angeles, CA	17,961,137
19) Yale University New Haven, CT	16,800,058
20) Michigan State University Lansing, MI	14,939,483

Source: Council For Aid to Education (CFAE)

COUNSELETTER

Counseletter is one of the best sources for information about Board enlistment and development, the high level involvement of Trustees, the fine points of fundraising and the strategy for developing large gifts. It covers governance management and policy, untangles philanthropic problems, and provides ideas for giving opportunities. It is not a "how-to" publication, but has practical ideas mixed with a happy combination of philosophical concerns. It is $48 a year, and there are 1,200 subscribers. It comes as an enclosure with the newsletter *Philanthropic Trends Digest,* published by Douglas Lawson & Associates. Keep *Counseletter* in a three-ring binder for future reference and use. **For more information: Arthur C. Frantzreb, Inc., 6233 Kellogg Drive, McLean, VA 22101.**

COMPREHENSIVE INSTITUTIONS

Comprehensive Institutions are those with strong postbaccalaureate programs, but no significant doctoral-level activity. Institutions in this group grant a minimum of 30 postbaccalaureate degrees, including master's and some doctorate and first-professional degrees.

PUBLIC COMPREHENSIVE INSTITUTIONS
TOP 15 IN DONATIONS—1987

Institution	Total Support (Dollars)	Alumni Giving (Dollars)	Property, Buildings & Equipment (Dollars)	Enrollment
1) San Diego State University San Diego, CA 92182	11,052,010	392,560		38,556
2) San Luis Obispo Polytechnical State University San Luis Obispo, CA 93407	7,425,169	1,621,679	3,983,771	15,750
3) Long Beach State University Long Beach, CA 90840	6,756,780	62,292	4,077,837	33,586
4) University of Maine – Orono Orono, ME 04469	6,390,224	2,794,523	1,149,262	10,954
5) University of Texas – El Paso El Paso, TX 79968	5,827,068	1,892,253	248,462	13,753
6) CUNY – City College New York, NY 10031	5,486,887	2,049,059	422,634	13,700
7) East Carolina University Greenville, NC 27858	5,423,199	516,062	388,772	14,459
8) Fresno State University Fresno, CA 93740	4,877,632	359,023	650,967	17,762
9) Northern Arizona University Flagstaff, AZ 86011	4,334,636	312,699	703,914	13,208
10) CUNY – Hunter College New York, NY 10021	4,220,452	1,121,812	200,000	19,577
11) Northridge State University Northridge, CA 91330	4,023,614	165,860	1,804,106	29,785
12) George Mason University Fairfax, VA 22030	4,022,207	108,362		17,652
13) University of Texas – Arlington Arlington, TX 76019	3,824,297	149,737	2,128,036	23,245
14) Central Michigan University Mount Pleasant, MI 48859	3,654,254	1,490,326	712,686	16,743
15) Oakland University Rochester, MI 48309	3,400,207	322,978	78,575	12,707

Source: Council for Aid to Education (CFAE)

If the column is blank, school did not provide information. Blanks can be interpreted as either information is not available or no support was reported.

THE WISE MR. FRANKLIN

The Reverend Gilbert Tennent went to Benjamin Franklin to ask his help in raising funds to build a Presbyterian Church in Philadelphia. Franklin felt that he could not accept, but he did send the good Tennent this counsel.

"In the first place, I advise you to apply to all those whom you know will give something; next, to those whom you are uncertain whether they will give anything or not, and show them the list of those who have given; and lastly, do not neglect those whom you are

sure will give nothing, for in some of them you may be mistaken."
Tennent took his advice "and asked everyone and we secured a
much larger sum than we expected." The campaign was over goal!

PRIVATE COMPREHENSIVE INSTITUTIONS
TOP 15 IN DONATIONS—1987

Institution	Total Support (Dollars)	Alumni Giving (Dollars)	Property, Buildings & Equipment (Dollars)	Enrollment
1) Wake Forest University Winston-Salem, NC 27109	66,255,408	5,919,579	52,565,630	5,049
2) Smith College Northampton, MA 01063	24,694,616	13,440,074	2,461,198	2,588
3) Baylor University Waco, TX 76798	21,637,613	7,463,665	4,327,371	11,556
4) Pepperdine University Malibu, CA 90265	18,344,149	328,855	2,033,469	6,834
5) Middlebury College Middlebury, VT 05753	16,874,321	4,577,209	1,549,580	1,950
6) Samford University Birmingham, AL 35229	15,643,199	548,826	2,161,089	3,835
7) Texas Christian University Fort Worth, TX 76129	15,416,790	2,925,377	4,403,077	6,916
8) University of Portland Portland, OR 97203	15,181,297	11,789,871	2,193,034	2,610
9) Rochester Institute of Technology Rochester, NY 14623	12,687,616	753,979	3,568,598	13,736
10) De Pauw University Greencastle, IN 46135	12,521,267	8,814,317	2,467,018	2,368
11) Colgate University Hamilton, NY 13346	12,497,477	8,793,416	2,923,657	2,696
12) Santa Clara University Santa Clara, CA 95053	11,585,083	2,401,073	3,002,194	7,745
13) Chapman College Orange, CA 92666	11,501,499	2,329,592	8,454,456	6,678
14) Stetson University Deland, FL 32720	11,143,068	7,741,923	4,406,215	2,841
15) Loyola Marymount University Los Angeles, CA 90045	10,912,141	1,691,638	3,234,209	6,476

Source: Council for Aid to Education (CFAE)

THE 20 COMPREHENSIVE INSTITUTIONS
REPORTING THE HIGHEST ENDOWMENTS

1) Smith College Northampton, MA	$299,624,813
2) Texas Christian University Fort Worth, TX	261,718,000
3) Wesleyan University Middletown, CT	258,131,000
4) Trinity University San Antonio, TX	248,788,000
5) Loyola University New Orleans, LA	236,795,000
6) Wake Forest University Winston-Salem, NC	226,072,000
7) Richmond, University of Richmond, VA	225,000,000
8) Baylor University Waco, TX	219,827,376
9) Middlebury College Middlebury, VT	202,583,000
10) Rochester Institute of Technology Rochester, NY	134,681,989

11) Trinity College		115,324,115
Hartford, CT		
12) Colgate University		104,312,764
Hamilton, NY		
13) DePauw University		95,877,959
Greencastle, IN		
14) Union College		87,063,081
Schenectady, NY		
15) Butler University		83,628,996
Indianapolis, IN		
16) Bucknell University		82,388,000
Lewisburg, PA		
17) Santa Clara, University of		79,794,000
Santa Clara, CA		
18) Mercer University		76,587,276
Macon, GA		
19) St. Thomas, College of		75,717,287
Saint Paul, MN		
20) Wheaton College		75,717,214
Wheaton, IL		

Source: Council For Aid to Education (CFAE)

THE 20 COMPREHENSIVE INSTITUTIONS
REPORTING THE HIGHEST CORPORATE SUPPORT

1) Wake Forest University	$51,183,428
Winston-Salem, NC	
2) Rochester Institute of Technology	6,613,718
Rochester, NY	
3) Chapman College	6,252,839
Orange, CA	
4) California State University at San Diego	4,826,374
San Diego, CA	
5) California State University at San Luis Obispo	4,493,485
San Luis Obispo, CA	
6) California State University at Long Beach	4,177,815
Long Beach, CA	
7) DePaul University	3,395,753
Chicago, IL	
8) Bradley University	3,269,164
Peoria, IL	
9) St. Thomas, College of	2,708,525
St. Paul, MN	
10) University of Texas at Arlington	2,663,538
Arlington,TX	
11) Santa Clara, University of	2,433,420
Santa Clara, CA	
12) Dayton, University of	2,336,115
Dayton, OH	
13) Hartford, University of	2,193,967
Hartford, CT	
14) New York Institute of Technology	1,974,888
New York, NY	
15) Pace University	1,666,047
New York, NY	
16) Drake University	1,663,679
Des Moines, IA	
17) Central Florida, University of	1,629,754
Orlando, FL	
18) California University of Pennsylvania	1,622,000
California, PA	
19) East Carolina University	1,565,012
Greenville, NC	
20) Bridgeport, University of	1,561,607
Bridgeport, CT	

Source: Council For Aid to Education (CFAE)

THE 20 COMPREHENSIVE INSTITUTIONS
REPORTING THE HIGHEST TOTAL ALUMNI
CONTRIBUTIONS

1) Smith College Northampton, MA	$15,440,074
2) Portland, University of Portland, OR	11,789,871
3) DePauw University Greencastle, IN	8,814,317
4) Colgate University Hamilton, NY	8,793,416
5) Stetson University Deland, FL	7,741,923
6) Baylor University Waco, TX	7,463,665
7) Wesleyan University Middletown, CT	6,731,239
8) Wake Forest University Winston-Salem, NC	5,919,579
9) Antioch University Yellow Springs, OH	5,782,705
10) Bucknell University Lewisburg, PA	5,247,572
11) Middlebury College Middlebury, VT	4,577,209
12) Hardin-Simmons University Abilene, TX	4,478,857
13) Rollins College Winter Park, FL	4,307,229
14) Abilene Christian University Abilene, TX	4,235,915
15) Trinity College Hartford, CT	3,982,349
16) American University in Cairo Cairo, Egypt	3,659,258
17) Mills College Oakland, CA	3,525,529
18) Richmond, University of Richmond, VA	3,320,934
19) Wheaton College Wheaton, IL	2,942,352
20) Texas Christian University Fort Worth, TX	2,925,377

Source: Council For Aid to Education (CFAE)

PREP SCHOOL RECORD SET

In 1979, Phillips Academy of Andover, Massachusetts raised $52 million in a capital program. For ten years, that stood as a record—the most raised by any preparatory school in the United States.

In 1988, Culver Educational Foundation (Culver Girls Academy, Culver Military Academy, and the Culver Summer Camps) successfully completed a campaign for $60.1 million—surpassing by 15 percent the record set by Phillips.

The Culver Institution is located in northern Indiana and is one of the earliest and largest of the military preparatory schools.

The largest gift to the campaign was an anonymous contribution of $5 million—which represented 8.5 percent of the amount raised—the classic size gift for a successful campaign.

INDEPENDENT SECONDARY SCHOOLS
TOP 15 IN DONATIONS—1987

Institution	Total Support (Dollars)	Alumni Giving (Dollars)	Property, Buildings & Equipment (Dollars)	Enrollment
1) Choate Rosemary Hall Wallingford, Connecticut	14,545,848	12,791,723	9,951,156	1,000
2) St. Mark's School of Texas Dallas, Texas	8,973,089	1,098,199	1,123,049	768
3) Lawrenceville School Lawrenceville, New Jersey	7,561,244	5,884,579	4,256,810	660
4) Phillips Exeter Academy Exeter, New Hampshire	7,327,028	5,791,222	183,469	982
5) Culver Academies Culver, Indiana	4,023,352	4,750,776	3,088,949	724
6) Deerfield Academy Deerfield, Massachusetts	6,650,347	4,688,147	350,455	576
7) Taft School Watertown, Connecticut	5,666,183	4,107,652	1,357,285	539
8) Milton Academy Milton, Massachusetts	5,354,733	988,764	179,690	905
9) Westminster Schools Atlanta, Georgia	4,899,482	1,132,473	477,903	1,677
10) Abington Friends School Abington, Pennsylvania	4,854,657	1,506,045	4,267,053	454
11) Groton School Groton, Massachusetts	4,682,191	2,834,394	10,172	320
12) Episcopal High School Alexandria, Virginia	4,655,403	3,285,123	1,990,792	297
13) American School in Japan Tokyo, Japan	4,367,813	36,775	1,153,701	1,401
14) Catlin Gabel School Portland, Oregon	4,103,542	177,475	136,309	572
15) Lakeside School Seattle, Washington	4,023,352	2,886,470	2,456,815	657

Source: Council for Aid to Education (CFAE)

Independent Elementary and Secondary Schools include boarding and day schools with students in grades pre-school through 12.

SPRING COMES TO TENNESSEE. BINGO!!!

The Supreme Court of Tennessee declared that bingo, raffles, and other games of chance would become illegal in March of 1989. As a result, Tennessee revoked the licenses of nearly 200 organizations running bingo games and told 750 others that operate raffles that they were in violation of the constitution.

It is estimated that in 1988, about $50 million was generated in Tennessee by organizations in bingo games—of which about $1 million actually went to charity.

And what are all of those bingo players doing now? They're arranging bus tours to Kentucky, Alabama, and North Carolina. According to the *New York Times,* the governor of Kentucky said: "...they're coming in by the busloads, those Tennessee bingo players are just swarming up here."

THE TEN BOARDING OR BOARDING/DAY SCHOOLS REPORTING THE HIGHEST TOTALS OF GIFTS FOR CAPITAL PURPOSES

1) Choate Rosemary Hall Wallingford, CT	$12,552,267
2) Lawrenceville School Lawrenceville, NJ	5,895,415
3) Culver Academies Culver, IN	5,395,178
4) Deerfield Academy Deerfield, MA	4,955,156
5) Phillips Exeter Academy Exeter, NH	4,536,568
6) Taft School Watertown, CT	4,426,680
7) Groton School Groton, MA	3,773,453
8) Episcopal High School Alexandria, VA	3,577,163
9) St. Mark's School Southborough, MA	3,374,070
10) Cheshire Academy Cheshire, CT	3,101,000

Source: Council For Aid to Education (CFAE)

THE TEN BOARDING OR BOARDING/DAY SCHOOLS REPORTING THE HIGHEST TOTAL OF TOTAL ALUMNI CONTRIBUTIONS

1) Choate Rosemary Hall Wallingford, CT	$12,791,723
2) Lawrenceville School Lawrenceville,NJ	5,884,579
3) Phillips Exeter Academy Exeter, NH	5,791,222
4) Culver Academies Culver, IN	4,750,776
5) Deerfield Academy Deerfield, MA	4,688,147
6) Taft School Watertown, CT	4,107,652
7) Episcopal High School Alexandria, VA	3,285,123
8) Cheshire Academy Cheshire, CT	3,173,327
9) St. Mark's School Southborough, MA	2,927,308
10) Groton School Groton, MA	2,834,394

Source: Council For Aid to Education (CFAE)

THE TWENTY DAY OR DAY/BOARDING SCHOOLS REPORTING THE HIGHEST ENDOWMENTS

1) St. Paul's School Concord, NH	$134,165,000
2) Phillips Exeter Academy Exeter, NH	121,319,697
3) Lawrenceville School Lawrenceville, NJ	85,589,153

4) Albuquerque Academy	78,650,000
Albuquerque, NM	
5) Hotchkiss School	72,101,759
Lakeville, CT	
6) Deerfield Academy	70,880,000
Deerfield, MA	
7) Milton Academy	60,990,626
Milton, MA	
8) Groton School	59,470,317
Groton, MA	
9) Choate Rosemary Hall	57,600,000
Wallingford, CT	
10) Culver Academies	49,277,711
Culver, IN	
11) Northfield Mount Hermon School	48,000,000
Northfield, MA	
12) Hill School	36,990,352
Philadelphia, PA	
13) Woodberry Forest School	36,478,939
Orange, VA	
14) Taft School	33,279,088
Watertown, CT	
15) Western Reserve Academy	29,159,594
Hudson, OH	
16) Iolani School	28,500,000
Honolulu, HI	
17) Baylor School	27,539,000
Chattanooga, TN	
18) Emma Willard School	26,200,000
Troy, NY	
19) Holland Hall School	25,831,040
Tulsa, OK	
20) Miss Porter's School	25,204,428
Farmington, CT	

Source: Council for Aid to Education (CFAE)

THE TEN DAY OR DAY/BOARDING SCHOOLS REPORTING THE HIGHEST TOTALS OF TOTAL ALUMNI CONTRIBUTIONS

1) Lakeside School	$2,886,470
Seattle, WA	
2) Pingry School	2,124,473
Martinville, NJ	
3) Baylor School	2,093,545
Chattanooga, TN	
4) Loomis Chaffee School	2,056,774
Simsbury, CT	
5) St. Francis Xavier High School	1,959,361
Bronx, NY	
6) McCallie School	1,691,924
Chattanooga, TN	
7) Dana Hall School	1,598,562
Wellesley, MA	
8) Abington Friends School	1,506,045
Abington, PA	
9) Darlington School	1,421,212
Rome, GA	
10) Regis High School	1,307,180
New York, NY	

Source: Council For Aid to Education (CFAE)

ADVANCEMENT-PROGRAM EXPENDITURES AS PERCENTAGE OF SCHOOL EXPENDITURES AND TOTAL VOLUNTARY SUPPORT, 1986–87

This table examines the relationship of fundraising expenditures to school expenditures and total giving. For all schools supplying this data, fundraising expenses were 4.1 percent of school expenditures and 14.8 percent of total giving in 1986–87.

Type of School	As Percent of School Expenditures		As Percent of Total Giving	
	No.	%	No.	%
Girls' Schools				
Day Elementary	2	4.5	2	26.0
Day Elementary/Secondary	36	4.1	36	14.6
Day Secondary	10	6.1	10	20.7
Day/Boarding	9	4.2	9	15.6
Boarding and Boarding/Day	15	5.8	15	17.1
Boys' Schools				
Day Elementary	7	3.6	7	9.0
Day Elementary/Secondary	14	4.5	14	11.5
Day Secondary	21	8.9	22	30.8
Day/Boarding	7	3.6	7	16.3
Boarding and Boarding/Day	24	6.6	24	14.4
Coed Schools				
Day Elementary	55	3.0	57	11.5
Day Elementary/Secondary	139	3.0	139	15.0
Day Secondary	36	4.3	37	15.3
Day/Boarding	34	3.9	35	15.0
Boarding and Boarding/Day	74	4.8	75	13.1
All Reporting Schools	483	4.1	489	14.8

Source: Council For Aid to Education (CFAE)

TOTAL VOLUNTARY SUPPORT BY TYPE OF INDEPENDENT SCHOOL, 1986–87

The breakdown of support by type of school, according to the level of program and type of student body, is shown in this table. Girls schools received the smallest amount of support, both in average per school and total dollars.

Type of School	Girls	Boys	Coeducational	Total
Day Elementary	$ 621,068	$ 6,273,541	$ 25,944,434	$ 32,839,043
	(2)	(8)	(70)	(80)
Day Elementary/ Secondary	31,643,364	23,299,403	130,238,876	185,181,643
	(37)	(15)	(152)	(204)
Day Secondary	6,855,943	18,975,109	27,105,024	52,936,076
	(13)	(22)	(39)	(74)
Day/Boarding	10,282,610	6,645,917	38,526,268	55,454,795
	(10)	(8)	(35)	(53)
Boarding and Boarding/Day	14,616,394	37,098,487	124,501,601	176,216,482
	(16)	(24)	(81)	(121)
GRAND TOTAL	$64,019,379	$92,292,457	$346,316,203	$502,628,039
	(78)	(77)	(377)	(532)

(Figures in parentheses show number of schools reporting.)

Source: Council For Aid to Education (CFAE)

TOTAL ENDOWMENT AND ENDOWMENT PER STUDENT, 1986–87

Type of School	Number Reporting	Endowment (000)	Average per Student*
Girls' Schools			
Day Elementary	—	—	—
Day Elementary/Secondary	36	$ 123,441	$ 6,855
Day Secondary	8	14,284	6,413
Day/Boarding	10	58,429	15,294
Boarding and Boarding/Day	16	114,427	30,191
Boys' Schools			
Day Elementary	7	23,065	10,717
Day Elementary/Secondary	15	104,659	10,209
Day Secondary	20	93,991	10,566
Day/Boarding	7	35,740	11,314
Boarding and Boarding/Day	23	268,667	32,376
Coed Schools			
Day Elementary	59	79,686	4,314
Day Elementary/Secondary	140	583,050	5,009
Day Secondary	36	43,303	2,908
Day/Boarding	33	233,925	11,915
Boarding and Boarding/Day	76	988,470	30,896
All Reporting Schools	486	$2,765,137	$12,344

*The average per student is the mean value of the endowment per student for all schools reporting in each category.

Source: Council For Aid to Education (CFAE)

JAPANESE ARE LEARNING TO GIVE

A handful of large Japanese corporations—led by Hitachi—are taking the lead and placing millions of dollars into foundations. Other Japanese companies are taking tentative, but definite, first steps—holding United Way drives, sponsoring cultural events, and donating products to local charities.

Japanese corporations are learning a lesson from their American brethren: the best way to polish your image is to give a little from corporation funds. Delwin Roy is president of the Hitachi Foundation and he says: "Hitachi realized how really bad its reputation and image was in the United States and became terribly concerned about it."

In 1983, Hitachi pleaded guilty to criminal charges of transporting stolen IBM technical documents to Japan. The Hitachi Foundation was organized 18 months later and remains the largest foundation estabished by any Japanese company. It has an endowment of $27 million.

Japanese companies have not been as active as they could be in the United States in corporate giving—but they are beginning to be. Last year, Japanese companies contributed about $150 million to charities, schools, and cultural groups—triple the amount given in 1986. More than half of the money went to universities.

Corporate giving is a perplexing concept for the Japanese. In their native land, the first responsibility of corporations is providing "cradle to grave" services to their employees. The government, in turn, takes care of other people's needs. In Japan, corporations do not get tax incentives for donations. But they are beginning to understand that a corporation in the United States is not simply an economic entity—it is a social entity. And that carries the implication of social and civic responsibility.

THE TEN DAY OR DAY/BOARDING SCHOOLS REPORTING THE MOST CORPORATE SUPPORT

1) American School in Japan Tokyo, Japan	$4,188,190
2) Deerfield Academy Deerfield, MA	875,208
3) Loyola Academy Wilmette, IL	518,419
4) Trinity Valley School Fort Worth, TX	506,650
5) Laurel School Cleveland, OH	451,979
6) North Carolina School of Science and Mathematics Durham, NC	413,406
7) Phillips Exeter Academy Exeter, NH	348,357
8) Culver Academies Culver, IN	255,041
9) Dwight-Englewood School Englewood, NJ	253,354
10) Baylor School Chattanooga, TN	244,211

Source: Council For Aid to Education (CFAE)

THE TEN DAY OR DAY/BOARDING SCHOOLS REPORTING THE HIGHEST TOTALS OF GIFTS FOR CAPITAL PURPOSES

1) St. Mark's School of Texas Dallas, TX	$8,462,228
2) Abington Friends School Abington, PA	4,460,782
3) Westminster Schools Atlanta, GA	4,014,482
4) Milton Academy Milton, MA	3,929,243
5) Catlin Gabel School Portland, OR	3,885,159
6) Morristown-Beard School Morristown, NJ	3,375,144
7) Lakeside School Seattle, WA	3,210,597
8) Pingry School Martinville, NJ	2,956,786
9) Baylor School Chattanooga, TN	2,440,494
10) Dana Hall School Wellesley, MA	2,321,529

Source: Council For Aid to Education (CFAE)

GIVING BY INDIVIDUALS

The following table shows individual giving trends over the last eleven years. It is interesting to note that in 1985–86, bequests rose a record $227 million, but increased by only $42.7 million the next year. Consequently, most of the extraordinary increase in individual giving during these years is attributable to living donors. Deferred gifts reached a record high of $425,297 in 1986–87, 74 percent more than the preceeding year.

BEQUESTS AND DEFERRED GIFTS, 1976–77 TO 1986–87
(thousands of dollars)

Year	All Individual Gifts	Bequests		Deferred Gifts	
1976–77	$1,025,301	$284,227	(27.7)	$ 69,554	(6.8)
1977–78	1,142,535	324,496	(28.4)	101,030	(8.8)
1978–79	1,202,496	296,993	(24.7)	95,946	(8.0)
1979–80	1,403,538	320,825	(22.9)	99,293	(7.1)
1980–81	1,611,232	374,054	(23.2)	103,153	(6.4)
1981–82	1,968,408	529,119	(26.9)	125,632	(6.4)
1982–83	2,054,133	437,961	(21.3)	154,508	(7.5)
1983–84	2,184,020	512,960	(23.4)	83,169	(3.8)
1984–85	2,411,244	485,000	(20.1)	194,028	(8.0)
1985–86	3,074,469	714,082	(23.2)	244,583	(8.0)
1986–87	3,795,699	756,795	(19.9)	425,297	(11.2)

(Figures in parentheses show percent of all individual gifts.)

Source: Council For Aid to Education (CFAE)

VOLUNTARY SUPPORT TO EDUCATIONAL INSTITUTIONS

Virtually all the gains in voluntary support over the last five years have significantly exceeded the rate of inflation, whether measured by the Consumer Price Index (CPI) or the Higher Education Price Index (HEPI), which measures the "market basket" of goods and services that educational institutions must buy. Between 1981–82 and 1986–87, voluntary support rose by nearly 75 percent while prices increased 19 percent (as measured by CPI) and 30 percent (HEPI). Only in the case of support from religious organizations was the increase less than the inflation rate.

VOLUNTARY SUPPORT OF COLLEGES AND UNIVERSITIES BY CORPORATIONS
(millions of dollars)

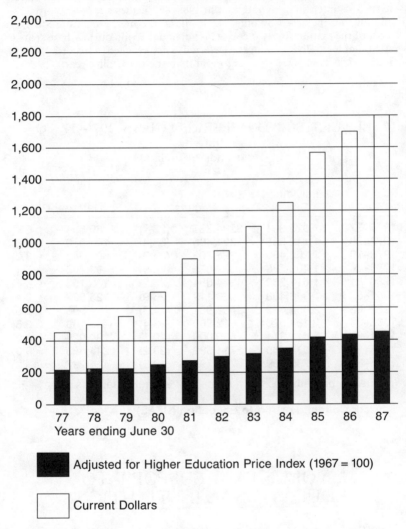

Adjusted for Higher Education Price Index (1967 = 100)

Current Dollars

Source: Council for Aid to Education (CFAE)

VOLUNTARY SUPPORT OF COLLEGES AND UNIVERSITIES BY ALUMNI
(millions of dollars)

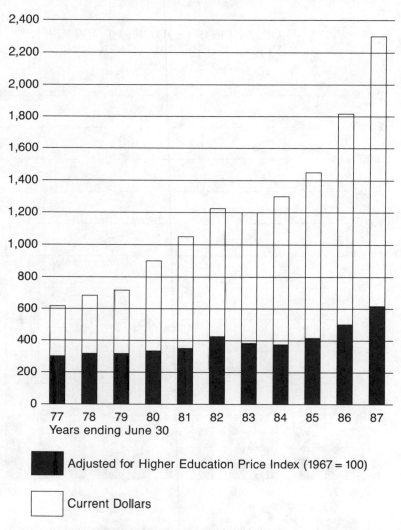

Adjusted for Higher Education Price Index (1967 = 100)

Current Dollars

Source: Council for Aid to Education (CFAE)

> *"In bestowing charity, the main consideration should be to help those who will help themselves; to provide part of the means by which those who desire to improve may do so; to give those who desire to rise the aids by which they may rise; to assist, but rarely or never to do all."*
>
> *Andrew Carnegie*

Our American tradition of neighbor helping neighbor has always been one of our greatest strengths and most noble traditions.
Ronald Reagan

VOLUNTARY SUPPORT OF COLLEGES AND UNIVERSITIES BY FOUNDATIONS
(millions of dollars)

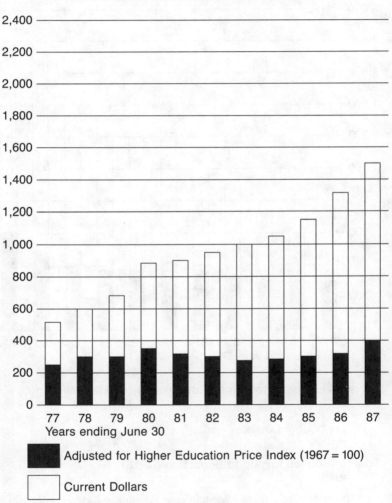

Years ending June 30

■ Adjusted for Higher Education Price Index (1967 = 100)

□ Current Dollars

Source: Council for Aid to Education (CFAE)

"The act of volunteering is an assertion of individual worth."
Edward C. Linderman (1885–1953)

"The question is not 'What can I get?' but 'What can I give in life?'"
Robert Baden-Powell (1858–1941)

TOTAL VOLUNTARY SUPPORT OF COLLEGES AND UNIVERSITIES
(millions of dollars)

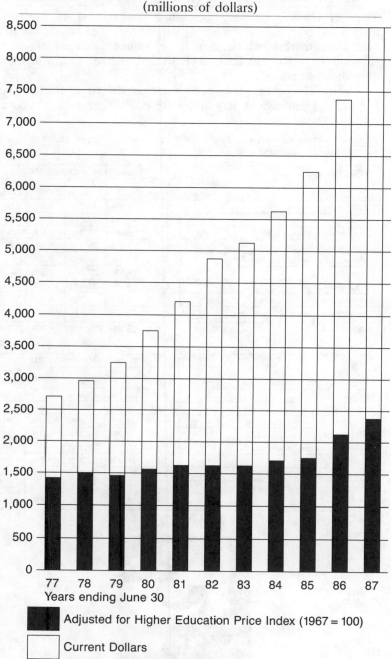

Years ending June 30

■ Adjusted for Higher Education Price Index (1967 = 100)

☐ Current Dollars

Source: Council for Aid to Education (CFAE)

THE FRI SURVEY SHOWS GREAT OPTIMISM AND IMPORTANT GROWTH

The *FRI Monthly Portfolio*, published by the Fund Raising Institute, is an extraordinary monthly newsletter filled with nuts-and-bolts information which can be a valued addition to every fundraiser's tool chest. Each issue is filled with material which can have direct application.

The FRI recently conducted a survey to determine the status of fundraising among a variety of not-for-profit agencies and organizations. The results follow.

Compared with a year or so ago, please rate the philanthropic income produced by your various fund-raising solicitations.

TYPE OF SOLICITATION	PHILANTHROPIC INCOME				
	much higher	higher	no change	lower	much lower
Capital gifts	19.8%	17.7%	17.7%	8.3%	1.0%
Annual gifts	7.3%	42.3%	19.8%	19.8%	1.0%
Gifts through giving clubs	5.2%	35.4%	19.8%	4.2%	1.0%
Deferred gifts via bequests	9.4%	21.9%	33.3%	8.3%	1.0%
Deferred gifts via trusts, etc.	6.3%	13.5%	34.4%	6.3%	—
Corporate gifts	8.3%	38.5%	22.9%	12.5%	—
Foundation gifts	6.3%	29.2%	32.3%	14.6%	1.0%
Government grants: federal	2.1%	18.8%	17.7%	4.2%	—
Government grants: state & local	3.1%	16.7%	16.7%	7.3%	—
1988 TOTALS—	11.1%	38.6%	35.3%	14.1%	.86%

TYPE OF SOLICITATION	PHILANTHROPIC INCOME				
	much higher	higher	no change	lower	much lower
Capital gifts	9.5%	26.7%	12.4%	5.7%	2.8%
Annual gifts	10.5%	48.6%	16.2%	11.4%	1.9%
Gifts through giving clubs	4.8%	24.8%	20.9%	3.8%	1.9%
Deferred gifts via bequests	13.3%	22.9%	27.6%	1.9%	2.8%
Deferred gifts via trusts, etc.	7.6%	14.3%	32.4%	—	1.9%
Corporate gifts	1.9%	36.2%	32.4%	11.4%	1.9%
Foundation gifts	7.6%	32.4%	33.3%	12.4%	0.9%
Government grants: federal	—	8.6%	22.9%	5.7%	—
Government grants: state & local	1.9%	11.4%	20.9%	6.7%	0.9%
1987 TOTALS—	9.9%	39.2%	38.0%	10.3%	2.6%

INDEPENDENT SECTOR

INDEPENDENT SECTOR IS A MAJOR FORCE AND PROPONENT OF PHILANTHROPY

Independent Sector is a not-for-profit coalition of 650 corporate, foundation, and voluntary organization members with a national interest and impact in philanthropy and voluntary action. It is the successor to the Coalition of National Voluntary Organizations and the National Council on Philanthropy. The organization's mission is to create a national forum capable of encouraging the giving, volunteering, and the not-for-profit initiative that will help all of us to better serve people, communities, and causes.

The group is one of the major forces in this country which provides focus and momentum to the nation's philanthropy. It helps greatly in the establishing of the nation's agenda for not-for-profit institutional initiatives and platforms. Many were involved in its development, but credit for the inspiration and founding is given primarily to John W. Gardner—Chairperson of the organizing committee and first Chairperson. Dr. Gardner is an author and former Secretary of Health, Education, and Welfare, and is held in high regard nationally.

Officers and Directors of Independent Sector follow.

Chairperson: **John H. Filer**
Partner, Tyler, Cooper & Alcorn
Former Chairman and CEO,
Aetna Life and Casualty

Vice Chairperson: **Linda Flores**
President, Puerto Rican Legal
Defense and Education Fund

Vice Chairperson: **John E. Jacob**
President, National Urban
League, Inc.

Vice Chairperson: **Boisfeuillet Jones**
President, the Woodruff
Foundation

Vice Chairperson: **David Mathews**
President, Charles F. Kettering
Foundation

Vice Chairperson: **Fern C. Portnoy**
President, Portnoy and
Associates

Vice Chairperson: **Cecile M. Springer**
Director of Contributions and
Community Affairs,
Westinghouse Electric
Corporation

Treasurer: **Astrid Merget**
Director, School of Public
Administration, Ohio State
University

Secretary: **Eugene R. Wilson**
President, ARCO Foundation

President: **Brian O'Connell**
Former President, National
Council on Philanthropy;
Former Executive Director,
Coalition of National Voluntary
Organizations

Brian O'Connell is the founding President of Independent Sector. He leads the coalition's work in generating new research on the sector, encourages the improvement of not-for-profit leadership and management, and creates mutually supportive relationships between government and voluntary organizations. Independent Sector is the country's leading advocate for giving and volunteering.

Early in his career, Mr. O'Connell was involved in rehabilitation programs for handicapped children. He worked with the American Heart Association, heading the state organizations in Maryland and California. He was National Director of the Mental Health Association. He is an author of note and a widely acclaimed speaker.

For more information: INDEPENDENT SECTOR, 1828 L Street, N.W., Washington, DC 20036 (202) 223-8100.

PUBLICATIONS AVAILABLE FROM INDEPENDENT SECTOR

Among its many services and activities, the Independent Sector offers a rich and worthy variety of publications.

From the Executive Office

Philanthropy in Action, by Brian O'Connell

Our Organization, by Brian O'Connell

Corporate Philanthropy: Getting Bigger, Broader and Tougher to Manage, a special issue of Corporate Philanthropy by Brian O'Connell

The Board Member's Book, by Brian O'Connell

America's Voluntary Spirit, by Brian O'Connell

Origins, Dimensions and Impact of America's Voluntary Spirit, by Brian O'Connell

From Daring Goals For A Caring Society

Daring Goals for a Caring Society, A blueprint for participating in the challenge to foster substantial growth in giving and volunteering in America

Involving Your Corporation or Foundation in the Program

Involving Your National Voluntary Organization in the Program

Starting a Coalition in Your Community

How to Survey the Level of Giving and Volunteering in Your Community— A Research Kit

From Government Relations

Charitable Giving and the Federal Tax Laws: Preserving a Vital Partnership for Public Purposes

Advocacy is Sometimes an Agency's Best Service: Opportunities and Limits within Federal Law

Regulation of Charitable Fund Raising: The Schaumburg Decision

Lobby? You? Of Course You Can...And You Should!

Valuation Guide for Donated Goods

Accountability with Independence—Toward a Balance in Government/ Independent Sector Financial Partnerships, a report of the task force on organizational and financial relationships, chaired by The Honorable Samuel Goddard

From Research

Dimensions of the Independent Sector: A Statistical Profile (Second Ed.) An overview of America's unique "third sector"

The Charitable Behavior of Americans, Commissioned by the Rockefeller Brothers Fund, conducted by Yankelovich, Skelly and White, published and distributed by IS

Americans Volunteer 1985, An updated version of the IS/Gallup survey on volunteering, including a dollar analysis of the value of volunteer time and a comparison with the survey done in 1981

Resource Raising: The Role of Non-Cash Assistance in Corporate Philanthropy, by Alex J. Plinio, President, the Prudential Foundation and Joanne B. Scanlan, Ph.D.

Major Challenges to Philanthropy, A keynote paper prepared for the 1984 IS Annual Meeting by Robert L. Payton, Associate Director and Scholar-in-Residence, Center for Public Affairs, University of Virginia and former President, Exxon Education Foundation.

Research-in-Progress (1986–85), A national compilation of 441 research projects on philanthropy, voluntary action and not-for-profit activity

Research-in-Progress (1985–84)

Research-in-Progress (1984–83)

Research-in-Progress (1983–82)

Working Papers for 1987 INDEPENDENT SECTOR Spring Research Forum—The Constitution and the Independent Sector

Working Papers for 1986 INDEPENDENT SECTOR Spring Research Forum—Philanthropy, Voluntary Action and the Public Good

Working Papers for 1985 INDEPENDENT SECTOR Spring Research Forum—Giving and Volunteering: New Frontiers of Knowledge

Working Papers for 1983 INDEPENDENT SECTOR Spring Research Forum—Since the Filer Commission. . .

Patterns of Charitable Giving by Individuals II, Research report based on the 1982 Gallup survey, commissioned by INDEPENDENT SECTOR, the 501(c)(3) Group, and The National Society of Fund Raising Executives.

From Effective Sector Leadership/Management

Nonprofit Management Series. A collection of nine reports by Brian O'Connell including: *The Role of the Board and Board Members; Finding, Developing and Rewarding Good Board Members; Operating Effective Committees; Conducting Good Meetings; The Roles and Relationships of the Chief Volunteer and Chief Staff Officers, Board and Staff: Who Does What?; Recruiting, Encouraging and Evaluating the Chief Staff Officer; Fund Raising; Budgeting and Financial Accountability;* and, *Evaluating Results.*

Aiming High on a Small Budget: Executive Searches and the Nonprofit Sector

Profiles of Effective Corporate Giving Programs, by E.B. Knauft, **IS** Executive Vice President, and former Vice President and Executive Director of the Aetna Life and Casualty Foundation

Series of Papers on Leadership, A collection of papers on various aspects of leadership prepared by John W. Gardner

Governance is Governance, Keynote address delivered at the second ESL/M Professional Forum, by Kenneth N. Dayton of the Oakleaf Foundation and former Chairman and CEO of the Dayton Hudson Corporation

An Independent Sector Resource Directory of Education and Training Opportunities and Other Services (Second Ed.)

INDEPENDENT SECTOR Professional Forum II Proceedings, Keynote speeches, highlights and panel discussions are included from the second annual Professional Forum which had the two-fold theme of "Governance/Board Development" and "Attracting and Retaining Talented People in the Field"

General Public Education

INDEPENDENT SECTOR ANNUAL REPORT

"TO CARE: America's Voluntary Spirit" Descriptive brochure/flyer on **IS** film, including complete rental/purchase information and order form

What Kind of Society Shall We Have? An INDEPENDENT SECTOR Occasional Paper prepared by Richard W. Lyman, President, Rockefeller Foundation, and former Chairperson, INDEPENDENT SECTOR

Giving: Big Bucks, Bare Basics and Blue Skies, A keynote address delivered by David Rockefeller at the 1985 **IS** Annual Membership Meeting and Assembly

Private Sector, Public Control and the Independent University, by A. Bartlett Giamatti, former President, Yale University

The Third Sector: Keystone of a Caring Society, by Waldemar A. Nielsen

For more information and a complete catalogue: INDEPENDENT SECTOR, 1828 L Street, N.W., Washington, DC 20036 (202) 223-8100.

THE NOT-FOR-PROFIT MAKES IMMENSE NATIONAL IMPACT

There are nearly 800,000 not-for-profit organizations in the arts, education, health, religion, and human and social services. This group enjoys tax-exempt status.

These organizations are an important part of the fiber and fabric of this country. They are all inclusive, more than 100,000 start with the foundations. Add to them museums, theaters, symphonies, zoos, aquariums, and other arts and cultural organizations. And all the health related institutions, special research centers, not-for-profit hospitals and medical centers, nursing homes, and rehabilitation centers. There are independent schools, church schools, colleges, and universities. And all the religious and health-related charities. Add to that the social and welfare organizations, the Girl Scouts, the YMCAs, Boys Clubs, Salvation Army, and the Red Cross. The list goes on. Twenty years ago, there were half the number. The figure grows and will continue to increase. In the next five years, the number of organizations will likely grow to one million. Each organization and institution affects the constituency it serves in a unique way.

Charitable and philanthropic organizations employ more than 6.6 million people. Working with them are 4.6 million volunteers.

In 1988, the operating expenses of these organizations totalled more than $23 billion. The group holds assets of more than $200 billion.

It received $93.7 billion in grants and gifts from all sources—corporations, foundations, individuals, and bequests. This is an all-time record for philanthropy.

Here are some even more amazing statistics. These not-for-profit organizations employ one out of every sixteen American workers—one out of eleven if you count volunteers. They account for one out of every 20 dollars of our country's income, and they generate nearly 20 percent of service revenue.

Source: Independent Sector & *Giving USA*

THE SHORT, INTENSIVE CAMPAIGN

Fundraising has come full circle. Today, we talk a great deal about "a development effort." Typically, this is a major capital effort that is designed to be carried on over an extended period. There was a time when this was the only way of raising funds!

The short-term, or intensive, campaign method of raising funds was "perfected" in the decade following 1905. It started with YMCAs. The genuis behind the idea was the ability to enlist and hold to a specific task a sufficiently large force of volunteers. Prior to those days, institutions would work for periods of several years, with a small handful of men, to raise building funds. The time was reduced to a month when a hundred volunteers concentrated on a project. There were some programs that were actually accomplished in a week or ten days.

In Canton, Ohio, the concept of selecting captains who would recruit workers was first tried. The idea spread. The intensive campaign was born. The ingredients: competition, division leaders, enlisted volunteers, announced time limits, careful record-keeping, plenty of good publicity, and definite objectives. Institutions learned that a large group of workers could be enlisted, and that by reporting on a regular and frequent basis, they were able to sustain the spirit of competition.

In 1905, $85,000 was raised in one month for the YMCA in Washington, DC—an extraordinary achievement at the time. And for the first time in such an effort, a "paid publicity agent" was employed. He was Charles S. Ward, a YMCA International Field Secretary.

There were others, but the man who had the most to do with promulgating the intensive campaign was Ward. A 1918 graduate of Dartmouth, Ward had been General Secretary of YMCAs in several medium-sized cities. In 1897, he went to Minneapolis where he reorganized a YMCA that had recently lost its building, and raised $25,000 that redeemed the property. From then on, it was one campaign after another.

Ward's dramatic career was set in motion. In three thirty-day campaigns, he raised $180,000 in Duluth, $225,000 in St. Paul, and $90,000 in Dallas. Over a weekend, he raised $30,000 in Lincoln. He said: "With team play, competition, and mass psychology and publicity—an entire city was made so interested and ready to give that a large number of men, many of whom were probably poor so-licitors, could successfully solicit subscriptions in a short length of time."

Ward insisted upon a carefully prepared list of prospects, a strong organization of workers with teams and captains, a dinner meeting at which the campaign was launched, and daily report meetings with effective publicity. With these devices, he raised nearly $30 million for YMCAs between 1910 and 1915. The climax of his career came in 1917, when he successfully directed the American Red Cross campaign for war funds of $100 million.

In every city where Ward managed a drive, it was characterized as the most remarkable campaign in the history of the city. Records were broken year after year as ever larger amounts were raised.

Charles Ward left the YMCA to start a company which would help colleges, universities and agencies raise funds. This was a totally new concept.

He asked another YMCA Secretary to join him, a man named Dreshman. Ward & Dreshman exist to this day, a firm with an extraordinary record, a distinguished past, and a talented group of men and women.

Many individuals and firms have contributed to the extraordinary record of philanthropy in this country. None is owed a greater debt than Charles Ward, and the firm he founded—Ward & Dreshman.

On December 5, 1988, the fundraising industry lost one of its great leaders. J. Richard Wilson died at his home in Alexandria, Virginia, at the age of 60.

He was an executive officer of the National Society of Fund Raising Executives for nine years—first as Executive Vice-President and later as President. It was during his tenure that membership grew from 2,000 to the current roster of 9,500 members. Chapters increased from 22 to 104. He was an impressive and articulate advocate of the profession and the field—and one of its most visible representatives. He gave generously of his time and talents.

Before becoming a staff member of the NSFRE, he was president of the Wisconsin Chapter of NSFRE in the 1970s and served on the National Board of Directors. He was also a member of the Board of Directors for the Independent Sector and the National Fund-Raising Advisory Committee for Special Olympics, Inc.

In recent years, his health was not good, but he never slackened his pace. For all in the field, his end came unexpectedly and too soon. He served the industry with distinction and in many ways, and left an indelible mark which history will record as of monumental proportions.

STATE LAWS REGULATING CHARITABLE SOLICITATIONS
(AS OF DECEMBER 31, 1987)

State/Regulatory Agency	Charitable Organizations						Fund Raisers/FR Counsel
	Registration or Licensing Requirements	Limitations on use of funds raised	Reporting Dates	Monetary Exemptions	Solicitation Disclosure Requirements		Registration/ Licensing Bonding Requirements
Alabama Attorney General Consumer Protection Div. Montgomery, AL 36130 (205) 261-7334	None	None	None	None	Solicitor must disclose name, % of proceeds allocated to charity.		None
Alaska Attorney General Dept. of Law 1301 W. 4th Avenue Anchorage, AK 99501 (907) 276-3550	None	None	None	None	None		None
Arizona Attorney General 1275 West Washington Phoenix, AZ 85007 (602) 255-1719	None	None	None	None	None		None
Arkansas Secretary of State Trademarks Department Little Rock, AR 72201 (501) 371-5167	Registration	None	March 31 or within 90 days after close of fiscal calendar year.*	Maximum proceeds of $1,000, if all soliciting is done by volunteers.	Solicitor must disclose % of gross proceeds allocated to charity.		Registration; $5,000 bond.
California Registry of Charitable Trusts 1718 3rd Street Sacramento, CA 94203-4470 (916) 445-2021	Registration	None	Financial report due same time as 990. 4½ months after end of accounting period. Annual report due May 15, if gross revenue or assets exceed $25,000 during year.	None	"Sale for charitable purpose card" must be shown prior to any solicitation.		None

State / Contact					
Colorado Attorney General Dept. of Law 1525 Sherman Street Denver, CO 80203 (303) 866-3611	None	None	None	Solicitor who knows that less than 50% of proceeds will be delivered to charitable organization must so disclose to solicitees—if the organization can prove that it is supposed to receive at least 50%.	None
Connecticut Attorney General Public Charities Unit 80 Trinity Street Hartford, CT 06106 (203) 566-5836	Registration	Within 5 months of close of fiscal year, on form prescribed by the Department. Independent CPA audit required if gross revenue less government grants and fees exceeds $100,000.*	Maximum proceeds of $25,000 if solicitors are not paid primarily to solicit.	Paid non-employee solicitors must disclose name of the soliciting firm, that firm is paid to solicit, and % of gross contributions allocated to charitable organization.	Registration; $20,000 bond if fund raiser has custody or control of contributions. Must file with Department a copy of contracts with charitable organizations.
Delaware Attorney General Civil Division The Wilmington Tower Wilmington, DE 19899 (302) 571-2528	None	None	None	None	None
District of Columbia Dept. of Consumer & Regulatory Affairs 614 H Street NW Washington, DC 20001 (202) 727-7086	Licensing	Within 30 days after end of licensing period and 30 days after a demand by the mayor.	Maximum proceeds of $1,500 if all soliciting is done by volunteers.	Solicitor must present to prospective donor a solicitation information card issued by Department.	None
Florida Department of State Division of Licensing The Capital-# 4 Talahassee, FL 32399 (904) 488-5381	Registration	Six months after organization's fiscal year. If gross contributions were: Greater than $10,000 but less than $50,000—on department-approved form or review/audit by independent	Maximum proceeds of $10,000, if solicitation is not done by professional solicitor.	Solicitor must disclose name and relationship to charitable organization, and advise solicitee that organization's disclosure statement is available upon	Licensing. $10,000 bond for professional solicitors. No bond requirement for Fund Raising Consultant.

State / Agency	Registration	Use of Funds	Financial Reporting	Exemptions	Disclosure	Bonding
(continued from previous page)			CPA; Greater than $50,000 but less than $100,000—review/audit by independent CPA; Greater than $100,000—audit by independent CPA.		request. Statement must be provided within 14 days of request.	
Georgia Secretary of State Office of Special Services 2 Martin Luther King Drive Suite 802-West Tower Atlanta, GA 30334 (404) 656-4910	Registration	None	Quarterly reports in first year of operation. Must be verified by independent CPA for proceeds over $50,000. Anual report within 180 days after close of organization's fiscal year.	Maximum proceeds of $15,000. Also religious and non-profit educational groups, civic and fraternal groups whose solicitation is confined to members; certain hunting and fishing groups.	Organization must disclose to donor names of solicitor and organization, and purpose of solicitation	Registration; $10,000 or 50% of fund raiser's income for preceding year, whichever is greater.
Hawaii Dept. of Commerce & Consumer Affairs P.O. Box 40 Honolulu, HI 96810 (808) 548-5319	Registration	None	With registration statement.	Maximum proceeds of $4,000 if all soliciting done by volunteers.	Solicitor must furnish authorization on request.	Licensing; $5,000 bond.
Idaho Attorney General Statehouse Boise, ID 83720 (208) 334-2400	None	None	None	None	None	None
Illinois Attorney General Charitable Trust Div. 100 West Randolph 12th Floor Chicago, IL 60601-3175 (312) 917-2595	Religious organizations also required to register, but may apply for exemption.	At least 75% of gross receipts after deducting ordinary and reasonable expenses must be used for charitable purposes. Not more than 25% of gross receipts may be used for unordered merchandise—e.g. fundraising gifts mailed to solicitees.	Within 6 months after end of fiscal year. Form 990 accepted but must be accompanied by a supplemental form. CPA opinion must accompany report if revenues exceed $50,000.	Maximum proceeds of $4,000, if all soliciting is done by volunteers.	None	Registration: $5,000 bond.
Indiana Attorney General Consumer	None	None	None	None	Paid solicitor and consultant must disclose—before	Registration

Protection Div. 219 State House Indianapolis, IN 46204 (317) 232-4522					solicitee agrees to make contribution—name of charitable organization, that solicitor is professional and is paid to solicit, amount (fee) of compensation, and % of contributions allocated to charitable organization.	None
Iowa Attorney General Consumer Protection Div. 1300 East Walnut Hoover State Off. Bldg. Des Moines, IA 50319	Registration with Secretary of State. [Requirement has been declared unconstitutional, but is still on the books.]	None	None		Attorney General recommends professional fund-raisers disclose % of proceeds allocated to charity. Consumer Fraud Act enforced.	None
Kansas Secretary of State Capitol Bldg.-2nd Floor Topeka, KS 66612 (913) 296-3751	Registration	15th day after close of organization's taxable year, on form prescribed by Attorney General. If books are not closed 12/31, organization must so notify Secretary of State. If proceeds exceed $75,000, report must be accompanied by opinion signed by independent CPA.	At least 75% of gross receipts must be used for charitable purposes and not more than 25% for the cost of unordered merchandise—e.g. fundraising gifts mailed to solicitees.	Maximum proceeds of $5,000, if all soliciting is done by volunteers	None	Registration; $5,000 bond.
Kentucky Attorney General Division of Consumer Protection Frankfort, KY 40601 (502) 564-2200	Registration if required to file 990.	No specific date. However, professional fund raisers must file annual report by Jan. 15 of the following year.	None		Opinion of Attorney General: Solicitors not employed by the charitable organization must disclose % of proceeds allocated to charity if so requested by solicitee.	Registration
Louisiana Attorney General	Registration	None	None		None	Registration

Dept. of Justice Consumer Protection Div. Baton Rouge, LA 70806 (504) 342-7013						
Maine Dept. of Business, Occupational & Professional Regulation Station # 35 Augusta, ME 04333 (207) 289-3671	Registration	None	Six months after close of fiscal year. If more than $30,000 raised, must be audited by independent CPA.	Maximum proceeds of $10,000 received from 10 persons or fewer in unsolicited funds by volunteers.	Proefssional solicitor must disclose to solicitee estimated cost of solicitation, where less than 70% of amount donated will be allocated to the specific charitable purpose. [Note: currently undergoing revision.]	Registration; $10,000 bond
Maryland Secretary of State State House Annapolis, MD 21401 (301) 974-3425	Registration	None	Most recent completed fiscal year. If proceeds are in excess of $100,000, audit is required by independent CPA applying accounting and financial reporting standards of voluntary health and welfare organizations.*	Maximum proceeds of $25,000 if solicitation is not done by professional solicitor.	Paid solicitor must disclose name, that s/he has been engaged as solicitor by charity, name of organization, purpose for which contribution is solicited, % of donations received by solicitor, % deductible for income tax purposes, and copy of organization's financial statement if requested.	Registration
Massachusetts Attorney General Division of Public Charities One Ashburton Place Boston, MA 02108 (617) 727-2235	Registration	At least 25% of proceeds allocated to charity. [Ruled unconstitutional 7/31/87.]	Form PC due on same date as federal form 990 or 990PF including extensions. For organizations not filing 990 or 990PF, form PC due on 15th day of the 5th month after the close of fiscal year. Organizations	None	Solicitor must disclose name of organization, that s/he is a paid solicitor, what funds will be used for, minimum % of gross receipts allocated to charity.	Licensing; $10,000 bond. Bond only for solicitors.

State						
Minnesota Attorney General Charities Division 340 Bremer Tower 7th Place & Minnesota St. St. Paul, MN 55101 (612) 296-6172	Registration	None	receiving over $100,000 annually must file audited financial statement. Within 6 months of close of fiscal year. Extension permitted if requested in writing. Annual report, financial statement, and copy of IRS 990. (990 may usually be filed in place of financial statement.) Audit required if public contributions exceed $100,000*.	Maximum proceeds of $25,000, if all soliciting is done by volunteers.	Solicitation card must be shown prior to solicitation. Solicitor must disclose identity of charity, tax deductibility of contribution, description of charitable program. Professional fund raiser must also disclose name, that s/he is a professional fund raiser, and a reasonable estimate of % of proceeds used for charitable purposes.	Registration; $20,000 bond (required if professional fund raiser has custody of funds).
Michigan Attorney General Charitable Trust Section 690 Law Building 525 West Ottawa Street Lansing, MI 48913 (517) 335-0855	Licensing	None	Within 6 months of end of fiscal year. CPA audit required where income from public support is at least $50,000.	Maximum proceeds of $8,000 if all soliciting is done by volunteers and annual report is given to contributors.	None	Licensing; $10,000 bond.
Mississippi Attorney General Carroll Gartin Justice Bldg. P.O. Box 220 Jackson, MS 39205-0220 (601) 359-3680	None	None	None	None	None	None
Missouri Attorney General P.O. Box 899 Jefferson City, MO 65102 (314) 751-2616	Registratoin	None	Annual report must be filed within 75 days of close of organization's fiscal year. Report must contain % of proceeds used for	Maximum proceeds of $10,000.	Solicitor must disclose that s/he is a professional fund raiser working on behalf of charitable organization; name of organization.	Registration

State						
Montana Secretary of State Room 225 Capitol Station Helena, MT 59620 (406) 444-3665	None	None	None	None	None	None
Nebraska Secretary of State Lincoln, NE 68509 (402) 471-2554	Certificate granted on basis of letter of approval obtained from county attorney of home office county.	None	At end of organization's fiscal year.*	None	Solicitor must show certificate, and issue receipts for donations of more than $2.00.	None
Nevada Attorney General Carson City, NV 89710 (702) 687-4170	None	None	By July 1 with Secretary of State.*	None	None	None
New Hampshire Attorney General Charitable Trust Concord, NH 03301 (603) 271-3591	Registration	None	Due 4 months and 15 days after close of fiscal or calendar year. 990 may be used in lieu of report.	None	Solicitor must disclose name, that s/he is a paid solicitor, and % of gross proceeds allocated to charity.	Registration (for fund raisers with custody of funds); $10,000 bond
New Jersey Charities Registration Section 1100 Raymond Blvd. Newark, NJ 07102 (201) 648-4002	Registration	None [Provision of no more than 15% of proceeds to solicitor remains law, but state has not sought to utilize it.]	Within 6 months after close of fiscal or calendar year.*	Maximum proceeds of $10,000 if all fund raising is done by volunteers.	Telephone solicitors must disclose name and address of organization; % of proceeds allocated to organization; tax exempt status, if any; % of donation tax deductible.	Registration; $10,000 bond.
New Mexico Attorney General/, Charitable Organization Registry P.O. Drawer 1508 Santa Fe, NM 87504-1508 (505) 827-6910	Registration	None	Within 75 days of the close of fiscal year. Report must disclose % of funds solicited spent on fund raising.*	Maximum proceeds of $2,500.	Solicitor must disclose that s/he is a professional fund raiser on behalf of organization.	Registration
New York Office of Charities	Registration	None	Within 135 days after close of	Maximum proceeds of $25,000 if all	Solicitors must disclose description	Registration; $10,000 bond.

Registration Department of State Albany, NY 12231 (518) 474-3720			organization's fiscal year. Where receipts are in excess of $150,000 for preceding year, report must be accompanied by opinion signed by independent CPA. Accountants "review report" required where receipts are between $75,000 and $150,000. Unaudited financial report required where receipts are below $75,000, due no later than 15th day of 5th month after organization's fiscal year.	fund-raising is done by volunteers.	of programs for which funds are being solicited.	
North Carolina Department of Human Resources Solicitation Licensing Branch 701 Balbour Drive Raleigh, NC 27603 (919) 733-4510	Registration [Some provisions of statute ruled unconstitutional by U.S. District Court. Case on appeal before U.S. Supreme Court.]	None	Fifth month after fiscal year. Financial statements by independent CPA required if gross receipts are over $250,000. If under $100,000 report by independent CPA acceptable."	Maximum proceeds of $10,000 if all soliciting is done by volunteers.	Solicitor must disclose % of all proceeds used for fund-raising expenses, purpose of organization, in writing upon request.	Licensing: $20,000 bond for fund raisers with custody of funds.
North Dakota Secretary of State Bismarck, ND 58505 (701) 466-3180	Licensing	None	Within 60 days after the close of fiscal or calendar year.	None	None	Registration
Ohio Attorney General Charitable Foundation Section State Office Tower 30 East Broad Street Columbus, OH 43266-0410 (614) 466-3180	Registration	None	Annual financial report due 15th day of the fifth month following close of trust's taxable year. Annual report due March 31. For organizations without calendar year, annual report due 90 days after close of fiscal year.	Maximum proceeds of $500.	None	Registration; $5,000 bond.

State / Agency		Allocation to Fundraiser	Reporting	Maximum Proceeds	Solicitor / Receipt Requirements	Registration / Bond
Oklahoma Income Tax Division Oklahoma Tax Commission 2501 Lincoln Blvd. Oklahoma City, OK 73194 (405) 521-4298	Registration	No more than 10% of total raised as payment to professional fund raisers.	Within 90 days of end of fiscal or calendar year.	Maximum proceeds of $10,000.	Receipts must be given in duplicate for contributions over $2.	Registration; $2,500 bond.
Oregon Attorney General Portland, OR 97204 (503) 229-5725	Registration	None	Within 4 months and 15 days of close of calendar or fiscal year.*	Maximum proceeds of $5,000.	Solicitor must disclose name of fund-raising firm, name of organization for which s/he is soliciting and % of proceeds allocated to charity.	Registration
Pennsylvania Dept. of State Bureau of Charitable Organizations Room 308, North Office Bldg. Harrisburg, PA 17120 (717) 783-1720	Registration	No more than 35% of proceeds for fund-raising expenses, excluding postage. Of the 35%, no more than 15% to professional solicitor unless higher authorized.	Annual and financial reports due 90 days after organization's fiscal year. For gross receipts under $15,000, audit or review is optional. For amounts over $15,000 and under $50,000, financial statements must be audited by independent CPA; over $50,000 complete audit required.*	None	Solicitor must produce authorization on request.	Registration; $10,000 bond.
Rhode Island Dept. of Business Regulations Providence, RI 02903 (401) 277-3048	Registration	No more than 50% of solicited funds allocated to expenses, of which a maximum of 25% may go to professional solicitor, unless higher authorized.	Within 90 days after end of fiscal year, audited by independent CPA. Where proceeds are less than $100,000, no audit required.	Maximum proceeds of $3,000, if all soliciting done by volunteers.	Solicitor must show ID card for each solicitation; card must contain name and address of organization, purpose for which, contribution is solicited, tax exempt status, % of contribution tax deducted.	Registration; $10,000 bond.
South Carolina Secretary of State Columbia, SC 29211 (803) 734-2169	Registration	"Reasonable percentage" allocated to professional	Within six months of the close of the fiscal year.*	Maximum proceeds of $2,000 for SC organizations only.	Solicitor must produce authorization on request.	Registration; $5,000 bond.

solicitor.

State / Contact	Registration	Limits	Reporting	Amount	Disclosure	Bond
South Dakota Attorney General State Capitol Pierre, SD 57501 (605) 773-3215	Registration	None	None	None	None	None
Tennessee Secretary of State James K. Polk Bldg. Suite 500 Nashville, TN 37219-5040	Registration	No more than 25% of proceeds for fund-raising costs; of which only 15% for professional solicitor, unless higher authorized.	No specific date submitted as part of annual registration process. Independent CPA audit required where proceeds are at least $10,000.	$5,000	Identification must be presented upon demand.	Registration; $10,000 bond.
Texas Attorney General Charitable Trust Section P.O. Box 12548 Austin, TX 78711 (512) 463-2002	None	None	IRS 990	None	None	None
Utah Dept. of Business Reg. Div. of Consumer Prot. P.O. Box 45802 Salt Lake City, UT 84145-0801 (801) 530-6601	Registration/Permit. (Application for permit must include estimate of % of proceeds allocated to charity.)	None	None	None	Professional solicitor must present to solicitee required permit card, which discloses name of charity, % of contribution allocated to charity.	Registration; $10,000 bond.
Vermont Attorney General 109 State Street Montpelier, VT 05602 (802) 828-3171	None	None	None	None	None	None
Virginia Office of Consumer Affairs P.O. Box 1163 Richmond, VA 23209 (804) 786-1343	Registration	None	No specific date. Reports submitted as part of annual registration process.*	Maximum proceeds of $5,000 if all soliciting is done by volunteers.	Solicitor must disclose name, employer, that s/he is a paid solicitor, that a financial statement is available from regulator, % of total solicitations allocatable to charity (if under	Registration; $20,000 bond.

70%).

State					
Washington Charities Division Office of the Secretary of State Legislative Bldg. (MS: AS-22) Olympia, WA 98504 (206) 753-7121	Registration	None	5 months and 15 days after close of accounting year.	Maximum proceeds of $5,000 if all activities, including soliciting, are done by volunteers.	Solicitor must disclose fund-raiser's name, organization, purpose of solicitation, name of charity, whether organization is registered, Secretary of State's toll-free number, % of funds received in the previous year which were applied to charitable purposes of organization.	Registration; $15,000 bond for paid counsel with custody of funds.
West Virginia Secretary of State Capitol Bldg. Charleston, WV 25305 (304) 345-4000	Registration	None	No specific date. Financial report must accompany annual registration statement. Where proceeds exceed $50,000 audit independent CPA required.*	Maximum proceeds of $10,000 if all soliciting is done by volunteers.	Solicitor must disclose, in writing, % of solicitation allocated to organization.	Registration; $10,000 bond.
Wisconsin Dept. of Regulation & Licensing P.O. Box 8935 Madison, WI 53708 (608) 266-0829	Registration	None	Within 6 months of close of 12 month accounting period on form prescribed by Department. Independent CPA audit required where proceeds exceed $50,000. 90 day extension may be granted upon request.	Maximum proceeds of $4,000.	Solicitor must disclose % of contribution allocated to charity.	Registration; $5,000 bond.
Wyoming Secretary of State Capitol Bldg. 200 W. 24th Cheyenne, WY 82002 (307) 777-7378	None	None	None	None	None	None

*Indicates states which accept IRS Form 990 in lieu of legislatively mandated annual report.

Source: AAFRC

259

RELIGION

GIVING TO RELIGION

In 1987, religious organizations and agencies received an estimated $43.61 billion. This is an increase in giving of nearly 5 percent over the previous year.

The amount represented nearly half of all philanthropy—46.55 percent.

The source for this information is *Giving USA*. They project the giving to religion as the amount remaining after donations to all other recipient categories are estimated. The problem is that many of the organized religions do not disclose the amount of contributions they receive. This is particularly true of some of the largest. There is clear evidence, however, that giving to religion far exceeds donations to any other type of charity.

TOTAL GIVING TO RELIGION

	Amount (Billions)		Amount (Billions)
1970	$9.34	1979	$20.17
1971	10.07	1980	20.28
1972	10.19	1981	25.06
1973	10.53	1982	28.06
1974	11.84	1983	31.61
1975	12.81	1984	35.43
1976	14.18	1985	37.46
1977	16.98	1986	41.68
1978	18.35	1987	43.67

RELIGIOUS GIVING AND INCOME

There is an important relationship between religious giving and family income. The higher the income, the more likely the gift to religious philanthropy. For example, 45 percent of respondents with incomes under $10,000 made no contributions to religion. In the case of those with incomes over $50,000, 13 percent did not make religious contributions. What this table demonstrates most significantly is the large range in both the amount and percentage of income contributed to religion, regardless of income level.

RELIGIOUS GIVING AND INCOME

Size of Religious Contribution	Under $10,000 (Percent)	$10,000– $19,999 (Percent)	$20,000– $29,999 (Percent)	$30,000– $39,999 (Percent)	$40,000– $49,999 (Percent)	$50,000 and Above (Percent)
None	45	34	24	22	20	13
$ 1–$ 100	36	23	18	17	10	9
$101–$ 250	11	15	18	14	13	9
$251–$ 500	6	13	20	19	26	21
$501–$1,000	2	9	11	13	14	17
More than $1,000	**	6	9	15	17	31
Total =	100	100	100	100	100	100
Mean Contribution						
All Respondents	$130	$280	$400	$620	$760	$1,190
Religious Givers Only	240	430	530	800	950	1,370

**Less than 0.5 percent.

RELIGIOUS GIVING AND INCOME—PERCENTAGE OF INCOME GIVEN

Percentage of Income Given	Under $10,000 (Percent)	$10,000– $19,999 (Percent)	$20,000– $29,999 (Percent)	$30,000– $39,999 (Percent)	$40,000– $49,999 (Percent)	and Above (Percent)
None	44	35	23	22	20	13
Less than 1 Percent	8	14	19	21	21	19
1 Percent	30	20	27	25	29	31
2 Percent	7	10	12	6	12	11
3–4 Percent	5	8	10	13	9	6
5 Percent or More	6	13	9	13	9	13
Total =	100	100	100	100	100	100
Mean Percentage of Income						
All Respondents	2.3	1.9	1.6	1.8	1.7	1.8
Religious Givers Only	2.7	2.9	2.1	2.2	2.1	2.1

Source: The Charitable Behavior of Americans; Independent Sector

RELIGIOUS GIVING AND AGE

Religious giving tends to increase with age, both the amount given and as a percentage of income. This table shows that even though the average total income drops after 65 years of age, the level of generosity remains constant. The most generous givers to religion are between 35 and 49 years old or 65 years and older.

RELIGIOUS GIVING AND AGE

Size of Religious Contribution	Under 30 Years (Percent)	30–34 Years (Percent)	35–49 Years (Percent)	50–64 Years (Percent	65 Years and Older (Percent)
None	33	37	25	27	23
$ 1–$ 100	27	20	12	18	30
$101–$ 250	13	12	16	14	13
$251–$ 500	13	17	19	14	19
$501–$1,000	9	5	12	13	8
More than $1,000	5	9	16	14	7
Total =	100	100	100	100	100
Mean Contribution					
All Respondents	$290	$350	$660	$570	$340
Religious Givers Only	440	560	880	780	440

RELIGIOUS GIVING AND AGE— PERCENTAGE OF INCOME GIVEN

Percentage of Income	Under 30 Years (Percent)	30–34 Years (Percent)	35–49 Years (Percent)	50–64 Years (Percent)	65 Years and Older (Percent)
None	34	39	27	29	27
Less than 1 Percent	22	18	14	12	12
1 Percent	22	21	26	30	28
2 Percent	7	9	13	6	12
3–4 Percent	8	7	11	11	7
5 Percent or More	7	6	9	12	14
Total =	100	100	100	100	100
Mean Percentage of Income					
All Respondents	1.2	1.2	1.9	2.0	2.3
Religious Givers Only	2.0	1.9	2.3	2.6	3.1

Source: The Charitable Behavior of Americans; Independent Sector

RELIGIOUS GIVING AND MANNER OF GIVING AMONG FREQUENT AND INFREQUENT CHURCH ATTENDERS

This table shows the impact of frequency of church attendance on contributions. The most generous giver to a church is one who attends nearly every week and pledges a proportion of his or her income to the church. These respondents gave a mean contribution of $1,300 and approximately 5 percent of their income to the church.

	Mean Dollar Contribution	Mean Percentage of Income
Givers Who Attend Religious Services on a Weekly Basis		
Give a Fixed Amount or Pledge Each Week	$ 990	3.4
Do Not Give a Fixed Amount or Pledge	630	2.8
Give a Percentage of Their Income	1,300	5.0
Do Not Give a Percentage of Their Income	560	1.9
Givers Who Attend Religious Services Once or Twice a Month		
Give a Fixed Amount or Pledge Each Week	$ 620	1.8
Do Not Give a Fixed Amount or Pledge	320	1.2
Give a Percentage of Their Income	670	2.6
Do Not Give a Percentage of Their Income	380	1.2
Givers Who Attend Religious Services Only a Few Times a Year		
Give a Fixed Amount or Pledge Each Week	$ 550	1.6
Do Not Give a Fixed Amount or Pledge	320	0.9
Give a Percentage of Their Income	810	2.5
Do Not Give a Percentage of Their Income	330	1.0

Source: The Charitable Behavior of Americans; Independent Sector

ANNUAL PER CAPITA GIVING BY FULL MEMBERS OF ALL PROTESTANT DENOMINATIONS— ADJUSTED TO 1967 DOLLARS

The graph that follows shows the impact of inflation on per capita giving to organized religion. The dollar amounts of giving have increased from $77.75 in 1965 to $344.42 in 1986, an increase of 343 percent. However, the increase in real terms—using constant 1967 dollars—is only from $82.38 in 1965 to $104.88 in 1986, an increase of 27.3 percent or only 1.3 percent a year on average. Full membership refers to those with full, communicant, or confirmed status.

DENOMINATIONAL PER CAPITA FULL MEMBER CONTRIBUTIONS ADJUSTED TO 1967 DOLLARS, 1961–1986

The table represents annual per capita giving of over forty of the major Protestant denominations in the United States. Each year has been adjusted to 1967 dollars.

Year	No. of Denoms.	Per Capita Full Member	Constant 1967 Dollars	Year	No. of Denoms.	Per Capita Full Member	Constant 1967 Dollars
1961	46	$69.00	$77.01	1974	44	$127.16	$86.09
1962	42	68.76	75.89	1975	43	138.54	85.94
1963	41	69.87	76.19	1976	43	149.07	87.43
1964	41	72.04	77.55	1977	45	159.33	87.78
1965	38	77.75	82.38	1978	42	176.37	90.26
1966		(Not Reported)		1979	44	197.44	90.82
1967		(Not Reported)		1980	40	213.41	86.47
1968	52	95.31	91.47	1981	45	239.71	88.00
1969	48	99.68	90.78	1982	40	261.95	90.60
1970	45	96.84	83.27	1983	40	278.67	93.39
1971	42	103.94	85.69	1984	39	300.40	96.56
1972	39	110.29	88.02	1985	42	321.77	99.87
1973	40	118.16	88.77	1986	44	344.42	104.88

RELIGIOUS GIVING AND MARITAL STATUS

Marital status is a factor in giving to religion. Whether a person is married, single, divorced, or widowed influences what proportion of their income goes to religious giving. The table shows that those who are divorced or separated give a smaller percentage of their income to religion than those who are single.

RELIGIOUS GIVING AND MARITAL STATUS

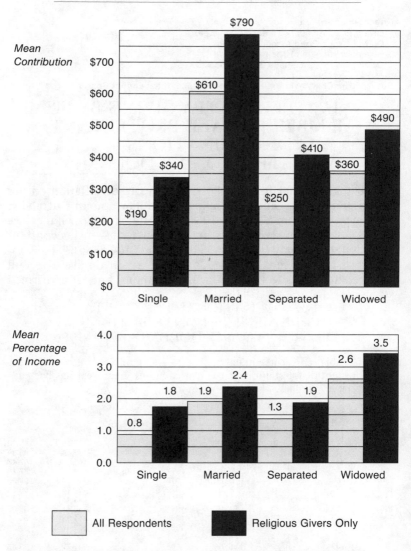

Source: The Charitable Behavior of Americans; Independent Sector

THE TOP TWENTY UNITED STATES CHURCHES RANKED BY PER CAPITA GIVING BY INCLUSIVE MEMBERS

Inclusive membership refers to those with full, communicant, or confirmed status plus other members listed as baptized, nonconfirmed, or noncommunicant. It is interesting that the church highest in per capita giving, the Reformed Episcopal Church, has a membership of 5,733 compared to the Presbyterian Church (U.S.A.) membership of 3,007,322.

Communion	Year	Per Capita Giving
Reformed Episcopal Church	1987	$1,228.78
Evangelical Mennonite Church	1987	952.60
The Wesleyan Church	1986	844.71
Evangelical Covenant Church	1986	836.48
Seventh-Day Adventists	1986	792.57
The Missionary Church	1986	779.11
Brethren in Christ Church	1986	778.62
Free Methodist Church of North America	1986	775.61
Presbyterian Church in America	1986	764.78
International Pentecostal Church of Christ	1987	741.96
Baptist General Conference	1987	736.12
Mennonite Church	1987	707.51
Conservative Congregational Christian Conference	1986	677.35
Evangelical Church of North America	1987	641.88
North American Baptist Conference	1986	640.24
Church of the Nazarene	1986	617.52
Church of God (Anderson, IN)	1986	571.95
Church of God General Conference (Oregon, IL)	1987	562.03
Christian and Missionary Alliance	1986	554.98
Presbyterian Church (U.S.A.)	1986	521.22

CONTRIBUTIONS TO FALWELL DROP

The nation's third largest "megaroller" experienced a major decrease in gifts in 1988. Contributions to Reverend Jerry Falwell's "Old-Time Gospel Hour" dropped by more than $10 million, and the ministry's net worth fell by nearly $5 million from the prior year.

In the 1988–1989 fiscal year, the organization will deliberately move away from dependence on direct public contributions and will put more emphasis on indirect support, programs, and business driven revenue.

This past year, contributions to the "Old-Time Gospel Hour" totaled $40.7 million. This was the lowest level since the 1981-1982 fiscal year.

All of the major TV evangelists experienced serious decreases in giving. This was a result of the well-publicized exploits of Jim and Tammy Bakker and the indiscretions of Jimmy Swaggart—two of the big-time evangelistic money makers.

THE TWENTY TOP PROTESTANT CHURCHES IN THE UNITED STATES RANKED BY TOTAL CONTRIBUTIONS

Between 38 and 52 religious bodies supply complete financial data annually on the total contributions they receive. This group represents the major Protestant denominations. The Roman Catholic Church does not supply figures for this comparison.

Communion	Total Contributions	Per Capita Contributions	Membership
Southern Baptist Convention	$4,116,321,455	$281.68	14,613,638
The United Methodist Church	2,333,928,274	253.90	9,192,172
Presbyterian Church (U.S.A.)	1,567,474,145	521.22	3,007,322
The Episcopal Church	1,134,455,479	452.97	2,504,507
Lutheran Church-Missouri Synod	717,706,885	272.83	2,630,588
Lutheran Church in America	681,121,693	235.19	2,896,138
The American Lutheran Church	530,788,865	228.84	2,319,443
Seventh-Day Adventists	528,009,727	792.57	666,199
United Church of Christ	493,148,330	294.22	1,676,105
Christian Church (Disciples of Christ)	330,304,890	298.47	1,106,692
Church of the Nazarene	327,849,894	617.52	530,912
American Baptist Churches in the U.S.A.	314,895,803	199.75	1,576,483
Presbyterian Church in America	143,842,638	764.78	188,083
Reformed Church in America	137,186,025	403.06	340,359
Christian and Missionary Alliance	132,492,973	554.98	238,734
Church of God (Anderson, IN)	107,905,502	571.95	188,662
Baptist General Conference	96,785,070	736.12	131,480
The Wesleyan Church	92,238,792	844.71	109,196
Free Will Baptist, National Association of	75,200,000	365.86	205,546
Evangelical Covenant Church	72,003,279	836.48	86,079

Source: Yearbook of American & Canadian Churches

THE COMPARISON IS FASCINATING

In the State of Rhode Island, there are approximately 1 million people. Eighty-three percent of that population is Roman Catholic—no other state in the union has as great a concentration of a single denomination.

The Archdiocese of the Church in Rhode Island raises nearly $5 million for Catholic Charities.

Also in Rhode Island are approximately 17,000 men, women, and children of the Jewish faith. That group gave $4.8 million to the Jewish Federation.

That makes the per capita giving for the Roman Catholics $13.16, and the per capita giving for the Jewish community $282.35—21 times higher.

FIVE LARGEST GIFTS TO RELIGION 1987-1988

Estate of Othel Fiers Brown & Dewitt Brown
$8,000,000 to the Christian Church Foundation,
Indianapolis, IN

Estates of Charles Tibby Hanna and Dorothy Hanna
$7,500,000 to Princeton University,
Princeton, NJ

Estate of Orlean Bullard Beeson
$2,300,000 to the Asbury Theological Seminary,
Wilmore, KY

Duke Endowment
$1,200,000 to the United Methodist Churches

Lilly Endowment
$1,100,000 to the Christian Theological Seminary,
Indianapolis, IN

Source: *Giving USA*

PER CAPITA GIVING TO
THE UNITED JEWISH APPEAL

City/State	Per Capita Giving by Jews	Total Giving (in millions)
1 Minneapolis, MN	$490.91	$10.8
2 Detroit, MI	348.57	24.4
3 Cleveland, OH	341.43	23.9
4 Hartford, CT	330.77	8.6
5 Milwaukee, WI	286.67	8.6
6 Montreal, Canada	285.15	28.8
7 Toronto, Canada	234.40	29.3
8 Pittsburgh, PA	208.89	9.4
9 Baltimore, MD	201.08	18.7
10 Chicago, IL	189.52	47.0
11 St. Louis, MO	175.70	9.4
12 Houston, TX	162.22	7.3
13 Sussex County, NJ	151.24	18.3
14 Denver, CO	139.13	6.4
15 Palm Beach County, FL	138.33	8.3
16 San Francisco, CA	134.38	17.2
17 Boston, CT	129.95	24.3
18 Bergen County, NJ	128.43	8.9
19 Philadelphia, PA	119.58	28.7
20 Washington, DC	106.67	17.6
21 Atlanta, GA	94.55	5.2
22 Los Angeles, CA	92.81	46.5
23 Miami, FL	87.97	21.2
24 New York City, NY	77.29	131.4

25 LARGEST JEWISH
CONGREGATIONS BY DUES PAID

Over 800 congregations comprise the Union of American Hebrew Congregations (UAHC). It is one of the largest Jewish groups. Rabbi Alexander M. Schindler, dynamic and world-renowned, is the leader of the hundreds of thousands of Reform Jews. The UAHC national headquarters are at 838 Fifth Avenue, New York, NY 10021. The UAHC has four Hebrew Union College-Jewish Institute of Religion Campuses located in Cincinnati, New York, Los Angeles, and Jerusalem.

Congregation	Dues Paid	Number of Members	Dues Per Member
1) New York, Congregation Emanu-El	$199,656	3,426	$58.28
2) Washington, Washington Hebrew Congregation	141,953	2,400	59.15
3) Miami, Temple Beth Am	112,180	1,700	65.99
4) Los Angeles, Stephen S. Wise Temple	110,676	2,642	41.89
5) Baltimore, Baltimore Hebrew Congregation	110,119	1,700	64.78
6) Houston, Congregation Emanu-El	98,236	2,100	46.78
7) Kansas City, The Temple Congregation B'nai Jehudah	97,714	1,696	57.61
8) Glencoe, North Shore Congregation Israel	96,564	1,413	68.34
9) Chicago, Temple Sholom	94,172	1,580	59.60
10) Seattle, Temple De Hirsch Sinai	93,127	1,584	58.79
11) West Bloomfield, Temple Israel	92,595	1,850	50.05
12) New York, Central Synagogue	91,917	1,345	68.34
13) Dallas, Temple Emanu-El	88,055	2,350	37.47
14) Beachwood, Anshe Chesed Fairmount Temple	87,508	2,330	37.56
15) Great Neck, Temple Beth El	87,407	1,735	46.48
16) Pittsburgh, Rodef Shalom Congregation	84,246	1,800	46.80
17) Houston, Congregation Beth Israel	83,467	1,810	46.11
18) Elkins Park, Reform Congregation Keneseth Israel	81,659	1,620	50.41
19) Boston, Temple Israel	80,647	1,735	46.48
20) Los Angeles, Wilshire Boulevard Temple	78,936	2,600	30.36
21) Denver, Congregation Emanuel	77,688	1,566	49.61
22) Wynnewood, Main Line Reform	76,567	1,200	63.81
23) New Rochelle, Temple Israel	75,174	1,100	68.34
24) Short Hills, Congregation B'nai Jeshurun	74,354	1,088	68.34
25) Philadelphia, Congregation Rodeph Shalom	74,001	1,743	42.46

Source: Annual Report of the Department of Maintenance of Union Membership, Union of American Hebrew Congregations

JEWISH GIVING IS TWICE
THE AMERICAN NORM

According to Barry A. Kosmin, Director of the Research Department for the Council of Jewish Federations, Jewish philanthropy is twice the American norm. His study, conducted over one year, showed Jewish giving at about $2.5 billion. This represented 5 percent of all philanthropy in the United States, even though the

Jewish community comprises only 2.5 percent of the total United States population. It is a commonly held belief that Jews give only to Jewish causes, but according to Kosmin, one-third of Jewish philanthropy goes to general or secular causes.

GIVING TO THE UNITED JEWISH APPEAL

City/State	1987 Campaign Results (in millions)	Jewish Population	Rank of City by Jewish Population
1 New York, NY	$131.4	1,700,000	1
2 Chicago, IL	47.0	248,000	3
3 Los Angeles, CA	46.5	501,000	2
4 Toronto, Canada	29.3	125,000	9
5 Montreal, Canada	28.8	101,000	11
6 Philadelphia, PA	28.7	240,000	5
7 Detroit, MI	24.4	70,000	14
8 Boston, CT	24.3	187,000	6
9 Cleveland, OH	23.9	70,000	13
10 Miami, FL	21.2	241,000	4
11 Baltimore, MD	18.7	93,000	12
12 Sussex County, NJ	18.3	121,000	10
13 Washington, DC	17.6	165,000	7
14 San Francisco, CA	17.2	128,000	8
15 Minneapolis, MN	10.8	22,000	24
16 Pittsburgh, PA	9.4	45,000	20
17 St. Louis, MO	9.4	53,500	18
18 Bergen County, NJ	8.9	69,300	15
19 Hartford, CT	8.6	26,000	23
20 Milwaukee, WI	8.6	30,000	22
21 Palm Beach County, FL	8.3	60,000	16
22 Houston, TX	7.3	45,000	21
23 Denver, CO	6.4	46,000	19
24 Atlanta, GA	5.2	55,000	17

ENDOWMENT DEVELOPMENT IN JEWISH FEDERATION PHILANTHROPY

From 1981 to 1987 endowment contributions to the Jewish Federation giving increased 158 percent—from $135.5 million to $344 million. This is in the form of bequests, philanthropic funds, lifetime gifts, and charitable trusts.

Approximately 10 percent of the Federation's annual campaign contributions now come from their endowments. In the fiscal year 1986–1987, endowment fund grants to agencies of the Federation totaled approximately $236 million.

Source: Norbert Fruehauf, Director of Campaign Planning Services, Council of Jewish Federations.

UNITED JEWISH APPEAL CELEBRATES JUBILEE YEAR

The United Jewish Appeal (UJA) traces its birth back to the night of November 10, 1938, when Jewish homes, synagogues, and stores were assaulted throughout Nazi Germany and Austria. The next morning, glass from shattered windows was everywhere. It literally covered the streets and sidewalks in all Jewish areas. The "Night of Broken Glass" (Kristallnacht) left wounds which would not heal among Jews in every nation of the world. But it also ignited their spirits in a common cause.

The Kristallnacht was the catalyst for the United Jewish Appeal—founded January 10, 1939. It was established as the Central American Jewish Fund Raising Organization. In its first campaign, it raised $28.4 million from American Jewry.

During the war years, the young organization raised $103 million from 1939 to 1944. The funds were used to rescue and resettle 162,000 Jews from Hitler's Europe.

In 1944 the incredible dimensions of the holocaust were finally discovered. In response to the plight of the survivors, UJA leadership raised $131 million on a goal of $100 million. Two years later, annual pledges swelled to $200.7 million. Annual contributions continue to grow, but at a gradual pace.

And then came the 1967 Six-Day War. The UJA initiated the largest of its special appeals and raised $322 million for the regular campaign and an emergency fund. The Six-Day War was a watershed—Jews around the world began seeing that their destiny was linked to the safety and well-being of Israel.

Contributions increased steadily from that point, and the United Jewish Appeal played a major role in strenghthening relationships and personal bonds with Israel.

The United Jewish Appeal campaign is comprised of 639 local and nonfederated Jewish communities which raise funds in partnership with the national UJA. The UJA is the primary fundraising vehicle for the support of humanitarian programs and social services for Jews in the United States, Israel, and 33 other countries.

The United Jewish Appeal has six regional offices and an office in Washington. Their national headquarters are in New York. The telephone number is (212) 818-9100.

SOME NAMING IDEAS

In its February 20, 1989, issue, *FORBES* described a number of gift opportunities they had uncovered. It is a glorious collection and should stimulate a flood of ideas for your own institution.

Julliard School will name a practice room for you for $50,000. If you would like your name on a new concert grand piano, it's yours for $25,000.

For $10 million, you can name the 3,600 seat auditorium at the Tampa Bay Performing Arts Center. Or you can have a chair with a plaque on the back of it for $2,500.

At the zoo in Los Angeles, you can name a cheetah for $15,000. In San Diego, the zoo will let you support a cheetah for $500 a year, a zebra for $200, and an elephant for $1,000.

For $1 million, you can name the new tropical pavilion at the Brooklyn Botanic Garden. And you can have ten acres of Montana's Little Bighorn Battlefield—that's where Custer made his last stand—for $6,000.

There's a Gothic pinnacle waiting for you at the National Cathedral in Washington. That will cost $400,000. Or you can have a carved angel for $6,000. The chapel at the Dallas-Fort Worth Airport is waiting for a donor—$100,000.

At the University of California, Berkeley you will be able to endow swimming lanes and baseball dugouts. At the University of Southern California, you can buy a position on the football team. Already named are the Chester H. Dolley quarterback and the Richard Alden center. One defensive back is still available for $250,000.

In 1988, Yale established the Joel E. Smilow Coach of Football for $1 million. Cornell, Princeton, and the University of Rochester have received endowments for coaching in several varsity sports.

In many universities, there are names on drinking fountains, silver tea services, benches, and trees. Princeton has the Mrs. C. Otto von Kienbusch Ladies' Lounge in the art museum, a Ralph Buchanan Albaugh carrel in the library, and the Henriette Foote Armour bed in the infirmary. There's also a Frederick Fox dogwood tree and an experimental flume, named for John Nicholson, at the water resources lab on the campus.

Leo Bernaek endowed the concert master-violinist's chair at the Boston Pops and an English horn chair at the Boston Symphony Orchestra. The total cost was about $1 million.

There is the Burt Reynolds Emminent Scholar Chair and Theater at Florida State University that cost $600,000. A chair at Harvard runs $1.5 million, and a university professorship, $2 million.

There's more. According to Don Betterton's *Alma Mater,* there are scholarships for: non-smokers, people named Murphy, Iowa farm girls who have played in the state basketball tournament, anyone born in Matapan, Massachusetts, and a generous fund for horticulture students with no better than a B average.

THEMES THROUGHOUT THE YEARS

The United Jewish Appeal has been campaigning actively for the past 43 years. The changing mottos and themes provide a fascinating collection—and help recall the times and events of the many challenges and historic endeavors of the Jewish Community.

1946 $100,000,000 Must Be Raised in 1946
1947 The Quota for 1947 Is $170,000,000
1948 Year of Destiny
The Dream of Generations—Our Challenge of the Hour
1949 The Exodus Campaign
We Raised $150 Million in 1948—We Must Raise $250 Million in 1949
1950 The Greatest Reconstruction Program in Jewish History
1951 The "Now or Never" Campaign
1952 The "Homemaking" Campaign
1953 Because Lives Depend on Us
1954 They Must Not Stand Alone
1955 Save Lives While There Is Still Time
1956 Stand by Those Who Stand for Freedom
1957 Yours to Give—Life and Hope
1958 A Second Chance to Save Polish Jewry
1959 A Job to Finish—A Job to Continue
1960 Year of Opportunity
1961 Year of Decision
To Save and Build Lives—To Strengthen the Settlements
1962 24th Annual Campaign for Life and Freedom
1963 A Quarter Century of Jewish Rescue and Rebuilding
Aid the Refugees—Turn the Human Tide Home
Keep Them Alive—Help Them Thrive—In UJA's Year 25
1964 Save Them Now, Absorb Them Now
1965 Give Life, Give Hope, Give Freedom to Jews All Over the World
1966 Bring Them All the Way Home
Children Are Israel's Future—Help Them Today
1967 To Build Lives for the Future
Your UJA Gift Opens the Door to Life for 827,600 Jews
1968 Ours Is the Generation
The Emergency Continues
1969 Israel Must Live
1970 We Hear You, Israel
1971 Survival Means Sacrifice
1972 Keep the Promise
1974 The Future Is in Our Hands
1975 We Are One
1976 Remembering Is Not Enough
1977 Around the Corner, Around the World
One in Mind—One in Spirit
1978 One People, One Heart
1979 Year of Renewal
1980 Now, More Than Ever

CONTRIBUTIONS GIVEN TO RELIGIOUS CHARITIES

Seventy-two percent of respondents report that they contributed to a church or synagogue. The median contribution to religious charity for all respondents was $470. The mean contribution for religious givers only (those who give to religious charities exclusively) was $660.

Amount Given to Religious Charity in the Past Year*	All Respondents (Percent)	Givers Only (Percent)
None	28	—
$ 1 – $ 50	9	13
$ 51 – $ 100	11	15
$ 101 – $ 250	14	20
$ 251 – $ 500	17	23
$ 501 – $1,000	10	14
$1,001 – $2,000	7	9
More than $2,000	4	6
Total =	100	100
Mean Contribution	$470	$660

Dash = Not Applicable

*Although 75 percent of total respondents reported that they contributed to a church or synagogue, these tables have been adjusted to exclude respondents who say they gave to religious charity in the past year, but did not report the specific amount.

Source: The Charitable Behavior of Americans; Independent Sector

In proportion to the population, Jews are 23 times as likely to establish a foundation dedicated to Jewish giving as Catholics are to their religious groups. The figures also indicate that Jews establish foundations at about 12 times the rate of Protestant religious givers.

UJA AND FEDERATIONS LAUNCH $75 MILLION CAMPAIGN FOR SOVIET JEWS

This year, United Jewish Appeals and Federations across the nation join in launching a combined effort to raise $75 million to assist Jews in leaving the Soviet Union. The campaign is called Passage To Freedom.

For years, American Jews demonstrated and petitioned on behalf of those in the USSR. Russian-Jewish history goes back 2,500 years, making Russia the site of some of the worlds oldest Jewish settlements. For some unknown reason, around 1979 the Soviets began withholding exit visas from some members of families while granting them to others, and denying visas to many Jews on the grounds of "state secrecy." Now Jews are at last being allowed out of the Soviet Union; some 30,000 to 40,000 are expected to leave in 1989.

The funds from the campaign will be used to support the care, housing, medical and social services, and cultural and religious activities of the emigres. The Soviet Jews who immigrate to the United States travel from Vienna to Italy to wait for American visas. They are allowed to take less than $200 with them when they leave their country.

JEWISH PHILANTHROPY TOPS MILITARY BUDGET OF CUBA OR TURKEY

Through careful analysis, it is estimated that 4 percent of all giving in the United States is by Jews. This represents totals of $3.1 billion in 1985, $3.5 billion in 1986, and $3.76 billion in 1987.

According to Barry A. Kosmin, Director of Research for the Council of Jewish Federations, the generosity of American Jews "thus exceeds the GNP of entire Third World countries such as Nepal and Madagascar, and the military budgets of Cuba or Turkey."

THE BIBLE SAID WE SHOULD

For centuries, the sought-after ideal for giving has been the tithe. The Bible says we should! The concept is that 10 percent of our income should go to charity. Both the Old and the New Testament are replete with admonishments to do so.

Many denominations preach the concept of tithing but only the Mormons, the Church of the Latter-Day Saints, truly practices the principle. It is one of the tenets of their religion. In their case, the tithe is not for charity in general, but the entire amount goes to the Church.

In actuality, even though Protestant churches emphasize the importance of tithing, few people do. It is a rare family that gives 10 percent to anything. As a matter of fact, according to a study made last year, only 9 percent of households gave 5 percent or more. One-third gave less than 1 percent. And nearly 29 percent gave nothing at all.

What is particularly fascinating about all of the statistics is that in general, the higher the income, the lower the percentage given to charity. According to the study, the rich give smaller percentages of what they earn, and thus appear to be less caring and less concerned than people who earn much less.

"I think we should organize a campaign
to raise money for air conditioning."

TWENTY PRESBYTERIAN CHURCHES REPORTING THE HIGHEST AMOUNT OF REGULAR CONTRIBUTIONS*

Church	Total Regular Contributions
1) Highland Park Presbyterian Church Dallas, TX	$6,614,538
2) Peachtree Presbyterian Church Atlanta, GA	4,956,134

3) First Presbyterian Church Orlando, FL	3,919,850
4) Menlo Park Presbyterian Church Menlo Park, CA	3,250,185
5) St. Andrews Presbyterian Church Newport Beach, CA	3,059,260
6) Second Presbyterian Church Memphis, TN	2,917,464
7) Village Presbyterian Church Prairie Village, KS	2,888,962
8) First Presbyterian Church Colorado Springs, CO	2,888,657
9) University Presbyterian Church Seattle, WA	2,778,904
10) First Presbyterian Church Houston, TX	2,765,037
11) Fourth Presbyterian Church Chicago, IL	2,433,723
12) Memorial Drive Presbyterian Church Houston, TX	2,371,196
13) Hollywood First Presbyterian Church Los Angeles, CA	2,275,346
14) First Presbyterian Church Ft. Lauderdale, FL	2,080,098
15) Lafayette-Orinda Presbyterian Church Lafayette, CA	2,076,925
16) College Hill Presbyterian Church Cincinnati, OH	1,994,550
17) First Presbyterian Church Berkeley, CA	1,921,157
18) Bel Air Presbyterian Church Los Angeles, CA	1,919,666
19) First Presbyterian Church Bethlehem, PA	1,834,137
20) Arcadia Presbyterian Church Arcadia, CA	1,772,899

Source: Presbyterian Church (U.S.A.) 1987 Minutes, Part II, Statistics

*Regular Contributions do not include capital and building funds or bequests.

THE TWENTY PRESBYTERIAN CHURCHES REPORTING THE HIGHEST AMOUNT OF CAPITAL AND BUILDING FUNDS CONTRIBUTED BY LIVING DONORS

Church	Building Funds
1) St. Andrews Presbyterian Church Newport Beach, CA	$3,494,876

2) Glenkirk Presbyterian Church Glendora, CA	2,189,520
3) Idlewild Presbyterian Church Memphis, TN	1,731,863
4) First Presbyterian Church San Antonio, TX	1,731,335
5) Westminster Presbyterian Church Oklahoma City, OK	1,728,057
6) First Presbyterian Church Dallas, TX	1,446,166
7) Preston Hollow Presbyterian Church Dallas, TX	1,368,265
8) Bel Air Presbyterian Church Los Angeles, CA	1,259,584
9) National Presbyterian Church Washington, DC	1,045,894
10) First Presbyterian Church Arlington, TX	1,039,261
11) Westminster Presbyterian Church Greensboro, TN	1,032,636
12) Germantown Presbyterian Church Germantown, TN	1,012,165
13) First Presbyterian Church Houston, TX	976,301
14) First Presbyterian Church La Grange, GA	924,315
15) University Presbyterian Church Seattle, WA	896,423
16) Peachtree Presbyterian Church Atlanta, GA	888,189
17) First United Presbyterian Church Ft. Collins, CO	859,928
18) Santa Ynez Valley Presbyterian Church Solvang, CA	844,659
19) First Presbyterian Church Greenville, SC	784,645
20) First Presbyterian Church Hayward, CA	775,417

**Source: Presbyterian Church (U.S.A.) 1987 Minutes, Part II
Statistics**

CATHOLIC DIOCESAN FUND APPEALS
INCREASE PRODUCTION
THIS PAST YEAR

The National Catholic Stewardship Council (NCSC) reported in June, 1988 that three out of four dioceses increased their goals this year from the previous one. Of the total group, 67 percent exceeded their goals. And the same number increased their total number of donors.

The study indicated that only 40 percent of the registered membership gave. The average gift rose from $68.29 the previous year to $70.67 this year.

Campaign costs were low; all dioceses averaged between 5 and 6 cents on the dollar.

The National Catholic Stewardship Council is a service center with executive headquarters in Albany, New York. The mission of NCSC is to assist parish, diocese, religious community, professional development consultants, and other church leaders in promoting the concept of Christian stewardship. This is achieved through an annual conference, newsletters, seminars, publications, exchange programs, and on-going consultation services.

For more information: Executive Director, NCSC, 1 Columbia Place, Albany, NY 12207.

PARTICIPATION RATES OF DONORS
TO THE CATHOLIC CHURCH

Arch/Diocese	Potential Donors	# of Gifts	Participation* Rate
1) Grand Rapids – Diocese of Grand Rapids, MI	34,514	27,286	79.1%
2) Gaylord – Diocese of Gaylord, MI	25,877	19,708	76.2
3) Harrisburg – Diocese of Harrisburg, PA	66,374	48,346	72.8
4) Springfield – Diocese of Springfield, MA	121,577	87,693	72.1
5) Providence – Diocese of Providence, RI	148,000	106,500	72.0
6) Baker – Diocese of Baker, OR	8,108	5,584	68.9
7) Saginaw – Diocese of Saginaw, MI	43,946	29,366	66.8
8) St. Louis Archdiocese of St. Louis, MO	148,123	95,912	64.8
9) Davenport – Diocese of Davenport, IA	33,898	21,701	64.0
10) Bismarck – Archdiocese of Bismarck, ND	26,386	16,425	62.2
11) Worcester – Diocese of Worcester, MA	100,000	62,167	62.2
12) Syracuse – Diocese of Syracuse, NY	115,006	70,794	61.6
13) Fargo – Diocese of Fargo, ND	30,800	18,900	61.4
14) Marquette – Diocese of Marquette, MI	28,500	17,327	60.8
15) Kalamazoo – Diocese of Kalamazoo, MI	25,200	15,285	60.7
16) Albany – Diocese of Albany, NY	110,000	65,231	59.3

	$ Amount Raised	Participation rate*
17) Springfield – Diocese of Cape Girardeau Springfield, MO	18,000	10,416	57.9
18) Crookston – Diocese of Crookston, MN	13,261	7,169	54.1
19) Milwaukee – Diocese of Milwaukee, WI	215,000	116,112	54.0
20) Peoria – Diocese of Peoria, IL	75,600	39,900	52.8

Source: National Catholic Stewardship Council

*Participation rate equals the number of gifts divided by the potential donors.

THE HIGHEST GIVING TO THE CATHOLIC CHURCH

Arch/Diocese	$ Amount Raised	Goal/Quota/ Target (dollars)
1) Detroit – Archdiocese of Detroit, MI	10,352,406	8,459,754
2) Boston – Archdiocese of Boston, MA	9,300,300	9,000,000
3) Toronto – Diocese of Toronto, Ontario, Canada	8,105,941	7,039,000
4) Rockville Centre – Diocese of Rockville Centre, NY	8,038,191	5,000,000
5) New York – Diocese of New York, NY	8,024,648	6,089,875
6) Philadelphia – Archdiocese of Philadelphia, PA	7,350,617	6,300,000
7) Cleveland – Diocese of Cleveland, OH	6,503,000	6,500,000
8) St. Louis – Archdiocese of St. Louis, MO	6,067,602	6,050,000
9) Miami – Diocese of Miami, FL	5,846,115	4,900,000
10) Milwaukee – Diocese of Milwaukee, WI	5,843,862	6,000,000
11) Newark – Archdiocese of Newark, NJ	5,478,000	5,000,000
12) St. Paul – Archdiocese of St. Paul, MN	5,137,604	5,072,815
13) Scranton – Diocese of Scranton, PA	4,800,000	3,000,000
14) Phoenix – Diocese of Phoenix, AZ	3,932,000	3,500,000
15) Galveston-Houston – Diocese of Houston, TX	3,887,048	3,600,000
16) Rochester – Diocese of Rochester, NY	3,869,403	3,584,000
17) Providence – Diocese of Providence, RI	3,791,938	3,736,000
18) Albany – Diocese of Albany, NY	3,524,000	3,524,000
19) Orlando – Diocese of Orlando, FL	3,442,396	3,000,000
20) Hartford – Diocese of Hartford, CT	3,342,814	3,000,000

Source: National Catholic Stewardship Council

THE LARGEST NUMBER OF CONTRIBUTORS
TO THE CATHOLIC CHURCH

Arch/Diocese	# of Gifts (dollars)	Ave. Gift (dollars)	Largest Gift (dollars)
1) Philadelphia – Archdiocese of Philadelphia, PA	202,096	36.37	50,000
2) Detroit – Archdiocese of Detroit, MI	166,154	60.02	NA
3) Toronto, Diocese of Toronto, Ontario, Canada	155,520	52.12	NA
4) New York – Diocese of New York, NY	122,648	65.42	NA
5) Milwaukee – Diocese of Milwaukee, WI	116,112	50.32	10,000
6) Cleveland – Diocese of Cleveland, OH	108,331	60.02	40,000
7) Providence – Diocese of Providence, RI	106,500	35.60	34,000
8) Boston – Archdiocese of Boston, MA	103,000	90.29	NA
9) St. Louis – Archdiocese of St. Louis, MO	95,912	63.26	25,000
10) Springfield – Diocese of Springfield, MA	87,693	34.50	10,000
11) Rockville Centre – Diocese of Rockville Centre, NY	87,478	92.40	30,000
12) St. Paul – Archdiocese of St. Paul, MN	84,422	60.85	20,000
13) Syracuse – Diocese of Syracuse, NY	70,794	36.73	NA
14) Albany – Diocese of Albany, NY	65,231	54.02	NA
15) Camden – Diocese of Camden, NJ	65,000	34.40	34,000
16) Rochester – Diocese of Rochester, NY	63,381	61.04	4,000
17) Cincinnati – Archdiocese of Cincinnati, OH	62,782	52.44	NA
18) Worcester – Diocese of Worcester, MA	62,167	45.11	33,000
19) Newark – Archdiocese of Newark, NJ	53,940	101.55	NA
20) Harrisburg – Diocese of Harrisburg, PA	48,346	52.71	NA

Source: National Catholic Stewardship Council

CONTROVERSIAL TREND—
BUT INCREASING

There is a trend in organizations and institutions toward rewarding fundraising performance with bonuses. The most definite rise in the practice is found among hospitals.

Although the incentive arrangement is controversial, it is becoming more prevalent. Last year, the National Association for Hospital Development (NAHD) officially recommended against such a practice. Historically, it has been unethical to relate awards and bonuses to production.

Those in the field predict that it will be commonplace to have the compensation of fundraisers related directly to the funds produced and generated, much like salespeople in business.

CATHOLIC CAMPAIGN EXPENSES

Arch/Diocese	Total Campaign Expenses (dollars)	Campaign Expenses as % of $ raised
1) Hartford – Diocese of Hartford, CT	339,895	10.1
2) Newark – Archdiocese of Newark, NJ	511,000	9.3
3) Rockville Centre – Diocese of Rockville Centre, NY	746,680	9.2
4) Providence – Diocese of Providence, RI	309,700	8.1
5) Scranton – Diocese of Scranton, PA	350,000	7.2
6) Springfield – Diocese of Springfield, MA	220,528	7.2
7) Toronto – Diocese of Toronto, Ontario, Canada	524,000	6.4
8) St. Paul – Archdiocese of St. Paul, MN	328,796	6.3
9) Palm Beach – Diocese of Palm Beach Gardens, FL	193,512	6.3
10) Philadelphia – Archdiocese of Philadelphia, PA	461,281	6.2
11) San Jose – Diocese of San Jose, CA	196,541	6.1
12) Cleveland – Diocese of Cleveland, OH	390,000	5.9
13) Miami – Diocese of Miami, FL	341,274	5.8
14) Cincinnati – Archdiocese of Cincinnati, OH	191,757	5.8
15) Detroit – Archdiocese of Detroit, MI	600,000	5.7
16) St. Louis – Archdiocese of St. Louis, MO	341,008	5.6
17) Milwaukee – Diocese of Milwaukee, WI	330,000	5.6
18) Rochester – Diocese of Rochester, NY	202,314	5.2
19) Boston – Archdiocese of Boston, MA	480,000	5.1
20) Seattle – Diocese of Seattle, WA	150,000	4.6

Source: National Catholic Stewardship Council

GIVING TO RELIGION

When looking at giving to religion by various demographic characteristics, some interesting trends emerge. Those that attend church regularly, have less than a high school education or are over age 65 are more likely to give a larger percentage of their charitable donations to religion. Income is another indicator of religious giving. As income goes up, respondents increase their giving to other charities. The table shows that persons with incomes above $50,000 give the smallest proportion of their total giving to religion.

All Respondents	Religious Charities (Percent)	All Respondents	Religious Charities (Percent)
Income	76	*Age*	
under $10,000		Under 30 Years	76
$10,000 – $19,999	82	30–34 Years	70
$20,000 – $29,999	77	35–49 Years	73
$30,000 – $39,999	76	50–64 Years	65
$40,000 – $49,999	72	65 Years and Older	85
$50,000 and Over	61		
		Marital Status	
Race		Single	61
White	72	Married	73
Black	70	Divorced/Separated	60
		Widowed	84
Religion			
Catholic	71	*Occupation*	
Protestant	75	Professional/Business Manager	69
		Clerical Sales/Service Worker	74
Education		Skilled Worker	80
Less than High School	85	Unskilled Worker/Other	77
High School Graduate	79	Housewife	77
Some College	75	Retired	76
College Graduate, Two-Year and Four-Year Degrees	68		
Postgraduate	62	*Volunteers*	
		Do Not Volunteer	73
Church Attendance		All Volunteers	71
Weekly or Nearly Weekly	85	Less than 3 Hours per Week	76
Once or Twice a Month	65	Three Hours or More per Week	68
A Few Times a Year	53		
Never	23		

Source: The Charitable Behavior of Americans; Independent Sector

ASIAN-AMERICAN PHILANTHROPY

Two important studies were conducted in 1988, reporting on the attitude towards and extent of giving among Asian-Americans. Both studies are significant not only in their findings and conclusions, but also because they are the first to analyze the generosity in this growing segment of the nation's population. The first was conducted by the Institute for Nonprofit Organization Management, the College of Professional Studies, at the University of San Francisco. You can receive a copy of the report by calling (415) 666-6867. It is entitled "Asian American Charitable Giving," by

Rosalyn Miyoko Tonai.

Respondents were well-educated (82.8 percent had at least a bachelor's degree), had a median gross personal income of $34,279, and median gross household income of $62,638. Fifty-five percent were professionals. Asians gave an average of $1,325.15 per household to charitable causes—an average of 2.7 percent of their household income. This is substantially higher than the national average. Individuals at lower income levels gave in significantly greater proportion than those at higher income levels. The levels ranged from a high of 6.6 percent (persons with incomes under $10,000) to 2.2 percent (those making between $20,000 and $60,000).

Most of the funds were given to charities with an Asian orientation. A positive attitude or participation in volunteering correlated with giving. The more not-for-profit organizations an individual volunteered with, the more likely he or she would be to give. Volunteers gave twice as much as non-volunteers.

The study also showed that as socio-economic status increased, giving increased. Older givers tended to give more than younger ones. Home owners gave more than non-home owners.

The results of the study are skewed due to the poor response to an otherwise excellent mail questionnaire. Although this is typical for a mail questionnaire, the report and the work is still immensely valuable.

The Chicago-based consulting firm of Jerold Panas, Young & Partners conducted another significant survey. It was undertaken for the United Way of Los Angeles, and involved interviewing 100 of the most influential and affluent Asian-Americans in the service area of the United Way. An executive summary is available by calling (312) 222-1212.

The Asian population, which includes Japanese, Chinese, Phillipinos and Koreans, now represents the largest minority in Los Angeles, and is growing each year. Among this group are individuals and corporations with immense financial resources. The United Way has a number of organizations and agencies that serve primarily an Asian population. Leadership in the country and the United Way is concerned because they do not feel they receive optimum financial support from American agencies.

There is not a unified "Asian community" that acts and reacts with a single mind and single focus. Each group (the Chinese, Japanese, Philippino, and Koreans) is diverse, independent, and usually does not interact with other Asian groups. There is often a great deal of diversity within each nationality.

Asians are intensely concerned about the education and welfare of their children. Total family welfare comes next. Philanthropy is not a part of their heritage. It needs to be taught.

A key factor is involvement. The more association a person feels with an organization, the greater his or her financial support. This is a direct relationship. Another important factor is that

Asians are often approached for a gift in what would be considered a typical fundraising scenario, and the survey group did not find this appealing or effective.

TAX EXEMPTION OF NOT-FOR-PROFITS UNDER ATTACK

In recent years, not-for-profits have been under increasing attacks regarding their current tax exempt status. Legislators are reviewing the situation more frequently and there are a significant number of "citizens' groups" becoming vocal. Without question, the matter will be scrutinized and intensively examined in the year ahead.

Hospitals in particular have been assaulted by those who challenge why an institution that may produce a net profit of $10 to $15 million, as many hospitals do, should still enjoy the benefits provided an eleemosynary institution. In Pittsburgh, for instance, city officials are demanding that hospitals now pay city taxes, following the example of many other communities.

In 1987 the YMCA lost a bench-mark suit; the court said the fitness center of the YMCA was no different than commercial health centers in Portland, Oregon, and the Y should not enjoy tax exempt status. Many other YMCAs (large cities particularly) are facing the same issue with their dormitories, food service, and fitness centers.

Following is a letter to the editor published in the *Wall Street Journal* on September 21, 1988, clearly stating the case opponents make against tax exempt status. Every not-for-profit must carefully evaluate its position and practices in this matter.

DO NON-PROFITS COMPETE UNFAIRLY?

As usual, Peter Drucker was quite perceptive in recognizing the significance of "The Non-Profits' Quiet Revolution" (editorial page, Sept. 8). It is gratifying to read that non-profits are performing more and more of the functions that government has proved itself incompetent with. But there are some facts about this "revolution" that suggest only cautious optimism is in order.

First, the so-called voluntary, nonprofit sector is, to a large extent, neither private nor voluntary. A multiyear research project by the Urban Institute in Washington revealed that as a whole the nonprofit sector receives more than 60% of its revenues from governmental grants. Since taxes are not voluntary, neither is the majority of the nonprofit sector.

Second, since many of the government-funded nonprofits are used to administer government programs, they may be viewed as just another arm of the government. The phrase "third party government" is routinely used by scholars of the nonprofit sector. Thus, neither is the nonprofit sector very "private."

This second fact has important implications because of another important development—the commercialization of the nonprofit sector. For the past 30 years or so non-profits have increasingly become commercialized, setting up private businesses to supplement their budgets. Non-profits compete with genuinely private businesses in myriad activities, including health and fitness training (YMCAs), audiovisual materials, magazine sales, hospital care, ambulance services, food preparation, research and testing labs, bookstores, taxi services, travel and tourism, and thousands of other services.

What one might call the commercial nonprofit sector is huge, comprising as much as 9% of gross national product according to my estimates. Commercial non-profits compete unfairly with private businesses, however, because as non-profits they pay no federal, state or local taxes, are granted low-interest, government-subsidized loans or outright direct subsidies, are exempt from most regulations their private competitors must comply with, pay lower postal rates, and can solicit tax-deductible donations and use volunteer labor.

The effects of these advantages are that in many industries commercial nonprofit enterprises such as the YMCA are able to crowd out their private-sector competitors. Thus, taxpaying businesses are replaced with non-taxpaying ones, which places stress on governmental budgets. Ironically, some of the tax money collected from private businesses is used to subsidize their nonprofit competitors that may eventually drive them out of the market.

The problem of "unfair competition" is so intense that the 1986 White House Conference on Small Business designated it as one of the top three problems (along with the deficit and the liability crisis) facing small business today. Since by far most of the jobs created in our economy are created by relatively small business, the crowding out of small business by unfair competition deserves to be closely scrutinized, as does the so-called nonprofit sector generally.

Thomas J. DiLorenzo
Professor of Free Enterprise
Center for Economic Education
University of Tennessee
Chattanooga, Tenn.

PolioPlus

ONE OF HISTORY'S MOST EXTRAORDINARY FUNDRAISING SUCCESSES HAPPENED IN 1988

In terms of fundraising, Rotary International has been a "sleeping giant." No longer!

Rotary International is the largest—and considered the most influential, prestigious, and affluent—of all the nation's service clubs. But over the years, it has not raised significant funds, although it has been active in awarding international scholarships and study programs. This year, it flexed its muscle! It raised $230 million on a goal of $120 million for a program called PolioPlus.

The potential has always existed for significant fundraising within the organization. This was really the first year Rotarians were properly and effectively challenged.

It all began in 1985 when PolioPlus surfaced in the consciousness of Rotarians. It symbolized the pledge of Rotary International to protect all the children of the world from the threat of the crippling and killing disease poliomyelitis. The roots of the current program to provide mass immunization for polio and other childhood diseases finds its antecedent in the work of the original Health, Hunger, and Humanity Committee of 1978. The project was explored at that time, and a recommendation made that a program be undertaken.

What Rotary ultimately wished to achieve in its audacious PolioPlus venture was the erradication of polio and other childhood diseases no later than the year 2005, to coincide with the 100th anniversary of the founding of Rotary International. Nothing like it had ever been undertaken by Rotary or any other service club group, and it raised the issue of whether such a commitment was truly appropriate as a collective expression of the will of the Rotary movement. In 1986, the question was settled and a resolution placed the collective will of Rotary behind PolioPlus with an endorsement of its goal as "a humanitarian service effort of great significance to improving child health worldwide."

There are 382,000 Rotarians in the United States, and their giving to the project averaged $312 per member.

The program was considered a notable achievement, one of monumental proportions—not only because the final amount will represent 190 percent of the original goal but also because Rotarians had never before been truly challenged or asked to make major gifts to one of their programs.

The PolioPlus project also helped swell the number of Paul Harris Fellows to 223,501—a record number of 46,990 were recorded this year. A person who makes a commitment of giving $1000 over a ten-year period is recognized as a Paul Harris Fellow.

ONE OF THE MOST IMPORTANT STUDIES OF ITS KIND PROVIDES OPTIMISM FOR INCREASES IN GIVING AND VOLUNTEERING IN THE FUTURE

In 1988, INDEPENDENT SECTOR commissioned a national study to assess the patterns, motivations, and satisfactions of giving and volunteering. The Gallup Organization conducted the study.

The results provide a benchmark for institutional planning and strategy. The survey revealed:

1. Seven out of ten households in America contribute an average of $790 to charitable organizations.

2. Forty-five percent of the adults surveyed volunteered an average of 4.7 hours per week to charitable causes and organizations.

3. Adults of low to moderate income are more generous than higher income individuals in their contribution of volunteer time and money.

4. Households with annual incomes below $10,000 gave an average of 2.8 percent to charitable organizations or causes. Those households with incomes between $50,000 and $75,000 gave 1.5 percent.

5. Almost half of all the money given comes from households with incomes below $30,000.

6. The total amount of time which is volunteered amounts to 80

million persons giving a total of 19.5 billion hours. Translated into wages, this would represent $150 billion.

7. There are countless Americans willing to volunteer, but they are not asked.

8. Three out of four Americans believe they should volunteer to help others.

9. Seventy-five percent believe it is an individual's responsibility to give to charity.

10. One out of three feel that they do not contribute enough.

11. One-quarter felt that they should strive to give 5 percent or more of their income to charity. Less than 10 percent are giving that much now.

12. Volunteering has a direct relationship to contributions. The more people volunteer and are involved, the more they give.

13. An overwhelming majority feel that charitable organizations play a significant role in American society and that charities are needed more today than five years ago.

Source: October 1988, "Update." INDEPENDENT SECTOR.
Copies of the summary report and the full report are available from INDE-
PENDENT SECTOR, 1828 L Street, NW, Washington, DC 20036.

HOURS WORKED PER WEEK BY FUNDRAISERS

	40 hours or less	41–55 hours	56–70 hours	Above 70 hours
Educational institution	13.3	74.0	12.2	0.6
Hospital/medical center	12.4	79.2	8.4	0.0
National health agency	12.8	75.7	11.6	0.0
National social agency	19.4	73.1	7.5	C.0
Regional/local service agency	28.0	66.0	6.0	0.0
Youth organization	15.2	78.2	6.5	0.0
Cultural organization	13.3	76.0	10.6	0.0
Religious organization	14.5	71.0	12.8	1.8
Conservation/wildlife	18.2	63.7	18.2	0.0
Environmental	33.3	33.3	11.1	22.2
Member of small consulting firm	13.3	57.7	28.9	0.0
Member of large consulting firm	0.0	61.8	26.4	11.8
Independent consultant	42.4	42.4	13.6	1.7
Composite	16.8	71.2	11.3	0.8

Source: NSFRE, 1988

THE FUND SEEKERS

The following list traces the founding and growth of some of the major fund-seeking organizations which represent some of the major agencies today in social, health, religious, and welfare programs.

GROWTH OF NATIONAL FUND SEEKERS
1900–1922

Increase in Number of National Organizations

Prior to 1900

Young Men's Christian Association	1866
National Women's Christian Temperance Union	1874
International Sunshine Society	1879
Salvation Army	1880
American Red Cross	1882
Needlework Guild	1885
Young Women's Christian Association	1886
American Humane Association	1889
Council of Jewish Women	1893
National Children's Home Society	1897
National Florence Crittenton Mission	1898
National Consumer's League	1899

1900–1916

Society for the Friendless	1900
National Child Labor Committee	1904
National Tuberculosis Association	1904
Boys' Club Federation	1906
Playground and Recreation Association of America	1906
National Probation Association	1907
Federal Council of Churches of Christ in America	1908
National Association for the Advancement of Colored People	1909
National Committee for Mental Hygiene	1909
Boy Scouts of America	1910
American Association for Organizing Family Social Work	1911
National Federation of Settlements	1911
Camp Fire Girls	1912
National Organization for Public Health Nursing	1912
American Rescue Workers	1913
American Society for the Control of Cancer	1913
American Social Hygiene Association	1914
Girl Scouts	1915
National Committee for the Prevention of Blindness	1915
National Congress of Mothers and Parent-Teacher Associations	1915

1917 and Since

National Association of Travelers' Aid Societies	1917
National Committee on Prisons and Prison Labor	1917
American Association for Community Organizations	1918

Community Service, Incorporated 1919
National Catholic Welfare Council 1919
National League of Girls' Clubs 1919
Circle for Negro Relief 1919
Jewish Welfare Board 1920
Child Welfare League of America 1920
American Federation for the Blind 1921
Big Brother and Big Sister Federation 1921
National Alliance of Legal Aid Societies 1922
American Child Health Associations 1922

Source: FUND RAISING IN THE UNITED STATES, Scott M.
Cutlip.

> *"Love grows by giving. The love*
> *we give away is the only love we*
> *keep. The only way to retain love*
> *is to give it away."*
> Albert Hubbard (1856–1915)

FIRMS AND INDIVIDUALS THAT SPECIALIZE IN DIRECT MAIL FUND RAISING

HUGH CHEWNING, 4 Candlebush, Irvine, CA 92715, (714) 845-2942

CONNIE CLARK, 218 North Lee Street, Alexandria, VA 22314, (703) 548-8206

E.J. COOPER, 506 E. Guenther, San Antonio, TX 78210, (512) 223-9903

JIM GENOVESE, P.O. Box 203, Tenafly, NJ 07670, (201) 871-4330

HERSCHELL GORDON LEWIS, P.O. Box 15725, Plantation, FL 33318, (305) 473-2044

STUART S. MAC LEAN, 7905 Hugh Mullen Drive, Manassas, VA 22110, (703) 368-9570

TOM PELLETIER, 165 Halls Village Road, Chester, NH 03036, (603) 887-2777

DEVELOPMENT DYNAMICS GROUP, INC., 1694 Larkin Williams Rd., St. Louis, MO 63026, (314) 349-0999

KILLION MCCABE & ASSOCIATES, 900 Coit Central Tower, 12001 N. Central Expressway, Dallas, TX 75243, (214) 239-6000

RESPONSE DEVELOPMENT CORP., 3837 Plaza Dr., Fairfax, VA 22030, (703) 273-5113

MAL WARWICK & ASSOCIATES, INC., P.O. Box 1282, Berkeley, CA 94701, (415) 843-8011

ZADOW & MEYERS, INC., P.O. Box 1554, Boston, MA 02118, (617) 482-9249

RUSS REID COMPANY, 2 North Lake Avenue, Sixth Floor, Pasadena, CA 91101, 1 (800) 423-3720, (818) 449-6100

NATIONAL COPY CLINIC, Conrad Squires, President, 220 Lake Avenue, Auburndale, Massachusetts 02166, (617) 332-3746

HUNTSINGER, JEFFER, VAN GROESBECK, INC., Jerry Huntsinger, Chairman, Richmond, VA (804) 264-1116

ROBERT J. BERRETTONE ASSOC., Icon Plaza, 10 Greenleaf St., Rochester, NY 14609, (716) 288-5200

CRAVER, MATHEWS, SMITH & CO. INC., 282 N. Washington St., Falls Church, VA 22046, (703) 237-0600

DIVOKY & ASSOCIATES, INC., 100 Main Street, Reading, MA 01867, (617) 944-4402

THE FOOTE SYSTEM, 266 Bloomfield Avenue, Box 430, Caldwell, NJ 07006, (201) 226-1212

GARTNER & ASSOCIATES, INC., 2 N. Riverside Plaza, Ste. 2400, Chicago, IL 60606, (312) 454-0282

MAILWORKS, INC., 230 North Michigan Ave., Chicago, IL 60601, (312) 263-0665

MCGRATH AND COMPANY, 900 Jorie Blvd., Oak Brook, IL 60521, (312) 990-1212

LOUIS NEIBAUER COMPANY, INC., 20 Industrial Drive, Warminster, PA 18974, (215) 322-6200

L.W. ROBBINS ASSOCIATES, 693 E. Central St., Fanklin, MA 02038, (508) 528-6333

KARL ROVE & COMPANY, 1609 Showal Creek, Ste. 203, Austin, TX 78701, (512) 479-6601

SANKY PERLOWIN ASSOCIATES, INC., 1501 Broadway, New York, NY 10036, (212) 921-0680

SPRINGDALE CONSULTANTS, 15052 Springdale St., Suite A, Huntington Beach, CA 92649, (714) 891-3344

CRAVER, MATHEWS, SMITH & COMPANY, 282 North Washington Street, Falls Church, Virginia 22046, (703) 237-0600

BEST OF CLASS

Competition for the philanthropic dollar has never been keener. At the same time, the generosity of Americans continues to increase from year to year. There has perhaps never been a time more exciting for fundraising, or a period of greater opportunity.

It is anticipated that in 1990, giving in this nation will outstrip even the $104 billion raised in 1989. In 1988, there was a dazzling array of "firsts" and "bests."

The one factor that seems to continue to propel philanthropy to greater heights is the increase in the number of applications for not-for-profit status. In each of the past few years, the Internal Revenue Service has approved nearly 50,000 new organizations for tax exemption. Each brings a new constituency, and each takes a bite out of the philanthropic pie, but also adds to it.

What stands out most of all is that America leads the way. There is no other country in the world that matches our generosity. Philanthropy is certain to continue to grow, in spite of any tax revisions of minor adjustments in the economy. This has been one of the most exciting years in philanthropic history—in many ways in a class by itself and the best of any year which has preceeded it.

INDIVIDUAL GIFTS THAT EXCEEDED $15 MILLION LAST YEAR

James L. Knight
$56 million to University of Miami

William Hewlett
$50 million to Stanford University

Ella S. Johnson
$31 million to Northeast Louisiana University

Maguire Thomas Partners
$28.2 million to Los Angeles Central Library

John W. Kluge
$25 million to Columbia University

Curt Carlson
$25 million to University of Minnesota

Anonymous
$17 million to Emory University

Charles Allen Jr. & Herbert Allen
$15 million to The Presbyterian Hospital

John E. Anderson
$15 million to University of California at Los Angeles

H. Carlos Grawemeyer
$15 million to University of Louisville

Leslie H. Wexner
$15 million to Ohio State University

Marion and John Anderson
$15 million to The University of California at Los Angeles

THE ELEVEN BEST IN PLANNED GIVING

There are a number of companies and individuals which provide excellent consultative services and value in the area of planned giving and estate planning. Here are eleven considered among the finest in the nation. The exclusion of any company or individual from this list does not in any way imply inferior service; these eleven are felt to be outstanding in the field.

Caswell, Schultz, Inc.
Golden Pacific Plaza #103
1601 Carmen Drive
Camarillo, CA 93010
(805) 987-0565

Charitable Funding Services Inc.
155 Canon View Road
Santa Barbara, CA 93108
(805) 969-0203

John Brown Ltd.
Noone Falls, Rte. 202
South Petersborough, NH 03458
(603) 924-3834

Kennedy Sinclaire, Inc.
810 Belmont Ave.
P.O. Box 8304
North Haledon, NJ 07538-0304
(201) 423-9133

National Committee on Planned Giving
620 Union Dr., Room 165
Indianapolis, IN 46202

Pentura, Inc.
8650 Commerce Park Place, Ste. G
Indianapolis, IN 46268
(317) 875-0910

Philanthropy Tax Institute
13 Arcadia Rd.
P.O. Box 299
Old Greenwich, CT 06870
(203) 637-4311

Philip Converse & Associates
2714 Union Ave.
Memphis, TN 38112
(901) 327-7170

R & R Newkirk
500 North Dearborn
Chicago, IL 60610
1-800/428-3852

Robert F. Sharpe & Company, Inc.
5050 Poplar Ave.
Memphis, TN 38157
(901) 767-2330

Trucker & Moerschbacker
456 Montgomery St.
Ste. 1100
San Francisco, CA 94104
(415) 788-3111

TEN LARGEST DONORS EACH YEAR, 1983–1988.

	Amount	Recipient	Donor
1988	$65,000,000	The Hawaii Foundation	Robert E. Black, Bequest
	50,000,000	*NY Hospital—Cornell Med. Cen.	Anonymous
	45,000,000	*Youth help in 5 cities	Annie E. Casey Foundation, CT
	33,000,000	*NY Hospital—Cornell Med. Cen.	M/M Marry B. Helmsley
	25,000,000	University of Rochester	Lady Warwick Fairfax
	23,000,000	Human Rights Now! (Tour)	Reebok International
	20,000,000	National Academy of Sciences	W.K. Kellogg Foundation
	20,000,000	University of Texas, Southwestern Med. Cen.	H. Ross Perot
	20,000,000	Natl. Geographic Society Ed. Foundation	National Geographic Society
	15,000,000	Harvard University	A. Alfred Taubman
1987	$750,000,000	Univ. of CA at Los Angeles	Norton Simon
	100,000,000	Rockefeller University	Hughes Medical Institute
	75,000,000	Stanford Research International	General Electric Co.
	50,000,000	Scholarships for Indiana Students	Lilly Endowment, Inc.
	50,000,000	Los Angeles Music Center	Lillian B. Disney
	40,000,000	Wake Forest University	RJR Nabisco, Inc.
	40,000,000	California Inst. of Technology	Arnold/Mabel Beckman Foundation
	40,000,000	European Universities	IBM
	30,000,000	United Jewish Appeal/Education	Joseph S. Gruss
	30,000,000	Harvard School of Business	John S.R. Shad & Friends
1986	$100,000,000	Washington University, MO	Danforth Foundation
	56,250,000	The University of Miami	James L. Knight
	55,000,000	Washington University	Danforth Foundation
	50,000,000	California Inst. of Technology	M/M Arnold Beekman
	50,000,000	Stanford University	William R. Hewlett, '34
	50,000,000	Stanford University	M/M David Packard
	45,000,000	Columbia University	Howard Hughes Medical Inst.
	40,000,000	Federal Republic of Germany	George Marshall Fund/USA
	40,000,000	California Inst. of Technology	Lilore Green Rains (Bequest)
	40,000,000	Loyola Marymount University	Lilore Green Rains (Bequest)
1985	$40,000,000	University of Illinois	Arnold O. Beckman
	20,000,000	Natl. Academy of Science and Engineering	Beckman Foundation
	20,000,000	Stanford University	M/M David Packard
	12,600,000	Stanford University	Hughes Memorial Institute
	12,000,000	Auburn University	Eleanor Ritchey
	11,500,000	Howard Univ. & M.I.T.	Aga Kahn
	10,900,000	University of So. California	Wm. M. Keck, (Bequest)
	10,900,000	Stanford University	Wm. M. Keck, (Bequest)
	10,000,000	Southern Methodist University	Mary K.H./C.H. Trigg
	10,000,000	Auburn University	H. M. Ware
1984	$70,000,000	California Inst. of Technology	W. M. Keck Foundation
	36,000,000	University of California	Marion O. Hoffman (Bequest)
	30–35,000,000	Dallas Museum of Fine Arts	Reeves Foundation
	25,000,000	The Hoosier Dome	Lilly Endowment
	20,000,000	Cornell University	M/M. S. C. Johnson
	15,000,000	University of Washington	Digital Equipment Corp.
	15,000,000	Massachusetts General Hospital	Arthur/Gullan Wellman
	15,000,000	Columbia University	Gannett Foundation
	14,500,000	University of Chicago	Bernard Mitchell
	14,000,000	Baylor University	Mattie L. Allen (Bequest)
1983	$50,000,000	Cornell University Med. School	Anonymous
	50,000,000	M.I.T.	Digital Corp. and I.B.M.
	40,000,000	Lincoln & Cheyney Universities	Provident Mutual Life Insurance Co.
	22,768,000	Miami-Dade Community College	Mitchell Wolfson (Bequest)
	21,400,000	University of Houston	Conrad Hilton Foundation
	21,000,000	Stanford University	System Development Foundation
	20,000,000	Stanford University Children's Hospital	David and Lucille Packard
	18,000,000	University of California at Berkeley	18 Hi-tech firms
	15,850,000	State of Florida	McKnight Foundation
	15,000,000	Duquesne University	Noble J. Dick (Bequest)

Source: Arthur C. Frantzreb "Million Dollar & Up Donors List"

MILLION DOLLAR AND UP DONORS

In 1987, there were 624 gifts of $1 million or more to philanthropic endeavors. This group represents a variety of educational institutions, hospitals and medical centers, and social and human-betterment institutions.

Amount	Recipient	Donor
$750,000,000	University of CA at Los Angeles	Norton Simon
100,000,000	Rockefeller University	Hughes Medical Institute
75,000,000	Stanford Research International	General Electric Co.
50,000,000	Scholarships for Indiana Students	Lilly Endowment, Inc.
	Los Angeles Music Center	Lillian B. Disney
40,000,000	California Institute of Technology	Arnold/Mabel Beckman Foundation
	European universities	IBM
40,000,000	Wake Forest University	RJR Nabisco, Inc.
30,000,000	Harvard School of Business	John S.R. Shad & Friends
	Undergraduate Biological Sciences Education Initiative	Howard Hughes Medical Institute
	United Jewish Appeal/Education	Joseph S. Gruss
	Undergraduate Biological Education Initiative	Howard Hughes Medical Institute
28,200,000	Los Angeles Central Library	Maguire Thomas Partners
27,500,000	University of Miami	Harcourt/Virginia Sylvester Foundation
25,000,000	Columbia University	John W. Kluge
	Ohio State University	Leslie H. Wexner
23,000,000	New York Public Library	Carl/Lilly Pforzheimer Foundation
20,000,000	Duke University	Disque D. Deane
	University of Richmond	M/M Robert Jepson, Jr.
	University of Mississippi	Standard Oil Co.
16,800,000	11 Public Secondary Schools	Robert Wood Johnson Foundation
15,200,000	Oregon Health Sciences Univ.	Howard Vollum
	University of Texas Institute	The Perot Foundation
	New York University	A.S. Onassis Public Benefit Foundation
	University of CA at Los Angeles	John E. Anderson
	Columbia Presbyterian Med. Ctr.	Charles Allen, Jr./Herbert Allen
15,000,000	The Indianapolis (IN) Zoo	Lilly Endowment, Inc.
	Cornell University	E. Vreeland Baker, Bequest
	University of CA at Los Angeles	John/Marian Anderson
	New York University	The Alexander S. Onassis Public Benefit Foundation
	University of CA at Los Angeles	Marion & John Anderson
	Ohio State University	Leslie H. Wexner
	Washington University, MO	John M. Olin Foundation
14,000,000	Agnes Scott College, GA	George W. Woodruff, Bequest
13,750,000	Univ. of CA at San Francisco	L.P. Markey Charitable Trust
13,000,000	Hartwick College, NY	A.L. & Mrs. K.B. Kellogg, Bequest
	College of Idaho	Anonymous
12,100,000	Yale University	L.P. Markey Charitable Trust
	Washington University, MO	L.P. Markey Charitable Trust
12,000,000	Food for the Hungry, Inc.	K-Mart Corporation
	Yeshiva University, NY	Sy Syms
	University of Louisville	H. Charles Grawemeyer
	Wichita State University	M/M W. Frank Barton
11,000,000	Harvard Medical School	L.P. Markey Charitable Trust
	Metropolitan Museum of Art, NY	Lila Acheson Wallace
10,700,000	University of CA at Los Angeles	Howard Huges Medical Institute
10,400,000	M.I.T.	William H. Ames, Bequest
10,000,000	University of Pittsburgh	Joseph M. Katz
	Choate Rosemary Hall, CT	Paul W. Mellon
	Emory University	M/M D. Wayne Rollins
	College of William & Mary, VA	Roy R. Charles, Bequest
	6 University Health Centers	Pew Charitable Trusts and Rockefeller Foundation
	University of CA at Los Angeles	M/M Eugene Rosefeld
		M/M James A. Collins
	Metropolitan Museum of Art	Henry R. Kravis
	University of North Carolina	Paul A. Johnson, Bequest
	Virginia Polytechnic Institute	Marion Bradley Via
9,000,000	Second Black Colleges Program	Pew Memorial Trust

Amount	Recipient	Donor
8,700,000	University of Chicago	Lucille P. Markey Charitable Trust
8,200,000	University of Southern California	Hedco Foundation
	Westbrook College, ME	John Whitney Payson
8,100,000	Pew Health Policy Program	Pew Memorial Trust
8,000,000	Indiana School of Medicine	The Winona Foundation
	8 Medical School Grants	Robert Wood Johnson Foundation
7,800,000	Among 100 organizations	Farm Aid
	Stanford University	Smith Kline Bechman Co.
7,500,000	Princeton University	2 Anonymous Donors
	Marquette University	Anonymous
	Dartmouth Medical School	M/M Robert C. Borwell
	Princeton University	Charles/Dorothy Hanna, Bequest
	US Tropical Rain Forests	MacArthur Foundation
7,100,000	Whitehead Institute for Biomedical Research	L.P. Markey Charitable Trust
7,000,000	Cold Spring Harbor Laboratory	Howard Hughes Medical Institute
	Eastern College & Eastern Baptist Theological Seminary	Dr./Mrs. C. Stanton Gallup
	Metropolitan Museum of Art	Iris/Gerald B. Kantor
6,800,000	Xavier University	Clara J. Schawe, Bequest
6,500,000	Institute of the Americas, CA	The Gildred Foundation
6,200,000	University of Miami	L.P. Markey Charitable Trusts
	Houston Symphony, TX	Wortham Foundation
	Stanford University	Cecil H. Green
6,160,000	University of Missouri at Kansas City	Board of Trustees (land)
6,000,000	University of Notre Dame	Robert/Raymond Siegfried
	University of Richmond	M/M Robert S. Jepson, Jr.
	Mount Sinai School of Medicine (NY)	Anonymous
	Middlebury College	Alexander Hamilton Fulton, Bequest
5,894,000	Mills College, CA	F.W. Olin Foundation
5,800,000	Carnegie-Mellon University	Digital Equipment Corporation
5,500,000	New York Medical College	Starrett Housing Coporation
5,300,000	DuPage County (IL) Forest Preserve District	The Forest Foundation of DuPage Co.
5,000,000	Northwestern University	Anonymous
	Cornell University	Anonymous group
	Hebrew Union College	Jack N. Skirball Foundation
	Dana Farber Cancer Institute	Louis B. Mayer Institute
	Witchita State University	Tom Devlin, Alumnus
	Berea College, (KY)	The Appalachian Fund
	Princeton University	Anonymous, Alumnus
	Lehigh University	Philip Rouch
	University of Alabama	Robert N. Alston, Bequest
	National Academy of Sciences	Howard Huges Medical Institute
	University of Illinois	Cary/Carlotta Bielfeldt
	Massachusetts Microelectronics Center	Digital Equipment Corporation
	Wesleyan University	Mansfield Freeman and Houghton
	Hole-in-the-Wall Gang, CT	Saudi King Faud
	Institute of Medicine	MacArthur Foundation
	Rand Corporation	Ford Foundation
	University of CA at Los Angeles	M/M Eugene S. Rosefeld
	Winrock International Institute Agricultural Development	MacArthur Foundation
4,700,000	Among 5 Libraries in Michigan	W.K. Kellogg Foundation
	Rochester Institute of Technology	Eastman Kodak Company
4,100,000	Center for the Study and Research in Philanthropy, Indiana University/Purdue University	The Lilly Endowment, Inc.
4,000,000	Boston Museum of Science	David Mugar
	Smithsonian Institution	Arthur M. Sackler
	University of Wisconsin at Green Bay	David/Mary Ann Cofrin
	University of Pittsburgh at Johnstown	Frank J. Pasquerilla
	Kalamazoo College	Herbert/Barbara Dow Foundation
	Williams College	Class of 1962
	Seattle University	Anonymous
	Oberlin College	Robert S. Danforth, Bequest
	University of Virginia	Tom G. Worrell
	University of Arizona	Curtis Cosden, Bequest
3,850,000	University of CA at Los Angeles	L.P. Markey Charitable Trusts
3,800,000	University of Pennsylvania	L.P. Markey Charitable Trusts
	Duquesne University, PA	Antonio J. Palumbo
	New York University	Jack N. Skirball Foundation
	College of Idaho	J.R. Simplot
	U.S. Memorial Holocost Museum	Helena Rubenstein Foundation

3,800,000	**University of Pennsylania**	Pew Charitable Trust
	Rollins College, Florida	M/M George D. Cornell
	California Institute of the Arts	Roy and Patty Disney
		Disney Family Foundation
	University of Chicago	Chicago Community Trust
	Child/Adult Literacy Programs	MacArthur Foundation
3,700,000	**Wake Forest University**	F.W. Olin Foundation
3,600,000	**University of Rochester**	Eastman Kodak Foundation
3,500,000	**University of Southern Mississippi**	Honeywell Bull Inc.
	Children's Defense Fund	Ford Foundation
	Adrian College	Anonymous
3,350,000	**International Health Policy Program**	Pew Charitable Trusts
3,302,650	**Stanford University**	Robert Wood Johnson Foundation
3,300,000	**Stanford University**	H.J. Kaiser Family Foundation
	University of Oregon	L.P. Markey Charitable Trusts
3,259,000	**4 Institutions of Higher Education**	W.M. Keck Foundation
3,240,000	**Chicago Community Trust**	John/Frances Searle, Bequest
3,200,000	**Columbus University**	A.L. Kellogg/Katherine B. Kellogg, Bequest
3,100,000	**University City Science Center (PA)**	Pew Charitable Trust
	Health Sciences Libraries Consortium	Pew Charitable Trust
3,000,000	**University of Minnesota**	Honeywell Foundation
	Lawrence School, New Jersey	Shelby Cullom Davis
	Rollins College, Florida	George/Harriet Cornell
	Columbia University, New York	Katherine B. Kellogg
	Alma College, Michigan	Herbert & Barbara Dow Foundation
	Indiana-Purdue University, Fort Wayne, Indiana	Foellinger Foundation
	California Community Foundation	J. Paul Getty Trust Foundation
	South Dakota Community Foundation	McKnight Foundation
	Transylvania University, Kentucky	Mar/Barry Bingham Fund
	Wisconsin Lutheran College	Schwans Sales Enterprises
	California Community Foundation	J. Paul Getty Trust Fund
	Ithaca College	Lois M. Smiddy, Bequest
	College of William & Mary, Virginia	Wendy Reves
	University of Chicago	Chicago Community Trust
	Massachusetts Institute of Technology	Knight Foundation
	Columbia University	Knight Foundation
	University of Arizona	M/M H. Porterfield & Daughter
	Abilene Christian University	Mabee Foundation
	Ohio State University	Raymond C. Firestone
	University of Houston	Japan Shipbuilding Industry Foundation
	Medical College of Wisconsin	Lynde/Harry Bradley Foundation
	University of Texas Science Center	John A. Hartford Foundation
	Children's Hospital Foundation	Bella Waxner
2,900,000	**University of Southern California**	M/M David R. Radell
2,850,000	**Johns Hopkins University**	W. John Kenney
	Center for Community Change	Ford Foundation
2,700,000	**University of Virginia**	AT&T
	Program for Integrating Economics and National Security	J. Howard Pew Freedom Trust
2,600,000	**Williams College**	Class of 1937
	Boston University/Brandeis University	Pew Charitable Trusts
	University of Oklahoma	Kerr Foundation
2,200,000	**Florida Hospital**	Anonymous
2,100,000	**University of Miami**	E.M. Findley, Bequest
	Culver-Stockton College	3 Anonymous Donors
	University of Utah	M/M Randall K. Fields
	University of Michigan	W.K. Kellogg Foundation
2,000,000	**Worcester Polytechnic Institute**	George/Sybil Fuller Foundation
	Duke University	RJR Nabisco Foundation
	Jackson Laboratory	Howard Hughes Medical Institute
	Stanford University	William & Flora Hewlett Foundation
	Stanford University	James Irvine Foundation
	South Dakota Community Foundation	#M
	American Chemical Society & American Institute of Chemical Engineers & University of Pennsylvania	Arnold/Mabel Beckman Foundation
	Memphis State University	Aaron B. Fogleman
	University of Rochester	Lynde & Harry Bradley Foundation
	University of Michigan	Upjohn Company
	National Fund for Medical Education	Pew Charitable Trusts
	Science Museum of Virginia	Ethyl Corporation
	University of Southern California	Anonymous

Amount	Recipient	Donor
2,000,000	Southern Education Foundation	Ford Foundation
	ICIS/The Door, New York	Ford Foundation
	Michigan State University	W.K. Kellogg Foundation
	Linfield College	Murdock Charitable Trust
	University of Minnesota & Public Schools	Super Value & McKnight Foundation
	Texas Christian University	T.J. Brown/C.A. Lupton Foundation
	Grove City College, Pennsylvania	Pew Charitable Trusts
	University of Southern California	Charles & Henry Greene
	Northeast Ventures Corporation, MN	Blandin Foundation
	Jackson Laboratory	Howard Hughes Medical Institute
	Morristown Memorial Hospital, New Jersey	M/M William Simon
	Morehouse School of Medicine, Georgia	Robert Wood Johnson Foundation
	National Academy of Sciences	Ford Foundation
	Flagler College, Florida	William Kenan Jr. Charitable Trust
	Southern Education Foundation	Ford Foundation
	University of Michigan	M/M William B. Searle
	University of Akron	Geraldine Staller, Bequest
	Stanford University	Pew Charitable Trust
	University of Nevada at Las Vegas	Peggy Gambarana, Bequest
	Nature Conservancy	The Champlin Foundation
	Community Health Promotion Program	Pew Memorial Trust
	The Public Broadcasting System	The Annenberg-CPB Project
	University of CA at San Diego	Sol Price & Family
1,900,000	Duke University	Duke Endowment
	American Association of Community & Junior Colleges	Sears Roebuck Foundation
	Drew University, New Jersey	Cleon/Elsie Fisher
	National Center for Neighborhood Enterprise	Amoco Foundation
1,800,000	Northern Illinois University Foundation	Aaron/Sylvia Scheinfeld Foundation
	The National Judicial College	MacArthur Foundation
	Maternity Center Association, New York	W.K. Kellogg Foundation
	League for Innovation	W.K. Kellogg Foundation
	Michigan 4-H Foundation	W.K. Kellogg Foundation
	Whitman College	Olin Foundation
	United Way of Southeast Delaware County	Pew Charitable Trust
1,750,000	Presbyterian School of Christian Education	Jeannette Early
	University of Puget Sound	Anonymous
	MGH Institute of Health Professions	James S. McDonnell Foundation
	Meharry Medical College, Tennessee	General Foods Fund
	George Washington University	Oliver T. Carr, Jr.
	North Texas State University	Meadows Foundation
1,700,000	University of Delaware	DuPont Company
	University of Missouri	W.K. Kellogg Foundation
	Duke University	Mabel Pew Myrin Trust
	Clemson University	P.W. McAlister, Bequest & Family
1,690,000	Duke University	Pew Charitable Trusts
1,671,250	National Academy of Sciences	Ford Foundation
1,650,000	Local Initiatives Management Assets Corporation	Ford Foundation
1,600,000	M.I.T.	Robert M. Metcalfe
	National Academy of Sciences	Ford Foundation
	University of Oxford, England	W.K. Kellogg Foundation
	National Academy of Sciences, DC	Ford Foundation
	University of Texas, El Paso	Lucille B. Pillow, Bequest
	M.I.T.	Ford Foundation
	Massachusetts Institute of Technology	Robert M. Metcalfe
	University of Texas	Edythe E. Gilbert/T.C. Gilbert
	Rand Corporation & University of CA at Los Angeles	Pew Charitable Trusts
	University of CA at San Francisco	Pew Charitable Trusts
1,500,000	California Institute of Technology	M/M Richard L. Hayman
	Yale University	Humana Foundation
	National Fund for Medical Education	Stuart Foundations
	University of Southern California	Bernard L. Simonsen
	Auburn University, Alabama	Edward Lowder Family
	Neighborhood Development Support Collaborative, Inc.	Ford Foundation
	Massachusetts Institute of Technology	Patrick J. McGovern

1,500,000	Ohio State University	John W. Galbreath Family
	Children's Hospital Foundation, Ohio	Nationwide Insurance Company
	California Institute of Technology	John J. Braun
	Bowman Gray/Baptist Hospital Medical Center	RJR Nabisco Foundation
	Columbia Presbyterian Medical Center	Charles A. Dana Foundation
	Memorial-Sloan Kettering Cancer Institute	Charles A. Dana Foundation
	University of Southern California	M/M Robert A. Maslund
	Oregon Coast Aquarium	Fred Meyer Charitable Trust
	West Texas State University	T. Boone Pickens, Jr.
	Worcester Polytechnic Institute	Marian B. Rutman
	Brown University	Kresge Foundation
	Howard University	American Express Company
	Institute of Medicine, DC	W.K. Kellogg Foundation
	Family Health Foundation of America	Norwich Eaton Pharm., Inc.
	Lycoming College, Pennsylvania	Luther D. Heim
	Columbia University	MacArthur Foundation
	University of New Hampshire	Oliver, Austin & Leslie Hubbard
	Lawrence University	Lynde & Harry Bradley Foundation
	University of Southern California	Gary A. Rosenberg
	Wayne State University	K-Mart Corporation
	Indiana State University	Hulman & George Families
	Arizona State University	Karsten Solheim & Family
	University of Notre Dame	Haggar Foundation
	Wayne State University	Jeanne Lusher
	Ripon College, Wisconsin	Lyne/Harry Bradley Foundation
	Salvation Army, Brooklyn	McKnight Foundation
	University of Michigan	Kresge Foundation
	Central Park Conservancy, New York	Doris/Jack Weiler
	Holmes Avenue, & 52nd Street Elementary Schools	C.A. Win—Rhodes Bea
	Institute of Medicine, DC	W.K. Kellogg Foundation
	Field Museum of Natural History	Kresge Foundation
	University of Southern California	Robert/Mildred Naslund
	Indiana Repertory Theatre	Lilly Endowment, Inc.
	Industrial Technology Institute, MI	Kresge Foundation
	University of Southern California	Hughes Aircraft Company
	McGill University, Canada	Mr. Samuel Bronfman & Children
	Harvard University	G. Ware Travelstead
	Carnegie Forum on Education and the Economy	Carnegie Corporation of New York
1,470,000	Carnegie Forum on Education and the Economy	Carnegie Corporation of New York
1,400,000	Stanford University	Carnegie Corporation of New York
	Public/Private Ventures, Pennsylvania	Ford Foundation
	United Way of America	W.K. Kellogg Foundation
	International Council for Adult Education	W.K. Kellogg Foundation
	10 Indiana School Systems	Lilly Endowment, Inc.
	Saint Louis University, Missouri	Chester Meyers, Bequest
	Washington University, Missouri	Monsanto Company
1,350,000	University of Vermont	Eugene W. Kalkin
	George Fox College	M.J. Murcock Charitable Trust
	Greater Cincinnati Community Foundation	The Appalachian Fund
	International Fertilizer Development Center	W.K. Kellogg Foundation
1,348,214	Ohio State University	Irene D. Hirsch Research Fund
1,300,000	Princeton University	John M. Olin Foundation
	Oral Roberts	Jerry Collins
	Meharry Medical College	Reader's Digest
	Pace University, New York	W.K. Kellogg Foundation
	University of Minnesota	Dayton Hudson Foundation
1,290,000	Dana Farber Cancer Institute, Mass.	Henry J. Kaiser Family Foundation
1,265,000	International Planned Parenthood Federation	MacArthur Foundation
1,250,000	Dartmouth Medical School	R. Borwell/K. Montgomery
	Columbia University	Warner-Lambert Company
	College of William & Mary	Lee Memorial Trust, DC
	Dana Farber Cancer Institute	Kresge Foundation
	Wichita State University	The Boeing Company
	Fort Wayne Fine Arts Foundation	Lincoln National Life Insurance Co.
	University of CA at Davis	Oak Tree Racing Association
	American Academy in Rome	Andrew W. Mellon Foundation

Amount	Recipient	Donor
1,250,000	Milliken University	F.W. Shilling, Bequest
	Yale University	M/M Adrian C. Israel
	Columbia University	A.W. Mellon Foundation
	University of Michigan	Kresge Foundation
	Hamilton College, New York	General Foods Fund
	Wichita State University	Lionel Alford
	Adult Literacy Programs	Gannett Foundation
	Williamette University	William B. Smullin
	University of Wisconsin, Madison	M/M Milton Shoemaker
	Hartwick College, New York	Anna B. Saxton, Bequest
1,200,000	New York University	S.H./Helen Scheuer Family Foundation
	Azusa Pacific University	Marie Roland, Bequest
	Meharry Medical College, Tennessee	Hospital Corporation of America
	Marquette University	Colemen/Fannie May Candies Foundation
	University of Minnesota	W.K. Kellogg Foundation
	Stanford University	Pew Charitable Trust
	Center for Research in Ambulatory Health Care Administration	W.K. Kellogg Foundation
	Fort Wayne Bible College, Indiana	College Board of Governors
	Waldorf College	M/M John K. Hanson
	Virginia Polytechnic Institute	W.K. Kellogg Foundation
	University of Minnesota	W.K. Kellogg Foundation
	Fine Arts Museum of San Francisco	Grover Magnin, Bequest
	Rollins College, Florida	Anonymous
	Alan Guttmacker Institute, New York	Ford Foundation
	Case Western Reserve University	Cleveland Foundation
	California Institute of Technology	Kenneth/Eileen Norris Foundation
	M.I.T.	Carnegie Corporation of New York
	Rollins College, Florida	Anonymous
	Georgia Southern College	Alan Paulson
	University of Amazon, Brazil	W.K. Kellogg Foundation
	Johns Hopkins University	Pew Charitable Trusts
	Stanford University	Hitachi America
	Randolph Macon College	J. Rives Childs, Bequest
1,189,159	Virginia Cooperative Extension Service	W.K. Kellogg Foundation
1,150,000	University of Oklahoma	Kerr Foundation
1,130,000	Johns Hopkins University	Charles A. Dana Foundation
1,100,000	University of Virginia	M/M John T. Neranc
	University of Michigan	Pew Charitable Trusts
	Harvard Medical School	Charles A. Dana Foundation
	University of Utah	FHP Foundation
	University of Pennsylvania	A.W. Mellon Foundation
	Fairfield University, Connecticut	Dominic R. Ciardi
	Gustavus Adolphus College	Delmar/Jean Pittman
	Edinboro University of Pennsylvania	Louis Porreco
	Texas Technological University	Joe/Beverly Pevehouse
	University of New Hampshire	W.K. Kellogg Foundation
	Christian Theological Seminary, Indiana	Lilly Endowment, Inc.
	Stanford University	Charles A. Dana Foundation
	Lehigh University	Bernard H. Jacobson
	New York University Medical Center	Hasbro Children's Foundation
	University of CA at Los Angeles	Charles A. Dana Foundation
	University of Virginia	Douglas Gordon
1,070,000	Health Education Center, Pennsylvania	W.K. Kellogg Foundation
1,050,000	International Women's Health Coalition	MacArthur Foundation
1,045,000	University of Texas	L.P. Markey Charitable Trusts
1,040,948	Montgomery General Hospital, Maryland	W.K. Kellogg Foundation
1,020,000	Commission for Improvement of Higher Education, Brazil	W.K. Kellogg Foundation
1,010,000	Group Health Cooperative of Puget Sound	W.K. Kellogg Foundation
1,006,000	Community Development Program, PA	Pew Memorial Trust
1,002,000	Fund for Camden, New Jersey	Pew Memorial Trust
1,000,000	Beloit College, WI	Coleman/Fannie May Candies Foundation
	Indiana Univ. School of Business	American United Life
	Columbia University	Marshall D. Shulman Friends and Colleagues
	Columbia University	Pepsi Co., Inc.
	Southgate, MI	Heinz Prechter
	Anderson College, IN	Glenn/Ruth Falls
	Hamline University, MN	William G. Kahlert

1,000,000	
Washington University, MO	Ruth M. Garber/N.G. Moore
Albany Medical Center, NY	Keycorp (banking)
Barry University, FL	Knight Foundation
United Foundation, MI	Kresge Foundation
Boston Plan for Excellence	Goodwin, Proctor, Hoar (attorneys)
University of Michigan	Ford Motor Co.
Univ. of Southern CA	Litton Industries Foundation
Educational Opportunities Council, South Africa	W. K. Kellogg Foundation
University of Minnesota	William I. Fine
University of Mississippi	Mobile Communications Corp. of America
Seton Hall Univ., (NJ)	Robert E. Brennan
University of Utah	Charles/Alice Hetzel
Centre College, (KY)	Anonymous
Wichita State University	M/M Charles Omer
University of Miami	Anonymous
University of Miami	Marta S. Weeks
University of Miami	Leslie O. Barnes
Lehigh University	Pepsico
University of Miami	Barnett Banks
CA Institute of Technology	James Irvine Foundation
Marquette University, WI	Haggerty Foundation
University of Minnesota	H. B. Fuller & Co.
Archdiocese of Chicago	Fannie May Candies Foundation
Smithsonian Foundation	Japan
Smithsonian Foundation	South Korea
Community Foundation of Southeastern Michigan	Elizabeth McCall Wight, Bequest
Marquette University, WI	Kimberly Clark Foundation
Washington University	Monticello College Foundation
University of Michigan	Dr./Ms. E. Gifford Upjohn
Natl. Council on Alcoholism	Joan B. Kroc Foundation
University of Michigan	Alex/Marie Manoogian
University of Utah	Francis A. Madsen Family
Univ. of MD, College Park	Ralph J. Tyser
Univ. of Southern California	Margaret Milligan
University of Notre Dame	M/M Peter Ruffin Foundation
University of Miami	Ryder System Charitable Foundation & Leslie O. Barnes
CA Institute of Technology	M/M Richard L. Hayman
University of Redlands	M/M Richard Hunsacker
Texas Lutheran College	M/M John A. Jackson
GA Institute of Technology	Evelyn G. Rankin
Lowndes Co. (AL) Public Schools	G.E.
Research Laboratories Group, Inc., CA	Pew Memorial Trust
Emory University	Blanche Hagan, Bequest
Reinhardt College	Blanche Hagan, Bequest
Univ. of CA at Los Angeles	Ahmanson Foundation
Yale University	Robert Wood Johnson Foundation
Albany Medical Center, NY	Keycorp
West Virginia University	Mylan Pharmaceuticals, Inc.
Bowman Gray School of Medicine & NC Baptist Hospital	J. T. Brooks & Jean B. Brooks
Duke University	Joseph M. Bryan
Walker Memorial Hospital, FL	Samuel Thomas Haywood
Layfayette College	M/M Eugene H. Clapp, II
Univ. of FL/Univ. of Missouri	Knight Foundation
University of Alabama	M/M Hudson Strook, Bequest
Creighton University	Philip/Ethel Klutzick
Pennsylvania State University	James/Barbara Palmer
Univ. of Southern California	J. Douglas/Marianne Palmer
Wittenberg University (OH)	Elizabeth Totten, Bequest
University of Texas System	M/M Ralph Meadows
VA Polytechnic Inst./St. Univ.	Hercules, Inc.
New York Public Library	Gladys/Jean Delmas
New York Public Library	M/M Gorden Getty
New York Public Library	Robert W. Wilson
Natl. Fund for Medical Ed.	Robert Wood Johnson Foundation
American Enterprise Institute	Lynde/Harry Bradley Foundation
CA Institute of Technology	Indianapolis Foundation
Fairfax Hospital, VA	Home Shopping Network
Notre Dame University	Humana Foundation
New York Public Library	Joseph Frank Bernstein
Rotary Foundation	John K. Evans
Science Museum of VA	M/M Wm. B. Thalhimer, Jr.

Amount	Recipient	Donor
1,000,000	Ripon College (WI)	M/M Charles Van Zoeren
	Palace of the Legion of Honor (CA)	Florence J. Gould Foundation
	Fine Arts Museums of S.F. (CA)	John/Dodie Rosekraus
	Boston Computer Museum	I.B.M.
	Fernbank Museum of National History, (GA)	Rankin Smith
	Colorado School of Mines	John Easthagen, Bequest
	University of Redlands	Richard/Ginnie Hunsaker
	Washington University, (MO)	Carl Neureuther
	Univ. of So. Dakota Foundation	Gannett Foundation
	Beloit College	Willard Mackey
	NJ Institute of Technology	Mentor Graphics Corp.
	Univ. of Southern California	Harold C. Moulton
	Augustana College	Robert/James W. Elmen
	Hendrix College	Reuben B. Hays
	Medical College of PA	Audrey Meyer Mars
	Midland Lutheran College	Hazel L. Keene, Bequest
	Ripon College, WI	Mrs. Erwin C. Uihlein
	Swarthmore College	Scheuer Family
	Wartburg College	Alvin & Clara Whitehouse
	Claremont University Center	J. Paul Getty Trust
	Univ. of CA, Los Angeles	J. Paul Getty Trust
	Marquette University	Rose Monaghan Charitable Trust
	VA Commonwealth University	Nathan/Sophie Gumenick
	Hartford Hospital, CT	Travelers Companies Foundation
	Johns Hopkins University	Pew Charitable Trusts
	Harvard University	Pew Charitable Trusts
	Hunter College, CCNY	Sylvia Fine Kaye
	Kalamazoo College	Anonymous
	University of Dayton	Beerman Foundation
	Univ. of NC, Chapel Hill	D. L. McMichael, Sr. Friends & Colleagues
	University of Arizona	Sally Lindholm, Bequest
	Univ. of Medicine & Dentistry, NJ	Becton, Dickinson & Co.
	Pennsylvania State University	Penn State Alumni Assn.
	University of Michigan	Everett E. Berg
	University of Maryland	Michael D. Dingman
	Univ. of TX, Health Science Ctr.	L. P. Markey Charitable Trust
	College of St. Thomas	Northwestern Bell Telephone
	Cornell University	Leo V. Berger
	Pennsylvania State University	Stanley/Flora Kappe, Bequest
	National Public Radio	Ford Foundation
	Wood Street Commons Assn., PA	Ford Foundation
	Stanford University	J. Howard Pew Freedom Trust
	CA Polytechnic State Univ.	Albert B. Smith
	Washington University, MO	Lee/Milford Bohm
	University of Oklahoma	Robt. S. & Grayce B. Kerr Foundation
	Eastern Illinois University	Lumpkin Foundation
	Beloit College, WI	James J./Joan Dahlquist Flood Foundation
	Beloit College, WI	Anonymous
	Beloit College, WI	Anonymous
	Bowdoin College	Wendy A./Leon A. Gorman
	University of Connecticut	M/M Harry A. Gampel
	Moravian College, PA	M/M Bernard Cohen
	Seattle University, WA	The Boeing Co.
	Seattle University, WA	Jesuit Community of Seattle
	Seattle University, WA	Theiline Pigott McCone
	University of Minnesota	William Find
	University of Alabama	Hudson/Theresa Strode, Bequest
	Washington University, MO & Technicon Israel Institute of Technology	Lee & Milford Bohm
	Ripon College, WI	M/M Charles Van Zoeren
	San Jose Museum of Art	M/M David Packard
	California Inst. of the Arts	Disney Co.
	California Inst. of the Arts	The Ahmanson Foundation
	California Inst. of the Arts	Capital Group Cos.
	California Inst. of the Arts	Walt Disney Co.
	California Inst. of the Arts	J. Paul Getty Trust
	California Inst. of the Arts	James Irvine Foundation
	California Inst. of the Arts	Jones Foundation
	Safe Motherhood Fund	The World Bank
	New York Public Library	Joseph Frank Bernstein
	Rochester Inst. of Technology	Gannett Foundation

Amount	Recipient	Donor
1,000,000	Annenberg Research Inst. for Judaic and Near East Studies	M/M C. W. Rothfeld
	Drury College	Jack/Melba Shewmaker
	West Virginia University	Ernest L. Hogan
	Wright State University	Dorothy Patterson Jackson
	Technology Center of Silicon Valley	Knight Foundation
	Challenger Center for Space Science Education	Gannett Foundation
	Civil Rights Project, Boston	Ford Foundation
	Reed College	Fred Meyer Charitable Trust
	Rockefeller University, NY	Pew Memorial Trust
	Wichita State University	Duane/Velma Wallace
	Roanoke College, VA	Anonymous
	Case Western Reserve University	B P America, Inc.
	Worcester Polytechnic Institute	Howard/Esther Freeman
	Babson College, MA	Roger Enrico
	City College/City Univ. of NY	Herman Goldman Foundation
	Princeton University	Merrill, Lynch & Co., Foundation
	Lehigh University	Kresge Foundation
	New York University	Kresge Foundation
	Houston Baptist University	Sun Exploration & Production Co.
	Trenton State College, NJ	Clara Kee Loser & Thomas and Carol Loser
	Morristown Memorial Hospital, NJ	Allied-Signal Foundation
	Morristown Memorial Hospital, NJ	Warner-Lambert Co.
	Urban Institute, DC	Ford Foundation
	Remediation & Training Inst., DC	Ford Foundation
	University of Minnesota	McKnight Foundation
	Chicago Public Library Foundation	Pritzker Foundation
	University of Houston	Japan Shipbuilding Industry Foundation
	Northeast Ventures Corp.	Northwest Area Foundation
	Institute of Medicine	A. W. Mellon Foundation
	Pennsylvania State University	Richard King Mellon Foundation
	Vassar College	Anonymous—2 Alumnae
	Lafayette College, PA	M/M Eugene H. Clapp, II
	American Council of Learned Societies	Ford Foundation
	Kalamazoo College	Upjohn Co.
	University of South Florida	Frederick H. Schultz
	West Texas State University	Mesa Ltd. Partnership and T. Boone Pickens, Jr.
	University of Houston	T.L.L. Temple Foundation
	University of Virginia	I.B.M.
	Democratic Party	Joan B. Kroc
	Bowling Green State Univ., OH	Harold/Helen McMaster
	University of Pennsylvania	A. W. Mellon Foundation
	California Inst. of Technology	Eastman Kodak Foundation
	California Inst. of Technology	M/M Samuel Oschin
	University of Washington	Jeff C.F. Shih
	Albany Medical Center, NY	Norstar Bancorp/Norstar Bank
	Hardin Simmons College	J.E./L.E. Mabee Foundation
	East Carolina University	C. B. Beasley/Lynn N. Kelso
	Chicago Capital Fund	MacArthur Foundation
	American Cancer Society	Robert W. Woodruff Foundation
	Marshall University	John/Elizabeth G. Drinko
	Reed College	Anonymous
	Claremont University Center	J. Paul Getty Trust Foundation
	U.C.L.A.	J. Paul Getty Trust Foundation
	Rand Corp. Institute for Civil Justice	Ford Foundation
	University of Iowa	Ben V./Dorothy M. Willis
	Hole-in-the-Wall Gang, CT	Anheuser-Busch Foundation
	Moravian College	Berte/Bernard L. Cohen
	Pennsylvania State Univ.	Robert/Stanley Holuba
	Univ. of CA at Los Angeles	Meridian Ruth Ball, Bequest
	Princeton University	Michael J. Scharf
	Palm Beach Art Center, FL	Raymond/Bessie Kravis
	Univ. of Pennsylvania	Pew Charitable Trust
	New York Public Library	Philip Morris Companies, Inc.
	Johns Hopkins University	Pew Charitable Trust
	Native American Rights Foundation	Ford Foundation
	Marshall University	Ashland Oil Foundation
	United Negro College Fund	Nabisco, Inc.
	New Mexico Military Institute	Anonymous

Source: Arthur C. Frantzreb

MILLION DOLLAR & UP DONORS
JANUARY 1 TO JUNE 30, 1988

During the first six months of 1988, there were 282 gifts of $1 million or more given to different organizations and institutions. This list, compiled by Arthur C. Frantzreb, represents giving and grants from all sources.

AMOUNT	RECIPIENT	DONOR
$65,000,000	The Hawaii Foundation	Robert E. Black, Bequest
50,000,000	NY Hospital—Cornell Med. Cen.	Anonymous
45,000,000	Youth help in 5 cities	Annie E. Casey Foundation, CT
33,000,000	NY Hospital—Cornell Med. Cen.	N/M Harry B. Helmsley
25,000,000	University of Rochester	Lady Warwick Fairfax
23,000,000	Human Rights Now! (Tour)	Reebok International
20,000,000	National Academy of Sciences	W. K. Kellogg Foundation
	University of Texas, Southwestern Med. Cen.	H. Ross Perot
	Natl. Geographic Society Ed. Foundation	National Geographic Society
15,000,000	M.I.T.	Howard Hughes Medical Institute
	Washington University, MO	John M. Olin Foundation
	Harvard University	A. Alfred Taubman
12,000,000	Indiana/Purdue Univ. Indpls.	Lilly Endowment, Inc.
11,000,000	Harvard Medical School	L. P. Markey Charitable Trust
10,580,000	Pew Scholars Program in Biomedical Sciences	Pew Memorial Trust
10,000,000	Police Foundation Third Decade Fund	Ford Foundation
	University of Kansas	Lied Foundation
	Penn State University	R. E. Eberly Family
	University of Nebraska	Richard H. Larson, Bequest
	NY Hospital—Cornell Med. Cen.	Peter S. Kalikow
	Mount Sinai Medical Cen., NY	Henry Kravis
9,000,000	Univ. of Missouri, Columbia	Donald W. Reynolds
	Univ. of Southern CA	Thomas/Dorothy Leavey Foundation
8,500,000	University of Florida	Arthur A. Jones
	NY Hospital—Cornell Med. Cen.	Wm S./Mildred Lasdon
8,200,000	University of Michigan	L.P. Markey Charitable Trust
7,600,000	Wichita State University	Oliver/Betty Elliott
6,000,000	NAACP Legal & Defense Educational Fund	Ford Foundation
	Pepperdine University	Arnold/Mabel Beckman Foundation
	Penn State University	H. Thomas Hallowell, Jr.
5,500,000	Case Western Reserve Univ., OH	L. P. Markey Charitable Trust
5,100,000	Michigan State University	W. K. Kellogg Foundation
5,000,000	Univ. of CA at Los Angeles	Pauley Foundation
	Univ. of Rochester	Xerox Corp.
	Southern Methodist Univ.	Nancy Harmon
	FL Institute of Technology	Harris Corp.
	Wellesley College	Katherine W/Shelby Cullom Davis
	Macalester College, MN	Reader's Digest Foundation
	Lehigh University, PA	Murray H. Goodman
	University of Denver	Frank H. Picketson, Jr., Bequest
	Elementary/Secondary Education in Chicago	Chicago Community Trust
4,700,000	Reed College	Edward/Sue Cooley John/Betty Gray
4,600,000	Augustana College, IL	Roy J. Carver Charitable Trust
4,500,000	University of Virginia	M/M David E. Harrison, III
	Philadelphia Museum of Art	Walter H. Annenberg
	Franklin Institute, PA	Pew Memorial Trust

4,500,000	Univ. of Southern Calif.	Kenneth/Eileen Norris Foundation
4,425,000	Wichita State University	Ron and Linda Tyler
4,000,000	Moraine Valley Community College	Grabill Corp. Foundation
	Univ. of Iowa Foundation	Edwin B. Green, Bequest
	Univ. of Southern California	John D. Lusk
	New York University	Baroness Zerillo-Marino
	University of Arizona	Curtis Cosden
3,800,000	University of Texas	L. P. Markey Charitable Trust
	Princeton University	Alfred L. Foulet, Bequest
3,500,000	Brandeis Univ., MA	Abraham D. Gosman
	Univ. of CA/San Diego	L. P. Markey Charitable Trust
	Southern Methodist University	Meadows Foundation
3,300,000	Natl. Institute for Dispute Resolution, DC	MacArthur Foundation
3,000,000	University of Akron	Firestone Tire & Rubber Co.
	Layfayette College, PA	W. B./P.T. Farion
	Watts Labor Community Action Committee, CA	Ford Foundation
	Southern Illinois University	Ralph E. Becker
	University of Virginia	John W. Kluge
	VA Wesleyan College	Marguerite & H.F. Lenfest
2,800,000	NYU School of Law	Anonymous
2,700,000	National Academy of Sciences	Ford Foundation
2,600,000	Natl. Academy of Education, MA	Spencer Foundation
	Natl. Academy of Education	Spencer Foundation
2,500,000	University of Arizona	Norman, Barbara, & Frances McClelland
	University of Southern CA	Herb & Lane Alpert
	Salisbury State College, DE	R. A. Henson
	University of Illinois	Clinton & Susan Atkins
	CA Institute of Technology	Weingart Foundation
	University of Southern CA	Weingart Foundation
	University of Utah	Jon M. Huntsman Family
	New York University	Starr Foundation
	NY Hospital-Cornell Med. Cen.	Mrs. Vincent Astor
	Institute of Civil Justice, CA	MacArthur Foundation
2,300,000	Fund for Theological Education, IN	Lilly Endowment
2,233,000	Harvard University	Pew Charitable Trusts
	Harvard University	Pew Memorial Trust
2,200,000	Museum of Contemporary Art, CA	W. M. Keck Foundation
2,200,000	Brandeis University	L. P. Markey Charitable Trust
2,100,000	CA State Univ. at LA	M/M Charles Luckman
	Hispanic Assn. of Colleges and Universities	Pew Memorial Trust
2,000,000	Cen. for the History of Chemistry	Arnold/Mabel Beckman Foundation
	Mental Health Law Project	MacArthur Foundation
	University of Hartford, CT	Harry/Helen Buckley
	WI Public Policy Institute	Lynde/Harry Bradley Foundation
	Temple University, PA	Pew Memorial Trust
	Univ. of WI at Madison	Grainger Foundation
	NY Hospital-Cornell Med. Cen.	Hays Clark
	Benedictine College	Order of St. Benedict
	Lawrence Inst. of Technology	W.H. Buell/Vita S. Buell-Craig
	College of William & Mary, VA	CSX Corporation
	Natl.-Community AIDS Partnership	Ford Foundation
	Western Michigan University	Gilmore Foundation
	Penn State University	J. Lloyd & Dorothy Huck
	Miami University	Reba Engler Daner
	Colorado School of Mines	Mrs. Janet Coors

AMOUNT	RECIPIENT	DONOR
2,000,000	Univ. of Oklahoma	S. R. Noble Foundation
	Univ. of South Carolina	N.G. & Wm. E. Gonzales
	Duke University	RJR Nabisco Co.
	Howard University, DC	W. H. Annenberg
	Univ. of Alabama	Hugh Culverhouse
	Greenville Technical College	T. Walter Brashier
	New York University	Yamaichi Securities Co.
1,900,000	NY Hospital-Cornell Med. Cen.	Nathan Cummings, Bequest
	Duke University	Duke Endowment
1,822,950	Haverford College, PA	Pew Charitable Trusts
1,800,000	League for Innovation in the Community College with University of TX at Austin	W. K. Kellogg Foundation
	Natl. Council of State Boards of Nursing	W. K. Kellogg Foundation
	City College/City of New York	Aaron Diamond Foundation
	Duke University	Duke Endowment
1,750,000	Guilford College	H. Curt Hege/Patricia S. Hege
	Anson County Hospital, NC	Duke Endowment
1,700,000	Lafayette College	Helen L. S. Hartsine, Bequest
1,650,000	Univ. of TX at Austin	Anonymous
1,614,704	Hospitals of NC & SC	Duke Endowment
1,600,000	Kalamazoo College, MI	Anonymous
1,500,000	Local Initiatives Support Corp.	Ford Foundation
	Boston Foundation	Ford Foundation
	United Way of America	Ford Foundation
	Rand Corp, CA	Ford Foundation
	National Endowment for Humanities	DeWitt Wallace Fund
	Yale University	Paralyzed Veterans of America
	M.I.T.	Mitsubishi Bank of Japan
	CA Institute of Technology	Bren Foundation
	NY Hospital-Cornell Med. Cen.	Gladys/Roland Harriman Foundation
	NY Hospital-Cornell Med. Cen.	Robert Wood Johnson Foundation
	NY Hospital-Cornell Med. Cen.	Michael Davidweill
	NY Hospital-Cornell Med. Cen.	M/M Stephen H. Weiss
	NY Hospital-Cornell Med. Cen.	Iris/B. Gerald Cantor
	University of Pittsburgh	Staunton Farm Foundation
	Stanford University	Kresge Foundation
	Univ. TX & Southwestern Med Ctr.	Greer Garson Fogelson
	TX Lutheran College	Houston Endowment
	Pacific University	Matsushita Electric & Indl. Corp
	University of Arizona	Karl & Stevie Eller
	St. Norbert College	Fort Howard Paper Co. with David Cofrin
	Julliard School, NY	Dorothy Richard Starling Foundation
	Univ. of TX at Austin	Natl. Endow. for the Humanities
	National Public Radio	MacArthur Foundation
1,400,000	Mexican/America Legal Defense & Educational Fund	Ford Foundation
	University of Pittsburgh	Westinghouse Educ. Foundation
	American Hospital Assn.	W. K. Kellogg Foundation
	NY Hospital-Cornell Med. Cen.	Warner Communications Foundation
	Museum of Fine Arts, MA	Digital Equipment Corp.
1,350,000	University of Florida	Arthur A. Jones
1,300,000	Univ. of IL at Chicago	A.T. & T.
	Augustana College, SD	H.F. Myklebust & Estate of M. Helen Myklebust
	Stanford University	Carnegie Corp. of Amer.
	NY Hospital-Cornell Med. Cen.	Dyson-Kissner-Moran Corp.

1,300,000	Neurosciences Research Foundation	L.P. Markey Charitable Trust
1,290,000	Harvard University	Carnegie Corp. of NY
1,250,000	University of Notre Dame	L. G. Balfour Foundation
	N.Y. Hospital-Cornell Med. Ctr.	M/M Jerome Fisher
	NY Hospital-Cornell Med. Cen.	M/M John L. Loeb
	NY Hospital-Cornell Med. Cen.	Mrs. J. Roy Psaty
	NY Hospital-Cornell Med. Cen.	Reliance Group Holdings
	NY Hospital-Cornell Med. Cen.	Anonymous
	NY Hospital-Cornell Med. Cen.	Bernard Chaus
	Illinois College	Ernest/Edna Witaschek
	Grand Valley State College, MI	L.V. Eberhard
1,200,000	University of WI, Madison	Anonymous
	Medical College of PA	Howard Heinz Endowment
	NC A&T University	W. K. Kellogg Foundation
	Alcorn State University, MS	W. K. Kellogg Foundation
	Waldorf Gardens of Garden City, NY	Pew Memorial Trusts
	University of Akron	Prudential Insurance Co.
	Fund for Theological Education	Pew Charitable Trusts
	National Public Radio, DC	Pew Memorial Trust
	University of Texas, Austin	Anonymous
	University of Pittsburgh	Upjohn Co.
	University of Wisconsin/Madison	Anonymous
	Bethany College	L. R. Hummel (groundskeeper) Bequest
	Haverford College, PA	Hughes Medical Institute
	Wesleyan University, CT	Hughes Medical Institute
1,182,000	M.I.T.	The Carnegie Corp.
1,127,000	Northwestern University, IL	Pew Charitable Trusts
1,125,000	Pomona College, CA	Pew Charitable Trusts
1,123,100	Northeast-Midwest Institute	The Carnegie Corp.
1,106,000	Child-Care Institutions NC & SC	Duke Endowment
1,100,000	NJ Institute of Technology	Valid Logic Systems
	Alcorn State University, MS	W. K. Kellogg Foundation
	TX College of Osteopathic Medicine	W. K. Kellogg Foundation
	M.I.T.	Carnegie Corp. of Am.
	60 Undergraduate Colleges	Research Corp.
	Christian Theological Seminary, IN	Lilly Endowment
	Block Nurse Program, St. Paul, MN	W. K. Kellogg Foundation
	Duke University	Duke Endowment
	Texas Lutheran College	Houston Endowment
1,075,500	Cornell University, NY	Pew Charitable Trusts
1,066,000	Stanford University	Charles A. Dana Foundation
1,050,000	Western MD College	Robert J. Gill, Bequest
1,000,000	Huntington Library	A. W. Mellon/W. M. Keck Foundation
	University of Alabama	James G. Brown Foundation
	Carnegie-Mellon University, PA	Pohang Iron/Steel Co. Korea
	Centre College, KY	Mary and Barry Bingham, Jr.
	University of Denver	Leo Block
	Ohio State University	Lewis Zirkle
	Catawba College	Elizabeth Stanback
	University of Minnesota	Deluxe Check Printers
	Natl. Boards for Professional Teaching Standards	The Carnegie Corp.
	Texas Wesleyan College	Mabee Foundation
	University of Illinois	Evans and Sutherland Co.
	Hunter College, NY	Sylvia Fine Kaye
	St. University of NY— Binghamton	Ford Foundation
	University of Dayton	Beerman Foundation

AMOUNT	RECIPIENT	DONOR
1,000,000	Natl. Board for Professional Teaching Standards	Carnegie Corp. of NY
	Natl. Institute for Dispute Resolution, DC	Ford Foundation
	Bedford-Stuyvesant Restoration Corp., NY	Ford Foundation
	Miss. Action for Comm. Education Fd.	Ford Foundation
	Allegheny Conference on Comm. Devlopment	Ford Foundation
	University of Notre Dame	Houston Endowment Inc.
	Babson College, MA	Pepsico
	Hartford Hosp., CT	Travelers Co. Foundation
	Fox Chase Cancer Center, PA	Anonymous
	Hamline University	Eliza A. Drew Mem. Foundation
	St. Univ. of NY, Binghamton	Ford Foundation
	St. Louis University, MO	Clara A. Dref Bequest
	Va. Commonwealth Univ.	T. A. Thomas Foundation
	So. Illinois University	Kenneth H. Pontikes
	Palm Beach Co. Center for the Arts	MacArthur Foundation
	Stanford University	Pew Charitable Trusts
	Drexel University, PA	Pew Memorial Turst
	Columbia University, NY	Pew Memorial Trust
	DePaul University, IL	Coleman/Fannie May Candies
	University of CA, LA	Audrienne H. Moseley
	University of the South, TN	Ogden D. Carlton, II
	Punahou School, HI	Sheridan C. F. Ing.
	Arizona State University	Pepsico
	Ohio State University	Robert/Ruth G. Wigor
	Saint Mary's Seminary & Univ.	Jacob/Annita France Foundation & Robert G./Anne M. Merrick Foundation
	Univ. of South Carolina	I.B.M.
	Southern Methodist University	Roy M./Phyllis G. Huffington
	University of Utah	Anonymous
	Harvard University	Caroline Z. Gross, Bequest
	Lamar University	M/M C. W. Conn
	Washington State Univ.	Wm. Emil Saupe
	New Milford Hospital, CT	Dominick Peburn
	Culinary Institute of Amer.	General Foods Fund
	Arkansas College	Anonymous
	NJ Institute of Technology	Versacad Corp.
	Pepperdine University	George C. Page
	Wayne State Univ.	Katherine Tuck Fund
	GA Institute of Technology	Motorola Corp.
	Abilene Christian Univ. TX	Anonymous
	Purdue University	Chyrsler Corp. Fund
	CA Institute of Technology	Shell Companies Foundation
	CA Institute of Technology	E. I. DuPont & Co.
	CA Institute of Technology	Eastman Kodak Co.
	CA Institute of Technology	3M Corp.
	Duke University	I.T. & T.
	Brandeis University	Sarge/Seymour Ruck
	College of Wooster, OH	Hughes Medical Institute
	Xavier University, LA	Hughes Medical Institute
	Catawaba College	Delhaize Co.
	Cornell University	George/Harriet Cornell
	Penn State University	Westinghouse Educ. Foundation with Robert E. Kirby
	Catholic University of AM	Dean W. Roach
	Northwestern University	Aon Corp.
	New York University	Wm. R. Kenan Charitable Trust
	Marshall University, WV	Sarah/Pauline Maier Foundation
	University of Florida	Alan Squitieri, Bequest
	University of Virginia	John Stewart Bryan Family

1,000,000	Yale University	Am. Collegiate Golf Foundation & Friends
	Center for Civic Education, CA	J. Howard Pew Freedom Trust
	University of Arizona	Del E. Webb Foundation
	University of Arizona	Donald and Joan Diamond
	Univ. of GA Bd. of Regents	Sally Lindholm
	Emory University, GA	John T. Lupton
	George Mason University, VA	William W. Hazel
	University of Kansas	Ken & Barbara Wagnon
	University of Kansas	Stanley Learned
	University of Miami	Anonymous
	Southern Education Fund	Bell South Foundation
	Pacific University, CA	Thomas J. Holce
	University of WI, Madison	Elmer/Janet Kaiser
	University of WI, Madison	Paul A. Elfers
	Wright State University	Dorothy Patterson Jackson
	Duke University	Duke Endowment
	YWCA of Fort Wayne, IN	Foellinger Foundation
	Virginia Commonwealth University	Theresa A. Thomas Mem. Foundation
	University of Texas	W. A. and Deborah Moncrief
	United Way of America	Lilly Endowment
	Bethany College, KS	Zona Richardson, Bequest
	Washington College	Alonzo G. Decker, Jr.
	Wichita State University, KS	Walter Morris & Cons Realtors
	Wake Forest University, NC	Kresge Foundation
	Lehigh University, PA	Kresge Foundation
	Group W. Television Stations	Metropolitan Life Insurance Co.
	University of Pittsburgh	George/Yolanda Barco
	NY Hospital-Cornell Univ. Med. Cen.	Florence J. Gould Foundation
	NY Hospital-Cornell Univ. Med. Cen.	Mrs. Samuel A. Seaver
	NY Hospital-Cornell Univ. Med. Cen.	John L. Weinberg
	University of Rhode Island	Eleanor M. Carlson

"But if I do give, how can I be sure the
money will actually get to you?"

TYPICAL NONPROFIT SALARIES

Position	Avg. 1988 Salary	Lowest Reported	Highest Reported
Executive director	$42,641	$ 8,000	$150,000
Deputy director	$35,928	$10,000	$100,000
Development director	$33,085	$11,466	$ 90,000
Controller	$30,294	$12,600	$100,000
Branch director	$29,712	$10,192	$ 84,350
Department director	$29,608	$ 6,750	$ 82,000
Program specialist	$21,195	$ 7,500	$ 49,500
Office manager	$18,716	$ 8,736	$ 38,000
Bookkeeper	$17,253	$ 9,000	$ 43,862
Technician	$16,712	$ 6,370	$ 25,000
Secretary	$15,770	$ 7,280	$ 32,000
Maintenance worker	$15,411	$ 6,097	$ 60,000
Receptionist/clerk	$13,250	$ 6,486	$ 20,456

Source: Survey of 660 501(c)(3)s around the country by Technical Assistance Center, Denver.

SALARIES AT MAJOR NATIONAL NONPROFITS

Position	Avg. 1988 salary	Highest salary reported
Top Executive Officer	$119,000	$360,000
Deputy Executive Officer	$83,800	$323,000
Top Administrative Position	$61,900	$144,600
Top Financial Position	$52,800	$129,800
Top Government Relations Position	$88,400	$240,700
Top Membership Position	$47,200	$105,000
Top Program Position	$55,800	$150,000
Top Development Position	$60,600	$117,200

Source: Survey of 288 major nonprofits and associations by TPF&C, Washington.

WHAT IS A 501(c)(3)?

The term is common and we use it often, and we know it has something to do with tax exemption—but not everyone is sure what it really means or where it comes from. Well here it is: the provision copied exactly from the Internal Revenue Code.

Sec. 501 [1986 Code]. (a) EXEMPTION FROM TAXATION.—
An organization described in subsection (c) or (d) or section 401(a) shall be exempt from taxation under this subtitle unless such exemption is denied under section 502 or 503.

(b) TAX ON UNRELATED BUSINESS INCOME AND CERTAIN OTHER ACTIVITIES—An organization exempt from taxation under subsection (a) shall be subject to tax to the extent provided in parts II, III and VI of this subchapter, but (notwithstanding parts II, III and VI of this subchapter) shall be considered an organization exempt from income taxes for the purpose of any law which refers to organizations exempt from income taxes.

(c) LIST OF EXEMPT ORGANIZATIONS.—The following organizations are referred to in subsection (a):

(1) Any corporation organized under Act of Congress which is an instrumentality of the United States but only if such corporation—

(A) is exempt from Federal income taxes—

(i) under such Act as amended and supplemented before July 18, 1984, or

(ii) under this title without regard to any provision of law which is not contained in this title and which is not contained in a revenue Act, or

(B) is described in subsection (1).

(2) Corporations organized for the exclusive purpose of holding title to property, collecting income therefrom, and turning over the entire amount thereof, less expenses, to an organization which itself is exempt under this section.

(3) Corporations, and any community chest, fund, or foundation, organized and operated exclusively for religious, charitable, scientific, testing for public safety, literary, or educational purposes, or to foster national or international amateur sports competition (but only if no part of its activities involve the provision of athletic facilities or equipment), or for the prevention of cruelty to children or animals, no part of the net earnings of which inures to the benefit of any private shareholder or individual, no substantial part of the activities of which is carrying on propaganda, or otherwise attempting, to influence legislation, (except as otherwise provided in subsection (h)), and which does not participate in, or intervene in (including the publishing or distributing of statements), any political campaign on behalf of (or in opposition to) any candidate for public office.

Ever wonder why it's a lower case "c"? Well, now you know. It is a subsection under section 501!

Here's something else. Just the fact that an organization is tax-exempt under code section 501 does not mean that a contribution to that organization is tax-deductible. There are many more organizations entitled to tax exemption than organizations for which a donor can take a deduction for the contribution. The qualification under (c)(3) makes the difference.

Check with your organization's attorney or accountant for a technical explanation—but here's one that a layman can understand: in order to qualify for exemption under 501(c)(3), an organization must file an application on Form 1023. And it must meet the following three conditions.

First—it must be organized and operated exclusively for religious, charitable, scientific, literary or educational purposes, for the prevention of cruelty to children or animals, or for the purpose of testing consumer products for public safety, or to foster national or international amateur sports competition.

Next—net income must not be for the benefit, in whole or in part, of private shareholders or individuals.

And lastly—it must not by any substantial part of its activities attempt to influence legislation by propaganda, except for certain lobbying activities.

The organizational exemption and the tax deductible status will continue to be challenged more aggressively in the years to come. Churches, YMCAs, and hospitals are being tested in court on a regular basis. It is interesting to note that just last year the Supreme Court ruled that a hospital does not need to provide medical care to indigents or provide care to needy persons at reduced rates to establish that it is exempt under 501(c)(3).

AT LAST, LEADERS WHO GIVE

In April 1989, President and Mrs. Bush and Vice-President and Mrs. Quayle filed their income tax returns. Their philanthropy represents the largest giving recorded by the nation's leaders since the institution of the income tax.

President and Mrs. Bush had income of $287,171 and donated $12,468. That was distributed among 39 charitable organizations and represents 4.3 percent of their income given to charity. Vice-President and Mrs. Quayle gave $17,403 to charity from an income of $156,546. This represents over 11 percent of their income given to charity. Better than tithing!

You may recall in the first year that Richard Nixon's giving was made public, it was reported that his philanthropy totaled about $100!

COMMEMORATIVE LABELS

The Stephen Fossler Company is a quality label company that can provide your organization with anniversary seals, commemorative labels, and seals to mark any special event or occasion.

For more information: Stephen Fossler Company, 439 South Dartmoor Drive, Crystal Lake, IL 60014 (815) 455-7900.

This is a good source, but there are a number of companies that can supply these for you. These are pressure sensitive seals that can be used on letters, your organizational literature, envelopes, etc.

MILLION DOLLAR DONORS IN 1988

Each year since 1982, *Town & Country* has issued a list of million dollar donors in its December edition. This is *Town & Country's* annual roster of individuals and foundations that have made contributions of a million dollars or more to art, science, scholarship, and the humanities. In 1988, *Town & Country* reported 175 gifts to a variety of colleges and universities, institutions, organizations, and agencies. The magazine titles the list the "Super Santas of '88."

INDIVIDUALS

David Packard: Gave $2,000,000,000 to the David and Lucile Packard Foundation.

Mr. and Mrs. Harry B. Helmsley: $33,000,000 to New York Hospital-Cornell Medical Center.

Albert B. Alkek: $25,000,000 to Baylor College of Medicine, Houston, Texas.

H. Ross Perot: $20,000,000 to University of Texas Southwestern Medical Center at Dallas.

A. Alfred Taubman: $15,000,000 to Harvard University's John F. Kennedy School of Government.

Peter S. Kalikow: $10,000,000 to New York Hospital-Cornell Medical Center.

Henry R. Kravis: $10,000,000 to the Mount Sinai Medical Center.

Arthur A. Jones: $8,500,000 to University of Florida.

Mildred and the late William S. Lasdon: $8,500,000 to New York Hospital-Cornell Medical Center.

Oliver and Betty Elliott: $7,600,000 to Wichita State University.

H. Thomas Hallowell Jr.: $6,000,000 to Pennsylvania State University.

Joan Kroc: $6,000,000 to University of Notre Dame.

Walter H. Annenberg: $5,000,000 to National Gallery, London.

Katherine and Shelby Davis: $5,000,000 to Wellesley College.

Murray H. Goodman: Gave $5,000,000 to Lehigh University.

Nancy Hamon: $5,000,000 to Southern Methodist University.

Jon M. Huntsman Family: $5,000,000 to University of Utah.

Mr. and Mrs. Robert S. Jepson Jr.: $5,000,000 to University of Richmond.

David Harrison: $4,500,000 to University of Virginia.

Ron and Linda Tyler: $4,425,000 to Wichita State University.

John D. and William Lusk: $4,000,000 to University of Southern California.

Sarah W. and W. David Stedman: $4,000,000 to Duke University.

Baroness Mariuccia Zerilli-Marimo: $4,000,000 to New York University.

Abraham D. Gosman: $3,500,000 to Brandeis University.

Ralph E. Becker: $3,000,000 to Southern Illinois University at Carbondale.

Fairleigh Dickinson Jr.: $3,000,000 to Fairleigh Dickinson University.

William B. and P.T. Farinon: $3,000,000 to Lafayette College.

George Rothman: $3,000,000 to Fairleigh Dickinson University.

Mr. and Mrs. Michael Steinhardt: $3,000,000 to Brooklyn Botanic Garden.

Herb and Lani Alpert: $2,500,000 to University of Southern California.

Mrs. Vincent Astor/The Vincent Astor Foundation: $2,500,000 to New York Hospital-Cornell Medical Center.

Iris and B. Gerald Cantor: $2,500,000 to Metropolitan Museum of Art.

Richard A. Henson: $2,500,000 to Salisbury State College.

Jon M. Huntsman Family: $2,500,000 to University of Utah.

Norman, Barbara & Frances McClelland: $2,500,000 to University of Arizona.

Pegeen Fitzgerald: $2,200,000 to the New York State Pegeen Fitzgerald Foundation.

Charles and Harriet Luckman: $2,100,000 to California State University, Los Angeles.

Walter H. Annenberg: Gave $2,000,000 to Howard University.

T. Walter Brashier: $2,000,000 to Greenville Technical College.

Hays Clark: $2,000,000 to New York Hospital-Cornell Medical Center.

Mrs. Janet Coors: $2,000,000 to Colorado School of Mines.

Hugh Culverhouse: $2,000,000 to University of Alabama.

Reba Engler Daner: $2,000,000 to University of Miami.

Harry J. and Helen Buckley Gray: $2,000,000 to University of Hartford.

H. Curt Hege Sr. and Patricia Shields Hege: $2,000,000 to Guilford College.

J. Lloyd and Dorothy Huck: $2,000,000 to Pennsylvania State University.

Iris and B. Gerald Cantor: $1,500,000 to New York Hospital-Cornell Medical Center.

David Cofrin: $1,500,000 to St. Norbert College.

Michel David-Weill: $1,500,000 to New York Hospital-Cornell Medical Center.

Karl and Stevie Eller: $1,500,000 to University of Arizona.

Yasuhiro and Hiroko Goh: $1,500,000 to the Phillips Collection.

Mr. and Mrs. Stephen H. Weiss: $1,500,000 to New York Hospital-Cornell Medical Center.

Dr. Helmer R. and the late M. Helen Myklebust: $1,300,000 to Augustana College.

Bernard Chaus: $1,250,000 to New York Hospital-Cornell Medical Center.

L.V. Eberhard: $1,250,000 to Grand Valley State College.

Mr. and Mrs. Jerome Fisher: $1,250,000 to New York Hospital-Cornell Medical Center.

Mr. and Mrs. John L. Loeb: $1,250,000 to New York Hospital-Cornell Medical Center.

Mrs. J. Roy Psaty: $1,250,000 to New York Hospital-Cornell Medical Center.

Mr. and Mrs. Alan C. Greenberg: $1,100,000 to United Jewish Appeal-Federation of Jewish Philanthropies of New York, Inc.

George J. and Yolanda G. Barco: $1,000,000 to University of Pittsburgh.

Philip and Muriel Berman: $1,000,000 to Philadelphia Museum of Art.

Mary and the late Barry Bingham: $1,000,000 to Centre College of Kentucky.

Leo Block: $1,000,000 to University of Denver.

Jacob Burns: $1,000,000 to George Washington University.

Iris and B. Gerald Cantor: $1,000,000 to The Brooklyn Museum.

Alan Caplan: $1,000,000 to United Jewish Appeal-Federation of Jewish Philanthropies of New York, Inc.

Eleanor M. Carlson: $1,000,000 to University of Rhode Island.

Ogden D. Carlton II: $1,000,000 to University of the South.

George D. and Harriet W. Cornell: $1,000,000 to Cornell University.

Alonzo G. Decker Jr.: $1,000,000 to Washington College.

Donald and Joan Diamond: $1,000,000 to University of Arizona.

Paul A. Elfers: $1,000,000 to University of Wisconsin at Madison.

Dr. Armand Hammer: $1,000,000 to National Cancer Institute.

William Hazel: $1,000,000 to George Mason University.

Thomas J. Holce: $1,000,000 to Pacific University.

Roy M. and Phyllis Gough Huffington: $1,000,000 to Southern Methodist University.

Walter J. Johnson: $1,000,000 to New York Botanical Garden.

Elmer Kaiser and Janet Ambach Kaiser: $1,000,000 to University of Wisconsin at Madison.

Robert E. Kirby: $1,000,000 to Pennsylvania State University.

John W. Kluge: $1,000,000 to National Cancer Institute.

Stanley Learned: $1,000,000 to University of Kansas.

Sally Lindholm: $1,000,000 to University of Arizona Board of Regents.

John T. Lupton: $1,000,000 to Emory University.

W.A. and Deborah Moncrief: $1,000,000 to University of Texas, M.D. Anderson Hospital and Tumor Institute.

Roger Pace: $1,000,000 to Atlantic Christian College.

George C. Page: $1,000,000 to Pepperdine University.

Dominick Peburn: $1,000,000 to New Milford Hospital, Litchfield, CT.

Milton Petrie: $1,000,000 to United Jewish Appeal-Federation of Jewish Philanthropies of New York, Inc.

Dr. Frederik Philips: Gave $1,000,000 to Emory University.

Kenneth N. Pontikes: $1,000,000 to Southern Illinois University at Carbondale.

Dean W. Roach: $1,000,000 to Catholic University of America.

Saul and Seymour Ruck: $1,000,000 to Brandeis University.

Mrs. Samuel A. Seaver: $1,000,000 to New York Hospital-Cornell Medical Center.

Frank P. Smeal: $1,000,000 to Citizens Budget Commission, New York, NY.

Joel E. Smilow: $1,000,000 to Yale University.

Elizabeth Stanback: $1,000,000 to Catawba College.

Mr. and Mrs. Saul P. Steinberg: $1,000,000 to United Jewish Appeal-Federation of Jewish Philanthropies of New York, Inc.

Ken and Barbara Wagnon: $1,000,000 to University of Kansas.

John L. Weinberg: $1,000,000 to New York Hospital-Cornell Medical Center.

Robert L. and Ruth Gooding Wigor: $1,000,000 to Ohio State University.

Lewis Zirkle: $1,000,000 to Ohio State University.

BEQUESTS

Richard H. Larson: $10,000,000 to University of Nebraska.

Frank H. Ricketson Jr.: $5,000,000 to University of Denver.

Curtis Cosden: $4,000,000 to University of Arizona College of Medicine.

Edwin B. Green: $4,000,000 to University of Iowa.

Alfred L. Foulet: $3,800,000 to Princeton University.

Wayne H. Buell and Vita S. Buell-Craig: $2,000,000 to Lawrence Institute of Technology.

Descendants of Ambrose, N.G. and William E. Gonzales: $2,000,000 to University of South Carolina.

Nathan Cummings: $1,900,000 to New York Hospital-Cornell Medical Center.

Howard J. Tracy: $1,300,000 to University of Utah.

Emert and Edna Witaschek: $1,250,000 to Illinois College.

Anna Ballard: $1,087,421 to Morris Animal Foundation.

John Stewart Bryan: $1,000,000 to University of Virginia.

Clara A. Drefs: $1,000,000 to Saint Louis University.

Kathleen Flynn Farness: $1,000,000 to University of Arizona.

Lawrence R. Hummel: $1,000,000 to Bethany College.

Dorothy Patterson Jackson: $1,000,000 to Wright State University.

R.J. and Oressa McCaslin: $1,000,000 to Boise State University.

Zona Richardson: $1,000,000 to Bethany College.

FOUNDATIONS
W.K. Kellogg Foundation: $20,000,000 to National Academy of Sciences and the Institute of Medicine.

Joseph and Bessie Feinberg Foundation: $17,000,000 to Northwestern University Medical School.

Howard Hughes Medical Institute: $15,000,000 to M.I.T.

John M. Olin Foundation: $15,000,000 to Washington University.

Starr Foundation: Gave $12,000,000 to New York Hospital-Cornell Medical Center.

The Pew Memorial Trust: $10,580,000 to Pew Scholars Program in the Biomedical Sciences, 1988–1991.

W.K. Kellogg Foundation: $10,000,000 to Michigan Biotechnology Institute.

Lied Foundation: $10,000,000 to University of Kansas.

Sealy & Smith Foundation: $10,000,000 to University of Texas Medical Branch at Galveston.

George S. and Dolores Doré Eccles Foundation: $9,375,000 to University of Utah.

Thomas and Dorothy Leavey Foundation: $9,000,000 to University of Southern California.

Donald W. Reynolds Foundation: $9,000,000 to University of Missouri at Columbia.

Lucille P. Markey Charitable Trust: $8,200,000 to University of Michigan.

The Pew Memorial Trust: $7,700,000 to Pew Science Program in Undergraduate Studies, 1986–1991.

Lucille P. Markey Charitable Trust: $6,500,00 to Columbia University.

Lucille P. Markey Charitable Trust: $6,500,000 to Purdue University.

Arnold O. & Mable M. Beckman Foundation: $6,000,000 to Pepperdine University.

Lucille P. Markey Charitable Trust: $5,500,000 to Case Western Reserve University.

F.W. Olin Foundation, Inc.: Gave $5,500,000 to Tufts University.

F.W. Olin Foundation, Inc.: $5,300,000 to Ursinus College.

W.K. Kellogg Foundation: $5,149,663 to Michigan State University.

Edwin W. Pauley Fund: $5,000,000 to University of California, Los Angeles.

Harcourt M. and Virginia W. Sylvester Foundation: $5,000,000 to University of Miami.

Roy J. Carver Charitable Trust: $4,600,000 to Augustana College.

Kenneth T. and Eileen L. Norris Foundation: $4,500,000 to University of Southern California.

Abell Foundation: $4,000,000 to the Greater Baltimore Committee.

Robert Wood Johnson Foundation: $4,000,000 to WGBH Television.

Lucille P. Markey Charitable Trust: $3,800,000 to University of Pennsylvania.

Duke Endowment: $3,650,000 to Duke University.

Ford Foundation: $3,600,000 to Fund for the City of New York.

Arnold O. and Mabel M. Beckman Foundation: $3,500,000 to Stanford University School of Medicine.

Lucille P. Markey Charitable Trust: $3,500,000 to University of California, San Diego.

Meadows Foundation: $3,500,000 to Southern Methodist University.

Herbert H. and Grace A. Dow Foundation: $3,000,000 to Albion College.

Ford Foundation: $3,000,000 to Enterprise Foundation, Columbia, MD.

Spencer Foundation: $2,600,000 to National Academy of Education, Cambridge, MA.

Ford Foundation: $2,500,000 to NAACP Legal Defense and Education Fund in New York.

John D. and Catherine T. MacArthur Foundation: $2,500,000 to Institute for Civil Justice, Santa Monica.

The Pew Charitable Trusts: $2,500,000 to the Greater Philadelphia Cultural Alliance.

The Pew Memorial Trust: $2,500,000 to Philadelphia Cultural Community Marketing Initiative.

Starr Foundation: $2,500,000 to New York University.

Weingart Foundation: $2,500,000 to University of Southern California.

Ford Foundation: $2,400,000 to Police Foundations Third Decade for Improving Public Safety in Washington, D.C.

Lucille P. Markey Charitable Trust: $2,400,000 to Children's Hospital Medical Center in Boston.

Lucille P. Markey Charitable Trust: $2,300,000 to Yeshiva University.

Kresge Foundation: $2,250,000 to Memorial Sloan-Kettering Cancer Center.

W.M. Keck Foundation: $2,200,000 to Museum of Contemporary Art, Los Angeles.

Lucille P. Markey Charitable Trust: $2,200,000 to Carnegie Institution of Washington.

Lucille P. Markey Charitable Trust: $2,200,000 to Brandeis University.

The Pew Charitable Trusts: $2,100,000 to Hispanic Association of Colleges and Universities, San Antonio.

Ford Foundation: $2,000,000 to National Community AIDS Partnership.

Gilmore Foundation: $2,000,000 to Western Michigan University.

Grainger Foundation: $2,000,000 to University of Wisconsin at Madison.

W.K. Kellogg Foundation: $2,000,000 to Council of Michigan Foundations.

J. Willard Marriott Foundation: $2,000,000 to University of Utah.

Samuel Roberts Noble Foundation: $2,000,000 to University of Oklahoma.

Skirball Foundation: $2,000,000 to Hebrew Union College-Jewish Institute of Religion.

Mary Flagler Cary Charitable Trust: $1,900,000 to New York Botanical Garden.

Aaron Diamond Foundation: $1,800,000 to City College of the City University of New York.

Howard Hughes Medical Institute: $1,800,000 to Xavier University.

W.K. Kellogg Foundation: $1,800,000 to National Council of State Boards of Nursing, Chicago.

Alfred P. Sloan Foundation: $1,780,000 to Duke University.

The Duke Endowment: $1,750,000 to Anson County Hospital, Wadesboro, NC.

GIVING USA

Giving USA, published by the AAFRC Trust for Philanthropy, is the nation's primary source of information on total philanthropic donations. It presents the earliest, most comprehensive, and most reliable annual estimates of who gives (by type of donor), how much, and who receives (by type of recipient). It also presents a yearly analysis of philanthropic issues and developments, and an annual listing of gifts of $1 million or more, by name of donors and recipients. Its giving estimates are derived from a specially commissioned econometric formula—the Personal Giving Estimating Model—and nationwide surveys of foundations, corporations, charities and other not-for-profit groups and causes. Estimates are revised yearly upon the acquisition of newly released data. *Giving USA* was first published in 1956 and has a total of 4,500 subscribers. Subscribers include corporate and not-for-profit CEOs, directors of development, foundation directors, government officials, fundraisers and students of philanthropy. The cost of subscription is $65. **For more information: American Association of Fund-Raising Counsel Trust for Philanthropy, 25 West 43rd Street, New York, NY 10036   (212) 354-5799.**

WHERE DONORS GAVE THEIR GIFTS 1955–1987

	Religion	Education	Health	Human Service	Arts, Culture & Humanities	Public/ Society Benefit	Other	Unallocated
1955	$ 3.48	$ .883	$ .746	$1.68	$ .349	$ .225	$ .347	—
1956	3.93	.817	1.10	1.60	.322	.250	.322	—
1957	4.22	1.07	1.21	1.70	.359	.279	.454	—
1958	4.34	1.17	1.33	1.66	.353	.272	.350	—
1959	4.76	1.54	1.35	1.63	.397	.290	.383	—
1960	5.01	1.72	1.35	1.63	.408	.314	.502	—
1961	5.23	1.79	1.40	1.69	.415	.318	.517	—
1962	5.45	1.88	1.56	1.77	.410	.312	.498	—
1963	5.84	2.19	1.74	1.97	.485	.374	.601	—
1964	6.14	2.28	1.68	1.92	.435	.387	.828	—
1965	6.72	2.47	1.67	2.07	.436	.383	1.01	—
1966	7.22	2.51	2.23	2.07	.536	.390	.861	—
1967	7.58	2.63	3.00	2.07	.559	.411	.790	—
1968	8.42	3.13	3.22	2.31	.604	.428	.848	—
1969	9.02	3.34	3.40	2.71	.718	.561	1.01	—
1970	9.34	3.28	3.44	2.92	.663	.455	.932	—
1971	10.07	3.65	3.74	3.01	1.01	.684	1.31	—
1972	10.19	3.83	3.94	3.16	1.10	.820	1.45	—
1973	10.53	4.11	4.16	3.07	1.26	.620	1.92	—
1974	11.84	4.04	4.19	3.02	1.20	.670	2.05	—
1975	12.81	3.75	4.22	2.94	1.56	.790	2.55	—
1976	14.18	4.35	4.79	3.02	2.27	1.03	2.40	—
1977	16.98	4.79	4.05	3.57	2.32	1.22	2.53	—
1978	18.35	5.45	5.38	3.87	2.40	1.08	2.44	—
1979	20.17	6.02	6.06	4.48	2.73	1.23	2.97	—
1980	22.23	6.86	6.67	4.91	3.15	1.46	3.46	—
1981	25.05	7.79	7.66	5.62	3.66	1.79	3.92	—
1982	28.06	8.44	8.41	6.33	4.96	1.68	2.16	—
1983	31.86	9.29	9.43	7.16	4.21	1.89	2.96	—
1984	35.43	9.95	10.30	7.88	4.50	1.94	3.30	—
1985	37.46	8.72	11.19	8.50	5.08	2.22	3.89	2.22
1986	41.68	10.08	12.26	9.13	5.83	2.38	3.99	2.65
1987	43.61	10.84	13.65	9.84	6.41	2.60	3.89	3.00

Note: Giving to some categories prior to 1985 cannot be compared to giving since 1985 because of different statistical tabulation and analysis procedures

Source: *Giving USA*

FUNDRAISING EXPENSE

The five largest charities in America, ranked by gross revenue, are: American Red Cross, The Salvation Army, UNICEF, Goodwill

Industries, and CARE. CARE spent the least on fundraising costs and administration, followed by the American Red Cross. Goodwill had the highest cost for fundraising among the group.

Charity	Revenues	Program Expenses	Fund-Raising Admin.
American Red Cross	$973 million	$796 (82%)	$ 76 (8%)
The Salvation Army	865 million	740 (86%)	123 (14%)
UNICEF	463 million	392 (85%)	45 (10%)
Goodwill Industries	447 million	342 (77%)	82 (18%)
CARE	397 million	376 (95%)	21 (5%)

Source: *Fortune* Magazine

SOME ALL-TIME LARGEST GIFTS

In 1988, twelve colleges and universities received the largest gifts in their history.

At the Illinois Institute of Technology, **William J. Stoecker**—Chairman and sole owner of the Grabill Corporation—gave $10 million to construct a high-tech campus in Chicago's research and development corridor. It is the largest gift ever received by the university, and supports a $4 million grant from the Rice Foundation, which purchased 19 acres of land where the new three-building campus will be built.

The J. Willard Marriott Foundation gave Brigham Young University $15 million for its School of Management. The school will be renamed to honor J. Willard and Alice S. Marriott. The foundation was established by the founder of the Marriott Corporation—also a leader in the Church of Jesus Christ of Latter-Day Saints.

Northwestern University received a $17 million gift to establish a cardio-vascular research institute at the Medical School. The grant was made by the **Joseph and Bessie Feinberg Foundation**, created by the sons of Joseph and Bessie Feinberg to honor the memory of their parents.

The University of Washington received a $5 million grant from the **John M. Fluke Endowed Technology Fund**, to support activities of the university's Technology Center. A new building at the center will be named for Mr. Fluke.

The W.K. Kellogg Foundation gave Michigan State a $10.2 million gift to establish a program of life-long education. It is the largest grant the university has received from a foundation. It will establish six regional centers throughout Michigan to determine the educational needs of the areas, and provide services to meet these needs.

The largest single gift in Harding University's history was made by the **Mabee Foundation** to help pay for the renovation and expansion of a residence hall, a library, and a center for American heritage. This challenge grant was for $1.25 million.

Leonard N. Stern gave $25 million to New York University to consolidate the business schools into one building on the Washington Square campus. The schools will be named for Mr. Stern. He received his undergraduate and graduate degrees from the university, where he is a trustee, and is Chairman of the Hartz Group, the parent of Hartz Mountain Pet Products.

A Denver attorney, Ira Rothgerber, Jr., gave $3 million to build a new research facility at the University of Colorado Health Science Center. The gift was made in honor of his two sisters.

Louise Lenoir Locke left a bequest of $10 million to the University of South Alabama—the largest gift ever received by any Alabama institution. The money will be used to establish a foundation to support scholarships and faculty positions at the university's medical school.

The Revlon Center will be built at the University of Pennsylvania as a result of a $10 million gift made by Ronald O. Perelman, Chairman and Chief Executive Officer of Revlon. The new building will be the hub for student organizations and activities, and will house administrative offices, meeting rooms, a performing arts center, restaurants, a movie theater, and the university book store.

A rancher gave Baylor College of Medicine a $25 million gift—one of the largest in the state's history. Albert B. Alkek, a Trustee of the college, placed no restrictions on how the gift might be used. Alkek's gift launches a $175 million fundraising drive for the college.

Paul Allen, co-founder of Microsoft Corporation, a computer software manufacturer, donated $10 million to the University of Washington. The gift is the largest individual donation ever given to the university. The donation will go toward the betterment of the university libraries. A new building will be named after Paul Allen's father, Kenneth Allen, who was the associate librarian for many years at the University of Washington.

EIGHT OF THE LARGEST FIRMS THAT SPECIALIZE IN EXECUTIVE SEARCH FOR DEVELOPMENT PROFESSIONALS

Ast-Bryant
2800 28th St., Ste. 321
Santa Monica, CA 90405
(213) 399-6978
51 Locust Avenue, Ste. 304
New Canaan, CT 06840
(203) 972-3863

Brakeley, John Price Jones Inc.
1600 Summer Street
Stamford, CT 06905
(203) 348-8100

Carolyn Paschal International
1237 Camino del Mar
Suite C506
Del Mar, CA 92014
(619) 587-1366

Ketchum Recruiting
Calvin Douglas, President
1030 Fifth Avenue
Pittsburgh, PA 15219
(412) 281-1481

Korn/Ferry International
Mr. James Heuerman
Managing Vice-President
The Transamerica Pyramid
600 Montgomery Street
San Francisco, CA 94111
(415) 956-1834

Snelling, Kolb & Kuhnle Inc.
2100 M Street N.W.
Suite 600
Washington, DC 20037
(202) 463-2111

Spencer Stuart
401 N. Michigan
Ste. 2500
Chicago, IL 60611
(312) 822-0080

Witt Associates
724 Enterprise Dr.
Oakbrook, IL 60521
(312) 574-5070

THE NATION COMMEMORATES THE THIRD ANNUAL NATIONAL PHILANTHROPY DAY

The third annual salute to America's great tradition of giving was celebrated on November 18, 1988.

Individuals and organizations throughout the nation were recognized for their generous contributions in money and time to philanthropic causes—ranging from arts and education to healthcare and social services.

No other nation in the world can match this country's commitment to philanthropy and sustaining the private sector. In 1988, Americans donated a record $93.68 billion, a major increase over 1987. In fact, philanthropy has always grown in this country, each year more than the year before. Over 350,000 organizations, institutions, and agencies were supported this past year. More than 80 percent of these contributions were made through individual donations—the remainder divided among bequests, foundations, and corporations.

National Philanthropy Day was established in 1986 by leaders from various not-for-profit groups. They organized and planned the first event which sparked celebrations across the country. This past year, it is estimated that 100,000 individuals from most of the states participated in Philanthropy Day.

The National Philanthropy Day committee members follow.

Chairman: Frank M. Hubbard, Former President and Chairman, Hubbard Construction Co.
President: John J. Schwartz, CFRE, Consultant
Vice President: Holly Stewart McMahon, Director of Government Programs, American Bar Association
Secretary: Cathlene Williams, National Society of Fund Raising Executives
Treasurer: Gale Clark, National Society of Fund Raising Executives

Robert Beggan, Senior Vice President, United Way of America
George A. Brakeley, Jr., CFRE, Chairman, Brakeley, John Price Jones Inc.
Virgil Ecton, CFRE, Executive Vice President/Chief Operating Officer, United Negro College Fund
Sarah Engelhardt, Executive Vice President, The Foundation Center
Douglas Freeman, President, The American Institute for Philanthropic Studies
Vivienne M. Lee, Vice President, Council for Advancement and Support of Education
William C. McGinly, Ph.D., President, National Association for Hospital Development
Marshall Monroe, CFRE, Chair, National Society of Fund Raising Executives
Milton Murray, FNAHD, CFRE, Director, Philanthropic Services, Seventh-Day Adventist World Headquarters
Dori Parker, Director of Fund Development Services, Girl Scouts of the USA
Arlie Schardt, Vice President of Communications, Council on Foundations
John Thomas, Vice President, Communications, INDEPENDENT SECTOR
Ernest Wood, Ed.D., CFRE, President, National Society of Fund Raising Executives Foundation
Sponsors: Lilly Endowment
   John D. Regan, General Services Life Insurance Company
Co-Sponsor: Thomas J. Doumani, Advanced Planning Concepts, Inc.

N A T I O N A L
PHILANTHROPY
DAY NOV. 18, 1988

PHI · LAN · THRO · PY
n. THE LOVE / OF HUMANKIND

DONOR RESEARCH MADE EASY

Every organization that solicits major gifts needs research support—but very few have the resources or are able to employ qualified professional researchers.

But research is important—in some situations, the difference between success and failure. Having full information about your prospects is the first step in soliciting properly and winning the gift.

There is one service which provides comprehensive information on your prospects—The Information Prospector. This group can furnish you with information about your prospect's financial status, personal interests, family connections, and philanthropic history.

For information: The Information Prospector, 306 North Washington Street, Falls Church, VA 22046 (703) 536-5900.

DONOR-RESEARCH SERVICES

COMPANIES THAT CONDUCT PROSPECT RESEARCH

Bentz Whaley Flessner
2660 Thayer Street
Kalamazoo, MI 49004
(616) 342-5116
Contact: Bobbie J. Strand,
Senior Associate

Bentz Whaley Flessner
5001 West 80th Street, Suite 201
Minneapolis, MN 55437
(612) 921-0111
Contact: Kathleen A. Foley,
Specialist

CDS International Inc.
1 American Square, Box 82040
Suite 1610
Indianapolis, IN 46282
(317) 637-1277
Contact: Wendy J. Shuler,
Program Officer

Development Research Systems
20 Olde Berry Road
Andover, MA 01810
(508) 470-1170
Contact: Elaine H. Lotto,
President

Fund Consultants Inc.
1 Richmond Square
Providence, RI 02906
(401) 751-4300
Contact: Donna L. Lancaster,
Research Specialist

**Bernard C. Harris Publishing
Company Inc.**
3 Barker Avenue
White Plains, NY 10601
(914) 946-7500; (800) 431-2500
Contact: Pauline Waller, Director
of Prospect Research

Patricia B. Hval
146 Button Rd
North Stonington, CT 06359
203-823-1225

The Information Prospector
306 North Washington Street
Falls Church, VA 22046
(703) 536-5900
Contact: David Lawson,
President

Staley/Robeson/Ryan/
St. Lawrence
635 West Seventh Street,
Suite 114
Cincinnati, OH 45203
(513) 241-6778
Contact: Lyn T. Day, Consultant

Thompson and Pendel Associates
911 South 26th Place
Arlington, VA 22202
(703) 684-7773
Contact: David M. Thompson,
Partner

Waltman Associates
1111 Third Avenue South,
Suite 460
Minneapolis, MN 55404
(612) 338-0772
Contact: Inez Waltman
Bergquist, President

Wiltshire & Associates
116 New Montgomery Street
Suite 640
San Francisco, CA 94105
(415) 543-2152
Contact: Kimery Wiltshire,
President

**Companies that provide
consulting and training services
for fund raisers who want to
research prospective donors:**

Brakeley, John Price Jones Inc.
1600 Summer Street
Stamford, CT 06905
(203) 348-8100
Contact: Aline F. Anderson,
Editor, or Gene M. Anderson,
Senior Vice-President

Source: The Chronicle of Philanthropy

John Grenzebach and Associates
211 West Wacker Drive
Chicago, IL 60606
(312) 372-4040
Contact: Martin Grenzebach,
President

Henderson & Associates
756 Coventry Road
Kensington, CA 94707
(415) 526-8643
Contact: Emily Pfizenmaier
Henderson, Consultant

Marts & Lundy Inc.
1280 Wall Street West
Lyndhurst, NJ 07071
(201) 460-1660
Contact: Bruce G. Freeman,
President

**Companies that publish
newsletters and directories about
prospect research:**

Fund-Raising Institute
P.O. Box 365
Ambler, PA 19002
(215) 646-7019

The Taft Group
5130 MacArthur Boulevard, N.W.
Washington, DC 20016
(202) 966-7086

IT SOUNDS AS IF HE'LL GET HIS WISH!

When Walter Annenberg, former Ambassador to the Court of King James, sold Triangle Publications last year for $4 billion, the already billionaire said: "I want to spend the rest of my life giving my money away." His office says that following that comment to the press, he receives 100 requests a week for funds.

MILLION DOLLAR PROSPECTING

One of the oldest companies in prospect research is Boyd's City Dispatch. They have been around for at least 160 years, assisting organizations and institutions in name development and prospecting.

While their research is not intensive and may not pass careful scrutiny—what they furnish can be of immense value in developing a beginning process.

Boyd's can provide the names, home addresses and phone numbers of affluent individuals. They can also furnish the names, business addresses, and phone numbers of top executives, and provide you with a file of small businesses.

Boyd's City Dispatch was the first mailing list house in America and is one of the oldest companies extant in this country. The company was established in 1830 as a first-class mail delivery service and issued its own postage stamps—and was an integral part of the Pony Express. At the time of the Civil War, it became the first mail-order catalogue company in the country.

For more information: Boyd's City Dispatch, Inc., Bank of Boston Building, Sharon, CT 06069 (203) 435-0861 or (800) 458-7664.

PROSPECT RESEARCHING INCREASES

In 1988, a new professional society was organized. It brought together men and women devoted to researching the giving capacity of potential donors. In a short time, the membership of the group has soared to over 400.

Some question the appropriateness and ethicacy of such research, claiming the donors' rights to privacy. While the debate continues, the research goes on and the society continues to grow.

An informal survey prepared by the association showed the average salary of prospect researchers grew to $25,000 in 1988. The survey used responses from 102 researchers. Forty-four said they earned between $19,000–$25,000, 42 said they earned between $25,000–$35,000. Five among the group earned more than $45,000 a year.

For more information about the Association or to apply for membership: Membership Director, American Prospect Research Association, Box 10179, Minneapolis, MN 55458-3179.

FUNDRAISING CERTIFICATION

The National Society of Fund Raising Executives (NSFRE) provides a program for certification. It gives experienced fundraisers the opportunity to be recognized as a Certified Fund Raising

Executive. This is accomplished by completing a written and oral examination, conducted by a body of peers. Once achieved, the highly recognized and coveted initials—CFRE—may be used following the fundraiser's name.

For more information: The National Society for Fund Raising Executives, 1101 King Street, Suite #3000; Alexandria, VA 22314 (703) 684-0410.

NSFRE IS LARGEST ASSOCIATION SERVING FUND RAISING FIELD

The National Society of Fund Raising Executives is an international organization. Its purpose: to foster the development and growth of professional fundraising executives. Currently, there are more than 9,000 members.

The society publishes an Annual Membership Directory. This includes not only a roster of members, but also a convenient guide for fundraising services and products. It also publishes a magazine and newsletter.

There are regular chapter meetings and an Annual International Conference, with an average attendance of over 1,000. There are also survey courses and a leadership institute.

Its national office includes a resource center and the National Fund Raising Library. The group also provides an important executive search service. This administers referrals from institutions seeking to hire development professionals. It also receives resumes from candidates searching for positions.

J. Richard Wilson, CFRE, headed the society as its Chief Executive Officer. He served as President from 1980 until 1988. Mr. Wilson was a graduate of California State University, and held a Masters from Temple University. He came to NSFRE from the Boy Scouts of America, where he was Development Director. J. Richard Wilson died on December 5, 1988.

For more information: National Office of NSFRE, 1101 King Street, Suite #3000, Alexandria, Virginia 22314 (703) 684-0410.

AWARDS FOR PHILANTHROPY—THE NATION'S HIGHEST HONOR

Awards Program

The National Society of Fund Raising Executives sponsors an annual Awards Program to identify and recognize outstanding achievement by individual, foundation, and corporate philanthropists, fundraising volunteers, professional fundraising executives, and civic and service philanthropic organizations.

These individuals and organizations form a vital partnership that philanthropy must have to maintain its contribution to mankind.

Selection Process

Nominations for each award are placed by an individual NSFRE member or a chapter. All nominations are endorsed by the chapter board of directors prior to submission. A Philanthropy Awards Committee makes a final selection for each award from among the nominees. If, in the judgment of the Awards Committee, no nominees meet the criteria, an award may not be given. The honorees selected receive their awards at the NSFRE International Conference on Fund Raising in April.

Awards and Criteria for Nomination

The **Outstanding Philanthropist Award** is presented to an individual or family with a proven record of exceptional generosity; who, through direct financial support, has demonstrated outstanding civic and charitable responsibility; and whose generosity encourages others to take leadership roles toward philanthropy and community involvement.

The **Outstanding Volunteer Fund-Raiser Award** is presented to an individual who has demonstrated exceptional leadership skills in coordinating groups of volunteers on one or more major fundraising project(s). The recipient demonstrates exceptional skills in coordinating and motivating groups of volunteers for fundraising projects for the benefit of charitable institutions and a commitment to the advancement of philanthropy.

The **Outstanding Fund-Raising Executive Award** is designed for a distinguished individual fundraising executive who practices his/her profession in an exemplary manner.

To qualify for the **Outstanding Philanthropic Organization Award,** a civic or service organization must demonstrate outstanding commitment to community through financial support and through encouragement and motivation of others to take leadership roles toward philanthropy and community involvement.

To qualify for the **Outstanding Foundation Award,** a foundation must demonstrate outstanding commitment through financial support, and through encouragement and motivation of others to take leadership roles toward philanthropy and community involvement.

The **Outstanding Corporation Award** is given to the corporate foundation that demonstrates outstanding commitment through financial support, and through encouragement and motivation of others to take leadership roles toward philanthropy and community involvement.

PAST RECIPIENTS

Outstanding Philanthropist Award

Frank M. Hubbard, Orlando, FL	1988
Jay Phillips, Minneapolis, MN	1987
H. Ross Perot, Dallas, TX	1986
Mr. & Mrs. Walter H. Hilmerich III, Tulsa, OK	1985
Dr. Arnold Beckman, Corona Del Mar, CA	1984
Dr. An Wang, Lowell, MA	1983
Prudential Insurance Co., Newark, NJ	1982
Samuel C. Johnson, Racine, WI	1980

Outstanding Philanthropic Organization Award

The Danforth Foundation, St. Louis, MO	1988
The J.L. Clark Foundation, Rockford, IL	1987

Outstanding Volunteer Fund-Raiser Award

David K. "Pat" Wilson, Nashville, TN	1988
Robert B. Shetterly, Clorox Co., Oakland, CA	1987
Muriel F. Smith, Chicago, IL	1986
James W. Aston, Dallas, TX	1985
Jane C. Freeman, New York, NY	1984
Mr. & Mrs. Whitney Harris, St. Louis, MO	1983
Millie Pastor, Bloomfield Hills, MI	1982
Betty Gerisch, Bloomfield Hills, MI	1981
Mrs. Donald S. Stralem, New York, NY	1980

Outstanding Fund-Raising Executive Award

Ian T. Sturrock, Ph.D., CFRE, Peoria, IL	1988
Lyle E. Cook, CFRE, Mill Valley, CA	1987
Henry Goldstein, CFRE, New York, NY	1986
Henry A. Rosso, CFRE, San Rafael, CA	1985
Philip S. Brain, Jr., CFRE, Minneapolis, MN	1984
Sandie E. Fauriol, CFRE, Falls Church, VA	1983
J.J. Guise, Jr. Dallas, TX	1982
Irl Mowrey, CFRE, Houston, TX	1981
Henry Endress, Washington, DC	1980

JERRY LEWIS SETS ALL TIME RECORD

Jerry Lewis raised $41 million in the 1988 Labor Day Telethon. It went for an uninterrupted 21.5 hours. It exceeded last year's record of $39 million.

Gifts, donations, and phone pledges poured in making, on average, $1.9 million an hour. There were two co-hosts, Tony Orlando in New York and Norm Crosby in Los Angeles. Lewis maintained a three-way conversation with them by satellite.

Jerry Lewis is the father of major telethons. His was the first, when 23 years ago he hosted the Muscular Dystrophy Telethon. Since that time, he has raised a total of $484.3 million for the organization.

The Heritage Collection . . .

During its 25th Anniversary Year, the National Society of Fund Raising Executives honored twenty-five authors who had written significant works contributing to the body of knowledge in fund raising. A permanent plaque was inscribed for the Library with the names of the books and the authors. The project was carried out by the Public Relations Committee of the External Affairs Division of the National Board.

An effort has been made to secure a copy of each book, with the author's autograph, to become a part of the NSFRE Heritage Collection. These will be marked as special books and not to be removed from the Library, but may be used by those who visit the Library at the NSFRE Headquarters in Alexandria, Virginia.

Each year, the National Board, through the Professional Advancement Division, may approve additional works to be added to the plaque, and the books will be added to the Heritage Collection.

The first 25 books to be honored are as follows:
- American Association of Fund Raising Counsel. GIVING U.S.A.
- Arthur Anderson & Company. TAX ECONOMICS OF CHARITABLE GIVING
- Balthaser, William F. CALL FOR HELP
- Barnes, David W. THE FUND RAISERS PLANNING & BUDGETING GUIDE
- Berendt, Robert & J. Richard Taft. HOW TO RATE YOUR DEVELOPMENT DEPARTMENT
- Brakeley, George A. TESTED WAYS TO SUCCESSFUL FUND RAISING
- Broce, Thomas E. FUND RAISING: A GUIDE TO RAISING MONEY FROM PRIVATE SOURCES
- Fink, Norman S. & Howard Metzler. THE COSTS AND BENEFITS OF DEFERRED GIVING
- Flanagan, Joan. THE GRASSROOTS FUND RAISING BOOK
- Gurin, Maurice. WHAT VOLUNTEERS SHOULD KNOW FOR SUCCESSFUL FUND RAISING
- Hopkins, Bruce G. CHARITY UNDER SIEGE
- Huntsinger, Jerald E. FUND RAISING LETTERS
- King, George V. DEFERRED GIFTS: HOW TO GET THEM
- Kiritz, Norton J. PROGRAM PLANNING & PROPOSAL WRITING
- Lautman, Kay & Henry Goldstein. DEAR FRIEND: MASTERING THE ART OF DIRECT MAIL FUND RAISING
- Lord, James Gregory. PHILANTHROPY AND MARKETING
- O'Connell, Brian. AMERICA'S VOLUNTARY SPIRIT
- Panas, Jerold. MEGA GIFTS: WHO GIVES THEM, WHO GETS THEM
- Semple, Lisa Pulling. THE DESK BOOK FOR FUND RAISERS
- Seymour, Harold J. DESIGNS FOR FUND RAISING
- Sharpe, Robert F. THE PLANNED GIVING IDEA BOOK
- Stuhr, Robert L. ON DEVELOPMENT
- Tatum, Liston. COMPUTER BOOK FOR FUND RAISERS
- Warner, Irving. THE ART OF FUND RAISING
- Whitcomb, Nike B. MONEY MAKERS

The 1986 additions to the collection are as follows:

- Dannelley, Paul. FUND RAISING AND PUBLIC RELATIONS
- Grasty, William K. & Kenneth Sheinkopf. SUCCESSFUL FUND RAISING
- Hodgkinson, Virginia A. & Murray S. Weitzman. DIMENSIONS OF THE INDEPENDENT SECTOR
- Kotler, Philip. MARKETING FOR NON-PROFIT ORGANIZATIONS
- Podesta, Aldo C. RAISING FUNDS FROM AMERICA'S 2,000,000 OVERLOOKED CORPORATIONS

The 1987 additions to the collection are as follows:

- Franklin, Beniamin. AUTOBIOGRAPHY AND OTHER WRITINGS
- Fund Raising Institute. FRI PROSPECT-RESEARCH RESOURCE DIRECTORY
- Jenkins, Jeanne B. & Marilyn Lucas. HOW TO FIND PHILANTHROPIC PROSPECTS
- Layton, Daphne Noibe. PHILANTHROPY AND VOLUNTARISM: AN ANNOTATED BIBLIOGRAPHY
- Non-Profit Network. THE INTERNATIONAL CERTIFICATE IN FUND RAISING VIDEOTAPES
- O'Connell, Brian. THE BOARD MEMBERS' BOOK

Some of the books in the Heritage Collection are now out-of-print, or cannot be obtained for sale, due to exclusive arrangements by the authors or publishers. The books described (alphabetically by title) are for sale through NSFRE and can be ordered at the NSFRE Annual Conference bookstore, by mail and by telephone (703) 684-0410.

CHARITABLE CONTRIBUTIONS DEDUCTION

Giving to charitable organizations and institutions entitles a person to a tax deduction. Certain organizations—including United Ways, not-for-profit agencies, foundations, churches, and most educational organizations—are classified as 501(c)(3) by the Internal Revenue Service (IRS). The classification exempts these organizations from taxes and enables people who contribute to them to deduct their gifts from their individual taxes.

Currently, because of the Tax Reform Act of 1986, only people who itemize on their income tax returns may deduct the money or value of property they contribute to tax-exempt organizations. Non-itemizers do not receive a charitable deduction.

DEDUCTIBLE EXPENSES

Aside from direct contributions, individuals also may deduct from their taxes any amount they paid over the fair market value for admission to benefit performances, charity balls, or banquets. For example, if a $20 ticket was purchased to attend a benefit concert, and the regular ticket price is $12, the IRS allows an $8 deduction.

While the Tax Reform Act of 1986 did not repeal the fair market value deduction, it does seek to strengthen the alternative minimum tax. The alternative minimum tax is a "back-up" tax applicable to high-income individuals who drastically reduce their tax liability by using deductions, credits, exceptions, and losses. As

begun January 1, 1987, the increased value of donated property (the difference between the cost to the taxpayer and the fair market value) must be added back into the taxpayer's income. A taxpayer must calculate his or her taxes first under the regular rules, then under the alternative minimum tax rules, and pay the greater of the two.

Expenses related to volunteering also are deductible. The purchase and upkeep of uniforms needed for volunteer service (e.g., as a firefighter or hospital aide) are deductible, as well as the cost of travel connected with volunteer service for a charitable organization. The IRS allows 12 cents per mile for volunteers using a vehicle for charitable business (e.g., driving disadvantaged youths to an event). Parking fees and tolls are deductible, as are reasonable payments for necessary meals and lodging during overnight trips while providing donated services.

People authorized to represent charitable organizations at conferences or meetings may deduct, as a charitable contribution, their unreimbursed expenses for travel and transportation, as well as a reasonable amount for meals and lodging during overnight trips. However, the cost for travel, meals, lodging, and other expenses for an accompanying spouse are not deductible.

For verification purposes, keep accurate records, receipts, cancelled checks, and other proof of charitable gifts or activities. For non-monetary contributions, indicate the original cost, the fair market value at the time of contribution, and the method of determining this value. For gifts of property valued at more than $5,000, the donor must obtain a qualified appraisal and attach a summary on the appropriate IRS form to the tax return.

NONDEDUCTIBLE EXPENSES

Appraisal fees for determining the fair market value of donated property are deductible under "miscellaneous deductions" rather than "charitable deductions." Expenses incurred while lobbying for a charity group, with the exception of churches, are not deductible. Direct contributions to needy or worthy individuals, money spent on raffles or bingo, blood donated to blood banks, and value of volunteer time contributed to a charitable organization are not deductible.

Source: United Way of America

A LETTER OF INTENT—THE PERFECT ANSWER TO THE "I'LL GIVE...BUT I WON'T PLEDGE" SYNDROME

It would be impossible to successfully complete a major campaign on the basis of cash gifts only. What is required is gift-payments over an extended period. Typically in a major campaign, this would extend over a three to five year period.

Many donors, however, are unwilling to sign a legally binding pledge card because they do not want to encumber their estate or they do not know what their income will be in the future. These are the two reasons most often given for not indicating future giving.

Many campaign programs and organizations have abandoned the pledge card in favor of a new form incorporating a line stating: "I will try to give..."

This often works best when the form is not printed, but typed or copied on the organization's stationery. It also helps to type in bold letters: "THIS IS NOT A PLEDGE."

Best of all, experience has shown that there is less attrition on letters of intent than there are on legally binding "official" pledge cards.

Here are two samples which worked very effectively for their organizations.

> "As a member of the Board of Trustees of the _____ Hospital, I recognize that the hospital must have major replacement and modernization of its buildings, facilities, and equipment to efficiently provide excellent in-patient care at reasonable cost. I know that sacrificial giving is required of Trustees and I, therefore, hope and plan on giving $_____ over the next five years. I understand that my gifts will be used to assist in the current capital campaign. It is my understanding that this document merely sets forth my intention to make the gifts but does not imply a legal obligation to complete the gifts. It is my understanding that I may cancel any or all of this commitment at any time. In the event of my death prior to the final payment, my estate will not have a legal obligation to complete this pledge, although they may wish to."

> "I recognize the needs of the _____ _____ in the Centennial Celebration Campaign. It is my hope to give $_____ over the next three years. This intention is subject to modification if changed conditions should warrant. It is understood that this does not obligate my family or my heirs, although they may desire to complete the payment knowing of my interest in the program. It is my serious intention to carry out the foregoing plan and to support the campaign. It is also understood that I may increase the gift I have indicated if I choose to."

If worded properly, this can become a sales piece rather than a frightening legal document or a casual excuse.

FINDING PRECISELY THE RIGHT WORD

Here is a list of words, all related to appreciation and forms of recognition. It will be an invaluable tool for fundraisers in designing awards, preparing recognition plaques, and choosing precisely the right word for important letters.

Accomplishments

achievements
acquirement
attainments
deed
efforts
feat
fulfillment
performance
realization

Achieve

accomplish
actualize
complete
execute
fulfill
perform

Actions

achievement
craftsmanship
creation
deed
deportment
effort
exploit
measure
movement
operations
performance
perpetration
representation
transactions

Aggressive

energetic
enthusiastic
go-getter
hustle
invasive
offensive
persistent
spirited
vigilant
vivacious
zealous

Award

accord
bestow
confer
give
grant
present

Cause

bring about
bring to pass
create
develop
establish
found
institute
make
originate
produce
sow the seeds of

Charity

almsgiving
benevolence
generosity
good will
kindness
liberality
philanthropy
tolerance

Commitment

consecration
constancy
dedication
devotion
fidelity
intrusting
loyalty
service
unreserved adherence

Completion

bring to maturation
close
compass

conclusion
consummation
culmination
denouement
finale
finishing touch
integration
perfecting
performance
realization
refine

Do

carry out
discharge
dispatch
enact
execute
make
perform

Donation

benefaction
bequest
contribution
endowment
gift
grant
gratuity
liberality
offering
present

Donor

benefactor
bestower
bequeathor
conferrer
contributor
giver
grantor
presenter
testator

Gratitude

acknowledgement
appreciation

gratefulness
sense of obligation
thankfulness
thanksgiving

Honors

salutation
compliments
congratulates
hails
pays homage to
salutes
thanks

Humanitarian

altruistic
benevolent
charitable
generous
good Samaritan
large-hearted
liberal
philanthropist
unselfish

Influence

actuate
affect
cause
create
determine
guide
impel
incline
induce
lead
magnetize
more
persuade

Lead

conduct, conduce
contribute
counsel
guide
head
induce
persuade
pilot

Love

admiration
affection
beneficence
benevolence
charitableness
endearment
fervor
fondness
passion
regard
sympathy
tenderness

Outstanding

celebrated
distinguished
eminent
illustrious
noted
prominent
renowned

Performance

achievement
action
creation
execution
representation
touch

Positive

cheerful
decided
emphatic
geniality
optimistic
sunny
unqualified

Profitable

advantageous
aid
beneficial
gainful
lucrative
productive
remunerative

Progress

advancement
betterment
development
forge ahead
forward
growth
ongoing
press onward
step forward
success

Recognition

acceptance
acknowledgement
appreciation
express gratitude
gratefulness
thankfulness

Serve, Service

aid
assist
dedication
devotion
duty
help
helpfulness
kindness
minister to
oblige

Volunteer (noun)

amateur
free-will worker
nonprofessional

Volunteer (verb)

come forward
express readiness
offer
present
present oneself
proffer
propose
stand for
undertake

Source: *Accent on Recognition.* **PSI.**

CHOOSING THE RIGHT PERSON TO HEAD YOUR CAMPAIGN

Selecting and recruiting precisely the right person to head your campaign program can be one of the most important decisions you make—a determining factor of the greatest significance for the success of your project.

Listed on this sheet are twenty-one criteria, essential characteristics in seeking a person to head your program. Grading is on a "one" to "ten" basis—10 being the highest mark. While perfection may be impossible, you should certainly seek the most effective person available. A perfect rating is 275.

The criteria are not listed in order of priority, although several are given added "weight" because of their importance.

For ease and flow of language—and for that reason only—we have used the male pronoun throughout the document. Obviously, women should be considered for this important post. Please substitute He or She where you see "He"—Him or Her where you see "Him."

Score 1 to 10...
ten being the
highest

1. He is an outstanding citizen, a well known and respected civic leader. **(Count two times the rating.)**

   _____

2. He occupies the top position in his firm, or at least no less than the next highest position.

   _____

3. Because of the kind of a man you seek, his business and his pleasures may often take him away from the city. This need not be a deterrent. The important factor is that when he is in the city, he has some flexibility and "give" in his schedule.

   _____

4. He should not be the President of your institution and often, it is desirable that he is not currently a member of the Board.

   _____

5. It is highly desirable that the candidate be knowledgeable about the institution but even this need not be necessary if he is willing to take the necessary time to learn about the program.

   _____

6. The person should be a good public speaker—though he need not chair every meeting. Most important, he must be sincere and convincing when he speaks about the institution.

   _____

7. He is the man in the community to whom it is

337

the most difficult to say "no" **(Count three times the rating).** _____

8. He has the ability to make or affect a number of major gifts. **(Count three times the rating).** _____

9. He has those characteristics to his personal and business life which makes his identification with the institution a desirable one. **(Count $1^1/_2$ times the rating.)** _____

10. He is a willing and enthusiastic delegator of responsibility. _____

11. He has an office staff capable of handling some of the telephoning and details of the campaign. _____

12. He does not have a primary identification with any other similar institutions and he should not have recently chaired another major drive. _____

13. He is not retired although he may now have reached the point where he is not as active in his business as he once was. _____

14. He is willing to give the campaign priority in his personal, business, and civic schedule. **(Count two times the rating.)** _____

15. He is capable of seeing "the big picture" and leave details and office mechanics to the campaign staff. _____

16. He is a secure person with a healthy personality and a high level of self-esteem. _____

17. The candidate is willing to lend more than his name to the campaign, although his name in itself adds luster to the total effort. _____

18. He is conscious of deadlines and schedules. _____

19. He is a team man, willing to listen and work with others. _____

20. The person enjoys good health and stamina. _____

21. He knows how to use and encourage good staff work. _____

22. He must be capable of enduring an insufferable number of roast chicken dinners. **(Count no points!)** ===============

TOTAL _____

_____

Name of Prospective General Chairman

262–275 points—An extraordinary choice. You cannot miss! Your campaign will be a success.

243–261 points—An excellent selection. Take all the care possible in recruiting this person. A victory is almost certain.

192–242 points—A good choice, but you may have some problems in recruiting some of the other leadership you require to reach your objective.

184–191 points—Marginal, but with the proper commitment and dedication, he may overcome deficiencies in other areas.

Source: Jerold Panas, Young & Partners Inc.

NATIONAL SOCIETY OF FUND RAISING EXECUTIVES
FOUNDING OF THE CHAPTERS

YEAR	CHAPTER	FOUNDING PRESIDENT
1964	New York: Greater New York	**John J. Schwartz**
1965	Greater Washington, D.C.	**K. Brent Woodruff**
1967	Massachusetts	**Bernard Delman**
1968	California: Greater Los Angeles Georgia Texas Society of Fund Raisers (1974–Southwest Society of Fund Raisers)	**George Johnstone** **Henry T. Wingate** **Byron Welch**
1969	Pennsylvania: Delaware Valley	**George King**
1970	Minnesota	**Robert J. Rees**
1971	California: Northern (Current Name: Golden Gate)	**Larry Dickson**
1972	Maryland	**Clifford Culp**
1973	Wisconsin	**C. Wilson Schroeder**
1974	California: San Diego New Jersey Missouri: St. Louis	**Clarke McElmury** **Frank Whitley** **William Keenan**
1975	Florida: Gold Coast (Current Name: South Florida)	**Thomas G. Sanberg**
1976	Illinois: Chicago	**Donald A. Campbell, Jr.**
1978	Arizona: Greater	**Skip Hobson**
1979	Michigan Ohio: Central Texas: Houston Texas: Dallas	**Robert Getz** **Kenneth Hoyt** **Jack Kehrberg** **Joyce Boyd**
1980	Alabama Arkansas Connecticut	**William Roth** **Edwin Shafer** **Joseph Coffey**

	Florida: Suncoast	Daniel Biggs
	Louisiana	Rose Marie Wilkinson
	Oklahoma	James Reid
	Pennsylvania: Central	Larry Merris
	Pennsylvania: Western	Jeanne Williams
	New York: Genessee Valley	Edward Moran/Robert Clinger
	Texas: Ft. Worth	William G. McDanel
1981	New York: Hudson-Mohawk	Paul Jones
	New York: Western	Patricia Ulterino
	Tennessee: Nashville	Delmar Staecker
	Rhode Island	Eva Heroux/Franklyn Cook
1982	Florida: Central	James Donovan
	Illinois: Central	Dr. Ian Sturrock
	Indiana	Dan Nicosan
	Iowa	Ellene Mitchell
	Kansas: Wichita	Charles Alberti, Ph.D.
	Nebraska	Richard Jennings
	New Mexico	James Robinson
	Ohio: Northern	Erwin Dieckmann
	Oklahoma: Eastern	Pauletta Henry
	Virginia: First	Claiborne Willcox, Jr.
	Wisconsin: Upper Mississippi Valley	Al Saterbak
	Colorado	Joseph Maloney
1983	California: Orange County	Dorothy Sutherland
	North Dakota	Paul Strawhecker
1984	Arizona: Southern	Barbara Levy
	California: Central Valley	David Barnes
	Delaware: Brandywine	J. Cameron Yorkston
	Florida: Palm Beach	Mary Bymel
	Illinois: Rockford	Thomas DuFault
	Missouri: Kansas City	Don Organ
	Missouri: Central	Dan Sullivan
	Nevada: Southern	Beverly Carlino
	New York: Central	William L. Corcoran
	New Hampshire/Vermont	Carolyn McNellis
	Oregon	Clifford Mansley
	Texas: Austin	Fred Bleeke
	Texas: San Antonio	Diane McAlister
	Texas: Waco	Thomas Strother
	Washington	Patricia Lewis
1985	Michigan: Western	Russell Gabier
	North Carolina: Charlotte	Kimm Jolly
	New Jersey: Mid-State	Jennifer Rice
	Tennessee: Memphis	Leo Arnoult

NSFRE FOUNDATION ADVANCES PHILANTHROPY

The NSFRE Foundation was initiated several years ago to encourage voluntary gifts to meet a variety of needs and to fund special projects of NSFRE. The foundation is responsible for the coordination of efforts to attract necessary support.

The goal of the 1988 annual fund was to strengthen existing programs and initiate new activiites which were identified by the society and the foundation boards.

The foundation sought $180,000 to fund a variety of activities: scholarships, the National Fund Raising Library, National Philanthropy Day, advanced certification, a membership career survey, long-range planning of the development of a survey course, and an emergency fund.

NSFRE FOUNDATION
BOARD OF DIRECTORS

Immediate Past Chair, J. Patrick Ryan, CFRE
Chair, Ernest W. Wood, Ed.D., CFRE
Vice Chair, President, Claudia A. Looney, FNAHD
Vice Chair, President, Milton Murray, FNAHD
Vice Chair, President, William D. Seelye, CFRE
Secretary, Sally Jean Smith, CFRE
Treasurer, Barbara H. Marion, CFRE
Acting Executive Director, Gale Clarke, CFRE
Development Chair, Linda Chew, CFRE

W. David Barnes, CFRE	J. Lloyd Horton, FNAHD
Marianne G. Briscoe, CFRE	James W. Krueger
Richard O. Buxton, CFRE	Kay Partney Lautman, CFRE
Donald A. Campbell, CFRE*	Charles E. Lawson, CFRE
Ralph E. Chamberlain, CFRE*	Frances A. MacAllister, CFRE
Franklin T. Cook, CFRE	Marshall Monroe, CFRE
Robert E. Corder	Stephen Morgan
Virgil E. Ecton, CFRE	Robert Pierpont, CFRE*
James L. Glass, CFRE	Russ Reid
Mark W. Glickman, CFRE	Thomas G. Sanberg, CFRE
James M. Greenfield, CFRE	C. Wilson Shroeder, CFRE
Maurice G. Gurin, CFRE	John J. Schwartz, CFRE
Duncan Hartley, CFRE	Del Staecker, CFRE
Gene M. Henderson	Ian T. Sturrock, CFRE
Virginia Hodgkinson	Eugene R. Tempel
Georgeann E. Hoffman, CFRE	W. Homer Turner, Ph.D.

*Past presidents and chairs of the Foundation who serve as ex-officio members of the Board of Directors. **NSFRE Foundation, 1101 King St., Suite 3000, Alexandria, VA 22314.**

"GIVE FIVE" CAMPAIGN IS LAUNCHED

The INDEPENDENT SECTOR has launched a "Give Five" campaign designed to help the American people realize that everyone should give at least 5 percent of their income, and five hours a week to the causes of their choice. This is the major thrust of the INDEPENDENT SECTOR's new project: Daring Goals for A Caring Society. The program has created great excitement and support around the country. The following was prepared as part of the "Metro Detroit Gives" campaign.

OFFICERS AND MEMBERS OF THE EXECUTIVE COMMITTEE OF THE NATIONAL SOCIETY OF FUND RAISING EXECUTIVES (NSFRE) FOUNDING TO PRESENT

1989

Chair
Marshall Monroe, CFRE
Director, Corporate Planning &
Financial Development
YMCA of the USA
101 North Wacker Drive
Chicago, IL 60606
(312) 269-0543

Vice Chair, Governance
Gerald M. Plessner, CFRE
President
Fund Raisers, Inc.
118-B La Porte
Arcadia, CA 91006
(818) 445-0802

Vice Chair, Professional
Advancement
Ian Sturrock, Ph.D., CFRE
Vice President for Development
& University Relations
Bradley University
Room 203, Swords Hall
1501 West Bradley Avenue
Peoria, IL 61625
(309) 677-3159

Vice Chair, External Affairs
Robert L. Thompson, CFRE
Chairman, CEO
Ketchum, Inc.
1030 Fifth Avenue
Pittsburgh, PA 15219
(412) 281-1481

Vice Chair, Member Services
Barbara M. James, CFRE
Consultant
2634 Hickman Street
Dallas, TX 75215
(214) 428-6447

Treasurer
Patricia F. Lewis, CFRE
Executive Director
Seattle-King County Council of
Camp Fire Girls
8511 15th Avenue, N.E.
Seattle, WA 98115
(206) 524-8550

Assistant Treasurer
Mary Kay Murphy, Ph.D., CFRE
Director of
Development/Foundation
Georgia Institute of Technology
Alumni Faculty House,
Room 301
Atlanta, GA 30332
(404) 894-2483

Secretary
Charles R. Stephens, CFRE
Vice President of Development
Clarke College
240 James P. Brawley Drive, SW
Atlanta, GA 30314
(404) 681-3080

Assistant Secretary
Stephen Wertheimer, CFRE
Vice President, Development
Baruch College
17 Lexington Avenue
New York, NY 10010
(212) 505-5891

1988

Chair
Marshall Monroe, CFRE
Director, Corporate Planning &
Financial Development
YMCA of the USA
101 North Wacker Drive
Chicago, IL 60606
(312) 269-0543

Vice Chairs, Governance
Gerald M. Plessner, CFRE
President
Fund Raisers, Inc.
118-B La Porte
Arcadia, CA 91006
(818) 445-0802

Professional Advancement
Ian Sturrock, Ph.D., CFRE
Vice President for Development &
University Relations
Bradley University
Room 203, Swords Hall
1501 West Bradley Avenue
Peoria, IL 61625
(309) 677-3159

External Affairs
Barbara R. Levy, CFRE
Director of Development
Arizona Theatre Company
P.O. Box 1631
Tucson, AZ 85702
(602) 884-8210

Member Services
Barbara M. James, CFRE
Consultant
2634 Hickman Street
Dallas, TX 75215
(214) 428-6447

Treasurer
Patricia F. Lewis, CFRE
Executive Director
Seattle-King County Council of
Camp Fire Girls
8511 15th Avenue, N.E.
Seattle, WA 98115
(206) 524-8550

Assistant Treasurer
Mary Kay Murphy, Ph.D., CFRE
Director of Development/Foundation
Relations
Georgia Institute of Technology
Alumni Faculty House,
Room 301
Atlanta, GA 30332
(404) 894-2483

Secretary
Charles R. Stephens, CFRE
Vice President of Development
Clarke College
240 James P. Brawley Drive, SW
Atlanta, GA 30314
(404) 681-3080

Assistant Secretary
Stephen Wertheimer, CFRE
Vice President, Development
Baruch College
17 Lexington Avenue
New York, NY 10010
(212) 505-5891

Chair, Chapter Presidents' Council
Mark W. Glickman, CFRE
Executive Director
T.O.P. Jewish Foundation, Inc.
235 S. Maitland Avenue
Maitland, FL 32751
(305) 740-7332

Chair, NSFRE Foundation
J. Patrick Ryan, CFRE
President
Staley/Robeson/Ryan/St. Lawrence
635 W. Seventh Street, #114
Cincinnati, OH 45203
(513) 241-6778

President, NSFRE Foundation
Ernest W. Wood, Ed.D., CFRE
Assistant Vice President
University of the Pacific
Burns Tower, 4tn Floor
Stockton, CA 95211
(209) 946-2503

Executive Committee
Members-at-Large
Marianne G. Briscoe, CFRE
Director, Corporate Relations
University of Chicago
5801 S. Ellis Avenue, Suite 601
Chicago, IL 60637
(312) 702-9767

Irwin Brod, CFRE
Senior Vice President
Brakeley, John Price Jones Inc.
1600 Summer Street
Stamford, CT 06905
(203) 348-8100

Sarah C. Coviello, CFRE
Senior Vice President
The Oram Group, Inc.
1730 Rhode Island, N.W.
Washington, D.C. 20036
(202) 296-9660

1987

Chair
John R. Miltner, CFRE
Vice Chancellor, University
Advancement
University of California, Irvine
Irvine, CA

Vice Chair, Governance
Del Staecker, CFRE
President
Saint Thomas Development
Foundation
Nashville, TN

Vice Chair, Professional
Advancement
Ernest Wood, Ph.D., CFRE
Assistant Vice President
University of the Pacific
Stockton, CA

Vice Chair, External Affairs
Barbara R. Levy, CFRE
Director of Development
Arizona Theatre Company
Tucson, AZ

Vice Chair, Member Services
Irwin Brod, CFRE
Senior Vice President
Brakeley, John Price Jones, Inc.
Stamford, CT

Treasurer
Benjamin F. Kelley, Jr. CFRE
Vice President of Development
LeBonheur Children's Medical Center
Memphis, TN

Assistant Treasurer
Patricia F. Lewis, CFRE
Executive Director
Seattle-King County Council of
Camp Fire Girls
Seattle, WA

Secretary
Charles R. Stephens, CFRE
Vice President of Development
Clark College
Atlanta, GA

Assistant Secretary
Stephen Wertheimer, CFRE
Vice President, Development
Baruch College
New York, NY

1986

Chair
John R. Miltner, CFRE
Vice Chancellor University
Advancement
University of California, Irvine
Irvine, CA

Vice Chair, External Affairs
Marshall Monroe, CFRE
Director of Corporate Planning &
Financial Development
YMCA of the USA
Chicago, IL

Vice Chair, Governance
Sally Smith, CFRE
Director of Development
The Corcoran Gallery of Art
Washington, DC

Vice Chair, Member Services
Irwin Brod, CFRE
Senior Vice President
Brakeley, John Price Jones, Inc.
Stamford, CT

Vice Chair, Professional
Advancement
Delmar Staecker, CFRE
Executive Vice President
St. Thomas Hospital Development
Foundation
Nashville, TN

Treasurer
Benjamin Kelley, Jr., CFRE
Executive Vice President
Baptist Health Foundation
Little Rock, AR

Assistant Treasurer
Marianne Briscoe, CFRE
Director, Corporate Relations Office
University of Chicago
Chicago, IL

Secretary
Carolyn Martchenke, CFRE
Director of Development
All Saints Espiscopal School
Ft. Worth, TX

Assistant Secretary
Ernest W. Wood, CFRE
Assistant Vice President
University of the Pacific
Stockton, CA

1985

Chairman of the Board
Barbara H. Marion, CFRE

Vice Chair—Governance
Irwin Brod, CFRE

Vice Chair—Professional
Advancement
Sarah C. Coviello, CFRE

Vice Chair—External Affairs
Marshall Monroe, CFRE

Vice Chair—Member Services
C.C. "Jitter" Nolen, CFRE

Treasurer
Delmar Staecker, CFRE

Assistant Treasurer
Benjamin F. Kelley, Jr., CFRE

Secretary
Carolyn Martchenke, CFRE

Assistant Secretary
Shirley A. Brown, CFRE

1984

Chairman of the Board
Barbara H. Marion, CFRE

Vice Chair—Professional
Advancement
C. Wilson Schroeder, CFRE

Vice Chair—External Affairs
Sarah C. Coviello, CFRE

Vice Chair—Governance
Linda L. Chew, CFRE

Vice Chair—Member Services
John R. Miltner, CFRE

Secretary
Jeanne Williams, CFRE

Assistant Secretary
Carolyn Martchenke, CFRE

Treasurer
Irwin Brod, CFRE

Assistant Treasurer
Thomas A. Frazier, CFRE

1983

Chairman of the Board
Thomas G. Sanberg, CFRE

Vice Chair—Education
Linda L. Chew, CFRE

Vice Chair—External Affairs
Sarah C. Coviello, CFRE

Vice Chair—Governance
C. Alvin Tolin

Vice Chair—Membership
John R. Miltner, CFRE

Secretary
Jeanne Williams, CFRE

Assistant Secretary
Carolyn Martchenke, CFRE

Treasurer
Frances MacAllister, CFRE

Assistant Treasurer
Irwin Brod, CFRE

1982

Chairman of the Board
Thomas G. Sanberg, CFRE

Vice Chairs
Linda L. Chew, CFRE
Sarah C. Coviello, CFRE
Samuel Rogers, CFRE
C. Alvin Tolin

Secretary
William G. McDanel, CFRE

Treasurer
Donald J. Johnson, CFRE

Assistant Secretary
Jeanne Williams, CFRE

Assistant Treasurer
Frances MacAllister, CFRE

1981

Chairman of the Board
Robert C. Blum

Assistant Secretary
David W. Canfield

Vice Chairs
Sarah C. Coviello
Barbara H. Marion
William G. McDanel
Thomas G. Sanberg

Treasurer
Donald J. Johnson

Assistant Treasurer
Marie M. Drummond

Secretary
Diane H. Carlson

1980

Chairman of the Board
Donald A. Campbell, Jr.

Assistant Secretary
Herbert G. Howard

Vice Chairs
William E. Arnold
Robert C. Blum
Jack R. Bohlen
Stephen J. Smallwood

Treasurer
C. Alvin Tolin

Assistant Treasurer
C. Wilson Shroeder

Secretary
Dorothy H. Sutherland

1979

Chairman of the Board
Donald A. Campbell, Jr.

Assistant Secretary
Herbert G. Howard

Vice Chairs
William E. Arnold
Robert C. Blum
Stephen J. Smallwood
Jack R. Bohlen
William Freyd

Treasurer
C. Alvin Tollin

Assistant Treasurer
C. Wilson Schroeder

Secretary
Dorothy H. Sutherland

1978

Chairman of the Board
Donald A. Campbell, Jr.

Secretary
Dorothy H. Sutherland

Vice Chairs
James L. Maxwell
William E. Arnold
Stephen J. Smallwood
Robert C. Blum

Assistant Secretary
Herbert G. Howard

Treasurer
C. Alvin Tolin

347

Assistant Treasurer
C. Wilson Shroeder

1977

Chairman of the Board
Byron Welch

Vice Presidents
William E. Arnold
Jack R. Bohlen

Secretary
M. H. "Skip" Hobson

Assistant Secretary
Helen O'Rourke

Treasurer
William Freyd

Assistant Treasurer
Stephen Smallwood

1976

Chairman of the Board
Henry Goldstein

President
Byron Welch

Vice Presidents
Jack R. Bohlen
William E. Arnold

Secretary
M.H. "Skip" Hobson

Assistant Secretary
Helen O'Rourke

Treasurer
Harold A. Ifft

Assistant Treasurer
Jess W. Speidel, II

1975

Chairman of the Board
Henry Goldstein

President
Byron Welch

Vice Presidents
M. H. "Skip" Hobson
Jack R. Bohlen

Secretary
C. Wilson Shroeder

Assistant Secretary
Helen O'Rourke

Treasurer
Harold A. Ifft

Assistant Treasurer
Jess W. Speidel, II

1974

Chairman of the Board
Norman C. Smith

President
Henry Goldstein

Vice Presidents
Byron Welch
M. H. "Skip" Hobson

Secretary
Donald F. Flathman

Assistant Secretary
Helen O'Rourke

Treasurer
Jess W. Speidel, II

Assistant Treasurer
Harold A. Ifft

1968

Chairman of the Board
Jess W. Speidel, II

Secretary
Harry Aschkinasi

President
Ralph E. Chamberlain

Assistant Secretary
Robert V. Donahoe

First Vice President
Aaron D. Duberstein

Treasurer
John L. Wallace

Second Vice President
Barnet M. Deutch

Assistant Treasurer
Ray Carmichael

1967

Chairman of the Board
Dr. Abel A. Hanson

Secretary
Harry Aschkinasi

President
Ralph E. Chamberlain

Assistant Secretary
Charles F. Isackes

First Vice President
Aaron D. Duberstein

Treasurer
John L. Wallace

Second Vice President
Barnet M. Deutch

Assistant Treasurer
Ray Carmichael

1966

Chairman of the Board
Dr. Abel A. Hanson

Secretary
Harry Aschkinasi

President
K. Brent Woodruff

Assistant Secretary
John L. Wallace

First Vice President
Ralph E. Chamberlain

Treasurer
Emanuel Greenfield

Second Vice President
Barnet M. Deutch

Assistant Treasurer
Ray Carmichael

1965

Chairman of the Board
Dr. Abel A. Hanson

Secretary
Mrs. Roy H. Fricken

President
Jess W. Speidel, II

Assistant Secretary
Harry Aschkinasi

First Vice President
K. Brent Woodruff

Treasurer
Emanuel Greenfield

Second Vice President
Benjamin Sklar

Assistant Treasurer
Ralph E. Chamberlain

1964

Chairman of the Board
Dr. Abel A. Hanson

President
Jess W. Speidel, II

ARTHUR C. FRANTZREB IS AT THE TOP OF THE FIELD

Arthur C. Frantzreb's business card says "Consultant in Philanthropy." He is indeed, and is likely one of the nation's most highly regarded. He is also one of the most active, prodigious, and effective writers for the field. He publishes *Counseletter*, a monthly newsletter. He also has a quarterly listing of all donors of $1 million and up gifts.

In 1988, he averaged more than two addresses and articles a month. A partial listing follows.

"Alternates to Feasibility Studies"

Chapter in new book, *The President and Fund Raising* by James L. Fisher and Gary H. Quehl

"Designing Philanthropic Success"

Philanthropic Action Council, Tampa, FL

"Management Preconditions for Philanthropic Success"

Gulf Coast Chap., National Society of Fund Raising Executives, Tampa, FL

"Philanthropy of the Future"

Fund Raiser's Institute, Council of Independent Colleges, Tampa, FL. Keynote Address

"Endowment Insures Quality"

The Board Letter, Associates for Board and Commission Development, P.O. Box 1017, Lake Oswego, OR 97034

"Mobilization of Philanthropic Resources"

New Jersey Chap., National Society of Fund Raising Executives

"Sometimes Quitting is the Best Answer"	Governance Column, April 7, *The NonProfit Times,* P.O. Box 7286, Princeton, NJ 08543-7285
"Planning for Fund Raising"	Annual Conference, DC, The National Council on the Aging
"Membership Benefits for Upper Levels"	Ninth Annual Art Museum Membership Conference, Kansas City, MO
"Training Your Board for Action"	In 3 Parts—May, June, July; *National Fund Raiser* (Newsletter), Barnes Associates, 603 Douglas Blvd., Roseville, CA 95678
"Philanthropy Begins with Governance"	Western New York Chap., Buffalo, National Society of Fund Raising Executives
"Success Begins with Attitudes"	Western New York Chap., Buffalo, National Society of Fund Raising Executives
"American Philanthropy: Who Gives? Who Gets?	Lead article, *Line on Design,* Newsletter, The Troyer Group, (Architects, etc.), Mishawaka, IN 46544-2297
"Fund Raising: The Motivation is Philanthropy"	Board Retreat, St. Elizabeth's Medical Center, Dayton, OH at French Lick, IN
"Girl Scouts Chief Speaks Out on Boards"	Governance article, *The NonProfit Times,* P.O. Box 7286, Princeton, NJ 08543-7285
"What do you mean: We're a Public Trust Major Gift Solicitations"	New Jersey Chap., NJ Conference on Philanthropy, National Society of Fund Raising Executives, Princeton

For more information: (703) 356-1266.

JEWISH WEALTH AND PHILANTHROPY

On the *Forbes* list of the 400 wealthiest American individuals, 40 percent of the top 40 names are Jewish-Americans. Twenty-three percent of the total list are Jewish. There are 5,148 private foundations in the country with either assets of over $1 million or annual giving of over $100,000. This represents 97 percent of all foundation assets and 92 percent of foundation giving in America. Of this group, 355 entries are for foundations with a Jewish orientation, compared with 437 for Protestant giving, and only 155 entries for Catholic philanthropy.

GLOSSARY OF WORDS AND TERMS

In 1986, the National Society of Fund-Raising Executives Institute published a *Glossary of Fund Raising Terms.* It is comprised of 935 entries and over 300 cross-references. Its purpose is to provide an authoritative source defining the specialized vocabulary most commonly used in philanthropy.

The book also attempts to provide a definitive answer to one of the most confusing and widely disputed issues, the term most often incorrectly used—it hyphenates the word "fund-raising." It points out that the only exceptions are organizations that are officially incorporated under non-hyphenated names. It states that "this treatment aligns with the recent decision by the American Association of Fund-Raising Council to promote consistent usage." (For an explanation of why it is consistently spelled as one word in this text, see *One Final Note.*)

We have listed the 100 terms most often used, but everyone in the field should order their own copy of the *Glossary of Fund Raising Terms.*

To order: National Society of Fund Raising Executives Institute, 1101 Kings Street, Suite #3000, Alexandria, Virginia 22314 (703) 684-0410.

AAFRC
American Association of Fund-Raising Counsel, Inc.

ACCOUNTABILITY
The responsibility of the donee organization to keep a donor informed about the use that is made of the donor's gift as well as the cost of raising it.

ACCOUNTING POLICY
A policy made by a gift-supported organization that specifies which types of gifts will be counted toward a campaign goal and which types will be excluded.

ACKNOWLEDGMENT FORM
An impersonal, printed form used to acknowledge relatively small gifts.

ACKNOWLEDGMENT LETTER
A letter sent by a donee, or on behalf of a donee, to the donor expressing appreciation for a gift and identifying the use that will be made of the gift. An acknowledgment letter may be a form letter, but it is usually personalized.

ACQUISITION MAILING (or PROSPECT MAILING)
A mailing to prospects to acquire new members or donors.

ACTION GRANT
A grant made to examine an operating program or project, as contrasted to a research grant.

ACTUAL VALUE
The price that property commands when sold on the open market.

ADJUSTED GROSS ESTATE
Determined by deducting a decedent's debts and estate settlement costs from his or her gross estate.

ADVANCE GIFTS
Gifts given or pledged in advance of a public announcement of a campaign. Advance gifts are solicited before a campaign is announced because the success or failure of a campaign may depend upon the size of advance gifts. (See also INITIAL GIFTS)

ADVISORY BOARD
A prestigious group of individuals, usually influential and prominent, whose endorsement of the campaign objectives implies credibility.

ANNUAL REPORT
A yearly report of financial and organizational conditions prepared by the management of an organization.

ANNUITY TRUST (or CHARITABLE REMAINDER ANNUITY TRUST)
A trust that pays (annually to the donor and/or another beneficiary) a fixed amount equal to not less than five percent of the initial fair market value of the property placed in trust. The income is paid for the donor or beneficiary's life or for a fixed term not exceeding twenty years. The Charitable Remainder Annuity Trust's ultimate recipient, after the donor or beneficiary dies, is a nonprofit charitable organization or institution. The donor's tax deduction is equal to the present value of the nonprofit organization's or institution's deferred charitable interest. The deduction depends on the rate of return of the annuity, the age(s) of the annuitant(s), and the number of beneficiaries. Basically, the value of the annuity is computed under IRS actuarial tables. The obligation of the trust is limited to the assets of the trust.

APPRECIATED SECURITIES GIFT
A gift of securities with a market value greater than the donor's cost or basis. Appreciated securities generally represent a potential capital gain and capital gain taxes unless given to a charitable organization. The gift value of a security that is traded on an exchange or in the over-the-counter market is established by the mean between the high and low prices on the date it is transferred to the nonprofit organization or institution.

APPRECIATION
The increase in market value of property over its original cost or tax basis; gratitude for a gift.

BARGAIN SALE
The sale of property at less than its fair market value. Frequently, a person will sell property to a 501(c)(3) organization or institution at a

"bargain" price (e.g., the individual's cost as opposed to its market value). The transaction, then, is partly a gift and partly a sale.

BELLWETHER
A gift given early in a campaign which, by its nature and size, tends to lead others to increase their levels of giving; a pace-setting gift.

BENEFACTOR
Contributor, usually at the highest level.

BEQUEST
A transfer, by will, of personal property such as cash, securities, or other tangible property.

BLUELINE
A specially processed photograph of an artist's mechanical that is reproduced on blueprint and cut and folded to actual size of final production.

BOILERPLATE
Text drawn from existing documents and presented in whole or part as original work.

BOOK VALUE
The amount of an asset stated in a company's records, not necessarily that which it could bring on the open market.

BROCHURE
A generic term describing a printed document of some substance and size used for promotional purposes in a campaign.

CAMPAIGN COSTS
Expenditures that are deemed essential to the mounting and operation of a campaign and that are directly related to campaign budget projections.

CAMPAIGN MATERIALS
General term used to denote campaign forms of all kinds: materials required for campaign workers, fact sheets, prospect lists, and numerous other items essential to the effective functioning of a campaign; printed materials such as pamphlets, brochures, leaflets, and flyers used to advance a campaign.

CAPITAL EXPENDITURE
An expenditure to acquire an asset with an expected useful life of more than one year.

CARRIER ROUTE PRESORT
Sorting mail before delivery to the post office (according to U.S. Postal Service regulations) so that it is bundled into individual carrier rates (abbreviated as Car-rt-sort).

CASE BIGGER THAN THE INSTITUTION
A thesis, long held in fund-raising circles, that a gift-supported

organization must be able to demonstrate its service to society; thus, the appeal for support presents financial needs in the context of the organization's overall service to society.

CASE STATEMENT
A carefully prepared document that sets forth, in detail, the reasons why an organization needs—and merits—financial support. In the context of the "case is bigger than the institution," it documents its services, human resources, potential for greater services, current needs, and future plans.

CERTIFIED FUND-RAISING EXECUTIVE (CFRE)
A credential granted to a fund-raiser by the National Society of Fund Raising Executives, which is based upon performance as a fund-raising executive, knowledge of the fund-raising field, tenure as a fund-raiser (minimum of five years), education, and service to the profession.

CFAE
The Council for Financial Aid to Education, Inc.

CHARITABLE LEAD TRUST
Provides for payments to a 501(c)(3) organization for a stipulated period of time, free from federal gift and estate taxes. At the end of the trust term, the trust assets go to a designated individual.

CHARITABLE REMAINDER TRUST
Provides income to donor for life (or term of years) with the remainder of the trust going to a 501(c)(3) organization at death. Provisions can be made also for survivors to receive the income during their lifetimes (or term of years). An income tax charitable deduction is available for the value of the remainder interest. Trusts can change appreciated investments without incurring any taxes or capital gains.

CHESHIRE LABEL
The most common type of label to which names and addresses are transferred by means of a heat process; most are printed "four across."

CORPORATE FOUNDATION
The philanthropic organization established to coordinate, over a period of time, the philanthropic interests of the founding corporation. Corporate foundations are very explicit as to their fields of interest, often limiting grants to causes related to corporate profits.

CORPUS
The principal or capital, as distinguished from the interest or income, of a fund, estate, investment, or the like.

CULTIVATION
The process of developing the interest of prospective contributors through exposure to institutional activities, people, needs, and plans to the point where they are considered ready to give at acceptable levels.

CY-PRES DOCTRINE
(pronounced CI-PRAY) When the restricted gift of a donor made
through a will cannot be carried out by an institution as intended, the
court can direct that donor's intent be carried out as nearly as possible.

DEEP WEALTH
Wealth accumulated over several generations by individuals and families;
often referred to as "deep pockets of wealth."

DEFERRED GIFT
A gift to be received in the future, although the transaction housing the
gift occurs in the present.

DEPRECIATED PROPERTY
Assets that qualify for annual deductions related to their becoming worn
out, exhausted, or obsolete and the cost of which is spread out over the
period of expected usefulness.

DEVELOPMENT
A term used to define the total process of organizational or institutional
fund-raising, frequently inclusive of public relations and (in educational
institutions) alumni(ae) affairs.

DONOR PROFILE (SINGULAR)
A description of basic information about an individual donor through
research.

DOOR-TO-DOOR SOLICITATION
A special activity, usually within a particular neighborhood, in which
volunteers go from house to house ringing door bells, briefly explaining
the purpose of an appeal, leaving literature, and asking for a
contribution.

ELEEMOSYNARY
Having to do with, derived from, or dependent upon philanthropy.

ENDOWMENT CAMPAIGN
A campaign to obtain funds specifically to create or supplement an
organization's endowment fund.

EVERY TUB ON ITS OWN BOTTOM
A phrase often used to describe a decentralized approach to
university-wide fund-raising where each school is responsible for raising
its share of a campaign goal.

FAMILY FOUNDATION
A foundation whose funds are derived from members of a single family.
Generally, family members serve as officers or board members of the
foundation and play an influential role in grantmaking decisions.

FAN-FOLD
A piece of paper that has been folded back and forth like a fan, leaving
no double edge for the machine to grip.

FEASIBILITY STUDY (or DEVELOPMENT PLANNING STUDY)
An objective survey of an organization's fund-raising potential that
measures the strength of its case and the availability of its leaders,
workers, and prospective donors. A written report includes the study
findings, recommendations, and (when the goal is feasible) a campaign
plan, timetable, and budget. The study is usually conducted by
fund-raising counsel.

GENERAL PURPOSE FOUNDATION
An independent private foundation that awards grants in many different
fields of interest.

GIFT ANNUITY
A contract between the donor and the charity wherein the donor
transfers property to the charity in exchange for the charity's promise to
pay the donor a fixed annual income for life or for some other mutually
agreed-upon period. Donor's right to income may be deferred for a
period of years. The annuity may be in joint and survivor form.

GIFT RANGE TABLE
A table of gifts that enables campaign leaders to know, in advance of a
capital campaign, the size and number of gifts that are likely to be
needed at each level in order to achieve the campaign goal. The table
focuses the attention of campaign leaders on the sequence of gifts that
will be needed.

HANGER
An additional appeal, usually smaller in size than the main letter and
usually signed by someone other than the signer of the main letter,
which is enclosed in the direct mail package (also called a lift note or
endorsement letter).

HONORARY CHAIRMAN, CHAIRPERSON
Individual of prominence or influence who agrees to lend his or her
name to a campaign organization with the understanding that he or she
will not be expected to assume an active role.

IMPACT PRINTER
A computer printer similar to an extremely high-speed typewriter.

INDEPENDENT SECTOR
A term used to described all not-for-profit organizations, as distinct
from government and corporations formed to make a profit; not to be
confused with the organization INDEPENDENT SECTOR. (See also
THIRD SECTOR.)

INDICIA
A mailing permit that appears in the upper righthand corner of an
envelope, which otherwise would be stamped or metered.

INITIAL GIFTS
Contributions, usually from trustees or directors of an organization or

institution, that demonstrate commitment to a campaign and provide momentum at the outset, before external solicitations are undertaken. (See also **ADVANCE GIFTS**.)

IN-KIND CONTRIBUTION
A contribution of equipment, suppliers, or other property in lieu of money. Some corporations may also donate space or staff time as in-kind contributions. The donor may place a monetary value on in-kind gifts for tax purposes.

INTERVIEW (UNSTRUCTURED)
An interview in which the interviewer does not determine the format or subject to be discussed, thus leaving the interviewee in major control of the conversation.

JOB DESCRIPTION (or POSITION DESCRIPTION)
A summary of responsibilities related to performance of a task or set of tasks.

KEY STATEMENT
A condensation of the case statement containing most of the substance of that document; often used for cultivation purposes.

KITCHEN-SINK APPROACH
The practice of crediting income from all philanthropic sources to a capital campaign without regard to the methodology used to attain that income.

LASER LETTER
A letter that has been personalized through a process where laser beam, toner, and fuser fix images on continuous computer forms.

LETTER OF INTENT
A letter that states a prospect's intention to make a specified gift or legacy; it is used when a prospect prefers to avoid making a pledge. Since it could possibly constitute a binding obligation under some circumstances, it is advisable for a prospective donor to seek legal counsel before executing such a letter.

LIVE STAMP
A postage stamp affixed by hand or machine to a carrier envelope.

LONG-RANGE DEVELOPMENT
The aspect of development concerned with future goals.

LOYALTY FUND
Designation applied to an annual fund to signify expectation of consistent support.

MAIL DROP
The delivery of bundled, bagged, and postage-affixed mail to the post office.

MAJOR BROCHURE
A campaign brochure that encompasses the generic case for support and is therefore applicable for use with all potential constituencies.

MARKETING RESEARCH
The process of gathering, recording, and analyzing information pertaining to the marketing of goods and services.

MEMORIAL
A gift to an organization commemorating either the donor or someone else, living or dead, designated by the donor for which a specific "memorial" will be set aside in accordance with the donor's wishes. Organizations often designate memorials and seek support from relatives and friends of the one being memorialized.

MERGE/PURGE
A computer operation that combines two or more files of names using a matching process to produce one file free of duplicates.

MINI-STATEMENT
A condensed version of a case statement. (See also **KEY STATEMENT**.)

MISSION STATEMENT
A concise description of the purpose of an organization. (See also **CASE BIGGER THAN THE INSTITUTION**.)

MONARCH SIZE STATIONERY
Stationery that measures $7^{1}/_{4}'' \times 10^{1}/_{2}''$.

MOTIVATION
The desire or need that causes volunteer leaders and workers to see a development program through to success.

NAHD
National Association for Hospital Development

NEEDS ASSESSMENT
Analysis of a campaign's table of needs, which becomes the basis for explaining why each project is needed; provides a rationale that is persuasive for the funder's consideration.

NSFRE
National Society of Fund Raising Executives

ORDINARY INCOME PROPERTY
Some property interests, that if sold at a profit, give rise to ordinary income as distinguished from long-term capital gains. A gift of ordinary income property to a tax-exempt organization or institution is deductible only to the extent of the donor's cost basis in the property.

PACESETTING GIFTS
Those gifts received during a campaign that set the standard for all

subsequent gifts; a category of gifts related to the gift range table of anticipated giving.

PERSONAL PROPERTY
Cash, stocks, bonds, notes, paintings, furniture, jewelry, and other similar property.

PHILANTHROPY
The philosophy and practice of giving to nonprofit organizations through financial and other contributions; all voluntary giving, voluntary getting, voluntary service, and voluntary association and initiative.

PHONATHON
A fund-raising effort in which volunteers solicit gifts or pledges by telephone. (See also **TELEPHONE CAMPAIGN**)

PLEDGE CARD
A printed form used by solicitors in seeking what is most often a legally binding commitment from a prospect.

PRIVATE SECTOR
Private, as opposed to governmental, sources of support of philanthropic causes.

PROPOSAL
A written request or application for a gift or grant that includes why the project or program is needed, who will carry it out, and how much it will cost.

PROSPECT LIST
A listing of prospective donors maintained by a development or campaign office.

PROSPECT PROFILE (or DONOR PROFILE)
A research report detailing all of the pertinent facts about a prospective donor, including resources, relationships, and past giving.

PROSPECT RATING COMMITTEE
Members of a campaign organization deemed capable of evaluating the giving capabilities of important prospects on a highly confidential basis.

PROSPECTUS
A plan of a proposed enterprise or project.

PYRAMID OF GIFTS
A reference to the distribution of gifts by size to a capital campaign within the context of the principle that larger gifts, although limited in number in relation to the total gifts received, will account for a larger and disproportionate share of the total objective; the classic gift pattern for a campaign that, graphically represented, resembles a pyramid.

QUESTION AND ANSWER FOLDER (Q&A FOLDER)
A folder containing questions pertaining to an organization, its needs,

and fund-raising plans, together with the answers, for distribution in support of a campaign.

REMAINDER INTEREST
The rights one holds in the remainder of a trust or other property.

RESTRICTED GIFT
A gift for a specified purpose clearly stated by the donor, such as for a research project.

REVOCABLE LIVING TRUST
The income from such a trust that is paid to the grantor during his or her lifetime, and to the family following the grantor's death. It can be canceled by the person granting or initiating the trust.

RIFLE-SHOT APPROACH
Solicitation narrowed down to a very select group of prospects, carefully planned and implemented, as opposed to "shotgun approach."

RULE OF THIRDS
A formula that has been widely used in constructing gift range tables: The rule of thumb is that about ten donors account for the first third of funds raised during a capital campaign; about one hundred donors provide the next third; and all remaining donors in the constituency furnish the final third. Any failure in achieving the objective of the top third can be compensated for by exceeding the objective of the middle third; the bottom third, however, cannot make up for failure in the top or middle thirds. (See also **PYRAMID OF GIFTS**.)

SEQUENTIAL GIVING
A cardinal principle of capital campaign fund-raising that gifts should be sought "from the top down," i.e., the largest gifts in a gift range table should be sought at the outset of a campaign, followed sequentially by the search for lesser gifts.

SHOTGUN APPROACH
Broad-scale and generally indiscriminate appeals for funds, the reverse of the "rifle-shot approach."

SIGHT RAISING
Calculated attempts employing various strategies to induce previous donors and prospects to raise their previous or expected levels of giving. (See also **UPGRADING**.)

SOLICITOR'S KIT (or WORKER'S KIT)
A packet of materials prepared for campaign workers for use in their calls on prospects, including list of assignments, solicitor's guide, copies of question-and-answer leaflet, campaign brochure, and pledge cards.

STANDARDS OF GIVING
Arbitrary but generally realistic assignment of giving potentials to groups or categories of prospects based on past performance and other criteria; a pacesetting level of giving to a campaign.

STEERING COMMITTEE
A committee of top leadership that bears overall responsibility for establishing a campaign or development program until a permanent campaign committee assumes this responsibility.

STRETCH GOAL
A goal seemingly in excess of an achievable goal, which is adopted because additional funds are needed and/or because it is necessary to raise prospects' giving sights.

SUSPECT
A potential donor whose interests in an organization are in an embryonic state and who therefore cannot be considered a likely prospect.

SUSTAINING FUND
One of several designations used by organizations to describe annual funding programs.

TANGIBLE PERSONAL PROPERTY GIFT
Gifts of antiques, art, jewelry, or other appreciated personal property. The charitable deduction is determined, in part, by the extent to which the use of the property is related to the charitable organization's mission as determined by its tax-exempt status.

TELEPHONE CAMPAIGN (or PHONATHON; TELEPHON)
A technique, employed especially in alumni(ae) fund campaigns, to obtain verbal commitments for gifts via telephone calls from teams of solicitors working out of a central headquarters.

THIRD SECTOR
A term used to describe all not-for-profit organizations and institutions. (See also **INDEPENDENT SECTOR.**)

TOKEN GIFT
A gift considerably below the capability of the donor and often reflecting inadequate cultivation or disinterest.

UNRESTRICTED GIFT
A gift made unconditionally; the reverse of a restricted gift.

UPGRADING
The process of increasing the level of giving of donors of record. (See also **SIGHT RAISING.**)

VARIABLE ANNUITY
An annuity contract providing lifetime retirement payments that vary in amount with the results of investment in a separate account portfolio.

VERBAL PLEDGE
An agreement made orally to contribute to a campaign. It is valid only as an expression of intent unless and until supported by a signed pledge

or letter of intent, actions creating a contractual or moral obligation, or the failure of timely withdrawal of the pledge, thereby raising the possibility of an estoppel.

"I'm sorry. Mr. Jones
cannot pick up the phone now.
He's raising money hand over fist."

COMPANIES WHICH SPECIALIZE IN NOT-FOR-PROFIT SOFTWARE PACKAGES TO ASSIST THE FUNDRAISING PROCESS.

A1-FUNDRAISER
Specs: IBM and compatible XT,/AT or 386-based machines, PC/MS-DOS, hard disk, 640K RAM. Software written in popular relational database (Rbase System V), which makes it easy for modification. Source code available. Single or multiuser versions.
Price: Software is modular; can be purchased separately or as a complete turnkey system. Consulting, training and support are priced separately. Modules start at $295.
Vendor: Strategic Consulting Group, 840 Via Casitas, Greenbrae, CA 94904 (415) 461-6309

ACCOUNTMATE
Specs: System runs on IBM and compatible XT,/AT or 386-based machines. PC/MS-DOS, hard disk, 512K RAM for single-user, 640K for multiuser LAN. Software written in dataBase III +. Software is modifiable by user. All data can be downloaded into Lotus for further analysis. Source code available at no charge. Single or multiuser versions available.
Price: $395–$695.
Vendor: Weber*Duffy*Weiss Services, Ste. 500, 230 Park Ave., New York, NY 10169 (212) 557-1322.

ADAM DONOR MANAGEMENT SOFTWARE

Specs: System runs on Data General desktop and requires 256K, MV Family, (2MB required), and also on the Data General NOVA compatible (512K required).

Price: Price is available on request.

Vendor: Campus America, Inc. 900 Hill Ave., Ste. 205, Knoxville, TN 37915-2523 (615) 523-9506.

ADVANCE SYSTEM, THE

Specs: VAX Advance runs on any VAX, including the desktop MV2000. IBM Advance runs on 937x, 43xx, 30xx mainframes. VM and MVS versions. Links with PCs. Versions for RDBMS environments. Source code is available.

Price: Based on client requirements, available on request.

Vendor: Business Systems Resource, Inc. (BSR) 1000 Winter St., Waltham, MA 02154 (617) 890-2105.

ADVOCATE VERSION

Specs: System runs on IBM AT or above, 286, 386 or PS/2. System is networkable and a hard disk is required. System also requires 640K. Source code is provided by special arrangements. Single-user or multiuser versions available.

Price: Available upon request.

Vendor: Advocate Development Corp., 186 S. St., 5th Fl., Boston, MA 02111 (617) 542-8489.

AGENCY DEVELOPMENT SYSTEM

Specs: Software operates under DOS 3.x on a variety of PCs, including IBM PS models. Source code is provided.

Price: $5,500.

Vendor: Karico Systems, Inc., 12601 Townepark Way, Louisville, KY 40243 (502) 245-8836.

ALUM

Specs: System runs on IBM PC, PS/2 and compatible; requires 640K and 20+ MB hard disk.

Price: $3,550 single-user; $6,500 multiuser.

Vendor: The Williamson Group, 129 Mt. Auburn St., Cambridge, MA 02138 (617) 497-6848; (800) 992-6848.

ALUMNI/DEVELOPMENT SYSTEM (ADS)

Specs: ADS runs on both IBM and Digital VAX mainframe/minis. Source code is provided.

Price: Prices range from $40,000–$100,000.

Vendor: Information Associates (an MSA company), 3000 Ridge Rd. E., Rochester, NY 14622 (716) 467-7740.

ALUMNI/FOUNDATION INFORMATION AND DEVELOPMENT SYSTEM

Specs: Operational on the Wang VS minicomputer, Hewlett-Packard 3000 minicomputer and all IBM compatible minicomputers running MS-DOS 2.1 or greater PC microcomputers. Source code kept in an escrow account.

Price: From $5,000

Vendor: Abacus Data Group, Inc. 921 S.W. Washington St., Ste. 410, Portland, OR 97205 (503) 224-2152. Other offices are in Los Angeles, Denver and Austin.

ALUMNI RECORDS AND DEVELOPMENT SYSTEM

Specs: Software operates under DOS 2.x on a variety of PCs

including IBM PS models. Source code is provided.

Price: $5,500.

Vendor: Karico Systems, Inc., 12601 Townepark Way, Louisville, KY 40243 (502) 245-8836.

AMT ESTIMATOR

Specs: System runs on any IBM PC or compatible or IBM PS/2, with a minimum of 256K internal memory and one 5¹/₄-in. or 3¹/₂-in. floppy disk drive, which runs MS-DOS or PC-DOS version 2.0 or higher.

Price: $300—Service agreement is an additional $50 per year for users of PGM, or $450 for non-users.

Vendor: PG Calc Inc., 129 Mount Auburn St., Cambridge, MA 02138 (617) 497-4970.

ARCLIST/THE DESKTOP DIRECT MARKETER

Specs: System runs on any IBM PC or compatible computer with a hard disk drive and 640K RAM.

Price: $695—Technical support costs $95 per year after a free initial 90-day period.

Vendor: Group 1 Software, 6404 Ivy Lne., Ste. 500, Greenbelt, MD 20770 (301) 982-2000; (800) 368-5806; (800) 368-6245 (Canada).

ARTIS

Specs: System runs on IBM PC, PS/2 and compatible. 640K, 20+ MB hard disk required. Altos, multiuser computers support up to 50 users.

Price: $7,800 single-user; $14,500 multiuser.

Vendor: The Williamson Group, 129 Mt. Auburn St., Cambridge, MA 02138 (800) 922-6848; (617) 497-6848 in MA.

BENEFACTOR

Specs: Benefactor runs on the Prime 50 Series of minicomputers providing a wide range of systems from under 10 users to more than 200 users. Prime systems offer compatibility and upward growth. Benefactor uses the Prime Information relational-like database. Source code is available.

Price: Software license fee starts at $85,000.

Vendor: Datatel Minicomputer Co., 3700 Mount Vernon Ave., Alexandria, VA 22305 (703) 968-9000.

CAMPAIGN

Specs: Hewlett-Packard 3000 minicomputers, all models, prices for multiuser systems start at $10,000 for a complete hardware. No extra cost or special system software required. Campaign software is interactive, on-line and batch reporting. Laser and dot matrix, or other letter quality printers supported. Source code held in escrow.

Price: Campaign prices range from $10,250–$42,500, varying by client size and modules acquired.

Vendor: Development Strategies, Inc., P.O. Box 807, Trabuco Canyon, CA 92678-0807 (714) 858-0664.

CAMPAIGN PLUS

Specs: Software designed for PCs with 640K memory, hard disk, and any common printer. System fully menu-driven with error trapping to assure data accuracy. Source code not included.

Price: Software is $895 complete, including manual and free telephone support for six months. Maintenance support contract available for $295 per year and includes at least two upgrades annually.

Vendor: Academy Computer Systems, Inc., 9520 Beauclerc Terrace, Jacksonville, FL 32217 (904) 398-1342.

CDS

Specs: Operates on Xenix, Unix or concurrent DOS operating systems. Price: $27,500–$128,000, depending on hardware configuration and number of users.

Vendor: The Williamson Group, 129 Mt. Auburn St., Cambridge, MA 02138 (617) 497-6848; (800) 992-6848.

CHARITABLE SCENARIO PLUS, THE

Specs: IBM PC, /XT, /AT, PS/2 and compatibles. Requires 640K RAM. Over 85 dot matrix printers and laser printers supported. Source code not provided.

Price: $2,490 (includes first-year maintenance).

Vendor: Philanthotec, Inc., 6135 Park Rd., Ste. 109, Charlotte, NC 28210 (704) 554-1646.

CHURCH GROWTH SYSTEM

Specs: Utilizing the PICK operating system, software can support one to 1,000 terminals. Software runs on 70 different models of computers manufactured by 30 different vendors. PC AT class hardware can support up to six terminals with minicomputers utilized for larger sites. Source code is kept in escrow.

Price: Software priced from $11,190 and up, depending upon the number of users. Turnkey depending upon the number of users. Turnkey systems $14,500 and up, depending on hardware required. Call to inquire about other products available.

Vendor: Information Services Group, 4431 S.W. 64th Ave., Ste. 114, Davie, FL 33314 (305) 581-4448.

COMMTACT

Specs; MacIntosh Plus, SE or II (min. 1MB RAM). Hard disk storage dependent on database size. Multiuser and local area network systems available. Source code can be purchased separately.

Price: Single-user price, $2,990; multiuser, $3,990. Turnkey CCS priced separately based upon database size, number of users and other pertinent considerations.

Vendor: Campagne Associates, Ltd., 9 Goldfinch Lne., Nashua, NH 03062 (603) 891-2129.

COMPLETE FUND RAISER, THE

Specs: Runs on all Data General MV-Series Systems (AOS/VS). Soon available for PCs, DEC, IBM and other hardware. Source code available.

Price: Turnkey system price starts from $17,500; or software only from $6,000 with one-year warranty.

Vendor: Complete Computer Systems, Inc., 1800 Byberry Rd., Huntingdon Valley, PA 19006 (215) 938-0191.

CONSULTANT, THE

Specs: The program is compiled dataBase III + code stand alone, which runs on any IBM XT, /AT, PS/2 or compatible systems under the MS-DOS and PC-DOS environments of which configuration includes a hard disk and 512K or more of RAM memory. Xenix and MacIntosh versions are now available—requires 1MB of RAM.

Price: $2,495, single-user price; $2,995, multiuser price; $2,995, MacIntosh price; $4,995, Xenix price; $25, demo disk.

Vendor: Gift Consultants, Inc., 3248 Matthews Dr., Fort Worth, TX 76118 (817) 589-7471.

CONTACT MANAGER, THE

Specs: System runs on 68000-based microcomputers and IBM

PC-compatible computers outfitted with an add-on board. Source code is available.

Price: Complete turnkey systems are available starting at $15,000 for three users.

Vendor: MegaPhone Systems, Inc., 7551 Sunset Blvd., Ste. 100, Los Angeles, CA 90046 (213) 850-6575.

CRUNCH STATISTICAL PACKAGE

Specs: System runs on most IBM PCs and compatibles.

Price: $495.

Vendor: Crunch Software Corp., 5335 College Ave., Ste. 27, Oakland, CA 94618 (415)420-8660.

DASCO II

Specs: Built on the popular Unix operating system, DASCO II can run on super micro-, mini-, supermini- and mainframe computers. It is currently available from Donor Automation on AT&T's 3B line and Digital Equipment Corp's VAX and MicroVax computers. Source code is not available.

Price: Software prices begin at $22,500.

Vendor: Doror Automation, Inc., 922 New York St., Ste. A, Redlands, CA 92373 (714) 793-1230.

DATAFLEX

Specs: Memory Requirement: 384K.

Price: $1,650 (per server) OS/2 version, 16-bit single-user; $1,250, 16-bit multiuser; $1,800 base price for Unix V and VAX/VMS.

Vendor: Data Access Corp., 14000 S.W. 119th Ave., Miami, FL 33186 (305) 238-0012.

DB DONOR

Specs: IBM PC, /XT, /AT or compatible computer with at least 512K. Supports color monitors. The source code is provided. DB Donor is written in dataBase III+.

Price: $2,500.

Vendor: Real Good Software, 300 N. Washington St., Falls Church, VA 22046 (800) 227-3117.

DEVELOPMENT SUPPORT SYSTEM-1 (DSS-1)

Specs: Single or multiuser, multitasking turnkey development system operating under either DOS or Xenix operating systems on IBM PC and compatible. Hard disk sized to fit user files. Larger disks as required by file sizes. Typical turnkey system includes hardware (NEC PC AT and Toshiba P-351 printer), software (DSS-1, general ledger, accounts payable, word processing, operating system). Source code held in escrow.

Price: Normally sold as a total turnkey system including hardware, installation and training. Turnkey system prices range from $9,995–$50,000 depending on scope of development program, size of mailing list and volume of response mail. A typical entry-level system would sell for $12,900 and would lease for $275 per month. It would comfortably provide total development support for a mailing list up to 50,000 names. Software only available starting at $4,900.

Vendor: National Data Systems, 635 Camino de Los Mares, San Clemente, CA 92672 (714) 496-9550.

DEV-MICRO

Specs: The DEV-Micro application module is built upon DMS-Micro, a relational database management system and 4GL. It includes a powerful report writer, information retrieval system utilizing multiple keys, screen

generation, and an English-like query language.
Price: DMS-Micro is $495 and DEV-Micro is $1,995.
Vendor: Campus America, Inc., 900 Hill Ave., Ste. 205, Knoxville, TN 37915-2523 (615) 523-9506.

DOLLARS
Specs: Available for IBM and compatible prsonal computers running MS-DOS 2.+ + or later and DEC Decmate/Rainbow running CP/M. Does not require recommended hard disk. Assembler language source code not available. Requires less than 64K for program execution.
Price: Base price is $695. Site licensed and tailoring included.
Vendor: Cottage Software, Inc. 4 Stewart St., Lewiston, ME 04240 (207) 783-3299.

DONORBASE III
Specs: IBM PC XT, AT System 2 and IBM compatibles. PC-DOS/MS-DOS operating systems; 512K RAM and minimum 10 MB hard disk. Single-user or multiuser. Source code provided without charge.
Price: $5,900–$8,900.
Vendor: H.A. Hanna Associates, 1319 Pennsylvania, Des Moines, IA 50316 (515) 263-5686.

DONORMASTER
Specs: Unix, Xenix, MS-DOS operating systems. For single-user micros, multiuser micros, supermicros and minicomputer. Altos, IBM, Unisys, NCR, AT&T, DEC, etc. Source code provided. Buyer has the option to purchase software only or a complete system with hardware and installation services.
Price: $3,995 and up.
Vendor: Master Systems, 1249 Pinole Valley Rd., Pinole, CA 94564 (415) 724-1300.

DONORPERFECT
Specs: System runs on any IBM PC, /XT, /AT or compatible with 512K RAM. DonorPerfect is written in compiled dataBase III +. Source code held in escrow.
Price: $1,995 (single-user version); $25 demo disk.
Vendor: Starkland Systems, 3327 Freeman St., San Diego, CA 92106 (619) 554-0772.

DONOR/PROSPECT-FILES (D/PRO)
Specs: The program can be in color if the user has a color graphics card. Written for IBM PC, /XT, /AT and/or compatible computers with at least 384K RAM and PC-DOS/MS-DOS operating systems. Source code not provided. Detailed user's guide with screens, reports and helpful hints included.
Price: D/Pro $997. C/Pro $499, and O/Pro is an additional $499. Demo disk, $53 (cost applied to purchase).
Vendor: McDanel and Associates, Inc., dba Data Pro-Files, 717 Havenwood Lne. St., Ft. Worth, TX 76112-1016 (817) 457-8111.

DONOR$
Specs: Unix, Xenix, and MS-DOS operating systems. Available for single-user and multiuser machines from AT&T, Altos, DEC, COMPAQ, and the IBM PC/AT and compatibles. Source code is negotiable.
Price: Software ranges from $995–$9,850.
Vendor: John Snow, Inc., (JSI) 210 Lincoln St., Boston, MA 02111 (617) 482-0485; (800) 521-0132.

DONOR-TRAC

Specs: Hardware requirements: IBM AT or compatible. Minimum 512K and 10MB hard drive. LAN version also available for IBM or compatible system. Donor-Trac can manage up to 60,000 active donors depending on size of hard drive. Source code included in package.

Price: Demo available for $10. Cost of program with ENABLE is $2,495. Cost to organizations currently using the system is $2,095. Prices do not include shipping and handling.

Vendor: Essential Systems, Inc., P.O. Box 29820, Minneapolis, MN 55429 (612) 566-3673.

ECHO'S DEVELOPMENT SYSTEM

Specs: IBM System 2, PC/XT, /AT supported. Minimum 512K RAM and 2MB of hard disk. Novell Netware version and other NETBIOS compatible networks available.

Price: Single-user $995; and multiuser $1,500.

EPOCH

Specs: Single-user system runs on any IBM PC compatible running MS-DOS 2.1 or higher; 640KB RAM and 10MB disk storage recommended. Multiuser systems run in the Pick or UNIX operating systems on IBM/XT, /AT compatibles; 640KB RAM, 40MB hard disk recommended. XT supports three users, one printer. AT supports 10 users, one printer. On 80386 machines, system supports 17 users, one printer. Also available for mini and mainframe computers.

Price: Single-user, $2,500. Multiuser begins at $8,000.

Vendor: North American Campaign Marketing, Inc., P.O. Box 477, Springfield, VA 22150 (703) 451-0551.

EXTERNAL RESOURCES MANAGEMENT (XRM) SYSTEM

Specs: Hardware necessary is a Hewlett-Packard 3000 minicomputer. Depending upon its configuration, these systems will support from 20 to 400 users. Source code is provided.

Price: Prices range from $20,000–$75,000, depending upon the hardware system purchased.

Vendor: Software Research Northwest, Inc., 17710 Ave. S.W., Vashon Island, WA 98070 (206) 463-3030.

FINALIST SYSTEM

Specs: Hardware requirements include IBM compatible 370 architecture, 30XX series and 43XX series mainframe computer, and IBM 9370 under all standard operating systems. Memory requirements vary based on execution of individual steps. Selected source code tables are provided.

Price: Perpetual license $20,000–$75,000.

Vendor: LPC, Inc., 1200 Roosevelt Rd., Glen Ellyn, IL 60137-6098 (312) 932-7000; (800) MAILERS.

FINANCE-DRIVE

Specs: System requires 512K memory, 30B hard disk, graphics card. Runs on IBM PCs and compatibles. VAX and MicroVAX. Written in BASIC. Runs on MS-DOS, Xenix, VAX, VMS and Unix operating systems.

Price: Available upon request.

Vendor: Applied Business Technologies, Inc., 500-A S. Roberts Road, Bryn Mawr, PA 19010 (215) 527-8900.

FOCUS FUND ACCOUNTING

Specs: System runs on the IBM/XT, /AT, PS/2, compatibles and multiuser networks. Minimum requirements are 512K RAM, a 20MB hard disk, and PC-DOS 2.x. QuickBASIC source code is available as an option.

Price: System starts at $750 with discounts for multisystem purchases.

Vendor: Focus on Business, a division of International Micro Systems, Inc. (IMS), 4331 Merriam Dr., Overland Park, KS 66203 (913) 677-1137; (800) 255-6223.

FRS—FUND RAISING SYSTEM

Specs: System supported on Digital MicroVAX 2000 through VAX 8800 models. Available on a time-share basis or as an in-house system.

Price: $15,000–$25,000 based on VAX CPU selected and optional modules needed.

Vendor: SIS, Inc. 90 Canal St., Boston, MA 02114 (617) 720-5500.

FUND-AL

Specs: All digital VAX and PDP-11 computers. Source code not normally provided, but exceptions can be made.

Price: From $26,300–$103,000, depending upon the constituency size, level of complexities for data conversion and special implementation considerations, if any.

Vendor: Quodata Corp., 266 Pearl St., Hartford, CT 06103 (203) 728-6777.

FUND ACCOUNTANT

Specs: Written in multiuser R/M COBOL for most Unix, Xenix or PC/DOS Systems, including networks.

Price: $3,000–$15,000.

Vendor: The Computer Center, 366 U.S. Rte. 1, Falmouth, ME 04105 (207) 781-2260.

FUND ACCOUNTING SYSTEM

Specs: System runs on the IBM family of products including the PC/XT, /AT, PS/2 (models 25, 30, 50, 60, 70 and 80). Multiuser version is available for operation on the IBM PC, IBM Token Ring and Novell Local Area Networks. Source code is not provided.

Price: Each module is priced at $2,000. Complete turnkey systems (hardware and software) start at $11,000.

Vendor: Blackbaud Microsystems, 160 E. Main St., Huntington, NY 11743 (516) 385-1420; (800) 443-9441.

FUND DEVELOPMENT SYSTEM, THE

Specs: Operates under the PICK operating system, which is compatible with IBM PCs and look-alikes, IBM 9370 with PICK/370, DEC, VAX and DEC MicroVAX with the Ultimate operating system, and all Ultimate computers.

Price: Software ranges from $8,000–$15,000.

Vendor: Paciolan Systems, Inc. (PSI), 2875 Temple Ave., Long Beach, CA 90806 (213) 595-1092.

FUNDER ENLIGHTENING

Specs: Software runs on IBM PC and compatibles with 640K and a hard disk drive.

Price: $1,000 for software with two weeks telephone support. Software is $2,000 with one year of telephone and update support.

Vendor: Resources, Inc., 1535 Lake-Cook Rd., Ste. 502, Northbrook, IL 60062 (312) 498-3990.

FUND-MASTER
Specs: Fund-Master runs on nearly any type of PC having a hard disk and at least 512K RAM. Multiuser versions for the IBM PC and Novell network as well as Data General minicomputers are available. Suitable for databases ranging in size from a few hundred donors to more than 500,000. Source code is kept in escrow.

Price: Starts at $4,900.

Vendor: Master Software Corp., 8604 Allisonville Rd., Ste. 309, Indianapolis, IN 46250 (317) 842-7020.

FUNDRAISER
Specs: Multiuser, multitasking system runs on minicomputers from Digital, Data General, IBM XT, /AT and compatibles and IBM PS/2. Software written in database management language and ANSI Standard. Source code is provided.

Price: Software license fees range from $4,900–$40,000.

Vendor: Inpact Systems, Inc., 11 DeAngelo Dr., Bedford, MA 01730 (617) 271-0300.

FUND RAISING SYSTEM
Specs: Hardware necessary is Digital VAX or MicroVAX computer. Source code is provided.

Price: Software prices start at approximately $40,000 for the Fund Raising System and $30,000 for a basic financial system including the product license, data conversion, installation and training. Quotes available upon request.

Vendor: Access International, Inc., 208 Union Wharf, Boston, MA 02109 (617) 367-3690.

FUND RAISING TOOL BOX
Specs: System runs on IBM PC/XT, /AT or compatibles running PC/MS-DOS 2.x or 3.x with 640K of memory and at least 10MB of disk storage and an 80-column printer. Upward compatible with Tool Box multiuser and local area network products. Source code provided.

Price: Network software starts at $4,895. Total hardware systems available on individual quotes.

Vendor: Fund Raising Tool Box Mfg. Co., Inc. (a subsidiary of Ketchum, Inc.), 2221 E. Lamar Blvd., Ste. 360, Arlington, TX 76006-7414 (800) 458-4392 (U.S.); (800) 548-8657 (Canada).

FUND-WARE SYSTEMS
Specs: MacIntosh SE, MacIntosh II, IBM System 2, IBM PC, /XT, /AT or compatibles. Minimum 256K, 640 preferred. Written in C programming language. Downloading/uploading from most computers. Source code not provided but can be put in escrow. Novelle Netware required for networking.

Price: Priced from $2,700–$6,000 for the single-user; $4,700–$7,900 for the network. Hardware is additional. Demo diskettes: $50.

Vendor: Insight Systems, Ltd., and FundWare Systems, Ltd., 3114 Thompson Ave., Des Moines, IA 50317-3145 (515) 263-0816.

GRANT SEEKER, THE
Specs: PC/MS-DOS ver 2.0, 2.1, 3.0, 3.1, multiuser, 256K, floppy or hard disk drive; floppy 200, hard unlimited; optimum number of records: 20,000–30,000.

Price: $1,500, demo price: $75.

Vendor: The Grants Manager, 800 W. End Ave., New York, NY 10025 (212) 678-7077.

IDS SYSTEM ONE

Specs: MS-DOS operating system version 3.0 or above, 648K RAM and a hard disk. Written in Clipperized dataBase III and Compiled BASIC. Source code is not available.

Price: $1,498.

Vendor: Institutional Data Systems, Inc., 2 Hamilton Ave., New Rochelle, NY 10801 (800) 322-IDS1.

IMS FUND RAISING SYSTEM

Specs: All multiuser Data General Systems. Handles up to 80,000 donor records with minimum memory requirement of 256K. Enhanced system can handle more than 100,000. One year software warranty. Programs written in Data General Extended BASIC. Source code is provided.

Price: From $9,950 for software only. Turnkey system including hardware, software, and training, from $24,950.

Vendor: Interactive Management Systems Corp., 555 E. Pikes Peak Ave., Ste. 205, Colorado Springs, CO 80903 (719) 634-7755.

MONEY-MACHINE DONOR MANAGEMENT SYSTEM

Specs: Versions available for IBM System/36, System/38 and AS/400 computers. System/36 can store up to 2.3 million donors. System/38 or AS/400 can store up to 20 million donors. Laser, matrix, line and letter-quality printers supported. Validation on all data entry. Hardware and software security. Source code is available.

Price: Starts at $12,000.

Vendor: Freedom Software Corp., 4251 Kipling St., Ste. 520, Wheat Ridge, CO 80033 (303) 422-7770; (800) 822-3112.

LEN BUCKLIN SYSTEM, THE

Specs: IBM PS/2, IBM PC, XT, /AT or compatibles. Minimum 256K RAM, 10MB hard disk storage and an 80-column printer. Capacity limited only by disk size and processor speed. Source code not provided.

Price: Three-year lease at $2,000 annually. Renewable for three additional years at same price. No extra charges. Multiple office installation price negotiable.

Vendor: The Len Bucklin System, P.O. Box U, York Harbor, ME 03911 (207) 363-4545.

LISTPRO

Specs: System runs on the MS-DOS and PC-DOS operating systems used by the IBM PC/XT, /AT and compatible microcomputers. Requires 512K RAM and hard disk.

Price: $745–$1,495.

Vendor: Sold via authorized dealers and directly from vendor: Peopleware, Inc., 1715 114th Ave. S.W., Ste. 212, Bellevue, WA 98004 (206) 454-6444.

MACTRAC

Specs: Software requires a MacIntosh Plus, Mac SE or a MacII, with at least 20MB hard disk. Source code available at additional cost.

Price: Software costs $750.

Vendor: The Technology Resource Assistance Center, Inc., 124 University Ave., Ste. 310, Palo Alto, CA 94301 (415) 321-0662.

MATCHMAKER-PC

Specs: Requires minimum 640KB and hard disk (minimum 40MB recommended). Written in DataFlex; runs under PC-DOS, MS-DOS, Unix, Xenix, Novell, 3Com and several other operating environments. Source code is not provided, but held in trust.

Price: Single-user $2,700; Multiuser/Networking $4,800.

Vendor: Heritage Computer Systems, Inc., 4020 N. 20th St., Ste. 101, Phoenix, AZ 85016-6024 (602) 265-4848; (800) 752-3100.

MAXIMIZER, THE

Specs: Designed to run under MS-DOS or PC-DOS 2.0 or higher. The system will operate on IBM XT, /AT or compatible computer, desktop or portable, with 640K, 3¹/₂-in. disk drives or hard drive. Written in C programming language. Source code is kept in escrow.

Price: $295 for a single-user; and $495 for each three additional users.

Vendor: Pinetree Software, 9th Fl., 8100 Granville Ave., Richmond, B.C. V6Y 3T6 (604) 270-3311; (800) 663-0375.

NAME BASE/DONOR BASE

Specs: System can operate in several environments from single-user PC (PC/MS-DOS with 512K memory and hard disk), multiuser Novell network, multiuser Unix and Xenix on various CUPs and on super-minicomputer environments, supporting from 12 to several hundred users.

Price: From $1,500.

Vendor: Execucomp, Inc., 11711 N. Meridian St., Ste. 730, Carmel, IN 46032 (317) 573-2999.

NAVASOFT FUND RAISING CONTROL SYSTEM (FRC)

Specs: NavaSOFT will operate on IBM PC/AT, /XT or compatible with 256K RAM. The system is PC-based for either stand-alone or network application, with no additional cost for installation or software.

Price: $1,000–$5,000.

Vendor: Navacel Enterprises, Inc., 385 Cleveland Dr., Ste. 202, Buffalo, NY 14215 (716) 835-6060.

PASS

Specs: IBM PC compatibles, requires 640K. Color monitor, light pen. Several ticketing, dot matrix and letter quality printers available. Documentation provided. Source code is not provided.

Price: Software starts at $5,000 for a single-user.

Vendor: Select Ticketing Systems, Inc., P.O. Box 959, Syracuse, NY 13201 (315) 479-6663.

PC-FUND

Specs: IBM PC, /XT, /AT and compatibles using MS-DOS, UNIX and XENIX. LAN's single-user or multiuser. Minicomputer for Data General systems using AOS/VS operating system. Source code not provided. Minimum of 640K memory. Hard disk (20MB) required, as well as 132-column printer.

Price: Microcomputer codules range from $695–$1,995, minicomputer comdules range from $2,995–$3,995. Multiuser price: add $500 per terminal for microsystem and $1,000 per terminal for minisystem.

Vendor: American Fundware, Inc., 1355 S. Lincoln Ave., P.O. Box 773028, Steamboat Springs, CO 80477 (303) 879-5770.

PC-GENERAL LEDGER

Specs: Will run on any IBM PC/AT or compatible with 256K memory and any version of PC or MS-DOS, and an 80-column printer. Can be used on single floppy, double floppy, or hard disk.

Price: $50, with a money-back guarantee.

Vendor: Charter Software, P.O. Box 70, Monticello, IL 61856 (217) 762-7143.

RAISER'S EDGE, THE

Specs: Runs on IBMs, including the PC/XT, AT, PX/2 (models 24, 30, 50, 60, 70 and 80). Multiuser version is available for operation on the IBM PC, IBM Token Ring and Novell Local Area Networks, Source code is not provided.

Price: System is priced at $6,000. Complete turnkey systems (hardware and software) start at $11,000.

Vendor: Blackbaud MicroSystems, 160 E. Main St., Huntington, NY 11743 (516) 385-1420; (800) 443-9441.

RAMS

Specs: System runs on DEC VAX 32-bit multiuser computers from the small Micro VAX with a few users to the largest VAX with hundreds of users. The end-user can upgrade the hardware without needing changes to the software.

Price: System is sold in modules and is priced depending on number of concurrent users. INGRES pricing based on CPU size. Quotes available upon request.

Vendor: Resources, Inc., 1535 Lake-Cook Rd., Ste. 502, Northbrook, IL 60062 (312) 498-3990.

RESULTS/PLUS

Specs: Created exclusively for the personal computer. Software runs on any IBM PC/XT, /AT, IBM PS/2 series or compatibles in a single-user or multiuser configuration. System requires a minimum of 512K RAM. Multiuser system requires the Novell Netware network connected with any of the above hardware.

Price: Results/plus starts at $4,995; multiuser $7,495.

Vendor: Metafile Information Systems, Inc., 15 E. 2nd St., Chatfield, MN 55923 (507) 867-4440.

RISS DONOR DEVELOPMENT SOFTWARE SOLUTION

Specs: Runs on any IBM PC compatible with a hard disk and on a number of networks, including Novell. Software also available on the NCR/ADDS Mentor and Microdata minicomputer systems. Source code held in escrow.

Price: Modular pricing starts at $2,400 for single-user RISS software; $400 for WordPerfect. Run time Revelation and 10 hours telephone technical support are included in base package. Multiuser network and minicomputer systems pricing is by quotation.

Vendor: Samuelson Computer Services, 350 S. Schmale Rd., Carol Stream, IL 60188 (312) 668-1598.

R$VP

Specs: R$VP can be used on any IBM System 38 configuration and requires about 20MB of disk storage. Source code is included at no additional charge.

Price: System costs $23,500. Annual support agreement is available for $2,820.

Vendor: Dynamic Programming, Inc., 10825 Financial Centre Pkwy., Ste. 400, Little Rock, AR 72211 (501) 224-9111.

SCI DONATION MANAGEMENT SYSTEM

Specs: DMS was designed for use with the Pick Operating System. System can be used with DEC, IBM (Series 1 and 9370), Altos, Honeywell, Fujitsu, ADDS, McDonnel Douglas, General Automation, and most IBM and compatible PCs. Source code is included in cost.

Price: Basic software for one to three users costs $7,500. From four to 30 users, add $1,000 per user; more than 30, add $500 per user.

Vendor: Software Co-Op, Inc., 122 Hillside Ave., Ste. 24, Hillside, NJ 07205.

SCOTT DONOR MANAGER
Specs: System requires IBM PC, PS/2 or compatible with a hard disk and minimum of 640K memory.

Price: Complete system including IBM hardware starts at $3,695. Software alone can be purchased for $1,995.

Vendor: Scott Computering Systems, 2780 Bert Adams Rd., Atlanta, GA 30339-3903 (404) 432-7000; (800) 241-7576.

SHELBY DONOR SYSTEM
Specs: System operates in several environments; single-user PC (DOS compatible), networked PCs, multiuser IBM systems S/36 and AS/400.

Price: Applications are modular and may be purchased individually, ranging from $175.

Vendor: Shelby Systems, 8601 Centerview Pkwy. #217, Cordova, TN 38018 (901) 757-2372.

STARMARK
Specs: Alpha Micro family of multiuser computers; PCs and compatibles. Unlimited number of records. Source code in escrow.

Price: Starts at $2,500.

Vendor: Starmark Systems, Inc., P.O. Box 1569, Phoenix, AZ 85061 (602) 258-1074.

TARGET/1 FUNDRAISER
Specs: Runs on any PC compatible and most networks. Requires 512K RAM. Unix V version available in Fall, 1988. Allow one MB of storage for each 2,000 donor/prospects/members and each 6,000 transactions. Source code in escrow.

Price: Single-user version $2,495; multiuser/network version, $3,495 and up.

Vendor: GT National Corp., 400 Center St., Auburn, ME 04210 (207) 786-0195; (800) 888-0111.

TEAM SYSTEM DEVELOPMENT
Specs: Software runs on all 100% IBM-compatible PC/MS-DOS microcomputers with 256K minimum RAM and hard disk storage. Optimal single-user capacity: up to 15,000 donors in the system; up to 9,000 donation records per fiscal year.

Price: Complete Team System Development package priced from $1,350 plus shipping and handling. No-risk, money back "Demo Package" available. All-in-one microcomputer system (hardware and software) for under $5,000. Quotes on request for software modifications and custom-written add-on applications.

Vendor: Burt Woolf Management, Inc., P.O. Box 1031, Cambridge, MA 02218 (617) 232-2580.

TIP$: THE INCOME PRODUCER
Specs: Versions available for IBM compatible PCs (including networks), Unix/Xenix multiuser systems, WANG VS microcomputers, and TIP$ Companion for laptops. Minimum hardware: DOS compatible PC with 256K and a hard disk. Laptop version is dual floppy. Source code negotiable on multiuser versions.

Price: $2,500–$7,995 on PC. $7,500–$30,000 on multiuser systems. Versatile report writer is included that can be used to design custom reports and graphs.

Vendor: Autocomp Systems Corp., 630 Third Ave., New York, NY 10017 (212) 599-2640.

TOOLKIT

Specs: Runs on IBM PC/XT, /AT or compatibles running PC/MS-DOS 2.x or 3.x with 640K of memory and at least 10MB of disk storage and an 80-column printer. Upward compatible with single-user system. Source code is provided.

Price: Versions at $695, $995 and $1,595.

Vendor: Fund Raising Tool Box Mfg. Co., Inc. (a subsidiary of Ketchum, Inc.), 2221 E. Lamar Blvd., Ste. 360, Arlington, TX 76006-7414 (817) 640-0900.

TOTAL CAMPAIGN SYSTEM

Specs: IBM PC/XT, /AT, or PS/2 or 100% compatibles. Requires 640K RAM, hard disk, 132-column printer. All programs written in dataBASE III+ and compiled with FoxVASE+ or Clipper (dataBASE III+ not required for operation). MS/PC-DOS 2.1 or greater (3.1 or greater for Variety Gift-Getter). Multiuser versions available for Novell and IBM PC Net. Source code not included.

Price: From $195 (VIP) to $5,995 (multiuser Top Giver Plus). (Call for further information on price availability.)

Vendor: Hewitt-Anderson Co., a division of Sidney-James Corp., 151 S. Tucson Blvd., Ste. 211, P.O. Box 41510, Tucson, AZ 85717-1510 (602) 326-5664.

TOTAL TELEMANAGEMENT SYSTEM-PLUS

Specs: The 386-based computer has 145MB disk and 4MB memory. Operating system is System Definition Language (SDL), developed by Source Data Systems, Inc. Operates to a maximum of 38 workstations per system and/or multiples of systems. Source code is provided to licensed users.

Price: Software license fee is $2,000 per work station, plus hardware installation and training.

Vendor: Source Data Systems, Inc., 122 2nd St., S.E., P.O. Box 5276, Cedar Rapids, IA 52406 (319) 366-7361.

WORK MANAGER—THE FUND RAISER

Specs: System runs on IBM PC/XT, /AT or PS/2 series as well as all compatibles with at least two floppy disk drives and 384K of memory.

Price: $695.

Vendor: Pyramid Software Publishing, Inc., 25422 Trabuco Rd., #105, Ste. A3, El Toro, CA 92630-2797 (714) 583-1060.

ZDS

Specs: Software is portable among all Prime 50 series computers. Novice users can communicate with system through English-like language. Software written in 4th generation language with source code provided.

Price: Software license fee starts at $22,400.

Vendor: Zoller Data Systems, Inc., 7525 Jefferson Hwy., Baton Rouge, LA 70806 (504) 928-7169.

Source: *Fund Raising Management Magazine*

AIMS RECOGNIZES EXTRAORDINARY DEVELOPMENT PROGRAMS WITH DEMONSTRATED EXCELLENCE IN PLANNING AND MANAGEMENT

In 1987, USX (formerly United States Steel) and CASE (Coun-

sel for the Advancement and Support of Education) established a
program for Achievement In Mobilizing Support (AIMS).

AIMS identifies and recognizes development programs with
demonstrated excellence in planning and management. The awards
replaced the Alumni Giving Incentive Awards, which the United
States Steel Foundation funded for 28 years. According to the official rules, judges "looked beyond purely monetary results in fund-
raising efforts, in recognition that adequate planning, good
management, and a concern for non-monetary as well as monetary
goals are required for long-term success in fundraising efforts."

Following are the winners in 1988.

1988 CASE/USX ACHIEVEMENT IN MOBILIZING SUPPORT (AIMS) AWARDS WINNERS

Total Development Category

Doctorate-granting Institution
University of Miami (FL)

General Baccalaureate Under 10,000 Alumni/ae
Huntington College (IN)

General Baccalaureate Over 10,000 Alumni/ae
Hope College (MI)

Two Year Institution
Spartanburg Methodist College (SC)

Free Standing Specialized or Other Professional Institution
Rhode Island School of Design (RI)

Private Secondary School Under 2,500 Alumni/ae
The Thacher School (CA)

Current Operations Category

Doctorate-granting Institution
University of Pittsburgh (PA)

General Baccalaureate Under 10,000 Alumni/ae
Whitman College (WA)

General Baccalaureate Over 10,000 Alumni/ae
Skidmore College (NY)

Private Secondary School Under 2,500 Alumni/ae
Lancaster Country Day School (PA)

Private Secondary School Over 2,500 Alumni/ae
Choate Rosemary Hall (CT)

Capital Purposes Category

General Baccalaureate Under 10,000 Alumni/ae
Claremont McKenna College (CA)

General Baccalaureate Over 10,000 Alumni/ae
Hobart and William Smith Colleges (NY)

Distinguished Achievement Category
Colleges and Universities

Clark College (GA)
Clark College Atlanta Capital Campaign

College of St. Scholastica (MN)
Alumni Annual Fund

Dordt College, Inc. (IA)
Current Operations

Gustavus Adolphus College (MN)
Total Development

Hartwick College (NY)
Citizen's Board Annual Fund Campaign

Linfield College (OR)
Partners-in-Progress Campaign

Marist College (NY)
Annual Giving

Middlesex County College (NJ)
Endowment Fund Development

Ohio State University (OH)
Annual Fund Program

Union College (NE)
Annual Giving

Williams College (MA)
Annual Giving

Distinguished Achievement Category
Secondary and Elementary Schools

Deerfield Academy (MA)
Total Development

Middlesex School (MA)
Annual Giving

Putney School (VT)
Annual Giving

Regis High School (NY)
Alumni Giving Program

In order for your institution to be eligible for the 1990 awards, you must submit material to CASE by October 31, 1988. The 1990 program will have only two categories—total development effort and individual programs.

For more information: Cheryl L. Martin, Director, CASE/USX AIMS Awards, 11 duPont Circle, Suite #400, Washington, DC 20036 (202) 328-5934.

GIVING BY BEQUEST
(in billions)

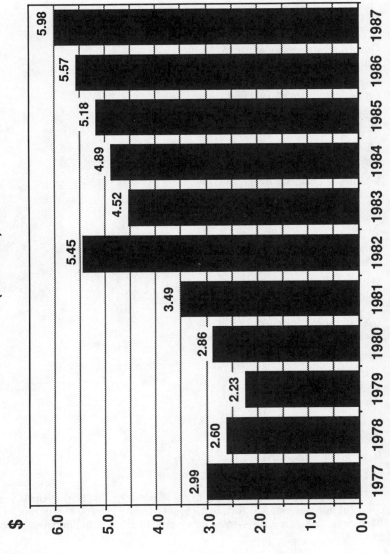

IN NORTH DAKOTA, THE GAME GOES ON

For an 18 month period ending in 1987, North Dakota not-for-profit organizations received $106,275,905 as a result of games of chance.

NORTH DAKOTA GAMES OF CHANCE

Analysis of Gaming Activity
For the Calendar Year Ended December 31, 1987

Game	Gross Proceeds	Prizes	Adjusted Gross Proceeds	Percent of Gross to Charity
Bingo	$32,209,823	$27,041,621	$5,168,202	16.1
Raffles	997,685	455,001	542,686	54.3
Rafflewheel Tickets	72,195	49,508	22,684	34.1
Charitable Gaming Tickets	136,624,390	113,959,920	22,664,471	16.5
Punchboards	68,414	50,455	17,958	26.3
Sports Pools	135,774	117,455	18,319	13.2
Twenty-one	19,110,540	14,275,891	4,834,649	25.2
Poker	311	–0–	311	100.0
Totals	$189,219,132	$155,949,852	$33,269,280	

NOTE: Of the Adjusted Gross Proceeds, nearly $16 million went for taxes and expenses other than prizes. The total amount which was actually used for contributions to the charities was $17,506,309.

TOP TWENTY CHARITABLE RECIPIENTS OF FUNDS

(Figures are for the year
October 1, 1987 through September 30, 1988)

Name of Organization	Proceeds
Prairie Public Broadcasting (Fargo)	$2,637,806
ND Association for Disabled (Grand Forks)	2,231,841
Plains Art Museum (Fargo)	1,967,892
North Dakota Special Olympics (Grand Forks)	1,280,231
Red River Human Services (Fargo)	839,005
North Dakota Safety Council (Bismarck)	646,029
Fort Abraham Lincoln (Mandan)	474,473
Blue Line Club (Grand Forks)	463,486
Development Homes (Grand Forks)	458,324
G. L. Jarrett Memorial Fund (Grand Forks)	447,565
Community Theater (Fargo)	447,089
Souris Valley Humane Society (Minot)	383,073
C.E.N.T.R.E (Fargo)	378,667
Community Betterment Club (Dunseith)	381,873
Share House (Fargo)	363,490
St. Wenceslaus School (Dickinson)	304,586

Cystic Fibrosis Association (Bismarck)   273,974
Multiple Sclerosis (Fargo)   252,891
Youth Commission (Fargo)*   236,884
American Red Cross (Grand Forks)*   220,319

*Data is for three quarters only.

Source: North Dakota Attorney General and the *Philanthropy Monthly*

A SUCCESSFUL FUNDRAISER

In a book published in late 1988, 88 criteria—skills, talents, characteristics, and attributes—were evaluated to determine the factors that make a successful fundraiser. An additional item, "Impeccable Integrity," was added later.

According to the author, after a careful selection process the original list was reduced to 30 criteria. The smaller, honed list is noted with an asterisk (*). This selected group of factors became the basis for a questionnaire which was distributed to and returned by 3000 fundraisers and development directors. It was also used for depth interviewing of 48 men and women who were part of a critical sampling. The complete list follows:

Be creative*
Have perseverance*
Have presence*
Enjoy pressure
Have high self-esteem
Be a long-range planner
Be a people-person*
Have personal style
Be a careful planner*
Be a conceptualizer*
Have a concern for society
Love the work*
Have a religious motivation
Be a good writer
Have a concern for people*
Be planning oriented
Be intense
Be spontaneous
Have a happy home life
Be a perfectionist

Be impulsive
Be self-sufficient
Be independent
Have spiritual motivation
Be decisive
Be a workaholic
Be assertive
Be a good speaker
Be physically attractive
Be a strong supervisor
Emphasize attention to detail
Be a good listener*
Be flexible
Be a strong strategist*
Be socially inclined
Be highly intelligent
Be persuasive*
Be active in professional society
Have ability to deal with rejection

Be a survivor
Have a quality of leadership*
Be well educated
Be convincing*
Have strong communication skills*
Have impeccable integrity (added later)*
Enjoy long-term relationships
Be hard working*
Need recognition
Seek challenges
Be a self-starter*
Be a risk taker
Be action oriented*
Have high expectations*
Be hungry to win
Be able to see the big picture*
Have a social concern
Have a committed

belief in the
organization
Be self-disciplined*
Have high physical
energy
Like people*
Be articulate*
Handle stress well
Have excellent health
Handle pressure well
Have high visibility
Have high energy*
Be an extrovert
Have ability to
motivate people*
Be goal oriented*

Know campaign
mechanics
Have class
Be resilient
Be aggressive
Be rigid
Be persistent
Have a sense of
humor
Have above average
intelligence
Be eager to succeed
Have good working
relationship with
other staff
Be consistent

Have ingenuity
Have ability to
inspire action*
Be an effective
salesman*
Have a business
sense
Be bright*
Be empathetic
Be well organized*

*used for the final
sampling

On the basis of his sampling and interviewing—and as a result of his own work in the field as a consultant for 20 years—the author listed the ten most significant factors in the order of their importance.

1. Impeccable Integrity

2. A Good Listener

3. Ability to Motivate

4. High Energy

5. Concern for People

6. High Expectations

7. Love the Work

8. Ability to Motivate

9. Have Perseverance

10. Presence*

11. Quality of Leadership*

*Tied

Source: *Born to Raise* by Jerold Panas; 1988; Pluribus Press

ONE FINAL NOTE

About midway through the writing of this book, it occurred to me that I didn't know how to handle the word. Come on now, you know what I'm talking about—THE word.

Is it one word, two words, or hyphenated?

There's an infallible rule that governs precisely this situation. If it's an adjective, it's one word: fundraising. If it's a noun, two words: fund raising. Or is it the other way around? In any case, I am certain that the rule is inviolable.

I called some people I consider authorities in our field. I spoke to Ursula Ellis, one of the senior officers at NAHD. She told me that she wasn't really sure how it was handled at headquarters. "We have no real policy around here about that and I guess each staff person handles the word as he or she chooses. I think I usually use two words for both the noun and the adjective. And I'm not sure about the verb—I guess two words, also."

I called Dick Wilson, executive director of the NSFRE. He always knows about this sort of thing.

"Dick, I have this serious problem. When you use it, is it fund-raising, fund raising, or fund-raising?"

There was a long pause. "I make it two words all the time. But hold on a minute, we have a glossary around here somewhere that we printed a couple years ago that governs that sort of thing. We felt that we needed a rule so that everyone would know the proper thing to do. There's been a lot of confusion about this. Let me see if I can find a glossary."

The phone was silent for a long time. Dick finally returned. "Well I'll be darned. In the glossary, we say that the word should be hyphenated all the time—for a noun, adjective, or verb. I guess I've been doing it wrong all this time."

"Well, do you think you'll change?"

"I guess I'll keep doing it the way I have."

I rather agree with Dick's sentiment regarding the matter. Glossary or not, seeing the word hyphenated just somehow doesn't look right to me.

I knew what to do. I called John J. Schwartz. For years, Jack was president of the AAFRC, and one of the nation's leading spokesmen on fundraising. (Or fund-raising, if you have a bias for the glossary.) If anyone would know, Jack would. I've never known him to equivocate on anything. And actually, never to be in doubt on anything. "Jack, I have this problem." And I explained my dilemma.

There was this long pause. Somehow in this investigation, I've learned a lot about long pauses!

"To tell the truth, I don't know if there is a rule about this sort of thing and I don't believe anybody is really consistent about it."

"How do you handle the word, John?"

"Well, I use two words. But that's just by preference. Let me see if I've got any material around here." Long pause. "Well, this is interesting. Here's a piece from AAFRC where it's hyphenated, and here's an article in a magazine where it is two words, and here's a folder where they use it both ways." We spoke some more and finally decided that I probably ought to make it two words. That seemed to make the most sense.

About 20 minutes later I had a telephone call. It was Jack Schwartz. He said that he had just checked with the office at AAFRC and there's definitely a rule and a style. The word— whether it's a noun, an adjective, or a verb—is to be hyphenated.

Good grief. I just don't like that hyphen.

So I called my publisher and reported the puzzle and the results of my investigation. He somehow didn't show the same kind of passion for the matter that I did. I said: "Aaron, it seems to me that no one really knows, and I definitely don't like the hyphen. Let's decide what to do. The important thing is that we be consistent.

"Let's make the noun and the adjective one word. I really like it that way and it looks good to me. And let's hyphenate the verb."

It really didn't matter a lot to me, hyphenating the verb. I don't use it very much—in fact, I don't think I used it as a verb once in my manuscript. And I didn't even know it was supposed to have a hyphen.

So I said to Aaron: "The important thing is to be consistent. Nouns and adjectives, one word. Verbs are hyphenated."

I believe it was Sally Rand, the famous fan dancer, who was asked to explain her immense success. "I owe it all to the two most important rules of advertising: Always be consistent and follow the principle of using plenty of white space."

Source: *Born to Raise* by Jerold Panas; 1988, Pluribus Press.

INDEX

Berkeley (CA) First Presbyterian Church,
276
Berman, Philip and Muriel, 315
Bernack, Leo, 271
Bernstein, Joseph Frank, 301–2
Berrettone (Robert J.) Associates, 291
Bethany College, 71
Bethel College and Theological Seminary,
185–86
Bethers, Bruce R., 4
Bethesda (MD) Boy Scout Council, 55–56
Beth Israel Medical Center, 77
Bethlehem (PA) First Presbyterian
Church, 276
Bethune Cookman College, 192
Betterton, Don, 271
Beyond Time Management, 222
Big Brother and Big Sister Federation, 290
Bingham, Jr., Mary and Barry, 297, 307,
315
Birmingham (AL)
Public Library, 129
Southern College, 183–84, 206
United Way, 39, 43
Birth defects, 72
Bismarck (ND)
Archdiocese, 278
Cystic Fibrosis, 382
Safety Council, 381
Black, Robert E., 294, 304
Blandford, Sister Margaret Vincent, 84
Blandin Foundation, 298
Blanshard (Paul) Associates, Inc., 156
Bleifeldt, Cary and Carlotta, 296
Blindness, 72
Block, Leo, 307, 315
Bloom, David, 140
Blum, Robert C., 341, 347
Boarding Schools
alumni contributions, 230–31
capital purposes gifts, 230, 234
corporate support, 234
endowments, 233
expenditures, 232
voluntary support, 232
Board Member's Book, 221, 244
Boeing Co., 299, 302
Boesky, Ivan, 140
Bohlen, Jack R., 347–48
Bohm, Lee and Milford, 302
Bondurant, William L., 242
Booth Ferris Foundation, 122

Born to Raise, 221
Borwell, Mr. and Mrs. Robert C., 296,
299
Boston (MA)
Archdiocese, 279–81
College, 180, 182
Foundation, Inc., 121
Girl Scout Council, 57–58
Library, 133
Pops, 271
Symphony Orchestra, 92–94, 271
United Way, 38, 43, 47
University, 183–84
YWCA, 22–23
Botts, Bill, 4
Botzum, Robert J., 4
Boulder Memorial Hospital, 74
Bowdich, Cary, 173
Bowdoin College, 204–6
Bowley, Jim, 4
Boyd's City Dispatch, 327
Boys' Club Federation, 289
Boy Scout Councils
endowments, 56
membership, 55
special events funds, 56
sustaining revenue, 55
United Way funds, 56
Boy Scouts of America, 60, 289, 328
BP America, Inc., 303
Bradley, Lynde and Harry, 120
Bradley, Marion, 295
Bradley Foundation, 297, 299, 301, 305
Bradley University, 277
Brain, Phillip S., 3, 10, 330
Brakeley Jr., George A., 324, 351
Brakeley, John Price Jones, Inc., 156, 189,
322, 326
Brashier, T. Walker, 306, 314
Braun, John J., 299
Bremer (Otto) Foundation, 120
Bren Foundation, 306
Brennan, Edward A., 37
Brennan, Robert E., 301
Bresnahan, Don, 84
Brethren in Christ Church, 265
Bridgeport (CT) United Way, 43
Brigham Young University, 321
Brigham & Women's Hospital, 76
Briscoe, Janey and Dolph, 53
Briscoe, Marianne G., 341, 344–45
Brod, Irwin, 344–46

North Dakota Special Olympics, 381
Grand Rapids (MI)
  Diocese, 278
  Junior College, 209
  Public Library, 134
  United Way, 40, 43
Grant (William T.) Foundation, 121
Grantmakers, 112–19
Grant-Seeking in North Carolina, 117
Grawemeyer, H. Charles, 293, 295
Gray, John and Betty, 304
Gray (Harry J. and Helen Buckley)
  Foundation, 314
Great Depression, 29
Great Oaks Communications Services,
  Inc., 186
Green, Cecil H., 296
Green, Edwin B., 305
Greenberg, Mr. and Mrs. Alan C., 315
Greene (John B., and Anne S.), 53
Greenfield, Emanuel, 350–51
Greenfield Jr., James M., 82, 341
Green Mountain College, 146
Greensboro (NC) United Way, 40, 42
Greenville (SC)
  First Presbyterian Church, 277
  United Way, 43
Greenwood, Thomas Leon, 6
Greenwood Press, Inc., 154
Grenzbech (John) & Associates, Inc., 159,
  326
Griffith (IN) United Way, 45
Grinnell College, 203–5
Grizzard Advertising, 163
Gross, Caroline Z., 308
Groton School, 229–31
Gruss, Joseph S., 294–95
GTE Foundation, 128
Guggenheim (John Simon) Memorial
  Foundation, 121
Guise, J.J., 330
Guide to Arkansas Funding Sources, 112
Guide to California Foundations, 112
*Guide to Charitable Foundations in the
  Greater Akron Area,* 117
*Guide to Charitable Trusts and
  Foundations in the State of
  Hawaii,* 113
*Guide to Corporate and Foundation
  Giving in Vermont,* 119
*Guide to Corporate Giving
  in Connecticut,* 113

  in Maine, 115
  in Massachusetts, 115
  in New Hampshire, 116
  in Rhode Island, 118
Guide to Foundations in Georgia, 113
Guide to Grantmakers, 116
Guide to Kentucky Grantmakers, 114
*Guide to Minnesota Foundations and
  Corporate Giving Programs,* 115
Guide to Oregon Foundations, 118
Gumenick, Nathan and Sophia, 302
Gund (George) Foundation, 120
Gurin, Maurice G., 162, 341
Gustavus Adolphus College, 187–89, 379

H

Haas, Peter, 195
Haas (Walter A.) School of Business, 195
Hackettstown Community Hospital, 74
Hagan, Blanche, 301
Haggar Foundation, 299
Haggerty Foundation, 301
Haken, Jerry Ten, 8
Haldane, Scott, 6
Hall, Elizabeth, 173
Hall, Frank R., 84–85
Hall Family Foundation, 121
Hallowell Jr., H. Thomas, 304, 313
Hamilton (Thomas Hale) Library, 132
Hamilton College, 203–5
Hammer, Dr. Armand, 315
Hamon, Nancy, 313
Hampton (VA)
  Public Library, 139
  United Way, 44
Hampton and Tuskegee, 170
Hanadiv (Bat) Foundation No. 3, 121
Hanaman, David B., 81, 85
Haney, K. Neil, 82
Hanify, Edward B., 52
Hanley, John W., 37
Hanna, Charles and Dorothy, 296
Hanna (Charles Tibby and Dorothy)
  estates, 267
Hanson, Dr. Abel A., 350–51
Hanson, Mr. and Mrs. John K., 300
Haralson, Jerry, 6
Hardesty, Sarah, 173
Harding University, 321
Hardin-Simmons University, 185–86, 228

Harmon, Gail, 6
Harmon, Nancy, 304
Harriman, Gladys and Roland, 306
Harrington, Sybil, 111
Harrington Cancer Center, 111
Harrington Foundation, 111
Harris, Joan W., 242
Harris, Pat, 6
Harris, Mr. and Mrs. Whitney, 330
Harris Jr., W.B., 80
Harrisburg (PA)
　Area Community College, 209–10
　Diocese, 278
　United Way, 40, 43
Harris Corporation, 304
Harris (Paul) and Fellows, 287
Harrison, David, 313
Harrison, Mr. and Mrs. David E., 304
Harris (Bernard C.) Publishing Company,
　Inc., 325
Hart, Dean H. Martyn, 34
Hartford (CT)
　Diocese, 279, 281
　Foundation for Public Giving, 122
　Metropolitan YMCA, 22
　Public Library, 131
　United Way, 39
Hartford (John A.) Foundation, Inc., 121
Hartley, Duncan, 314
Hartsine, Helen L.S., 306
Hartwick College, 204, 379
Hartz Group, 322
Harvard, John, 59
Harvard University, 84, 170, 200–2, 217,
　222–24
　Law School, 196, 198, 200
Harvey Mudd College, 196, 200
Hasbro Children's Foundation, 300
Hauser, Fred, 5
Hawaiian Foundation, 132
Hayes, JoAnne, 162–63
Hayman, Richard L., 301–2
Hays, Reuben B., 302
Hayward (CA) First Presbyterian Church,
　277
Haywood, Samuel Thomas, 301
Hazel, William W., 309, 315
Healthcare
　awareness, 73
　contributions per victim, 72
　organizations, 62–85

Hearst (William Randolph) Foundation,
　121–23
Hebrew Congregations. *See* Jewish
　Congregations
Hebrew Union College-Jewish Institute of
　Religion, 89, 268
Hedco Foundation, 296
Hege Sr., H. Curt, 314
Hege, H. Curt and Patricia S., 306
Hege, Patricia Shields, 314
Heim Jr., Charles W., 81
Heim (Bill) Company, 159
Heinz (Howard) Endowment, 120, 307
Heinz (Vira I.) Endowment, 121
Heisner, Bernie, 5
Hellman, Sandra, 84
Helm, Luther D., 299
Helmken, Charles Michael, 172
Helmsley, Harold and Leona, 140, 294,
　304, 313
Hemberger, Harold J., 6
Henderson & Associates, 326
Henson, Richard A., 305, 314
Hercules, Inc., 301
Heritage Collection, 331–32
Herman, Jack, 81, 85
Herrick Foundation, 121
Herron, Douglas, 6
Hesselbein, Frances, 242
Hesston College, 208, 210
Hetrick, Tom, 6
Hetzel, Charles and Alice, 301
Hewlett, William R., 292, 294
Hewlett (William and Flora) Foundation,
　120, 125–26, 297
Higher Education
　contributions, 190
　See also Colleges and universities
Higher Education Price Index, 235
Highland Park Presbyterian Church, 275
Hill, Lyda, 242
Hillary, Charles R., 82
Hillman Library, 138
Hill School, 231
Hilmerick, Mr. and Mrs. Walter H., 330
Hilton (Conrad H.) Foundation, 121
Hinsdale Hospital, 74
Hirsch (Irene D.) Research Fund, 299
Hirschfeld, Trueman, 6
Hitachi, 233, 300

Jones, Myldred, 53
Jones (W. Alton) Foundation, Inc., 121
Jones Foundation, 302
Joseph, James A., 242
Jossey-Bass, Inc., 154
Joyce Foundation, 120
Joyner, Margie, 173
Juilliard School of Music, 196, 200, 271
Junior Achievement
  revenue, 59
Junior League
  of Phoenix, 112
  of San Jose, 130
Juvenile Diabetes Foundation, 63

K

Kahleri, William G., 300
Kahn, Aga, 294
Kaiser, Elmer and Janet, 309, 315
Kaiser (Henry J.) Family Foundation, 120,
  297, 299
Kalamazoo (MI)
  College, 185–86
  Diocese, 278
  United Way, 42–43
Kalikow, Peter S., 304, 313
Kalkin, Eugene W., 299
Kanawha County (WV) Public Library,
  139
Kandel, Lynn E., 81
Kansas City (MO)
  Lyric Opera, 95
  Metropolitan YMCA, 23
  Public Library, 134
  United Way, 39, 42
Kantor, Iris and Gerald B., 69, 296
Kappe, Stanley and Flora, 302
Katz, Joseph M., 295
Kaye, Sylvia Fine, 302, 307
KCET (Los Angeles), 93
KCRW (Santa Monica), 90
Keck (W.M.) Foundation, 120, 126, 294,
  318
Keeler, Most Rev. William H., 53
Keene, Haxel L., 302
Keller, Charles, 53
Keller, Helen, 205
Kelley Jr. (Benjamin) Foundation, 345–46
Kellogg, Al and Katherine, 295, 297
Kellogg, Katherine B., 297

Kellogg, (W.K.) Foundation, 33, 120,
  125–26, 294, 298–300, 304,
  306–7, 317–19, 321
Kelly, Robb B., 53
Kelso, Lynn N., 303
Kenan Jr. (William R.) Charitable Trust,
  121, 123, 298, 308
Kenedy, W. John, 297
Kenedy Sinclaire Inc., 293
Kenedy (John G. and Marie Stella)
  Memorial Foundation, 122
Kennedy, President John F., 30, 86
Kenney, Edward F., 84
Kentucky State University, 204
Kerr, James R., 37
Kerr Foundation, 297, 300, 302
Ketchum, Carlton G., 152, 162
Ketchum, Inc., 152, 159
Ketchum Recruiting, 322
Kettering (Charles F.) Foundation, 122
Kettering Medical Center, 74
Keycorp, 301
Keystone Junior College, 207–8
Kidd, Sandra, 173
Kidney disease, 72
Killion McCabe & Associates, 290
Kimberly Clark Foundation, 301
King Jr., Martin Luther, 117
Kirby, Robert E., 308, 315
Kirby (F.M.) Foundation, Inc., 121
Kirksville College of Osteopathic
  Medicine, 198
Klewit (Peter) Foundation, 121
Klinkhart, Emily, 351
Kluge, John W., 292, 295, 305, 316
Klutzick, Philip and Ethel, 301
K-mart Corp., 295, 299
Knight, James L., 292, 294
Knight Foundation, 120, 297, 301, 303
Knoxville (TN)
  –Knox County Public Library, 138
  United Way, 44
Koenig, Stella, 351
Koret Foundation, 121
Korn-Ferry International, 323
Korpi, Wilson, 173
Kosmin, Barry A., 268
Kotler, Philip, 331
KPFA (Berkeley), 90
KQED (San Francisco), 93
Kraft Foundation, 128
Kravis, Henry R., 33, 89, 295, 304, 313

Community College, 209
Community Foundation, 120
Marion, Barbara H., 341, 346–47
Marist College, 379
Mariuccia, Baroness, 314
Marketing Imagination, 222
Markey (L.P.) Charitable Trust, 295–97,
   302, 304, 307, 317
Marquette (MI) Diocese, 278
Marquette University, 139, 180, 182
Marriott Corp., 321
Marriott (J. Willard) Foundation, 319, 321
Mars, Audrey Meyer, 302
Marshall, James G., 85
Marshall (George) Fund/USA, 294
Martchenke, Carolyn, 345–46
Martin, Cheryl L., 379
Marts, Dr. Arnaud C., 162
Marts & Lundy, Inc., 152, 159–60, 326
Mary Washington College, 205
Maslund, Mr. and Mrs. Robert A., 299
Mason (Virginia) Hospital, 70
Massachusetts Grantmakers, 115
Massachusetts Institute of Technology,
   200–2, 217, 222–24
Massey Foundation, 151
Massiollon Plaque Company, 100
Matching gifts, 47–48, 171
Mathers (G. Harold and Lella Y.)
   Charitable Foundation, 122
Mathews, David, 241
Matsushita Corp., 306
Maxwell, James L., 347
Mayer (Louis B.) Institute, 296
Mayo Clinic, 70
Mayo Medical School, 200
May Stores Foundation, Inc., 151
McAllister, Edith, 53
McAllister (P.W.) & Family, 298
McCallie School, 231
McCarthy, Mary Joan, 173
McCarty, Harry R., 7
McCaslin, R.J. and Oressa, 317
McClelland, Norman, Barbara and
   Frances, 305, 314
McColough, C. Peter, 37
McCormick (Robert R.) Charitable Trust,
   120
McCune Foundation, 121
McDanel, William G., 347
McDermott, Brig. Gen. Robert F., 53
McDonnell (Douglas) Foundation, 151

McDonnell (James S.) Foundation, 298
McGarvey, Ray L., 53
McGinly, Dr. William C., 80, 82, 324
McGovern, Patrick J., 298
McGrath and Company, 291
McKinney, J.V., 7
McKnight Foundation, 120, 125–26, 294,
   297–99, 303
McLaughlin, Kenneth, 7
McMahon, Holly Steard, 323
McMaster, Harold and Helen, 303
McMichael Sr., D.L., 302
Meadows, Mr. and Mrs. Ralph, 301
Meadows Foundation, Inc., 120, 123, 298,
   305, 318
Medallions, 98
Medical College of Georgia, 197
Medical College of Wisconsin, 198–200
Medical University of South Carolina, 197
Mega Gifts, 221
Meharry Medical College, 183–84, 199–200
Meierjohan-Wengler, Inc., 100
Meikle, James A., 82
Mellon, Andrew, 60, 89
Mellon, Paul, 89, 295
Mellon (Andrew W.) Foundation, 120,
   125–26, 299–300, 303, 307
Mellon (Richard King) Foundation,
   125–26, 303
Memel, Sherwin L., 84
Memorial Drive Presbyterian Church, 276
Memorial gifts, 145–46
Memorial Sloan-Kettering, 85
Memphis (TN)
  –Shelby County Library, 138
  United Way, 39, 43
Menlo Park (CA) Presbyterian Church,
   276
Mennonite Church, 265
Mental Health Association, 243
  bequests, 66–69
  contributions, 63–66
Mental illness, 72
Mentor Graphics Corp., 302
Mercer University, 185–86, 227
Merget, Astrid, 241
Merrick Foundation, 308
Merrill Lynch & Co. Foundation, 303
Metal Decor, 99–100
Metcalfe, Robert M., 298
Metropolitan Arts Fund, 91

Metropolitan Association for
    Philanthropy, 134
Metropolitan Life Insurance Co., 309
· Foundation, 128, 151
Metropolitan Museum of Art, 33, 89
Metropolitan Opera, 111
Meyer, Eugene L., 82
Meyer (Fred) Charitable Trust, 121, 299,
    303
Meyerhoff, Harvey, 79
Meyerhoff (Joseph) Family, 89
Meyers, Chester, 299
Miami (FL)
  –Dade Community College, 207, 209–10
  –Dade Public Library, 131
  Diocese, 279, 281
  Opera Guild, 95
  United Way, 39, 45
Michigan Foundation Directory, 114–15
Michigan Metropolitan Girl Scout
    Council, 57–58
Michigan State University, 194–95, 224,
    321
Michigan Technical University, 197–98
  Library, 134
Microsoft Corp., 322
Middlebury College, 226, 228
Middlesex County College, 379
Middlesex School, 379
Milligan, Margaret, 301
Milliken, Christine Topping, 242
Milliken University, 206
Mills, James T., 145
Millsaps College, 183–84, 228
Milltown (NJ) United Way, 41, 45
Milstein, Paul and Seymour, 146
Miltner, John R., 344
Milton Academy, 31, 34, 229
Milton Hood Ward & Co., Inc., 161
Milwaukee (WI)
  Diocese, 279
  Junior Achievement, 59
  Metropolitan YMCA, 22
  School of Engineering, 199
  United Way, 39, 43
Miner Jr., T. Richardson, 81
Minneapolis (MN)
  de Tocqueville Society, 55
  Girl Scout Council, 57–58
  Metropolitan YMCA, 21
· Public Library, 134
  –St. Paul Junior Achievement, 59

United Way, 39, 42
YWCA, 23
Minnesota Foundations Directory, 115
Minnesota Opera, 95
Minnesota Symphony, 92–94
Minot (ND), Souris Valley Humane
    Society, 381
Minter, Steven A., 242
Missionary Church, 265
Mississippi College, 185–86
Missouri Western State College, 204
Miss Porter's School, 231
Mitchell, Bernard, 294
*Mitchell Guide to Foundations,
    Corporations and Their
    Managers,* 116–17
Mitsubishi Bank of Japan, 306
Mnookin, I.J., 80
Mobil Corporation, 92
Mobile Communications Corp., 301
Mobile (AL) United Way, 44
Mobil Foundation, Inc., 128
Moncrief, W.A. and Deborah, 309, 316
Monaghan (Rose) Charitable Trust, 302
Monroe, Marshall, 324, 341–43, 345–46
Monsanto Co., 299
  Fund, 128
*Montana and Wyoming Foundation
    Directory,* 115
Montana State Library, 134
Montgomery, K., 299
Monticello College Foundation, 301
Montreal-Anderson College, 207–8
Moody Foundation, 120
Moore, Michael E., 82
Moore, N.G., 301
Moran, William M., 82
Moran (Martin J.) Company, Inc., 160
Mormons, 274
Morris, Mervin G., 84
Morris (Hugh) Library, 131
Morristown-Beard School, 234
Morristown (NJ) United Way, 40, 44
Morse Jr. (Lester S.) Lobby, 145
Moseley, Audrienne H., 308
Motorola Corp., 308
Mott, John R., 2
Mott (Charles Stewart) Foundation, 120,
    125–26
Moulton, Harold C., 302
Mount Holyoke College, 203–6
Mount Olive College, 207

Rochester (NY)
  Diocese, 279–81
  Community Chest, 29
  Institute of Technology, 226–27
  Metropolitan YMCA, 13, 22
  Public Library, 134, 136
  United Way, 35, 39, 42
Rockefeller, David, 53
Rockefeller, John D., 60
Rockefeller Jr., John D., 60
Rockefeller Brothers Fund, 121, 124
Rockefeller Foundation, 120, 125–26, 295
Rockhurst College, 180, 182
Rock Island (IL) United Way, 44
Rockville Centre (NY) Diocese, 279–81
Rockwell International Corporation Trust,
    128, 151
Rodef Shalom Congregation, 268
Rodger, George E., 3, 8
Roland, Marle, 300
Rollins, O. Wayne, 79, 295
Rollins, Inc., 79
Rollins College, 228
Roman Catholic church. *See* Catholic
    church
Rooks, Charles S., 243
Roosevelt, Eleanor, 29, 206
Roosevelt, President Franklin D., 86
Roosevelt, President Theodore, 86–87
Roosevelt Center for American Policy
    Studies, 90
Rosario, Juan, 243
Rose, William, 83
Rosefield, Mr. and Mrs. Eugene, 295–96
Rose-Hulman Institute of Technology, 196,
    198
Rosekraus, John and Dodie, 302
Rosenberg, Gary A., 299
Rosso, Henry A., 212
Rotary International, 79
  PolioPlus campaign, 286–87
Roth, William S., 81, 85
Rothfield, Mr. and Mrs. C.W., 303
Rothman, George, 314
Rouch, Philip, 296
Rouse, James W., 152
Rove (Karl) & Company, 291
Rowe, Ted, 85
Roy, Delwin, 233
Royal Restaurant, 152
Rubinstein (Helena) Foundation, 89, 296
Ruffin, Mr. and Mrs. Peter F., 301

Ruotolo Associates, 160–61
Rush-Presbyterian-St. Luke's Medical
    Center, 76
Rush University, 196, 199–200
Ruskin, John, 203
Russ Reid Company, 291
Russellville (AL) United Way, 26
Rust College, 192
Rutman, Marian B., 299
Ryan, J. Patrick, 341
Ryder, Rita, 53
Ryder System Charitable Foundation, 301

S

Saario, Terry T., 243
Sackler, Arthur M., 296
Sacramento (CA) United Way, 40, 45
Safeway Stores, 71
Safford (AZ) United Way, 26
Sage (Russell) Foundation, 122
Saginaw (MI) Diocese, 278
St. Andrew's Presbyterian Church, 276
St. Augustine's College, 192
St. Francis Xavier High School, 231
St. George, Dale E., 9
St. Helena Hospital, 74
St. John Baptist De La Salle, 175
St. Joseph Medical Center, 76
St. Joseph's Hospital (CA), 77
St. Joseph's Hospital (TX), 77
St. Louis
  Archdiocese, 278–81
  Art Museum, 96
  Boy Scout Council, 55–56
  Girl Scout Council, 57–58
  Junior Achievement, 59
  Opera Theatre, 95
  United Way, 38, 43
  YMCA, 21
  YWCA, 23
St. Louis University, 180, 182
St. Mark's School of Texas, 229–30, 234
St. Mary's College (CA), 176–77
St. Mary's College (MN), 176–77
St. Mary's College at Maryland, 204
St. Olaf College, 187–88
St. Paul (MN)
  Archdiocese, 279–81
  Foundation, 122
  Public Library, 134

Temple Israel, 268
Temple Sholom, 268
Temple University, 193, 328
Tennent, Rev. Gilbert, 225
Tennessee Directory of Foundations and Corporate Philanthropy, 118
Tennessee Supreme Court, 229
Terry, I. Brewster, 81, 85
Tested Ways to Successful Fund Raising, 222
Tetreault, Diane, 9
Texaco Philanthropic Foundation, Inc., 128, 151
Texas A & M University, 202, 216, 222, 224
Texas Christian University, 226, 228
  Funding Information Center, 139
Texas Lutheran College, 187–89
Texas State Technical Institute, 210
Thacker School, 378
Thalhimer Jr., Mr. and Mrs. Wm. B., 301
Thebault, Ried, 9
Therese, Sister Marie, 53
Thiel, Kenneth A., 9
Third Sector, 246
Third Sector Press, 155
Thomas, Danny, 197
Thomas, John, 324
Thomas (T.A.) Foundation, 308–9
Thomas Jefferson University, 196, 198, 200
Thompson Jr., Joseph M., 9
Thompson, Robert L., 343
Thompson and Pendel Associates, 326
Thoreau, Henry David, 137
3M Corp., 308
Timken Foundation, 121
Tisch, Lawrence, 33
Tisch, Robert, 33
Tisch Foundation, 89
Tithing, 274–75
Tobin, Mrs. Edgar, 53
Tobin, Robert, 53
To Care, 246
Toledo (OH)
  –Lucas County Public Library, 137
  United Way, 40, 43
Tolin, C. Alvin, 346–47
Tonai, Rosalyn Miyoko, 283
Topeka (KS)
  Public Library, 132
  YMCA, 20
Toronto (Canada) Archdiocese, 279–81

Totten, Elizabeth, 301
Town & Country, 111, 313
Towsley, MD, Harry Albert, 52
Towsley, Margaret Dow, 52
Tracy, Harold, 317
Transaction Books, 155
Travelers Co. Foundation, 302, 308
Travelstead, G. Ware, 299
Trefethan Jr., Eugene E., 53
Triangle Publications, 326
Trigg, Mary K.H., 294
Trinity College, 170, 210, 227–28
Trinity Valley School, 234
Tri-State (NY) United Way, 38, 45
Tri-State University, 206
Trucker & Moerschbacker, 293
Truman, President Harry S., 86
Tuck (Katherine) Fund, 308
Tucson (AZ) United Way, 40
Tufts College, 170
Tulsa (OK)
  City-County Library System, 137
  United Way, 40, 43
Tuolomne County Library, 130
Turner, Robert, 9
Turner, W. Homer, 341
Tuskegee Institute for Negroes, 60
TV evangelists, 265–66
Two-year institutions
  highest endowments, 207
  highest total alumni contributions, 208
  highest total support, 210
  top private, 208–9
  top public, 209
Tyler, Ron and Linda, 305, 313
Tyser, Ralph J., 301

U

UCFCA. *See* United Community Funds and Councils of America
Uhlein, Erwin C., 302
UNICEF, 320
Uniform Federal Fund-Raising Program, 30
Union of American Hebrew Congregations, 268
Union College, 175, 227, 379
Union Theological Seminary, 196
Union University, 185–86
United Cerebral Palsy Association

Health Center
  Dallas, 197
  Houston, 197
  San Antonio, 197–98
  Medical Branch, Galveston, 197, 199
  System Cancer Center, 196–97, 199
University of Virginia, 216
University of the Virgin Islands, 140
University of Washington, 200–2, 216,
  224, 321–22
University of Wisconsin
  at Green Bay, 89
  at Madison, 139, 200, 202, 216, 224
Upjohn, Dr. and Mrs. E. Gilford, 301
Upjohn Co., 297, 303, 307
UPS Foundation, Inc., 151
Urbanch, 89
Ursuline Convent, 59
USX, 377, 379
  Foundation, 128, 151

V

Valencia Community College, 209
Valid Logic Systems, 307
Valparaiso University, 187–89
Valuation Guide for Donated Goods, 244
van der Voort, Roberta, 243
Van Gorder, Bill, 9
Van Zoeren, Mr. and Mrs. Charles, 302
Vassar College, 203, 205
Venereal disease, 72
Ventura (CA) United Way, 45
Vermont Medical Center Hospital, 78
Vermont State Department of Libraries,
  139
Victorian Community Foundation, 140
Village Presbyterian Church, 276
Virginia Military Institute, 204–5
Virginia Polytechnic Institute & State
  University, 201, 223
Virginia University, 192
Vitello, John R., 81, 85
Vittel, Bob, 173
Vollum, Howard, 295
Voluntary support
  education institutions, 235–39
  by source, 199
  top 20 colleges and universities, 200
Volusia County Public Library, 131
von Kienbusch, Mrs. C. Otto, 271

W

Wabash College, 203
Wagnon, Ken and Barbara, 309, 316
Wake Forest University, 185–86, 201–2,
  226–28
Waldorf College, 208
Walker, Norma, 173
Wallace, Duane and Velma, 303
Wallace, John L., 349–50
Wallace, Lila Acheson, 295
Wallace (DeWitt) Foundation, 306
Walla Walla College, 175
Wall Street Journal, 284
Wall units, 99
Walpole Public Library, 133
Walsh, John E., 84
Waltman Associates, 326
Wang, Dr. An, 330
Ward, Charles S., 247–48
Ward, William Arthur, 262
Ward & Dreshman, 248
Ward, Dreshman & Reinhardt, Inc., 152,
  161
Ward, Wells & Dreshman, 152
Wardley, Alfred, 84
Ware, H.M., 294
War Fund, 101
Warhol, Andy, 89
Warner, Irving, 183
Warner Communications Foundation, 306
Warner-Lambert Co., 299, 303
War on Poverty, 30
Warren (William K.) Foundation, 121
Wartburg College, 187–89
Warwick (Mal) & Associates, Inc., 291
Washburn University, 204
Washington, Booker T., 60, 206
Washington (DC)
  Community Chest, 29
  Girl Scout Council, 57–58
  Hebrew Congregation, 268
  National Monument Society, 60
  United Way, 38, 43, 47
Washington Adventist Hospital, 74
Washington and Lee University, 205
Washington State Community College,
  209, 210
Washington University (St. Louis), 22–23,
  200, 217
Washoe County Library, 135
Watkins Sr., Jerry, 349